TREES

TREES

AN ILLUSTRATED IDENTIFIER
AND ENCYCLOPEDIA

TONY RUSSELL & CATHERINE CUTLER

Special Photography: Peter Anderson & Sidney Teo

This edition is published by Hermes House, an imprint of Anness Publishing Ltd,
Blaby Road, Wigston, Leicestershire LE18 4SE; info@anness.com

www.hermeshouse.com; www.annesspublishing.com

If you like the images in this book and would like to investigate using them for publishing, promotions or advertising,
please visit our website www.practicalpictures.com for more information.

Publisher: Joanna Lorenz
Editorial Director: Helen Sudell
Editor: Simona Hill
Text Editor: Daniel Gilpin
Design: Nigel Partridge
Tree Illustrators: Peter Barrett, Penny Brown, Stuart Carter,
David More and Stuart Lafford
Map Illustrators: Anthony Duke, Sebastian Quigley
Editorial Readers: Penelope Goodare, Kate Humby, Jay Thundercliffe,
Lindsay Zamponi
Production Controller: Ben Worley
Jacket Design: Nigel Partridge

Ethical Trading Policy
Because of our ongoing ecological investment programme, you, as our customer, can have the pleasure and reassurance of knowing
that a tree is being cultivated on your behalf to naturally replace the materials used to make the book you are holding.
For further information about this scheme, go to www.annesspublishing.com/trees

Picture Credits
The publishers would like to thank the following for
permission to use their images in this book:

Oxford Scientific Films: page 41 bottom right, 45 bottom,
49 top and 55 top

Peter Anderson: page 2, page 31 and page 53 top

Edward Parker: page 7 bottom right, page 8–9,
page 15 top left and bottom middle, page 16 bottom left,
page 28 bottom left, page 29 top right, page 30 top,
page 32 bottom left, page 33 top, page 34 top right, page 35,
page 37 top right, page 38 top right, page 42 all,
page 60, and page 61 bottom left and bottom right

Acknowledgements
The publishers would like to thank Daniel Luscombe and
Bedgebury Pinetum, Kent; Westonbirt, The National Arboretum,
Gloucestershire; Kew Gardens, Surrey; Tortworth Park,
Gloucestershire; Batsford Arboretum, Gloucestershire;
RHS Garden, Wisley, Surrey; and RHS Garden, Rosemoor, North Devon.

Publisher's Note
Although the advice and information in this book are believed to be accurate and true at the time of going to press, neither
the authors nor the publisher can accept any legal responsibility or liability for any errors or omissions that may have been made.

CONTENTS

INTRODUCTION

Trees are the most complex and successful plants on earth. They have been around for 370 million years and quite likely will be around for many millions of years to come. Today, they cover almost a third of the earth's dry land and comprise more than 80,000 different species ranging from small Arctic willows that are just a few inches high to the lofty giant redwoods, which stand at an amazing 113m/368ft.

Trees are the oldest living organisms on earth. In California, USA, there are Bristlecone pines which are known to be over 4,500 years old and in the United Kingdom there are yew trees of a similar age. Ever since the first primates appeared in the Palaeocene epoch, 65 million years ago, trees have played an integral part in human development, providing food, shelter, safety, medicines, timber and fuel among other things.

Trees are indeed essential to all life. They reduce pollution by absorbing vast amounts of carbon dioxide from the atmosphere while at the same time replacing it with 'clean' oxygen. Each day 0.4 ha/1 acre

Above: Palms trees survive in the heat. They usually have large, attractive, compound leaves and a single trunk.

of trees will produce enough oxygen to keep 18 people alive. Forests of trees help to regulate water flow and can reduce the effects of flooding and soil erosion. They also influence weather patterns by increasing humidity and generating rainfall.

With their myriad shades of green, trees make our cities and towns more colourful. They increase wildlife diversity and create a more pleasant living and working environment. They provide shade in summer and shelter in winter. It is a fact that post-operative hospital stays are shortened when patients are in rooms with views of trees.

For centuries poets, writers and artists have been inspired by the beauty of trees. Works such as Wordsworth's *Borrowdale Yews* and John

Left: Robinia pseudoacacia trees have been used to create avenues for at least 400 years. Pollarding keeps the shape neat and even.

Above: Ancient trees are important points of reference in our towns and the countryside, and help to determine the character of an area.

Constable's majestic elms in *The Hay Wain* will live on long after the original trees depicted have died. Trees help to bring beauty to our gardens and parks. Chosen well, they will provide stunning flowers, foliage, fruit and bark every day of the year. Nothing brings structure and maturity to a garden more successfully than a tree.

With so many obvious values it should be safe to assume that trees are venerated the world over. Unfortunately that is not the case. Over ten per cent of the world's tree species are now endangered. More than 8,750 species are threatened with extinction – some are literally down to their last one or two specimens. Across the world we are losing at least 40 ha/100 acres of trees every minute.

This book is a celebration of trees in all their forms from hardy evergreens and deciduous broadleaves, to desert survivors and tropical palms. It reveals what incredible organisms trees are and describes the diversity that exists throughout the world and how they each contribute to the planet. The first chapter describes the origins of trees, how they have evolved, how they live, grow, reproduce and why they die. It looks in detail at their leaves, bark, fruit,

flowers, buds, cones and seeds and details the fascinating role each plays in the life of the tree. Trees inhabitat many natural landscapes, from the highest mountain ridges all the way down to sea level, and have adapted to different circumstances. The heat of the tropics, the biting cold of northern lands, the salt and wind of the sea and the pollution of the city have all contributed to the evolution of the tree.

The second section of this book features a comprehensive encyclopedia of the most well-known, unusual, or economically and ecologically important species from around the world. Each entry provides a detailed description of the tree, its height, habit, colour and leaf shape and whether it produces flowers, fruit or cones. Its habitat and most interesting features are described to aid identification and a map helps to locate wild populations for each entry.

This book aims to bring a greater understanding and appreciation of trees to a wider audience. It should encourage you to look more closely at the diversity of trees in your own locality and if you have the opportunity to visit far-flung countries to appreciate the diversity that exists on the planet.

Below: The monkey puzzle tree, Araucaria araucana, *has a distinctive and instantly recognizable silhouette.*

HOW TREES LIVE

Trees have three obvious features that together distinguish them from all other living plants. First, they produce a woody stem, roots and branches which do not die back each winter but continue to grow year upon year. This means that from the time a tree begins to germinate until the time it dies it is always visible. Be it the smallest Arctic willow or the largest Californian redwood, this basic principle of growth remains the same.

Second, trees live longer than any other living organism on the planet. It is not exceptional to find living trees that are more than 1,000 years old and many are considerably older. Third, trees are the largest living organisms on the planet. Around the world there are trees in excess of 100m/328ft tall or 1,500 tonnes in weight.

Trees have been growing on earth for 370 million years and today can be found growing almost everywhere from the Arctic Circle to the Sahara Desert. For much of the world, trees are the climax species of all plants – which in simple terms means if land is left untended long enough it will eventually become colonized by trees.

So why are trees so successful? Well, as with all plants, trees need light to survive. Without light, photosynthesis cannot take place and food for growth cannot be made. Trees are superb competitors for light; their woody stem enables them to hold their leaves way above the leaves of any other plant. This means they can absorb vast quantities of light while shading out other plants in the process.

Such is the extensive nature of a tree's root system that it can access moisture from deep in the subsoil – something few other plants can do. As such, trees are well equipped to survive periods of drought, particularly as their structure and size allows them to store food and water for times of deficiency. All in all trees are an incredibly competitive and successful group of plants – which is why they have been around so long. They are also a fascinating group of plants, as the following pages will clearly show.

Left: Cedars of Lebanon, Cedrus libani, in the remnants of a forest in the Bcharre Valley, in Lebanon. This species is known to live for over 2,000 years.

THE EVOLUTION OF TREES

The first trees evolved more than 300 million years ago. By 200 million years ago they were the most
successful land plants on earth, growing in all but the most inhospitable places, such as the Polar regions.
Their ability to produce vast amounts of oxygen has enabled other life forms, including humans, to evolve.

The first living organisms appeared on earth 3,800 million years ago. These primitive, single-celled life forms were followed 500 million years later by the earliest cyanobacteria or blue-green algae. Also single-celled, these were the first organisms able to harness the sun's energy to produce food. This process, known as photosynthesis, had an important by-product – oxygen, which gradually began to accumulate in the earth's atmosphere.

Archaeopteris: the first tree
The first known land plant, which was called *Cooksonia*, evolved around 430 million years ago. *Cooksonia* was erect and green-stemmed with a simple underground root system. It was followed about 60 million years later by *Archaeopteris*, the first real tree.

Below: The timeline below shows the evolution of life forms from the first ammonites of the Devonian period, 417–360 million years ago, through to the development of flowering trees such as magnolias during the Cretaceous period, 144–65 million years ago.

With a woody trunk up to 40cm/16in across, *Archaeopteris* had branches and a large root system. It also had the ability to produce buds and continue growing year after year. Fossils of *Archaeopteris* found recently suggest that it may have been able to live for as long as 50 years. As forests of *Archaeopteris* spread across the earth, the amount of oxygen in the atmosphere rapidly increased, paving the way for an explosion in the evolution of new land animals.

The Carboniferous period
During the Carboniferous period, the earth's climate was warm and humid. Great forests and swamps of trees, ferns and mosses covered the land. One of the most common trees was *Lepidodendron*. Known as the scale tree, it reached heights of 30m/98ft and had a trunk more than 3m/10ft across. It looked like a palm tree, but instead of fans of long, thin leaves it had fern-like fronds, each ending with cone-shaped structures containing spores for reproduction.

At the close of this period, the first primitive conifers, or gymnosperms, began to appear. These plants protected their seeds in cones and had a much more efficient reproductive system than their predecessors. None of these early conifers survives today. Their nearest relatives are species of *Araucaria* (monkey puzzle), *Podocarp* and *Taxus* (yew).

Pangaea
A vast supercontinent that existed 280–193 million years ago was known as Pangaea. The northern part, called Laurasia, comprised the landmasses of North America, Europe and Asia all joined together. The southern part, Gondwanaland, was made up of South America, Africa, Arabia, India, Australia and Antarctica.

Since they were part of Pangaea the continents have moved. Fossil evidence taken from samples of ice deep in the Antarctic ice cap show that relatives of *Nothofagus moorei*, the Antarctic beech, grew in that region more than 200 million years ago.

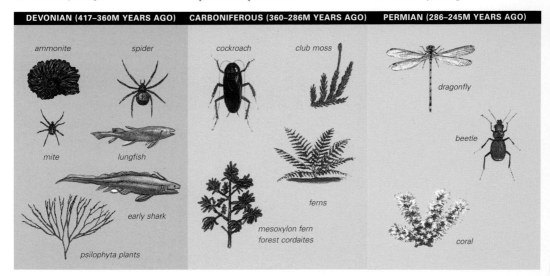

| DEVONIAN (417–360M YEARS AGO) | CARBONIFEROUS (360–286M YEARS AGO) | PERMIAN (286–245M YEARS AGO) |

ammonite *spider* *cockroach* *club moss* *dragonfly* *beetle*

mite *lungfish* *ferns* *early shark* *mesoxylon fern forest cordaites* *coral*

psilophyta plants

Above: One very early tree that is still around today is the deciduous Ginkgo biloba, *or maidenhair tree. It is the last surviving member of a family of trees called the ginkgos; along with conifers, they dominated the land for the next 250 million years.*

The Mesozoic era

This era lasted from 245–65 million years ago. It was the age of dinosaurs and saw dramatic fluctuations in world climate. Conifers adapted to these changes so successfully that different species evolved for almost every environment. Today they survive in some of the coldest and hottest parts of the planet.

Ginkgos were also successful: fossils show that they grew throughout the Northern Hemisphere, from the Arctic Circle to the Mediterranean and from North America to China. Fossils of the Jurassic period (208–144 million years ago) also show the dawn redwood, *Metasequoia glyptostroboides.* Previously thought to have been extinct since that time, the dawn redwood was discovered growing in China in 1941. During the Cretaceous period (144–65 million years ago) flowering plants (angiosperms) evolved and began to exert their dominance over conifers. Among the earliest were magnolia, which are common today.

The Tertiary era

Many of the trees that grew during the Tertiary era (65–2 million years ago) still grow today. The main difference between the Tertiary and the present was the scale of the forests. During the early Tertiary era the planet was warmer than it is today. Europe and North America had a similar climate to that of present-day South-east Asia and vast swathes of forest covered virtually every available piece of land. Oak, beech, magnolia, hemlock, cedar, maple, chestnut, lime and elm occurred alongside tropical trees such as the nypa palm. As the era progressed however, the climate began to cool.

The ice ages

By 1.5 million years ago the climate had cooled so much that the first of four ice ages began. Trees that we now regard as tropical began to die at the far north and south of their ranges. As the temperature dropped further so more temperate species succumbed. Only those trees close enough to the Equator were able to survive. Each glaciation was interspersed with warmer inter-glacial periods lasting anything up to 60,000 years. During these warmer periods, many trees recolonized their previous ranges. Every continent suffered; however, some fared better than others because of differences in topography. In North America, for example, the mountain ranges all run from north to south. Heat-loving trees were able to spread south as the ice sheets advanced, using the valleys between mountain ranges to reach refuges nearer the Equator. The trees were able to recolonize their old ranges back along these same routes. In Europe, however, recolonization was impossible. The Pyrenees and the Alps, which stretched from east to west meant that many trees were unable to move south ahead of the ice. Once trapped they perished, leaving Europe with a far less diverse tree flora than that of North America or Asia.

The modern era

Since the last ice age began to wane 14,000 years ago, the temperature of the earth has gradually increased and trees have begun to recolonize temperate areas of the world. Today there are over 80,000 different species of trees on earth.

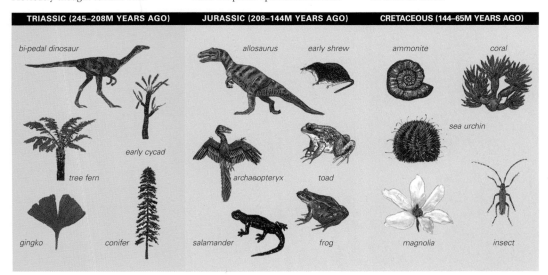

TRIASSIC (245–208M YEARS AGO)　**JURASSIC (208–144M YEARS AGO)**　**CRETACEOUS (144–65M YEARS AGO)**

bi-pedal dinosaur

allosaurus　*early shrew*

ammonite　*coral*

sea urchin

early cycad

tree fern

archaeopteryx　*toad*

magnolia

gingko　*conifer*

salamander　*frog*

magnolia　*insect*

CLASSIFICATION OF TREES

Classification is the process by which plants or animals are grouped and named according to their specific similarities. The theory and practice of classification is called taxonomy and those that work in this field are known as taxonomists.

There are over 300,000 different species of flowering plants and gymnosperms or conifers in the world. Botanists have classified them in order to try and make sense of the way that they are related to each other. Rudimentary grouping of trees has occurred for centuries, not always with great accuracy. For example the English oak, *Quercus robur*, and the holm (evergreen) oak, *Q. ilex*, have always been regarded as being closely related because of the fruit they produce. However, the sweet chestnut, *Castanea sativa*, and the horse chestnut, *Aesculus hippocastanum*, which were also once classified on the basis of their fruit, are now thought to belong to two quite different families.

The science of classification starts to become ever more complex as botanists study trees more closely. Where once trees were classified on the basis of just one or perhaps two characteristics, now many more of their features are compared before a degree of relatedness is decided.

Below: The horse chestnut (left) and sweet chestnut (right) were once thought to be related.

Carl Von Linné (1707–1778)

Ever since the time of the Greek philosopher Aristotle (384–322BC) it had been recognized that, both in the plant and animal world, there was a natural order where everything had its place and was linked to other species by a common thread. However, it was not until the 18th century that the Swedish botanist Carl Von Linné (also known as Linnaeus – the Latin name that he gave himself) made the first attempt to link all plants by one specific feature. He classified them by the way they reproduced themselves and the make-up of their reproductive systems – in the case of flowering plants, their flowers. As he admitted, his choice of feature for classification was artificial. Linnaeus had not found the common thread, the natural order of all living things. Nevertheless, he did create a system of classification that is still in use today.

Linnaeus invented the principle of using two Latin words to name a species. He chose Latin because it was the language of scholarship, and was understood across the world but no longer used as a spoken language, so

Above: Trees often have common names that refer to their place of origin, colouring, or use.

the meaning of its words would not change over time. The first of the two words is known as the generic (genus) name and the second the specific (species) name. The generic name gives a clue to the species' relationship with others. Closely related species are given the same generic name but different specific names. For example, the English oak is called *Quercus robur* and the closely related turkey oak is called *Quercus cerris*. All species with the same generic name are said to belong to the same genus.

Similar genera (the plural of genus) are combined into larger groups known as families. For example the oak genus, *Quercus*, belongs to the same family as the beech genus, *Fagus*. This family is called Fagaceae, and is commonly known as the beech family. Similar families are gathered together in turn into larger groups called orders. The beech family, Fagaceae, combines with the birch family, Betulaceae, to make the beech tree

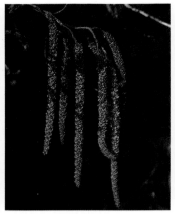

order Fagales. Similar orders are then combined into subclasses. The beech order is part of the hazel subclass, which is called Hamamelidae. In turn, Hamamelidae is combined with all of the other plant subclasses that are characterized by embryos that contain two seed leaves, to form a group that is known as the dicotyledons. This group is then joined together with all plants that have an embryo that contains only one seed leaf (monocotyledons) into one group that contains all flowering plants – the Magnoliophytina. Finally, this is gathered together with all of the other groups of seed-producing plants and then combined with the non seed-producing plants, such as ferns, into the Plant Kingdom.

Charles Darwin (1809–1882)

The 'common thread' or natural order of all living things was left for Charles Darwin to discover. Darwin recognized that plants, or animals for that matter, were usually alike because of their common ancestry.

Trees alive today can be classified in terms of their relatedness because they have all evolved over time from a single common ancestor that existed millions of years ago. The science of the ancestry of all living things is called phylogeny and it goes hand in glove with taxonomy.

Once the interrelatedness of all plants was understood, scientists began to trace back the evolution of trees. In many ways this process is similar to tracing back one's own family tree. The major difference is that fossil records are used. The different characteristics of trees living today compared to fossils of those from the past reflect the evolutionary changes that have occurred to the common ancestral line over millions of years. Each evolutionary change has been in response to a different environmental condition and has resulted in a different tree.

For most of us, classification only becomes pertinent when we are trying to identify a species.

Below: The cork oak (left) and common beech (right) look different, but in fact they are both members of the beech family, Fagaceae.

Above: It is possible to recognize trees that belong to the same family by certain obvious characteristics. For example hazel (above left), alder (above centre), birch (above right), hornbeam (not shown) all belong to the birch family, Betulaceae, and all produce catkins.

For botanists and taxonomists however, classification is an everyday procedure and a frequent cause of disagreement. It is now more than 200 years since Linnaeus developed his system of classification and 150 years since Darwin announced his theory of evolution. Nevertheless taxonomists still move species from one genus to another and some botanists cast doubt on whether plant classification should be based upon the evolutionary process at all.

ROOTS

Tree roots provide anchorage, ensuring that the tree does not fall over. They obtain water, the lifeblood of any tree, by sucking it from the soil. Roots provide the tree with minerals, which are essential for growth. They also store food, such as starch produced by the leaves, for later use.

Roots have the ability to influence the size of a tree. Around 60 per cent of the total mass of any tree is made up by its trunk. The remaining 40 per cent is split evenly between the branches and the root system, each having a direct relationship with the other. If there are not enough roots, the canopy and leaves will not be able to obtain enough water and branches will start to die back. In turn, if branches are damaged or removed and there are fewer leaves to produce food, a tree's roots will begin to die back.

A shallow existence

Contrary to popular belief, tree roots do not penetrate deep into the soil. In most cases the roots of even the tallest tree seldom reach down more than 3m/10ft. In reality the overall shape of a tree will look like a wine glass, with the roots forming the shallow but spreading base.

More than three-quarters of most trees' roots can be found within 60cm/24in of the surface. They seldom need

Below: Few trees can survive indefinitely in waterlogged conditions such as these.

to go deeper: the top layers of the soil are normally rich in organic material, minerals and moisture, which are just the ingredients that roots require.

However, roots do spread outwards considerably within the upper layers of the soil. The bulk of a root system will be found within 3–4m/10–13ft of a tree's trunk. However, very fine roots may spread anything up to twice the radius of the canopy, which in a large tree can mean anything up to 30m/98ft away from the trunk.

Tap root

Tap roots

The first root that every tree grows from its seed is called a tap root. Tap roots grow straight down and from day one have the ability to extract moisture and minerals from the soil. Within days of the tap root emerging from a seed, side roots (known as laterals) grow off the tap root and begin to move horizontally through the top layers of the soil. On some trees,

such as oak, the tap root will persist for several years. In most species, however, the tap root withers and the lateral roots take over.

Lateral roots

Lateral roots

Most lateral roots stay close to the surface for the whole of a tree's life. Although sometimes they may develop from the tap root or grow directly from the base of the trunk; in the latter case they can be over 30cm/12in across. Within 1m/3ft of the trunk they taper to around 10cm/4in across, and at 4m/13ft away they are usually under 5cm/2in in diameter and far more soft and pliable.

Allies and enemies

Within the soil, tree roots come into contact with the living threads, or *hyphae*, of numerous fungi. Quite often this association is beneficial to both the tree and the fungus. Usually the tree acquires hard-to-obtain nutrients such as phosphorus from the fungus and the fungus gets carbohydrates from the tree. These structures formed between tree roots and fungi in these mutually beneficial, or symbiotic, associations are known as mycorrhiza. Sometimes, however, contact with fungus can be damaging for a tree.

Roots and water

Tree roots require water to survive but they also need to obtain a supply of oxygen. It is important that they have water readily available, but roots will not do well if they are continually submerged. In constantly waterlogged conditions roots will not be able to obtain enough oxygen from the soil and a tree will effectively drown.

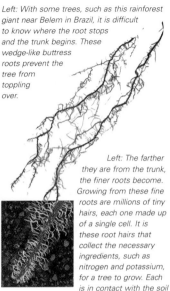

Left: With some trees, such as this rainforest giant near Belem in Brazil, it is difficult to know where the root stops and the trunk begins. These wedge-like buttress roots prevent the tree from toppling over.

Left: The farther they are from the trunk, the finer roots become. Growing from these fine roots are millions of tiny hairs, each one made up of a single cell. It is these root hairs that collect the necessary ingredients, such as nitrogen and potassium, for a tree to grow. Each is in contact with the soil particles around it and is able to absorb both the moisture and the diluted minerals that surround each particle. Root hairs have a lifespan of no more than a few weeks, but as they die, new ones are formed.

Knee deep

As its name suggests, the swamp cypress from the south-eastern United States grows in wet conditions. To counter the lack of soil oxygen, its roots have strange knobbly growths, called knees. These grow out of the water or wet ground to gain access to the air, and therefore to a supply of oxygen. Swamp cypress knees can reach a height of 4m/13ft. They not only absorb oxygen, but also provide support to the tree, making it less likely to blow over in strong wind.

Stilt roots

Stilt roots

Mangroves grow throughout the tropics on coastal mudflats. Many species of mangrove have stilt-like roots that arch from the main stem down into the mud. Once these have taken root, they help to anchor the tree so that it remains stable in the constantly moving mudflat silt. The stilt roots graft together, creating a three-dimensional framework that holds and supports the mangrove tree clear of the mud.

Pillar roots

Pillar roots

Both the weeping fig, *Ficus benjamina*, and the banyan, *F. benghalensis*, have roots that grow and hang down from the branches. These roots grow remarkably quickly – up to 1cm/½in a day – and once anchored in the soil they form prop-like pillars, capable of bearing the weight of the spreading branches they grew from originally. This system enables the tree

Below: The breathing roots of this mangrove protrude through the sand on Mafia Island.

to continue to grow outwards almost indefinitely. A single banyan tree planted in the Royal Botanic Garden of Calcutta in 1782, for example, now covers an area of 1.2ha/3 acres (larger than a football pitch) and has 1,775 pillar roots.

Below: Honey fungus, Armillariella mellea, is one of the biggest killers of trees in the temperate world. Once it has made contact with a tree's roots, it rapidly spreads through the entire vascular system of the tree, killing tissue as it goes.

TRUNK AND BARK

What makes a tree different from all other plants is the tough, woody framework it raises above the ground: a framework, made up of a trunk and branches, that lasts for the entire life of the tree. As each year passes, this framework gets bigger as the trunk and branches expand upwards and outwards.

The main purpose of the trunk is to position the leaves as far as possible from the ground. The higher they are, the less competition there is from other plants for light. Without light trees die. The trunk supports the branches and the branches support the leaves.

The trunk and branches have two other functions. They transport water, which has been collected by the roots, up through the tree to the leaves. Second, they move food, which is produced in the leaves, to every other part of the tree, including the roots.

Considering the importance of the functions that the trunk and branches perform, it is extraordinary that more than 80 per cent of their mass are made up of dead cells. The only living cells in a tree's trunk and branches are those in the area immediately beneath the bark. It is here that all of the activity takes place.

The inner tree

A tree's bark is like a skin. It is a corky waterproof layer that protects the all-important inner cells from disease, animal attack and, in the case of redwoods and eucalyptus, forest fires.

Some barks, such as that of the rubber tree, exude latex to 'gum up' the mouths of feeding predators. Pine trees have a similar defence mechanism, exuding a sticky resin, which can literally engulf a whole insect. Some trees, such as the South American quinine tree, *Cinchona corymbosa*, produce chemicals in their bark, which are poisonous to attackers.

Bark is perforated with millions of tiny breathing pores called lenticels, which pass oxygen from the outside atmosphere through to the living cells beneath. In cities and along busy roads these lenticels get clogged up with dirt and carbon. Some trees, such as the London plane, *Platanus x hispanica*, have adapted by regularly shedding their old bark. All trees are constantly growing and their girth expanding. This is reflected in the cracks and crevices that appear in the bark of many trees. As bark splits, new corky cells are produced to plug the gap.

Beneath the outer bark is the inner bark, or phloem. This is a soft spongy layer of living tissue that transports sap – sugary liquid food – from the leaves to the rest of the tree.

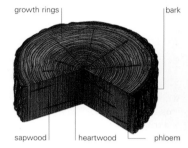

/ bark

sapwood / heartwood / phloem

Above: A section through the trunk of a larch tree showing the darker heartwood and the lighter sapwood.

Beneath the phloem is a thin tissue known as the cambium. Although it is only one cell thick, the cambium is extremely important. It is here that all tree growth takes place. Cambium cells are constantly dividing, producing phloem cells on the outside and on the inside wood cells, or xylem.

Xylem has two parts: the sapwood, made up of living cells, and the heartwood, composed of dead cells. The sapwood transports water and minerals from the roots to the leaves. Most of these are carried in sapwood made by the cambium during that year. The heartwood forms the dense central core of the trunk, supporting the tree and giving the trunk rigidity. The two main constituents of xylem are cellulose and lignin. Cellulose, a glucose-based carbohydrate, makes up three-quarters of the xylem and is used in the construction of cell walls. Lignin comprises most of the remaining quarter and is a complex organic polymer. It is lignin that gives wood its structural strength. If water and air reach the heartwood as a result of damage to the outer layers of the trunk, decay will occur and in time the tree may become hollow.

Left: Most trees over 500 years old are hollow. Eight people sitting around a table can fit inside the trunk of this tree.

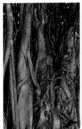
Banyan tree

Cola nut

Kapok

Papaya

Flame of the forest

Tembusu

Bark invaders

While bark exists to provide a protective barrier over the living tissue of a tree's trunk and branches, there are plenty of creatures capable of penetrating that barrier. Bark beetles and wood-boring insects eat cellulose and excavate breeding chambers and galleries for egg-laying purposes. Often the damage inflicted by insects is much greater than just the physical effects of their mining. Insects may carry fungal diseases such as Dutch elm disease. Beetles that bore into infected trees become coated with fungal spores and then carry those spores to other, healthy trees. Once underneath the bark, the fungus quickly blocks the cells transporting food and water, leading to the tree's demise.

How we use bark

Bark not only forms protection for trees, it can also be incredibly useful to

Below: Trees grow from terminal and lateral buds positioned towards the tip of the branches.

us. Much of the wine that we drink is sealed in bottles with bark from the cork oak tree, *Quercus suber*. In Mediterranean regions, cork oaks are grown in orchards. Every ten years or so, the outer corky bark is carefully removed, leaving the cambium layer intact. The cambium then produces more cork cells to replace the bark lost.

Bark also provides us with food and medicine. The spice cinnamon is made from the dried and ground bark of the Sri Lankan cinnamon tree, *Cinnamomum ceylanicum*, while the bark of the Pacific Yew, *Taxus brevifolia*, contains a substance called taxol, which has been highly effective in the treatment of some forms of cancer.

Some trees have very attractive bark, making them ideal ornamental plants for parks and gardens. The Tibetan cherry, *Prunus tibetica*, has highly polished mahogany-red bark, for example, and the Himalayan birch, *Betula utilis*, has bark the colour of freshly fallen snow.

Himalayan cherry

Indian horse chestnut

Floss silk tree

Eucalyptus

Paperbark maple

Birch 'Snow Queen'

BUDS

Buds act as protective sheaths for the growing tips of trees during the coldest months of the year. In winter, even though deciduous trees will have shed their leaves, they can still be readily identified by their buds.

For trees to grow they need water, minerals, nutrients and the right growing conditions, namely sunlight and warmth. In parts of the world where there is little seasonal variation, such as the tropics, favourable climatic conditions may allow growth to continue all year round. However, even in tropical rainforests very few trees grow non-stop. The normal pattern for most trees, particularly those in temperate regions, is for a period of growth followed by a period of rest. The period of rest coincides with the time of year when the climate is least favourable to growth. Across Britain, Europe and North America this is during the cold and dark of winter.

Throughout the winter resting period, the growing tips of a tree, known as the meristem, are vulnerable to cold winds and frost. Prolonged low temperatures can very easily damage or even kill the meristem. Trees have therefore evolved ways to protect this all-important tissue.

Protective sheath

During early autumn, as the growing season approaches its end, the last few leaves to be produced by the tree are turned into much thicker but smaller bud leaves, known as scales. These

Above: A lime tree breaking bud.

Above: A sycamore breaking bud.

toughened leaves stay on the tree after all of the other leaves have fallen off and form a protective sheath around the meristem. This sheath is known as a leaf-bud. Its thick scales are waterproof and overlap each other, creating a defence system able to withstand the onslaught of winter. Often a coating of wax, resin or gum is used to strengthen these defences.

Inside the bud

Winter buds contain all that the tree will need to resume growing once the days lengthen and the temperature increases in spring. Inside is a miniature shoot, miniature leaves all carefully folded over one another and, in some species, such as the horse chestnut, *Aesculus hippocastanum*, miniature flowers.

Trees without buds

Not all trees produce buds, even in temperate regions. Some, such as the wayfaring tree, *Viburnum lantana*, have 'naked buds' with no bud scales. At the end of the growing season in this species, the last leaves to be formed stop growing before they are

fully developed. A dense layer of hair then forms on them to protect them from the cold and they proceed to wrap themselves around the meristem. When spring arrives the protective leaves simply start growing again from where they left off.

Eucalyptus trees also have 'naked buds' but as back-up they produce tiny concealed buds beneath the leaf base. These are only activated if the growing tip gets damaged.

Below: An Indian horse chestnut bud opening to reveal long, thin, down-covered leaves.

Below: Some buds contain all of the cells needed for the whole of the following year's growth. Others contain just enough to start growing in spring and then produce more growth cells once the leaves have emerged from the bud.

Some conifers, such as western red cedar, *Thuja plicata*, and lawson cypress, *Chamaecyparis lawsoniana*, have no distinct buds at all; instead they produce little packets of meristematic cells, which are hidden beneath the surface of each frond of needles.

The growing season

As spring arrives, buds open and the leaves begin to emerge. For all trees the trigger for this to happen is increasing warmth and light. Individual species each have their own trigger point, which is determined by their geographical origins. Species that originated in colder regions, such as birch or willow, burst bud earlier than those such as horse chestnut or sweet chestnut, which evolved in warmer parts of the world. Birch instinctively knows that northern European summers are relatively short affairs, and that it needs to get going as quickly as possible to make the most of the growing season. Sweet chestnut, on the other hand, instinctively expects a long, Mediterranean summer, so is in less of a rush to get started.

Trees that have everything for the coming year's growth pre-packaged inside the bud tend to have a single growth spurt immediately after their leaves

Day one

Day two

Left: The sticky buds of horse chestnut will open over a period of three days in springtime.

Day three

Bud arrangements

Even in winter, when deciduous trees display bare branches, trees can still be identified by the shape, size, colour and arrangement of the buds on the twigs.

Opposite buds

The buds of trees such as sycamore and ash are said to be opposite – that is, in pairs on each side of the twig, exactly opposite each other. Ash buds are easily recognizable by their distinctive black colouring.

Alternate buds

The buds of trees such as beech and willow are arranged alternately on different sides of the twig. Willow buds are generally longer and more slender than those of beech.

Hairy buds

Magnolia buds are very distinctive and easily recognized by their covering of thick grey fur. Magnolia buds are some of the largest found on any tree.

Clustered buds

Oak buds appear almost randomly on the twig, but always with a cluster of buds at the tip. Cherries also adopt this clustered approach.

Whiskered buds

As well as being clustered, some oaks, such as the turkey oak, also have thin whiskers surrounding the buds.

Naked buds

The wayfaring tree does not have a true bud. Instead it has immature hairy leaves which surround the growing tip to protect it from the cold.

emerge. This can mean that they achieve virtually all their growth for the whole year within the first four weeks of spring. Those trees that over-winter with just enough growth cells in the bud to aid emergence in spring grow more slowly but grow for a longer period of time. In some instances these species may continue growing for more than 100 days. However, by the end of the season the overall growth of each will be similar.

Below: Sweet cherry buds.

Below: Magnolia bud.

Below: Wingnut bud.

Below: Horse chestnut bud.

LEAVES

Each leaf on a tree is a mini power station, generating food, which the tree uses to provide the necessary energy for living and growing. The process by which leaves produce food is called photosynthesis. During this process the leaves absorb carbon dioxide and emit oxygen.

Leaves contain a green pigment called chlorophyll, which absorbs light energy from the sun. This energy is used to combine carbon dioxide, which the leaf absorbs from the atmosphere, with water taken from the soil. The resulting products are glucose and oxygen. Glucose provides the energy to run the tree and can be turned into starch for storage or cellulose, which form the tree's cell walls. The oxygen is released by the leaf back into the atmosphere. A mature tree can produce the same amount of oxygen every year as that used by ten people.

Leaf structure
Each leaf is covered by a skin of tightly packed cells known as the epidermis. This skin is coated by a waxy covering called the cuticle. The cuticle acts as waterproofing, preventing the leaf from losing any more water than is necessary. The transfer of oxygen and carbon dioxide to and from the atmosphere takes place through tiny holes in the cuticle known as stomata. Stomata are concentrated on the underside of the leaf away from the direct heat of the sun to minimize water loss. The cells around the stomata have the ability to enlarge and decrease the size of the hole. Despite this, water is lost from the leaf through the stomata. This loss of water is known as transpiration. Even though stomata normally

cover less than one per cent of a leaf's total area, the amount of water lost in this way can be astonishing. A large deciduous tree can lose up to 300 litres per day in summer. The lost water is usually replaced by water drawn from its roots. In times of drought however, the amount of water lost may exceed that available to the roots. When this happens the leaves wilt and die, stopping the tree from producing food.

Inside the leaf cells, the chlorophyll is contained in millions of tiny cell-like vessels called chloroplasts. Most of these are found in the upper part of the leaf, which receives the most light. Beneath the chloroplasts are the vascular tissues that make up the xylem, and which transport the raw ingredients for photosynthesis, such as water and minerals, all the way from

Above: In autumn, when chlorophyll production ceases and any residue decays, other pigments are revealed in the leaves.

Below: In spring new leaves form.

Below: Summer.

Below: The changing tones of autumn.

Above: Winter profile.

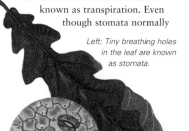

Left: Tiny breathing holes in the leaf are known as stomata.

Below: Cross section of a leaf.

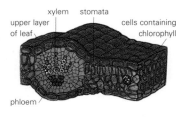

upper layer of leaf — xylem — stomata — cells containing chlorophyll — phloem

the roots to the leaf. Alongside the xylem is the phloem, which transports the sugary products of photosynthesis from the leaf to all other parts of the tree. Both vascular systems rely on a process called osmosis to move liquid. Osmosis is a process whereby liquid moves from one cell to another. The catalyst for this to happen is the fullness, or turgidness, of each cell. As one cell becomes full, so the liquid within it permeates through the cell wall into a neighbouring cell that is less turgid. Once this cell is full, liquid starts to permeate from it into the next empty cell and so on.

Leaf size and shape
One of the most interesting things about leaves is the incredible range of shapes and sizes. The smallest so-called broad leaf is produced by the Arctic willow, *Salix nivalis*. This tundra species has leaves less than 5mm/¼in long. Some conifers have needles that are even smaller.

All broad-leaved tree leaves have one thing in common: a network of visible veins, which spread out across the leaf from its base. It is within these veins that the xylem and phloem are found. The veins join together at the leaf base to form the stalk, or petiole.

Simple leaves
These come in a wide variety of shapes. At their most basic they may be entirely round or heart-shaped, or have no indentation around the leaf edge. Many leaves, such as those of cherry trees, are oval in shape and have small serrations around the edge. On others the serrations may be more pronounced, as with the sweet chestnut, *Castanea sativa*. Some trees, such as the oak, produce leaves with distinctive lobing. These lobes may be rounded, or more angular.

Compound leaves
At first glance the leaflets of compound leaves look like separate leaves growing off the same stalk. However, closer inspection of a new compound leaf reveals that the whole stalk and its leaflets all emerge from the same leaf bud. It is in essence all one leaf. Many of the trees in our cities have compound leaves. One of the most easily recognized is the horse chestnut, which has seven or nine large leaflets all attached to the same point of the main leaf stalk. The golden-leaved robinia, *Robinia pseudoacacia* 'Frisia', has paired leaflets that come off the leaf stalk opposite each other (pinnate leaflets), as does the European ash, *Fraxinus excelsior*. Occasionally the leaf stalk to which the leaflets are attached may sub-divide, producing side stalks and a bipinnate leaf. One of the best examples of a tree with bipinnate leaves is the Japanese angelica tree, *Aralia elata*, which has leaves in excess of 50cm/20in long.

Evergreen leaves
A deciduous tree keeps its leaves for only part of the year; they grow in the spring and fall off in the autumn. By contrast, evergreen trees, which include most conifers and trees such as holly, box and laurel, have leaves all year round. This does not mean the same leaves stay on the tree for the whole of its life. Evergreen leaves fall from trees and are replaced throughout the year. The real difference between evergreen and deciduous trees is that the leaves of deciduous trees all fall at around the same time, while those of evergreens do not. On average, evergreens keep their leaves for between three and five years, although on some firs and spruces the needles may be retained for up to ten years.

Needles
Conifers such as pines, firs, larches, spruces and cedars all have needles, as do yews and redwoods. Although visually quite unlike other leaves, needles are in fact just compact versions of simple leaves, and do the same job of producing food for the tree. Needles lose far less water than the leaves of broadleaf trees. They are therefore better equipped to survive in areas where water is in short supply, such as northern temperate regions where the ground is frozen for months at a time.

Below: The soft, feathery needles of the western red cedar.

Below: The 1m/3ft-long leaves of the tropical breadfruit tree.

Below: The fine pencil-like leaves of Eucalyptus champmaniana.

FLOWERS

Flowers contain the tree's reproductive organs. Some trees, such as cherry, have both male and female reproductive organs within the same flower. Others, such as hazel, have separate male and female flowers on the same tree. Some trees only produce flowers of one sex.

Flowers are the sex organs of a tree. What happens in them determines the ability of the tree to reproduce itself. Trees are passive organisms; they cannot actively go out and search for a mate, so they have to engage in sex by proxy. Each tree needs a go-between to get its pollen either to another tree or from the male to the female part of its own flowers. Depending on the species of tree, this go-between may be wind, water or an animal, such as a bird or insect. Over countless generations each species has developed its own flower to suit a specific go-between. The African baobab tree, *Adansonia digitata*, for example, has developed large flowers that produce vast quantities of nectar at night. These flowers attract bats, which feed on the nectar and in the process get covered in pollen. The bats transfer that pollen from flower to flower and tree to tree.

Inside the flower

There are almost as many different forms of tree flower as there are trees. Indeed the whole classification system for trees (and other flowering plants) is built around the design of the flowers. Although outwardly tree flowers may look very different, their basic components are all the same. Most flowers have four main parts: the stamen, which is the male reproductive organ and produces the pollen; the stigma, which receives the pollen; the

Below: Magnolia flowers are pollinated by insects.

style, which links the stigma to the ovary; and the ovary, which contains ovules that, after fertilization, develop into seeds. A few tree flowers have only male or female parts.

If both male and female components are present in the same flower, then the flower is said to be 'perfect'. The tree is then capable of self-pollination and it is known as an hermaphrodite. Self-pollination is far from ideal, and can lead to genetic weaknesses in the same way as inbreeding does in animals. Cross-pollination with another tree is better because it enables different genes to mix. Trees that are hermaphrodites include cherry, laburnum and lime.

To avoid self-pollination, some trees have developed separate male and female flowers. Such trees are known as monoecious and are particularly common where the main vector for pollination is the wind. Monoecious trees include beech, birch and hazel.

Some species only produce male or female flowers on any one tree. These species are 'dioecious'. This division of trees into sexes overcomes the problem of self-pollination but raises a new problem. Trees of opposite sexes must be relatively close together to have any chance of breeding at all. Trees that are dioecious include yew, holly and the New Zealand kauri pine. Holly berries are found only on female trees and then only when there is a male tree not too far away.

Below: The flowers of the Italian alder are pollinated by the wind.

Life cycle of a flower from bud

Left: In winter the flowers are protected within buds.

Left: The flowers emerge as the temperature rises in spring.

Right: Once fully open the flowers are pollinated by insects.

Left: Fertilized flowers produce berries in summer.

Right: Birds eat the berries and the seed they contain are dispersed within the birds' droppings.

Welcoming guests

Tree flowers come in all manner of sizes, shapes and colours. Much of this diversity is linked to the pollinator. In general, flowers that are pollinated by animals tend to be larger and showier then those that are pollinated by wind. The wind is indiscriminate but animals need to be attracted. Some animal pollinators are attracted to flowers of certain colours and a few trees actually alter the colour of flowers once they have been pollinated to discourage further visitors. For example the colour of the markings inside the flowers of the horse chestnut, *Aesculus hippocastanum*, changes from yellow to red after pollination. To a bee, red looks black and very unattractive, so it visits a flower that has yet to be pollinated instead.

Sometimes tree flowers themselves may be quite inconspicuous but are surrounded by showy sterile flowers or leaf bracts to draw pollinators to them. The pocket handkerchief tree, *Davidia involucrata*, from China, for example, has large white bracts that guide pollinating moths to its flowers.

Gone with the wind

Most wind-pollinated trees evolved in places where there was a shortage of insects. Wind pollination is common in the colder northern temperate regions of the world. All conifers are wind pollinated and most produce such large amounts of tiny-grained pollen that on breezy days, clouds of the stuff may fill the air around them. Conifer stamens are positioned at the tips of the branches to aid dispersal. Those of pine trees are bright yellow and stand upright from the needles like candles.

Alder, birch and hazel are also wind pollinated. Rather than having erect

Below: Burmese fish tail palm is pollinated by insect and by wind.

Above: Magnolia grandiflora has some of the largest flowers borne by any tree.

stamens like those of pines they have drooping catkins, each containing millions of pollen grains. In many places, these catkins are one of the first signs of spring. They are made all the more conspicuous by the fact that they appear before the tree comes into leaf. Oak also has pollen-bearing catkins but these are hardly ever seen because they open in late spring after the tree's leaves have emerged.

Insect pollinators

Pollination by insects is by far the most common method of reproducing among trees. More than 60 per cent of tree species in equatorial regions are pollinated by some kind of insect. Trees that use insects as pollinators tend to produce flowers with copious amounts of sugar-rich nectar. Their pollen grains are larger than those of wind-pollinated species and also quite sticky so that they adhere to insects' bodies.

Below: Male and female persimmon flowers are borne on separate trees.

Birds and mammals

In the tropics, birds are important pollinators of tree flowers. Flowers that are pollinated by birds tend to be tubular in shape (to keep the nectar out of reach of other animals), brightly coloured and unscented, since most birds have a poor sense of smell. Hummingbirds use their long beaks to reach inside the flowers of trees such as the angel's trumpet, *Brugmansia*, from Brazil. In Australia and South Africa, bottle-brush trees, *Banksia*, have masses of protruding pollen-covered stamens, which brush against birds' feathers as they collect nectar. Few temperate trees are pollinated by birds. The giraffe is the most unique pollinator of all. It transfers pollen between the flowers of the knobthorn acacia, *Acacia nigrescens*, which grow high up in the tree's branches.

Below: The Prunus x yedoensis is grown for its stunning display of spring flowers.

SEEDS

Seeds are the next generation of tree. They contain all that is necessary for the creation of a mature tree virtually identical to its parents. Seeds come in a variety of forms; they may be contained within nuts, fruit or berries, or have 'wings' to aid dispersal by the wind.

Every tree seed has the potential to develop to become part of the next generation. 'From little acorns mighty oak trees grow' is a well-known and accurate saying, although it has to be said that a tiny proportion of all acorns will ever have the opportunity to become mighty oaks. A mature oak tree can produce up to 90,000 acorns in a good year, but fewer than 0.01 per cent will grow to become anything like as mighty as their parent. Most acorns will be eaten by mammals or birds (a wood pigeon can eat up to 120 acorns a day), or simply land in a spot where germination and growth are impossible. It is because of this low success rate that the oak produces so many acorns. In terms of seed production 90,000 is actually quite modest; alder trees will produce around 250,000 seeds a year.

Different seed types
Seeds are produced from the female part of the flower once it has been pollinated and one or more of its ovules fertilized. Just as tree flowers have evolved over millions of years in their quest to find the most effective method of pollen dispersal, so tree seeds also take on many different forms. The fundamental problem facing pollen is exactly the same as that for seeds; trees cannot move, so they have to find other ways of distributing what they produce.

Some trees wrap their seeds inside brightly coloured, sweet tasting fruits or berries. The fruit or berry has two

Left: Apple seeds are contained within an edible, fleshy, protective fruit.

Left: The first year's growth from an acorn.

roles; firstly to protect the seed and secondly to tempt animals to take it away from the tree. After a fruit or berry is eaten, the seed passes through the animal's digestive system and is excreted, often far from the parent tree, in its own ready-made package of fertilizer.

Other trees enclose their seeds within tough outer casings as nuts. Once again, these casings help to protect the seed, but in this case it is the actual seed inside that is the attraction. Squirrels will collect and hoard the nuts, eating some in the process, but many of the nuts are never eaten and wherever the squirrel has stored them they will proceed to germinate and grow.

Conifer seed is known as 'naked seed' because each individual seed is produced without a protective coat or cover. Conifer seeds are encased together in a cone but the scales of each cone can be bent back to reveal the unprotected seed inside. Each seed is often equipped with light, papery wings, which enable it to "fly" away from the parent tree on the wind.

Below: The seeds of the crab apple are contained within a berry loved by birds.

Other seeds, such as those of alder, are contained in cones, but rely on water for their distribution.

Whatever the method of dispersal there is always one aim: to get the seed as far away from the parent plant as possible. There is no point competing for living space with one's own progeny. Dispersal also reduces the risk of cross-pollination between parent and offspring in years to come.

Matters of time
Most ovules are fertilized within days of pollen landing on the stigma. How long seed takes to ripen varies from tree to tree. Elm seed can be ready for dispersal less than ten weeks after fertilization.

Most temperate broad-leaved trees disperse their seed in the autumn of the year in which their flowers were fertilized. In many conifers, on the other hand, seed takes two years to develop. This is because fertilization is delayed for a year after pollination. Some conifers will hold seed in a sealed cone for many years after it has ripened, waiting for a special event to trigger its release. For the giant redwood this trigger is forest fire, which kills off all competing vegetation and provides a thick bed of nutrient-rich ash for its seeds.

Below: The seeds of the Douglas fir are paper-thin and borne on bracts within a woody cone.

Above: Tamarind pods grow to 18cm/7in long and contain a soft pulp.

Above: The nuts or seeds of the cream nut tree are edible, but difficult to find because they are also irresistible to monkeys.

Above: Some seed heads are incredibly attractive, such as these remarkable magnolia seed capsules.

Right: The seeds of sweet chestnut are contained within a spiny casing to protect them from predation.

Berries and fruit

Most fruit and berries are brightly coloured to attract birds. Bright red rowan berries are loved by starlings, while red holly berries attract waxwings and fieldfares. The berries of hawthorn provide a vital source of food for many different birds in the middle of winter.

Normally, the flesh of berries is digested but the seed is not, and it gets passed out in the bird's droppings.

Fruits range in size from large tropical varieties, such as mango and papaya, to the small, glossy, black berry of the European elder tree. Many fruits are eaten regularly by humans, and some trees, such as apple and olive trees, are farmed specifically for their fruit. Some fruits only become good for human consumption as they begin to rot, such as the fruit of the medlar tree, *Mespilus germanica*.

Nuts and other seeds

Essentially, nuts are edible seeds. Some, such as hazelnuts,

Above: Seeds such as this of the sycamore are attached to wings to aid dispersal.

Right: Walnut seeds are protected within a hard wooden casing.

are encased in a woody shell. Others, like chestnuts, are surrounded by an inedible but more fleshy outer coating. They are distributed by birds and mammals. Squirrels and jays both bury those nuts that they are unable to eat straight away. Some of the store is never returned to and these may germinate. Some seed casings are impenetrable to all but the most determined of foragers. The Brazil nut has one of the toughest cases of all but it is staple food for the agouti, a cat-sized rodent. Agoutis collect up Brazil nuts and bury them, just like squirrels do in temperate forests.

Many dry seeds rely on wind for their dispersal. Eucalyptus seed is like fine dust and can be borne considerable distances on the wind. Some heavier seeds also ride on the wind. Those of maple and ash trees have extended wings known as keys, which help to keep the seed airborne. Sycamore seeds have paired keys.

Alder trees grow alongside rivers and watercourses. Each of their seeds is attached to a droplet of oil, which acts like a tiny buoyancy aid. After falling from the tree into the water, the seed floats downstream until it is washed ashore. Wherever it lands it will attempt to grow.

The world's largest seed comes from the coco de mer palm, *Lodoicea maldivica*, which is found in the Seychelles. It looks like an enormous double coconut and takes ten years to ripen. The heaviest of these seeds can weigh up to 20kg/45lb.

Germination

Inside every ripe tree seed are the beginnings of a root, a shoot and two specialized leaves, which are known as cotyledons. If a seed is fortunate enough to end up in a suitable location it will either germinate straight away or lie there until conditions become right for it to do so. In temperate regions this is usually in spring, when both the air and soil temperatures begin to rise.

Below: The first thing to emerge from the seed is the root. No matter which way the seed is lying, the root will instinctively grow downwards into the soil. Once the root has become established and is providing additional food and moisture, the two cotyledons emerge and begin the process of photosynthesis. Shortly afterwards, true leaves appear from a bud between the cotyledons and the tree begins to grow.

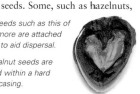

LIFE CYCLE OF TREES

The life cycle of a tree is a fascinating, and in many cases very long, process of change and development. From the initial struggle, coupled with rapid growth, while a sapling establishes itself, through a middle period of relative inactivity, to an eventual slow decline into old age and death.

There is a saying that 'an oak tree spends 300 years growing, 300 years resting and 300 years dying'. Although these time spans may be optimistic for some oaks and very optimistic for most other tree species, there are, in fact, several important truths within this statement.

There is no doubt that trees have the potential to live for a very long time. They include by far the oldest living organisms on earth. The oldest tree in the world is a bristlecone pine, *Pinus longaeva*, growing 3,050m/10,000ft up in the White Mountains of California and has been verified as 4,700 years old. Close on its heels is Scotland's Fortingall yew, which is estimated to be somewhere between 3,000 and 5,000 years old.

Trees go through various stages of growth in much the same way as humans. In our early years we develop and grow at a relatively fast rate. By

Below: This sweet chestnut is in the final stages of its life cycle. It is still alive even though its trunk is hollow.

the end of our teens, growth slows down and stops and our bodies stay pretty much the same for the next 40 years or so. Then, as our three score years and ten approaches, we begin our decline into old age and eventual demise. This is similar to a tree's life cycle, the only real difference being the amount of time that it takes.

So how do trees grow?

As with any living organism, it all begins with a birth. In the case of trees it is the germination of a seed. However, it can also occur naturally when a piece of an older tree breaks away, develops its own root system and grows as a completely new tree. This frequently happens with willows growing along riverbanks. When the river floods, a lower branch may be broken off by the force of the water and swept downstream. Eventually this branch will come to rest and from it roots will develop, grow down into the mud and a new willow tree will grow. A tree grown in this way is known as a

Above: Some trees in old age need a helping hand to prevent their branches from crashing to the ground.

cutting. Cuttings have the same DNA as the tree they were once part of.

Seeds do not have the same DNA as the tree that produces them. A seedling tree will develop its own genetic identity, taking on characteristics from both its male and female parent or, in the case of a self-fertilized tree, the characteristics contained in the genes of the male and female sex cell that initially produced it.

Once a seed or cutting has put down roots and sprouted its first leaves, the process of growth begins. The first few years, known as the establishment years, are critical in the life of any tree and the odds are stacked against survival. A young tree is vulnerable to being eaten or trampled by animals, its root system may not be able to withstand drought and it is far more vulnerable to forest fire than a larger tree. Other major threats include long periods of frost or waterlogging, which a fully grown tree would survive more easily.

The growing years

Once a tree is established, it can get down to some serious growing. Trees grow upwards, downwards and outwards. The rate of growth will be determined by many factors, including the availability of water, light and climatic conditions.

Upward growth

There is a popular misconception that trees grow from the bottom up and are continually moving skywards. In other words, if you were to go to any tree and paint a ring around it 2m/6½ft above the ground and then return to it five years later when the tree was 2m/6½ft taller then the ring would be 4m/13ft above the ground. Well, this is not the case; the tree may well be 2m/6½ft taller but the painted ring will still be 2m/6½ft above the ground. Growth occurs year on year only from the tips of the previous year's growth.

At the tip of each branch are growing cells. As these divide, they make the branch grow longer, so the tree becomes taller and wider. How fast these cells divide will depend on the species and many other external factors, such as the availability of water and light. Some plants, such as bamboo, can grow more than 50cm/20in a day, but there are no trees that grow at anywhere near this rate. The fastest-growing trees come from tropical parts of the world, simply because there are no seasonal changes and so growing conditions remain good throughout the year. One species of tropical eucalyptus from New

Below: Tree growth is determined by the amount of sunlight the leaves can absorb and the uptake of water through the roots.

Guinea, *Eucalyptus deglupta*, can grow 10m/33ft in just over a year, as can *Albizia falcata*, another tropical tree, from Malaysia. Willow is one of the fastest growing temperate trees. When it is coppiced (the stem is cut back down to the stump) it can grow more than 3m/10ft in a year.

Growth in any tree is affected by age; as trees get older their growth rate decreases until they eventually stop growing altogether.

Downward growth

There is a direct relationship between growth put on above ground by the branches and that achieved below ground by the roots. This relationship is known as the root:shoot ratio. The leaves on the branches provide food for the roots and in turn the roots provide water and minerals for the leaves. As a tree grows, it produces more leaves. These require more water and minerals, so the root system needs to grow in order to provide these minerals. To do that it needs more food from the leaves. The balance is a fine one; if leaves or roots fail, the tree will suffer and may even die.

Outward growth

As the branches grow longer, so the trunk, branches and roots become thicker. In temperate regions a mature tree trunk increases in diameter by about 2.5cm/1in every year. This growth is a result of the need for the tree to be able to transport increasing amounts of water and food to and from its branches. This process occurs immediately below the bark surface in the vascular system, which contains the phloem and xylem. Throughout a tree's life, the cambium constantly produces new phloem and xylem cells, which cover the inner wood. As these cells are added, so the tree's girth expands. In tropical regions this growth continues throughout the year. In temperate areas, growth only occurs in the spring and summer.

Growth rings

The cycle of growth in a temperate tree can be clearly seen when the tree is cut

Above: Saplings without competition for light from other trees will establish much more quickly than those trying to grow in the shade.

down. Each year the new cells that are produced under the bark create a new ring of tissue, visible in a cross section of the trunk. Each ring has light and dark sections. The light tissue is less dense and is made up of cells produced in the spring when the tree is growing fastest. The dark part of the ring is composed of cells laid down in the summer when the rate of growth has slowed. These rings are known as growth rings. By counting them it is possible to work out the age of a tree.

Old age

As a tree gets older, so its rate of growth slows down and eventually it stops. In theory, provided that the root:shoot ratio remains stable the tree should live for many years. However, as a tree ages and its growth slows, so it also loses the ability to defend itself from attack. Opportunistic fungi will exploit this and eventually disease and decay upset the root:shoot ratio and the tree starts to decline.

Rejuvenation

Some trees are able to respond to hard pruning or coppicing. The re-growth is effectively young wood and displays all the characteristics of a tree still in the early growing years of its life. In theory, and often in practice, coppicing carried out on a regular basis can extend a tree's life almost indefinitely. At Westonbirt, the National Arboretum in England, there is a coppiced small-leafed lime, *Tilia cordata*, at least 2,000 years old, which is still growing as a juvenile.

TREES AND WEATHER

Climate is the main controlling influence over where and how trees grow. Throughout time, climate changes have dictated the pattern of tree distribution and evolution across the world. In times of intense cold, such as the ice ages, billions of trees perished.

The relatively settled climate of the last 12,000 years has resulted in fairly static patterns of tree distribution over that time. However, even minor changes in the earth's climate now, perhaps due to the greenhouse effect, could have a dramatic effect on future patterns of tree distribution and growth. An increase in the mean temperatures of just 2°C/35°F would result in a significant northward migration of temperate trees in the Northern Hemisphere. Thousands of acres of sugar maple plantations in New England would disappear as the climate became too warm for them. Spruce would have difficulty surviving in the United States, Great Britain and central Europe for the same reason. Deserts would expand into the Mediterranean regions of the world, threatening the natural diversity of trees in California, Spain and France. In the Southern Hemisphere more than half of the rainforest of northern

Australia would disappear, along with vast areas of rainforest in central Africa and South America.

Influencing weather patterns

Whereas the climate controls tree distribution on a global scale, trees actually influence weather patterns on a regional or local level. The process of photosynthesis raises humidity in the air. Where trees are found in large numbers, such as in equatorial rainforests, this humidity has an effect on daily rainfall. In the morning the sun warms up the forest and warm, moist air rises from the trees. As the air rises, it cools and condenses into water droplets, causing clouds to form, and it begins to rain. This process is repeated daily throughout the year all around the world's equatorial regions.

Reducing the effects of weather

Ever since man evolved, trees have been used to reduce the effects of cold and wind exposure. Forests and woodlands provided natural shelter, and many original human settlements

Above: Palm trees are well equipped to cope with the heat and drought of the tropics.

were created in clearings cut from the forest. Trees were also used to shelter stock. The practice of 'wood pasture' – grazing cattle or sheep within a forest – has been going on in Britain since the 2nd century. Timber from trees has been used to build shelters and dwellings for thousands of years and early man discovered that wood from trees could be burnt to provide heat.

Today, our use of trees to control the extreme effects of the weather has become far more sophisticated. We now know which are the best species to include within wind shelter belts, for example. We know how tall, how wide and how dense the belt should be. We also know how far away it should be from the area we wish to shelter. On average, a shelter belt 20m/66ft wide and 20m/66ft tall will provide wind protection on the leeward side for a distance of 400m/1,312ft. Such protection can increase cereal crop production by as much as 20 per cent.

Trees also help reduce the effects of frost. If tree shelter belts are planted across a hillside, cool air descending the slope will become 'trapped' by

Below: In areas of severe exposure trees will grow away from the direction of the prevailing wind.

the trees. Frost 'ponds up' above the trees rather than travelling farther down the hillside or into the valley bottom. The same principle applies to snow. Strategic planting of trees on lower mountain slopes dramatically reduces the chance of avalanches occurring and their effects if and when they do occur.

Another important function trees have is the stabilization of soil and prevention of erosion. Tree roots help bind soil to the ground and soak up rainfall, while leaves and branches reduce the effects of wind on the ground. The latter is particularly important in areas of low rainfall where soil is often dry and loose. One of the biggest causes of soil erosion is deforestation. Once trees have been felled, fragile topsoil becomes exposed to both wind and rain, and is soon washed or blown away. Once the soil

Above: Reducing temperatures in autumn will trigger an explosion of colour as the leaves begin to die.

Below: Many conifers have adapted to regular heavy snowfall by developing weeping branches, which are able to shed snow.

Above: Welwitschia mirabilis *has adapted successfully to the Namibia Desert, where less than 3cm/1¼in of rain falls each year.*

has gone so has the opportunity to grow food crops. Trees are now being re-planted in the Sahel region of Africa to try to reduce the effects of soil erosion and also the expansion of the Sahara Desert.

Trees also help protect against the effects of heavy rainfall and flooding. Those planted in water catchment areas soak up excessive amounts of rain, enabling the soil to release smaller volumes of water into the watercourses gradually, thus reducing the possibility of flash-flooding farther downstream. Trees such as willow, planted alongside riverbanks, reduce the effects of riverbank erosion when water levels are high.

Indicators of climate change

In many parts of the world where there are seasonal differences in rainfall and temperature, trees form clear annual growth rings in their trunks. The width of these rings varies depending on the growing conditions in any one year. In cold, dry years, tree growth is slow, producing a narrow ring. In warm, wet years, tree growth is faster and the ring produced wider. As tree rings build up, they provide a year-by-year record of changes in climate. Because trees live for such a long time, these records may cover hundreds or thousands of years.

TREES AND POLLUTION

Trees are the air filters of the world. They absorb carbon dioxide from the air and replace it with oxygen. They also trap airborne particle pollutants, which are one of the main causes of asthma and other respiratory problems.

The process by which trees produce food and thereby harness energy for growth is called photosynthesis. As part of the process, trees absorb vast amounts of carbon dioxide from the atmosphere and break it down. The carbon is effectively locked up within the trees' woody structures of roots, trunk and branches. A healthy tree can store about 6kg/13lb of carbon a year. On average, 0.4ha/1 acre of trees will store 2.5 tonnes of carbon per year. Trees are the most effective way of removing carbon dioxide from the atmosphere and thereby reducing the effects of global warming.

When trees die naturally, the carbon they contain is gradually released back into the atmosphere as carbon dioxide. This happens so slowly that the gas can be reabsorbed by the next generation of trees growing alongside. However, when trees, or coal (fossilized wood), are burnt, the carbon they contain is released much more quickly. Living trees and other plants are only able to reabsorb some of it – the remainder stays in the atmosphere. Continual burning means a continual build-up of carbon dioxide.

The practice of 'slash and burn' agriculture, carried out in tropical rainforests to create agricultural land,

Below: Across the world 40ha/100 acres of forest are felled every minute.

Above: One of the biggest threats to the tropical rainforests is the ongoing expansion of agriculture.

releases hundreds of thousands of tonnes of carbon dioxide back into the atmosphere. Even more serious is the large-scale burning of fossil fuels, such as coal and oil, in the West. The carbon dioxide produced traps more of the sun's energy than normal inside the atmosphere and so contributes to global warming.

During the photosynthesis process trees not only remove carbon dioxide from the atmosphere, they also replace it with oxygen, effectively producing clean air. Every day 0.4ha/1 acre of trees produces enough oxygen to keep 18 people alive.

Biological filters
As well as removing carbon dioxide from the atmosphere, trees absorb sulphur dioxide produced by the burning of coal; hydrogen fluoride and tetrafluoride released in steel and phosphate fertilizer production; and chlorofluorocarbons, which are produced by air-conditioning units and refrigerators. Trees also trap other particle pollutants, many of which are by-products of the internal combustion engines in cars. These particles are one

of the main reasons for the increasing incidence of asthma and other respiratory illness in people across the world. Research has shown that trees act as excellent biological filters, removing up to 234 tonnes of particle pollutants every year in cities the size of Chicago.

Trees cause pollution
Some trees emit large amounts of certain volatile organic compounds (VOC), which react with nitrogen oxides and sunlight to form ozone – a significant ground-level air pollutant. Volatile organic compounds exist in fossil fuels, such as petrol. Most petrol nozzles are fitted with filters to stop the VOC from escaping into the atmosphere. It is of course impossible to stop trees from emitting high rates of VOC, but some tree species produce more than others. Scientists suggest that these trees should not be grown in large quantities where high levels of nitrogen oxides already exist, such as in and around towns and cities.

Trees that produce high levels of VOC include eucalyptus, oaks and poplars. The blue haze often seen over the Blue Mountains near Sydney, Australia, is in part caused by the release of VOC by eucalyptus trees. Ten thousand eucalyptus trees will emit about 10kg/22lb of VOC an hour, which is equivalent to that released by the spilling of 54 litres/12 gallons of petrol an hour.

There is evidence to suggest that certain tree species, particularly conifers such as spruce and fir, increase acidification of streams, rivers and lakes. This increased acidification can cause the decline of freshwater flora and deplete stocks of freshwater fish. The evidence for this effect is not clear-cut however. Acid deposition from the atmosphere (acid rain) can increase acidification in freshwater, and therefore the decline of freshwater flora and fauna may be attributable to that. There is much debate over whether conifer plantations in water-catchment areas actually do increase the level of acidification. Long-term studies are currently underway in North America, Great Britain and Scandinavia to establish the truth. In the meantime, forest policy in Great Britain at least has been revised so that coniferous tree species are no longer being planted directly adjacent to lakes and rivers.

Trees are subject to pollution

Although trees can act as natural "air filters", ideally they need clean air to live and grow. Photosynthesis becomes more difficult for trees in areas of high air pollution. In highly polluted cities such as Mexico City, it is estimated that less than ten per cent of the tree population is healthy. Some trees, such as the London plane, *Platanus* x *hispanica*, are able to cope with relatively high levels of air pollution, but it is estimated that more than half of the trees in large cities are in decline due to air pollution. In New York City the average lifespan of trees is less than 40 years.

In many parts of the world the air is now highly polluted. Pollutants such as sulphur dioxide reach high into the atmosphere where they vaporize and mix with other chemicals and moisture to form acid rain. The damage caused by acid rain affects both coniferous and broad-leaved trees. The effects are more obvious on evergreen trees than deciduous ones because their needles or leaves are replaced less often. Discoloration of foliage is the first sign of acid rain damage. This is followed in extreme cases by defoliation and death. Nutrients are stripped from the leaves as acid rain falls through the canopy and the roots are slowly killed as the acid soaks into the soil.

There are a range of other sources of pollution that affect trees. Too much ozone disrupts the process of photosynthesis and can sterilize pollen, so reducing seed production. Particles of soot are also harmful because they coat leaves and thus prevent vital sunlight getting through. Even salt that is spread to de-ice roads can affect the chemistry of the soil around the roots of roadside trees.

Below: Views of greenery makes travelling by road less stressful for motorists, but the pollution emitted by vehicles is ultimately damaging to the trees.

ANCIENT TREES

The oldest living things in the world are trees. The life span of most is measured in centuries rather than years and there are some that have existed for millennia. Temperate trees generally live longer than tropical trees; although there are baobabs in South Africa said to be more than 3,000 years old.

Until recently we knew more about the ages of trees in temperate than tropical regions (because there are no annual growth rings to count in tropical trees), but now evidence suggests that tropical trees can live just as long as their temperate counterparts. For many years it was thought that the rapid growth and decay that occurs in tropical rainforests meant that tropical trees rarely lived for more than 200–300 years. However, recent advances in carbon-dating have clearly shown that many tropical trees are capable of living for more than 1,000 years.

Ancient tropical trees

There is speculation that some tropical trees may be more than 1,500 years old. The oldest tropical tree recorded with any certainty is a *castanha de macaco* (monkey nut), *Cariniana micrantha*, which is related to the Brazil nut. One specimen of this

Below: Africa's oldest known tree is a baobab growing in Sagole, South Africa. It could be over 5,000 years old.

Amazonian rainforest tree is known to be 1,400 years old. The cumaru tree, *Dipteryx odorata*, from Brazil, is also known to live for more than 1,000 years. One of the best known and largest of all tropical rainforest trees, the Brazil nut, *Bertholletia excelsa*, regularly attains heights in excess of 50m/164ft, but none of those carbon-dated so far has been found to be more than 500 years old.

Africa's oldest known tree is a baobab, *Adansonia digitata*, growing in Sagole, in South Africa's Northern Province. Near its base it is 13.7m/45ft in diameter, and it is thought to be more than 5,000 years old.

The oldest tree in the world with a known and authenticated planting date is a fig tree, *Ficus religiosa*. It grows in the temple gardens in Anuradhapura, Sri Lanka, and was planted as a cutting taken from another fig tree given to King Tissa in 288BC. King Tissa planted it and prophesied that it would live forever: over 2,000 years later it is still going strong.

Above: English oaks, Quercus robur, have been known to live for more than 1,000 years.

The world's oldest?

People have a fascination for the oldest and biggest. Over the years ancient trees have grabbed their fair share of the headlines. An 11,700-year-old creosote bush, *Larrea tridentata*, was said to grow in California's Mojave Desert. A 10,000-year-old huon pine, *Dacrydium franklinii*, was 'discovered' in Tasmania. The most incredible is a king's holly, *Lomatia tasmania*, also from Tasmania, which was reported to be up to 40,000 years old. These are all great stories, but are they true?

Close scrutiny reveals that these are all clones that have grown from plants that were on the same site before. In terms of the age of the growth that can be seen above ground today, none is any older than 2,000 years. Whether or not they qualify for the title of oldest living trees is debatable. They have the same genetic material as the seedlings that first grew on the same spot all those millennia ago, but then all living things that reproduce asexually have the same genetic make-

up as their ancestors. We would not consider a female aphid produced asexually to be the same animal as its mother. No doubt the veracity of these claims will continue to be debated for some time to come.

Ancient temperate trees

The oldest living tree in the temperate world is the bristlecone pine, *Pinus longaeva*. Bristlecone pines originate from the White Mountains of eastern

Below: Olive trees will live for centuries; the oldest in the world is believed to be 2,000 years old.

California. The oldest are found in an area known as Schulman Grove, named after Dr Edward Schulman, who spent more than 20 years studying the trees there. In 1957 he discovered that many of them were over 4,000 years old and one of them, which he christened Methuselah, was considerably older. These trees all have solid centres, so Schulman was able to bore right into the centre of each tree and take out pencil-thick radial cores, from which he was able to count the growth rings. Carbon-dating since then has confirmed Dr Schulman's original age for these trees and Methuselah is verified as being 4,700 years old.

For many years the giant redwoods, *Sequoiadendron giganteum*, were assumed to be the oldest trees because they were the biggest. We now know that isn't the case. The oldest redwood is a giant known as General Sherman, which stands in the Sequoia National Park, California, and is approximately 2,700 years old.

The oldest tree in Europe is believed to be the Fortingall Yew, which stands

Above: Methuselah, the world's oldest bristlecone pine, grows in the White Mountains of eastern California.

in a churchyard in Perthshire, Scotland. Although much of its trunk has rotted away, its girth suggests that it is at least 4,000 years old. There are many contenders for the oldest oak tree, *Quercus robur*, and in truth we will probably never know for certain which is the oldest. Oaks have a habit of looking more ancient than they actually are. England and Wales have possibly the best collection of ancient oaks in western Europe. There are several oaks in Britain and across Europe that are believed to be up to 1,000 years old, but their exact age is anyone's guess. Three oaks are locally proclaimed as being 1,500 years old: one in Brittany, France, another one in Raesfeld, Germany, and a third in Nordskoven, Denmark. The oldest olive tree, *Olea europaea*, grows in the Garden of Gethsemane, at the foot of the Mount of Olives in Jerusalem. It is said to have been planted at the time of Christ.

GIANT TREES

Trees are by far the largest living organisms on earth. Some of the tallest specimens would dwarf the Leaning Tower of Pisa in Italy, or Big Ben in London. A single banyan tree in India covers an area that is larger than a football pitch.

Not only are trees the oldest living things on earth, they are also the largest. The world's biggest trees include the most famous individual trees of all. Some of these arboreal giants are local celebrities, others nationally famous and a few known about around the world.

Almost every country has its dendrologists (tree buffs) and tree measurers, who can always be readily identified by their measuring tapes and skyward gaze. Countries such as Britain and the United States even have their own tree registers, which detail the largest specimen of just about every tree species that grows in that country. Books are written about the biggest trees and photographs taken. Champion trees are big news and interest in them is growing.

What is a champion tree?

A champion tree is the tallest or fattest living example of a species. In order to be proclaimed champion it must have been accurately measured and those measurements recorded in an agreed way. The height is taken to be the distance from the ground to the top of the tallest living part of the tree. Girth is considered to be the distance around the trunk, and is read at 1.3m/4ft 3in from the ground.

Right: Compare the height of trees to the Leaning Tower of Pisa, which stands 58m/190ft tall. From the left: Montezuma cypress, 35m/115ft; New Zealand kauri, 51m/167ft; giant redwood, 83m/272ft.

Tropical giants

The tallest tropical tree, which is called *Araucaria hunsteinii*, is a relative of the monkey puzzle and grows in New Guinea. When last measured the largest specimen was 89m/293ft tall. In Africa, Dr David Livingstone (1813–1873), camped under a baobab tree, *Adansonia digitata*, which had a girth of 26m/85ft. This tree appears not to exist now and the largest baobab alive today is 13.7m/45ft in circumference.

One of the largest trees in the world is found in the Calcutta Botanic Garden in India. It is a banyan tree, *Ficus benghalensis*, that was planted in 1782. In not much over 200 years it has grown into an arboreal titan with vital statistics that are simply astounding. The tree covers an area of about 1.2ha/3 acres and can provide shade for more than 20,000 people. It has 1,775 'trunks' (pillar roots) and an average diameter of more than 131m/430ft.

Temperate giants

For sheer volume, the largest single living thing on earth is a giant redwood, *Sequoiadendron giganteum*, called

Above: One of the largest trees in South America is this Fitzroya cupressoides, which has a height of 44.5m/150ft.

General Sherman. The tree, which stands in the Sequoia National Park, California, has a diameter of 17.6m/58ft, is 95m/311ft tall and weighs 1,200 tonnes.

General Sherman is not the tallest tree in the world, however. This accolade belongs to a specimen of its cousin, a coastal redwood, *Sequoia sempervirens*, which goes by the simple but appropriate name of 'Tall Tree'. It grows on the Californian coast and when last measured, in October 1996, was 112.2m/368ft tall. If transported to London and placed next to the Houses of Parliament, this tree would be more than 14m/46ft taller than Big Ben.

General Sherman is not the fattest tree in the world either. That title is held by a Montezuma cypress,

Taxodium mucronatum, growing in the grounds of a church at Santa Maria del Tule, near Oaxaca in southern Mexico. This enormous tree is made even more impressive by its very close proximity to the church and other buildings, which take on toy-town proportions in its shade. The Santa Maria del Tule Montezuma cypress has a girth of 36.3m/119ft, outstripping even the mighty African baobabs.

Two trees from New Zealand also deserve a mention. They are the kauri, *Agathis australis*, which grows in the north of the North Island, and the totara, *Podocarpus totara*, which grows on both the North and South Islands. Both trees are antipodean giants, reaching ages approaching 2,000 years, girths of 13m/43ft and heights approaching 60m/197ft. They hold great religious significance for the Maori people, who believe that important spirits live within the trees.

Both species have suffered at the hands of the loggers over the last 200 years and many of the biggest specimens have gone. Those that remain are protected within special sanctuaries, such as Waipoua State Forest, north of Auckland.

The tallest tree ever recorded was an Australian eucalyptus called the mountain ash, *Eucalyptus regnans*, measured in 1872 in Victoria. Unfortunately it never qualified as a champion tree because when it was measured it was already on the ground. It was 132.6m/435ft tall at the time, and thought to have been over 150m/500ft tall when it was at its peak. At one time giant mountain ash clothed the valleys that run from Melbourne to Tasmania. Today, only remnants of this mighty forest remain. There are still some big eucalyptuses in Australia, but nothing approaching these dimensions. There are now no trees over 100m/328ft tall.

There are no world-record-breaking trees in Britain but there is plenty of time for that situation to change. Britain has a good climate for tree growth. It is moist with few extremes of temperature as a result of its proximity to the Gulf Stream. A large number of exotic trees have been introduced into Britain in the last 200 years and many of them are world-beaters in their native habitats. The British examples are still babies but their growth rates so far suggest that some have the potential to develop into record-breaking giants. The title of tallest tree in Britain is currently shared between two Douglas firs, *Pseudotsuga menziesii*, both growing in Scotland. Each measures 62m/203ft tall – taller than the Leaning Tower of Pisa, which stands at 58m/190ft.

Below: In southern California, the giant redwoods regularly attain heights in excess of 100m/328ft.

THE PLANT HUNTERS

For centuries man has sought out new tree species; firstly for food, medicine and timber and latterly for ornamental purposes. Over the last 200 years plant hunters have scoured the world in search of previously unknown species to introduce to gardens and arboreta.

Ever since they first appeared on earth, trees have spread to new places by natural means. Sometimes their movements have been the result of large-scale geological events, such as the break up of the supercontinent Pangaea, which began to occur around 193 million years ago. Sometimes they have been in response to changes in global climate. For example successive ice ages saw a migration of plants away from the poles and towards the Equator. Interglacial warm periods saw a movement back towards the poles but also away from low-lying land, which became flooded as the polar caps melted and sea levels rose. These movements occurred over many plant generations and sometimes took tens of thousands of years.

Later, the development of human civilization brought an accompanying quickening in the rate at which trees migrated and species settled in entirely new areas. Humans quickly realized that trees were useful. They could be used to make basic tools, produce food and provide shelter and fuel. As humans moved around the earth, they

Below: The Royal Botanic Gardens at Kew, England, has one of the finest ornamental tree collections in Europe.

started using the trees that surrounded them and took parts of other trees with them, sometimes in the form of their fruits and berries. Inadvertently to begin with, but then consciously, humans became the vehicle for seed distribution and then, ultimately, tree movements. Trees took on new importance, becoming symbols for pagan worship. As time passed, their medicinal properties became better understood too.

The early plant hunters

The first record of plant hunting and tree collecting dates from 1495 BC. Queen Hatshepsut of ancient Egypt sent out expeditions to Somalia to collect the incense tree, *Commiphora myrrha*, which produced a resin that was burned in Egyptian temples.

The Romans sped up the process of distribution, taking many trees with them as their empire expanded. Later, during medieval times, monks were also responsible for moving trees right across Europe, as they developed a network of monasteries from Russia to Portugal.

As civilization developed, so did the aesthetic appreciation of trees. Trees were considered an integral part of

Above: The Oriental plane is indigenous to Albania and Greece. It was introduced to much of Europe by the Romans.

garden creation and from the 16th century onwards, European plant hunters started to look outside their own continent for new introductions. One of the first trees to be brought in was the horse chestnut, *Aesculus hippocastanum*, which was introduced into Vienna and then into France and England from Constantinople by the Austrian botanist Clusius in 1576. It was followed shortly afterwards by the Oriental plane, *Platanus orientalis*, introduced into Britain from Greece in the late 1590s.

It was in the early 1600s, as the exploration of North America began, that plant hunting really started to take off. Stories of amazing new trees swept through Europe and everyone with influence and money wanted their own collection. John Tradescant, (1570–1638) and his son, also called John (1608–1662), were the first organized plant hunters. After starting out as gardeners for the rich and famous (including King Charles I), they introduced a phenomenal range of plants including dogwoods, *Cornus* species; lilac, *Syringa* species; red maple, *Acer rubrum*; the tulip tree,

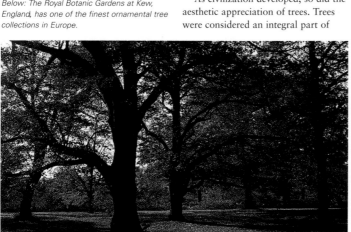

Liriodendron tulipifera; and the false acacia, Robinia pseudoacacia, from North America into Britain.

The past 200 years

As travel became easier, European plant hunters ventured farther and farther away in search of ever more exotic and wonderful trees. North America, South America, the Himalayas, China, Japan, Australia and New Zealand all contained huge, largely unexplored tracts of land, ripe for discovery. Expeditions were funded by wealthy landowners or botanical institutions such as London's Kew Gardens, keen to build up their collections of botanical rarities. Arboreta sprang up all over Europe. Among the first was the magnificent Westonbirt Arboretum in England, created by Robert Holford in 1829.

David Douglas (1799–1834)

Born in Perthshire, Scotland, David Douglas was probably one of the greatest tree collectors of all time. From an early age he displayed a great interest in all things horticultural. By the time he was ten he was apprentice gardener to the Earl of Mansfield at Scone Palace. In his early twenties he was commissioned by the Horticultural Society in London (later to become the Royal Horticultural Society), to collect for them in North America. Over the

Below: The tulip tree, Liriodendron tulipifera, *was introduced into Europe from America by John Tradescant in 1650.*

next ten years Douglas walked almost 10,000 miles, exploring the Pacific coast of North America. Along the way he collected over 200 species never seen in Europe before, which included the Monterey pine, *Pinus radiata,* from Southern California; the noble fir, *Abies procera;* the grand fir, *Abies grandis;* and perhaps the finest tree of them all, the Douglas fir, *Pseudotsuga menziesii.*

William Lobb (1809–1864)

A Cornishman, William Lobb was the first plant hunter employed by Veitch and Sons, nurserymen of London and Exeter. His first journey for the company in 1840 took him to the South American Andes, where, among other things, he collected more than 3,000 seeds from the monkey puzzle tree, *Araucaria araucana.* The seed was dispatched to Veitch and Sons, and by 1843 the first seedlings were on sale. In 1849 Lobb was sent on his second trip, this time to North America, with the aim of picking up from where Douglas had left off 20 years before. It was on this trip that he discovered the western red cedar, *Thuja plicata,* and collected seed from the coastal redwood, *Sequoia sempervirens.* Lobb's third trip in 1852, again to North America, was the one for which he is best remembered. It was on this trip that he discovered the largest tree in the world, the giant redwood, *Sequoiadendron giganteum.* Lobb arrived back at Veitch and Sons with seed from this remarkable tree just before Christmas in 1853. The tree was immediately named 'Wellingtonia' in honour of the Duke of Wellington, who had recently died. The Victorians fell in love with Wellingtonia and virtually overnight it became the most sought-after tree for estates across the British Isles.

Ernest Wilson (1876–1930)

Another employee of Veitch and Sons, Ernest Wilson was sent to China in 1899 to find what had been described as "the most beautiful tree in the world" – the pocket handkerchief tree, *Davidia involucrata.* When he

Above: General Sherman, the world's tallest giant redwood. This species was introduced to Europe by William Lobb.

arrived in China, he was presented with a scruffy piece of paper with a map on it. The map covered an area of roughly 51,200km^2/20,000 miles^2. On it was marked the rough position of a single pocket handkerchief tree. Amazingly Wilson found the tree's location, but all that was left was a stump. The tree had been cut down and its timber used to build a house. Undaunted, Wilson continued to search the area and eventually found another pocket handkerchief tree, from which he collected seed to send back to England. In 1906 Wilson left the employment of Veitch and Sons to became a plant hunter for the Arnold Arboretum in Boston, USA. From there he carried out further trips to China and to Japan. During his plant-hunting career Wilson introduced more than 1,000 new species to the western world.

Charles Sargent (1841–1927)

Born in Boston, USA, Sargent created the Arnold Arboretum. A botanist and plant hunter, he collected mainly in North America and Japan. Sargent had several plants named after him. Perhaps the best-known is the Chinese rowan, *Sorbus sargentiana.*

TREE CULTIVATION

People grow trees for several reasons. Foresters plant on a large scale to produce trees for timber, while farmers and landowners cultivate them for their fruit. Many trees are grown for pure ornament, to brighten up parks or add structure to gardens.

Ever since people first appeared on earth they have lived in a world dominated by trees. When modern humans finally arrived 35,000 years ago, trees covered more than two thirds of all dry land on the planet. The other third was covered by ice or occupied by grassland or desert.

Modern humans have grown up alongside trees and forests. People have used them for shelter, as a source of food, fuel and all the necessary implements for life. In the beginning,

Above: Fruit trees have been cultivated in orchards for more than 2,000 years.

Below: The first roadside tree planting was carried out by the Romans, to provide shade for their marching legions.

they would have used whatever tree happened to be near to them. Gradually, however, awareness grew that certain tree species were better used for specific purposes. Harvesting trees from the wild had one serious disadvantage however – the more that were taken, the farther people had to travel from home to find the right tree for the job.

Semi-natural forests

Eventually people learnt that trees could be 'managed'. Seed could be collected, seedlings grown and trees planted in more convenient locations closer to human settlement. These were the first artificial plantations. At the same time, people realized that some trees did not die once they had been cut down, but re-grew from the stump. They learned that regular cutting (coppicing) provided a ready supply of thin, straight sticks, which could be used for a variety of purposes. The trees were all native to the area, and had been part of the original natural forest, but now that people were managing them in these ways, the forest had become semi-natural.

Above: The para rubber tree is indigenous to the Amazon rainforest but is grown in plantations throughout South-east Asia.

Early plantations

The idea of growing specific trees together in one place for a clearly defined purpose dates back almost to prehistory. Ancient Egyptians grew plantations of sandalwood so that they could have a ready supply of incense, for example. Both the ancient Greeks and Romans planted groves of olives, as well as orchards of cork oak. Fruit, such as apples and pears, have been grown in orchards in much of western Europe since early medieval times. In Britain from the 16th century, forests of oak were planted to supply timber to build wooden ships for the navy. One large warship could consume as many as 3,000 trees.

With the advent of the Industrial Revolution came the need for vast quantities of raw materials, many of which came from trees. One tree that typifies this change is the para rubber tree, *Hevea brasiliensis*, which originates from the Amazon rainforest. As early as the 15th century, rubber

was being extracted from this tree to make shoes, clothes and balls. In 1823, Charles Macintosh, a Scottish inventor, coated cloth with rubber and invented the raincoat we now know as the mackintosh. Just 16 years later, an American, Charles Goodyear, discovered that heating rubber with sulphur caused the rubber to stabilize. This led to many new uses for rubber, including the manufacture of tyres. In 1872, Joseph Hooker, director of the Royal Botanic Gardens at Kew in England, sent plant hunter James Wickham to Brazil to collect seed from the para rubber tree. There, Wickham collected more than 70,000 seeds. Out of these seeds, 9,000 grew into young saplings, which were then shipped to Sri Lanka and Singapore. These saplings began rubber growing on an entirely new continent and formed the basis for plantations that now cover more than a million ha/2,500,000 acres across South-east Asia.

Plantation forestry

The form of tree cultivation that we are most familiar with is the growing of trees in man-made forests for timber. Around 1.2 billion ha/3 billion acres of the temperate world are now covered with commercial timber plantations. More than 80 per cent of

Below: In many areas, timber-producing, fast-growing conifers have replaced traditional broad-leaved woodlands.

these are plantations of softwood trees – fast-growing conifers, such as the Monterey pine, *Pinus radiata*, which is widely planted in New Zealand, Australia and South Africa, and sitka spruce, *Picea sitchensis*, which is grown in the Northern Hemisphere. Both of these species have the potential to grow more than 1m/3ft in height per year. They are both harvested at 20–60 years of age, depending on growth rates, for use in construction or to create pulp for papermaking. Once harvested the forest is re-planted and the whole process begins again.

This 'sustainable' forestry has far less impact on the environment than the wholesale destruction of natural forests, such as that which occurs in many parts of the tropics. Even so, it does have its disadvantages. Conifer plantations are normally made up of just one species, often not native to the country it is being grown in. The trees are planted close together in rows, thus creating poor habitats for wildlife. Some organizations have begun to acknowledge that this is unacceptable, and have taken steps to remedy the problem. In Britain, the Forestry Commission, for example, now ensures that at least 20 per cent of the ground is left unplanted and that other, native tree species are also grown within the conifer plantation.

Plantation forestry is not restricted to temperate countries, though. Large

Above: There are more than 20 different varieties of fir, which are now cultivated for Christmas trees.

areas of Java are now planted with teak, for instance, to provide wood for furniture-making. Like the softwoods from conifer plantations, this timber is sustainably produced – the trees are replaced with new saplings immediately after they are cut down. Sustainable forestry is now being developed all over the world and is actively encouraged by organizations such as the Forestry Stewardship Council (FSC), based in Oaxaca, Mexico. Consumers are also better informed about where wood comes from – most products made from timber grown in certified sustainable forests now carry an FSC label.

Christmas trees

Growing Christmas trees is now big business, with thousands of acres being devoted to their cultivation. These are 'short rotation crops' being harvested normally in less than ten years from planting. Traditional Christmas trees, such as the Norway spruce, *Picea abies*, now have competition from many other species, such as the Nordman fir, *Abies nordmanniana*, which has citrus-scented needles that remain on the tree for longer after it has been felled.

TREES FOR TIMBER

Wood is humanity's oldest natural resource. It has provided us with food, fuel, weapons, shelter and tools for thousands of years. Wood can be easily shaped, it has great strength and is durable, hard-wearing and naturally beautiful.

If you look around any room, you will see several things that are made of wood. Furniture, panelling, doors and window frames are the most obvious, but even the paint on the doors, the paper this book is printed on and the photographic film the photographs were taken with, all have a proportion of wood in them.

Wood is unique because it is the one basic natural resource that mankind can renew. When all of the world's oil, gas and coal has been exhausted, there will still be trees and we will still have wood – that is, as long as we manage our forests and woodlands properly.

What is wood?

Wood is a type of tissue produced within trees by a specialized cell layer known as the cambium. Cambium encircles a tree, producing on its outside phloem cells, which transport food manufactured in the leaves to other parts of the tree, and on its inside xylem cells, or living sapwood, which transport water and minerals from the roots to the leaves. This sapwood is constantly being renewed,

Below: Teak is indigenous to India and South-east Asia. It produces a strong, durable timber.

overlaying the existing sapwood and so enlarging the core of the tree. As each growing season passes, so the core of the tree gets larger. Only the xylem cells in the current year's sapwood are able to transport water and minerals; the cells beneath gradually die. As they die the old cells undergo a chemical change, turning drier, harder and normally darker. It is this change that creates the visually distinctive banding in a sawn log, demarcating the boundary between the young, soft sapwood and the older, harder inner wood, or heartwood.

Is there a difference between wood and timber?

No, both refer to the woody cells that make up the structure of a tree. The difference between the two words is a matter of timing. When a tree is standing and growing, its bulk is referred to as wood. Once the tree has been cut down and sawn up, that bulk becomes timber. We buy planks from a timber merchant, but once the planks have been turned into something, the object that they have been turned into is generally referred to as being made of wood, rather than timber.

A global business

Timber is produced by almost every country in the world. In general, softwood timber, such as spruce, larch and pine, is more likely to have been grown in temperate regions, whereas hardwood timber, such as teak, mahogany and ebony, is more likely to have come from the tropics. Some countries, such as Canada and Brazil, are virtually self-sufficient in timber supplies. Others, such as Great Britain and Japan, must import up to 90 per cent of their timber requirements. Over the last 100 years or so, the global trade in timber has increased dramatically. For many developing

countries, timber is financially by far their single most important export. Unfortunately, this reliance on timber has resulted in the destruction of millions of hectares of natural forest. It is estimated that 80–200 million hectares/200–500 million acres of natural forest were destroyed in the last ten years of the 20th century.

Timbers of the world

The world's most famous types of timber are household names. But, perhaps surprisingly, not every type is sourced from trees of just one species. Ebony, for instance, may come from any one of five different trees.

Mahogany

Ever since the 16th century, when it was first brought to Europe by the Spanish, mahogany has been the most prized wood for cabinet- and furniture-making in the world. Mahogany is the collective name for the timber of several species of tree in the genus *Swietenia*, which originate from Central and South America. The most

Below: The red-brown colouring of mahogany timber has long been valued for cabinet and furniture production.

Above: Pine timber is used for general construction work and economy furniture.

favoured species is *S. mahoganii*, but because this tree is now very rare most commercial supplies of mahogany now come from *S. macrophylla*. Mahogany has distinctive, rich red-brown colouring, complimented by dark figuring. As well as being beautiful, it is also very durable and is quite impervious to rot and woodworm.

Teak
Indigenous to India, Burma and Indonesia teak, *Tectona grandis* has been introduced to Central America, where it is widely planted. Its timber has beautiful golden brown heartwood and is extremely strong and durable. Teak timber is used to make all manner of things, including furniture, boats, staircases and sea defences.

Ebony
Certain species of *Diospyros* provide the timber known as ebony. There are two main types: African ebony, produced by trees that originated from West Africa and Madagascar, and East Indian ebony, produced by trees from Sri Lanka and southern India. Both types have a distinctive almost jet-black colouring. Ebony has always been used for furniture and sculpture, but it is best known as the timber used to make the black keys of pianos.

Oak
There are more than 450 species of oak, most of which occur in temperate regions. The most important group for timber production is known as the "white oaks" and includes the English oaks, *Quercus robur* and *Q. petraea*; the American oak, *Q. alba;* and the Japanese oak, *Q. mongolica*. Timber from white oak has a creamy fawn sapwood and yellow-brown heartwood with silver-grey veining. It is one of the world's most popular timbers. Oak beams were used in the construction of many of the most important old buildings in western Europe, including the majority of tythe barns, churches and cathedrals.

Spruce
This is a group of 20 evergreen conifers found growing naturally in most of the cool temperate regions of the Northern Hemisphere. Of those, only two are commercially important: Norway spruce or 'whitewood', *Picea abies*; and sitka spruce, *Picea sitchensis*. Norway spruce occurs in the wild throughout much of northern Europe, while sitka spruce originates from the Pacific coast of North America. Both timbers are widely used for interior building work, general joinery and the manufacture of pallets. Sitka spruce produces a significant amount of the world's virgin pulp supply for newspapers.

Pine
European redwood, red deal and Scots pine are just three of the names given to the timber of *Pinus sylvestris*, a tree that occurs right across Eurasia from Spain to Siberia. Pine is one of the heaviest softwoods and has attractive pale red-brown heartwood. It is often used in the manufacture of economy furniture, as well as for general building work. In Britain, pine has been used for many years for making railway sleepers and telegraph poles.

Elm
The elm occurs naturally throughout northern temperate regions of North America, Europe and Asia. Although different species grow in different regions, the characteristics of the timber are broadly similar. The heartwood is dull brown with a reddish tinge and has prominent, irregular growth rings, which give an attractive figuring. Elm is very water-resistant – in Roman times it was used as a conduit for water, the heartwood being bored out to create a basic drainpipe. The Rialto bridge in Venice stands on elm piles. Sadly, because of Dutch elm disease, elm timber is in short supply across much of Europe and elm trees are much rarer than they once were.

Below: Oak was the traditional timber for building ships and for roofing beams.

GENERAL USES OF TREES

It is easy to take wood for granted because it features in almost every area of life. Humans have had a long association with trees and consequently there is an impressively wide range of useful products that can be obtained from trees.

Over the centuries and to the present day, tree products have found their way into the larder, medicine cupboard, wine cellar, paint store, garage, garden shed, wardrobe, bathroom, library and jewellery box.

Medicinal uses

Although the bark and wood of trees is seldom edible, extracts from them have given rise to some of the world's most important medicines. Malaria is said to have killed more people than all of the wars and plagues in history combined. Oliver Cromwell and Alexander the Great are two of the better-known people to have died at its hands. For centuries the only known treatment was quinine, an alkaloid found in the bark of the evergreen cinchona tree, which grows in the tropical forests of Peru and Bolivia. Quinine was first used to treat malaria by the Quechua Indians and in the 16th century the Spanish Conquistadors realized its potential. Called the 'miracle cure' when it finally arrived in Europe, it was used to cure King Charles II, King Louis XIV and the Queen of Spain, among countless others. Quinine has been chemically reproduced since the 1940s; however, in recent years some forms of malaria have developed resistance to synthetic quinine and the

Below: Aspirin was originally derived from the bark of the white willow, Salix alba.

Above: Extracts of the leaves of Gingko biloba *have been used to improve memory loss.*

cinchona tree has once again become the centre of attention.

If you have ever had a headache then the chances are that you will have reached for a bottle of aspirin, the world's most widely used drug. Before aspirin came in bottles, aches and pains could be cured by walking to the nearest river and finding a piece of willow bark to chew on. Aspirin is a derivative of salicylic acid, which comes from the bark of the white willow, *Salix alba*. Nowadays aspirin is produced synthetically.

The last remaining member of a family that existed when dinosaurs roamed the earth, the maidenhair tree, *Ginkgo biloba*, has long been used for medicinal purposes. The leaves have traditionally been a staple of Chinese herbal medicine and used to treat everything from asthma to haemorrhoids. Now maidenhair tree leaves have found their way into western medicine and are used to treat memory loss and coronary conditions. Fluid extracted from the leaves helps

to improve blood circulation. It relaxes blood vessels, enhancing blood flow throughout the body but in particular that going to the brain.

More than 2,000 different trees are currently used for medicinal purposes. Many, such as the Pacific yew, *Taxus brevifolia*, are helping in the fight against cancer. *Castanospermum australe*, the Australian Moreton Bay chestnut, contains an unusual alkaloid called castanospermine, which is able to help neutralize the Aids virus HIV. Witch hazel, *Hamamelis virginiana*, is a tree with strong antiseptic qualities. Native American tribes such as the Cherokee made a 'tea' of the leaves, which they used to wash sores and wounds. Another important medicinal tree species is *Eucalyptus globulus*. Its leaves contain the oil cineol, which is very effective in the treatment of coughs, sore throats, bronchitis and asthma.

Trees in the home

One of the world's favourite drinks – coffee – is made from the seeds (beans) of three small evergreen trees, *Coffea arabica, C. canephora* and *C. liberica.* Now cultivated extensively throughout the tropical world, they originate from the montane forests of Ethiopia, where they grow to approximately 6m/20ft tall.

Products made from the Amazonian tree *Hevea brasiliensis* have found their way into just about every home in the world. Better known as the para rubber tree, its cultivation accounts for about 90 per cent of the world's raw rubber supply. *Hevea brasiliensis* produces a gummy, milky white sap beneath its bark as a natural defence against attack from wood-boring insects. This sap, known as latex, is tapped and collected once the tree reaches seven years old. An experienced tapper can harvest about

Above: A mature cork oak may produce up to 4,000 bottle stoppers per harvest.

Above: Olive trees provide an important crop of fruit for many Mediterranean regions.

450 trees a day. *Hevea brasiliensis* is cultivated on more than 7 million ha/17 million acres of land across the tropics. These plantations yield about 6.5 million tonnes of natural rubber every year.

Cork comes from the outer bark of the cork oak tree, *Quercus suber*. An evergreen tree, the cork oak is grown in Mediterranean countries, such as Portugal, Spain and Italy. Cork is a great insulator and it protects the tree's inner bark from forest fires and hot dry summer winds. It is also resistant to moisture and liquid penetration. The Romans used cork to insulate their houses and beehives, as soles for their shoes, stoppers for bottles, jugs and vases, floats for fishing nets and buoys for navigation purposes. Today its main use is in the wine industry. The cork oak is not stripped of its bark until it reaches 25 years old. After that, the cork is harvested every nine to twelve years, giving the tree time to grow a new 'skin'. Cork oaks are long-lived trees, regularly exceeding 200 years old. A mature tree provides enough cork to make 4,000 bottle stoppers per harvest.

Much of the food that stocks our supermarket shelves comes from trees. Citrus fruits, such as oranges and lemons, are produced by evergreen trees of the *Citrus* genus, originally from South-east Asia. The species that yields Seville oranges, *Citrus aurantium*, was introduced to Spain in the 12th century and its fruit became a valuable provision on long sea voyages, helping to prevent scurvy among the sailors. Today the orange is the most widely grown fruit in the world – every year more than 70 million tonnes are harvested.

Olive trees, *Olea* species, have been grown for their fruit for more than 5,000 years. Originally from Europe's Mediterranean region, they are now cultivated across the world, from Australia to California. The fruit is either eaten whole or pressed for its oil, which has significant health benefits. A ripe olive is about 20 per cent oil.

Even when we brush our teeth we are using products from trees. Toothpaste contains carboxymethal cellulose, which is basically pulped up wood. In Africa, small sticks made from the wood of a tropical tree called *Diospyros usambarensis* are chewed to clean teeth. The wood contains anti-fungal bacteria, which help to combat gum disease and tooth decay.

Below: Lightweight timber has been used for boat building and aircraft.

NATURAL DISTRIBUTION OF TREES

The natural distribution of trees around the world is influenced by the weather. Over millions of years each tree species has adapted to a particular set of climatic conditions and so their distribution is limited to where those conditions exist.

Trees in different parts of the world all function in much the same way. They all require the same things to survive, namely water, minerals, air and light. They all have leaves, roots and a persistent woody stem containing a vascular transport system, which takes water and minerals from the roots to the leaves and food from the leaves to the rest of the tree. That, however, is where the similarity ends.

Throughout the world, trees have adapted to the climate that surrounds them. The amount of rainfall, the temperatures they have to endure, the amount of daylight hours and the angle of the sun all influence both the behavioural patterns of trees and their natural distribution across the planet.

Trees growing in the tropics look very different to those found in temperate parts of the world. In a large number of cases they represent very different groups of plants. In general, conifers dominate the colder and drier areas of the world, and broad-leaved trees are more common in warmer and wetter regions.

Below: The world is broken up into zones that experience different climatic conditions. Individual tree species seldom occur within more than one zone.

Equatorial rainforest

Five degrees latitude north and south of the Equator is the area where Equatorial rainforest exists. The conditions in these rainforest areas are perfect for tree growth: the morning sun heats up the vegetation, causing water to evaporate from the leaves. Warm, wet air rises from the trees, forms clouds and produces rain in the afternoon. This happens on every day of the year and there are no major seasonal changes. Numerous trees thrive here, among them rosewood, *Dalbergia nigra*, and the gaboon, *Aucoumea klaineana*.

Monsoon forest

Moving away from the Equator, the climate becomes drier. Within 5 and 25 degrees north and south of the equator there is a marked dry season during the winter months when the air is colder and clouds do not form. Trees can only grow during the summer months when warm air allows clouds to form and causes rain to fall. This seasonal change is known as monsoon and the forest that grows in these regions is monsoon forest. Monsoon forest covers a vast proportion of the Indian subcontinent, parts of Central America, East Africa, Madagascar and south-eastern China. Trees of the monsoon forest include Indian rosewood, *Dalbergia latifolia*, and East Indian ebonys, among them *Diospyrus melanoxylon*.

Savannah and desert

Between 25 and 35 degrees of latitude, clouds seldom form, rain rarely falls and the climate becomes progressively drier. Savannah grassland, which borders the monsoon areas, eventually gives way to desert. Few trees can survive in this harsh environment. Those that do include the giant saguaro cactus, *Carnegiea gigantea*, from North America, and the dragon's blood tree, *Dracaena cinnabari*, from Yemen.

Mediterranean forest

Beyond latitudes of 35 degrees, the conditions for tree growth gradually improve. At 40 degrees from the Equator, the Mediterranean forest region begins. This region contains most European Mediterranean countries, California, Chile and parts of Australia. Typically, the climate is characterized by hot, dry summers, and winters with moderate rainfall. Mediterranean trees include the holm oak, *Quercus ilex*, and the olive tree, *Olea europaea*.

Temperate forest

Between 40 and 50 degrees of latitude the climate becomes damp and windy, with cold temperatures in winter months restricting tree growth. This temperate region covers central and western Europe (including the British Isles), central North America, New Zealand, Japan and parts of China. The natural tree cover of this area is primarily broad-leaved. Trees that thrive here include oak, beech, ash, birch and maple.

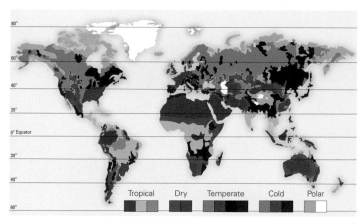

Tropical   Dry   Temperate   Cold   Polar

Above: Conifers are particularly well adapted to cold conditions.

Boreal forest

From 50 to 70 degrees of latitude, the length of the tree growing season diminishes and winter lengthens. Known as the boreal region, this area covers by far the greatest landmass of all the forest regions. It includes most of central Canada, northern Europe and Russia, right across to the Pacific coast. The natural tree cover of this region is primarily conifer and includes Scots pine, *Pinus sylvestris*, and sitka spruce, *Picea sitchensis*. The tree density of this region is greater than in temperate or Mediterranean regions, but less than both Monsoon and the Equatorial regions.

Tundra

Above 70 degrees, winter lasts almost all year and very few trees are able to survive. Known as tundra, this area includes northern Canada, Iceland, Greenland and the far north of Europe and Russia. One tree that does survive is the dwarf willow, *Salix reticulata*.

Micro climates

There is always some blurring at the edges of every climatic forest region. Land that is close to the sea will generally be warmer than that which is landlocked. Consequently a greater diversity of tree species will grow here

than would be expected for the same latitude. The west coasts of Britain and Ireland benefit from the Gulf Stream, which brings warm, moist air from the Caribbean. This allows trees that grow naturally in the Mediterranean forest region to survive and sometimes to flourish. One Mediterranean forest tree that tends to grow well in gardens in Cornwall, the Isles of Scilly and the west coast of Scotland is the Chilean azara, *Azara lanceolata*.

Montane forest

In mountainous areas, trees typical of regions farther from the Equator thrive. Because of their latitudes, both the Alps of central Europe and the

Rocky Mountains of North America are technically within the temperate region. But because of their high altitude, which decreases average temperatures and effectively shortens the summers, the tree cover is more typical of boreal forest. In the Alps, Norway spruce, *Picea abies*, is the dominant species.

Tree zoning

Whether or not a tree will survive in any region, given its basic requirements of water, minerals, air and light, depends on the lowest temperatures it will have to endure. Over the years, through trial and error, botanists and horticulturalists have identified the average annual minimum temperatures that individual tree species can withstand. Maps of the world have been produced that put countries or regions into zones, according to the average annual minimum temperatures that occur in them. Most of Britain is suitable for tree species rated at zone eight – trees that are capable of surviving average annual minimum temperatures of around 5°C/41°F. Tree species rated at zone nine would find this average fairly chilly. They prefer the average temperatures not to fall below 10°C/50°F.

Below: Savannah grassland is the harsh intermediate zone between Mediterranean forest and desert. The closer conditions are to a desert, the fewer trees exist.

TEMPERATE TREES

*Temperate trees are found in the bands 40 to 50 degrees north and south of the Equator. These areas
include most of North America, Britain and Europe, southern Russia, northern China, Japan,
New Zealand, Tasmania, southern Argentina and Chile.*

In temperate regions the climate is suitable for tree growth for six months of the year, when temperatures average more than 10°C/50°F. There are well-defined seasons but few extremes in either temperature or rainfall.

Although the temperate regions are suitable for both deciduous and evergreen trees, it is deciduous broad-leaved trees, such as oak, which predominate. Many trees that live in the windy conditions of the world's temperate regions are wind pollinated.

Temperate diversity
There is far less tree diversity within temperate regions than in the tropics. This is partly because the climate is less favourable and partly due to historical climatic changes.

Temperate trees have been forced to migrate towards the Equator and back again several times during the last two million years because of successive ice ages. Inevitably these mass movements had casualties. Some tree species perished as they were unable to successfully disperse their seeds with enough speed to escape the freezing conditions expanding outwards from the polar regions. Other species became extinct because their escape routes were blocked by high mountain ranges, such as the Alps and Pyrenees.

Temperate pioneers
The density of temperate woodlands is such that light is rarely in short supply and there are few other plants, such as climbers, that have the ability to stifle tree growth. Temperate pioneer trees have large canopies and their branches

and leaves are free to grow right down the trunk. Their wood is light in colour. Birch is one of the most successful temperate pioneer tree species. It will colonize land far more readily than any other species and is quite often found growing on disused industrial sites, spoil heaps, landfills and railway embankments. Willow, poplar and pine are also early colonizers of inhospitable land.

Other temperate species
The temperate tree species that has been around longer than any other is the maidenhair tree, *Ginkgo biloba*. Today it grows wild in a small area of Chekiang province, China, although it has been widely planted elsewhere.

There are more than 450 species of oak tree across the temperate world. In Europe the two main species are the English oak, *Quercus robur*, and the

1 Oak
2 Beech

Above: Oak is the predominant tree species in temperate regions of the world.

Below: Species such as oak and beech (below) are slow to establish on new sites and move in only after pioneer species, such as birch, willow, pine and poplar, have improved soil conditions with their fallen leaves. Oak and beech are the predominant woodland species of Great Britain.

One of the most recognizable temperate trees is the monkey puzzle or Chile pine, *Araucaria araucana*. This hardy evergreen grows up to the snow line in its native Andes Mountains. It has rigid, spiny and prickly leaves.

One temperate tree that looks like it belongs in the tropics is the tree fern, *Dicksonia antarctica*. Native to Tasmania, it grows well in warm, moist temperate regions, such as southern Ireland, where frosts are not too severe. *D. antarctica* is a very exotic-looking tree with a fibrous trunk and large fern-like fronds, which can reach over 3m/10ft long. In Tasmania there are tree fern forests with specimens growing to more than 10m/33ft tall.

Perhaps the most beautiful of all temperate trees is the tulip tree, *Liriodendron tulipifera*. It is native to North America, where it grows from Nova Scotia to Florida. The tulip tree is a large species, growing to heights in excess of 40m/131ft. It has flowers that resemble greenish orange tulips. Quite often a mature tree will be covered with a stunning spectacle of flowers.

sessile oak, *Q. petraea*. The holm or evergreen oak, *Q. ilex*, originates from the Mediterranean but also grows well in southern temperate regions of Europe and America.

Close to 80 species of oak are native to North America, including the red oak, *Q. rubra*, which has large, sharply pointed leaves that turn red in autumn.

TROPICAL TREES

Tropical trees are found in three main parts of the world: central Africa, Amazonia in South America, and South-east Asia. The total area they cover amounts to about 9 million square kilometres (3½ million square miles) and represents 7 per cent of the earth's land surface.

In the rainforest, levels of rainfall, warmth and sunlight are constant, creating ideal conditions for tree growth throughout the year. Most tropical trees have evergreen leaves with pointed tips. These 'drip tips' help the trees to keep their leaves dry, shedding excess water during tropical rainstorms. Tropical trees include the fastest growing trees in the world; 5m/16½ft of vertical growth per year is commonplace. Fast growth means a fast metabolism; consequently everything happens at a fast rate, including the advent of senility. Very few of the tropical trees live beyond 500 years of age, whereas many temperate trees are much older.

Tropical diversity

The range of tropical species is amazing – there are over 2,000 different tree species, for example, in Madagascar alone.

The reason for so many different species is not fully understood. However, the fact that today's tropical rainforests have existed for millions of years means that there has been plenty of time for new species to evolve. Evolution takes place primarily as a response to outside influence. It is possible there are so many tropical tree species because there are so many potential killers of trees in tropical forests. The climate is ideal for tree growth and for insects, fungi and viruses. New tree species may have evolved specifically to repel attackers.

Despite their great species diversity, most tropical rainforest trees look very similar to one another; they have tall, thin trunks supported by roots with prominent buttresses. The crowns of these trees are comparatively small and bear large, thick, evergreen leaves not dissimilar to those of laurel. Most tropical trees have thin bark because there is no need to provide protection against frost or water loss. Often, however,

the wood of tropical trees is stained dark with chemicals for protection against fungal attack.

Tropical pioneers

Such is the competition for space and light in a tropical rainforest that only those trees that can react quickly to changes in the density of the canopy survive. If a gap opens up in the canopy when a mature tree dies, light reaches the forest floor and there is a scramble by other plants to fill that gap. The first species to colonize gaps are herbaceous plants and climbers. These plants do their best to smother the ground to prevent another tree from filling the gap because they need the light to survive. Eventually a branchless, umbrella-like tree shoot with a thick, slippery trunk will emerge

Below: Rainforests are characterized by layers of planting. At the top are the tallest trees, usually with large leaves to take any moisture and light, and buttress roots to anchor them into the ground. Below these are smaller trees with glorious flowers and luscious fruit to attract pollinators.

1 Kapok
2 Palm tree
3 Brazil nut

from the ground. At the top of this trunk a huge canopy of leaves unfolds, desperate to capture as much light as possible. The thick, slippery trunk provides nothing for climbing plants to grip on to and the tree's leaves are held well out of reach of grasping tendrils. These pioneer trees can grow up to 10m/33ft tall in their first year, quickly filling the space left by the fallen tree.

Tropical species

Outside the tropics most tropical trees are known for their products. Brazil nut, *Bertholletia excelsa*, is probably one of the best-known tropical trees because of the nuts it produces. It grows wild in Brazil and throughout Peru, Columbia, Venezuela and Ecuador. The Brazil nut is among the largest tropical trees, reaching heights in excess of 40m/131ft. It has thick, leathery, oval-shaped leaves up to 20cm/8in long. Brazil nuts flower in November, producing fruit pods at the end of thick branches the following June. Up to 25 individual nuts can be found in each large, spherical, woody fruit pod. Each tree can produce up to 300 fruit pods a year and

thousands of tons of Brazil nuts are exported from South America each year. In economic terms, the Brazil nut is second only to rubber in importance to Brazil as an export cash crop.

The weeping fig, *Ficus benjamina*, originates from the tropical forests of South-east Asia and today is grown from India through to northern Australia. It is an attractive tree with narrow, leathery leaves, which can be

Above: Such is the diversity of the Amazon rainforest that over 500 different species have been found within a single hectare (2½ acres).

up to 12cm/4¾in long. Mature weeping figs can have dramatic twisting, branches. In temperate areas this species is grown as a conservatory or house plant. In the warmer tropical regions it produces small red figs in pairs along its twisting branches.

Palm trees have different leaf shapes from both Brazil nuts and weeping figs. Long, narrow and strap-like, the leaves branch out from the tree top. There are around 3,000 species of palm in the world, and the vast majority of them grow in the tropics.

DESERT TREES

There are few places on earth, other than the polar regions, where plants will not grow. Even in the harsh environment of the desert, plants – including trees – somehow manage to cling to life. Deserts are very inhospitable places for trees.

Trees that survive in the desert have developed unique ways of coping with the day-to-day difficulties of survival. The main problems facing desert trees relate to water – or lack of it. Hot sun, drying winds and low, erratic rainfall make it difficult for tree roots to supply enough water to make up for that lost by transpiration from the leaves. Desert trees have adapted to the extremes of heat and aridity by using physical and behavioural mechanisms.

Plants that have adapted by altering their physical structure are called either xerophytes or phreatophytes. Xerophytes, such as cacti, usually have special means of storing and conserving water. They often have few or no leaves, which helps them to reduce transpiration. Phreatophytes are plants, such as the African acacias, that have adapted to parched conditions by growing extremely long

roots, allowing them to acquire moisture from the water table.

Other plants have altered their behaviour to cope. They have to make the most of the times of greatest moisture and coolest temperatures, remaining dormant in dry periods and springing to life when water is available. Many germinate after heavy seasonal rain and then complete their reproductive cycle very quickly. These plants produce heat- and drought-resistant seeds that remain dormant in the soil until rain eventually arrives.

The Joshua tree

The *Yucca brevifolia*, or Joshua tree, grows in the Mojave Desert of California, Nevada, Utah and Arizona. It has spiky, leathery, evergreen leaves at the tips of the branches, thus reducing the effects of transpiration. The leaves have a hard, waxy coating

that also helps to reduce water loss. Originally considered a member of the agave family, the Joshua tree is now known to be the largest yucca in the world. It can grow up to 12m/40ft tall with a trunk diameter of 1m/3ft.

Welwitschia

A dwarf species from Africa, *Welwitschia mirabilis* is one of the strangest trees on earth. It grows on the dry gravel plains of the Namib Desert in southern Angola and is a throwback to the prehistoric flora that existed on the supercontinent of Gondwanaland millions of years ago. Its shape and growing characteristics are so unusual that there is no comparable living plant. It is a unique species occupying its own genus.

The bulk of *Welwitschia's* 'trunk' grows under the sand like a giant carrot. Its girth can be up to 1.5m/5ft

1 Baobab
2 Date palm
3 *Welwitschia mirabilis*

Above: Mormon pioneers are said to have named this species the Joshua tree because it reminded them of the Old Testament prophet Joshua, with arms outstretched, waving them on towards the promised land.

Below: Tropical Africa is home to deserts and savannah. Trees that live in these habitats are exceptionally good at storing water. The Welwitschia mirabilis has a long tap root that can reach down to the water table. Succulents have few leaves and are best adapted to the desert. The baobab of the savannah can store vast amounts of water in its trunk.

and its height (or in this case length) up to 4m/13ft, less than a third of which appears above ground. Its subterranean trunk is a water storage organ made of hard wood and covered with a cork-like bark. Broad, leathery leaves emerge from the part of the trunk that appears above ground. The leaves, which can reach 2m/6½ft long, sprawl across the desert floor. They have specially adapted pores to trap any moisture that condenses on the leaves during the night when the temperature falls. As rain falls about once in four years in the Namib Desert this method of moisture collection is vital. Recent carbon-dating has established that some of these trees are more than 2,000 years old.

Other desert trees

The acacias and tamarisks, which grow in African deserts, are phreatophytes – they have developed incredibly long root systems to cope with the absence of surface water. These roots take water from the permanent water table, which may be anything up to 50m/164ft below the desert surface. Once mature, they have little trouble combating harsh desert conditions – the difficulty is in establishing themselves, as the roots have to first grow through great depths of bone-dry soil before they reach the water. Phreatophytes grow in places where the soil is occasionally wet, such as dried-up riverbeds, as these are the only spots where they can get started.

Perhaps the most successful desert plants are cacti. The giant saguaro cactus, *Carnegiea gigantea*, is the ultimate desert tree. It has no leaves at all but does have a thick green trunk, which is capable of photosynthesis and storing water. The giant saguaro can grow to heights in excess of 10m/33ft.

The Socotran desert-rose tree, *Adenium obesum*, grows in desert conditions on the Indian Ocean island of Socotra, Yemen. It has a swollen grey trunk, which looks like a sack of potatoes. This trunk has the ability to expand in size on the rare occasions that rain falls, enabling it to store huge quantities of water for the drought period to follow.

MOUNTAIN TREES

Mountains tend to be covered with conifers and most are members of the Pinaceae family –
pines, spruces, hemlocks and firs. The higher the elevation, the slower the trees grow. The point beyond
which no trees will survive is known as the tree line.

In many ways mountains have the same climate as subarctic regions, having short summers, cold winters and a mean temperature that rarely rises above 10°C/50°F. Wind speeds tend to be greater at high altitudes. These drying winds and shallow soils, often frozen for long periods of time, mean that only those trees that are protected against water loss and frost damage will survive.

Conifers and evergreens

A characteristic that conifers and broad-leaved evergreens share is leaves that are resistant to water loss and cold. Broad-leaved evergreens often have thick, leathery leaves with a waxy coating.

Conifers further reduce water loss by having fine, rolled, needle-like leaves, that expose a small surface area to the elements.

Conifers and other evergreens are efficient at functioning in low light and temperature conditions. Once deciduous trees have lost their leaves in autumn they cannot produce food or grow until the next year's leaves grow – anything up to six months. Yet, during this time there are periods when the temperature and light is sufficient for photosynthesis to occur. Evergreens and conifers take advantage of this. Deciduous trees are also vulnerable when their young leaves are bursting from the bud in spring. These new leaves are sensitive to frost and can easily be damaged. Evergreens have tough leathery leaves that are never so vulnerable.

Mountain characteristics

Trees become progressively shorter as they approach the tree line. The reason for their shortness is not cold but increasing wind – constant stem movement stunts a tree's growth. High winds can also damage trees and to avoid this some species have evolved a low-growing, almost sprawling habit.

Many mountain trees have adopted characteristics to cope with this harsh environment. They are conical or spire-shaped with branches and twigs that point downwards. This prevents snow from building up on the branches and breaking them. Instead it simply slides off the tree to the ground.

Mountain trees will also grow away from the direction of the prevailing wind, giving them a windswept appearance. The reason for this is that the waxy coating on the leaves or needles on the windward side gets worn away by the sandpaper effect of harsh winds carrying ice particles. Once the coating has gone the leaves and shoots are open to dehydration,

1 Sitka spruce
2 Brewer spruce

Above: As trees approach the elevation beyond which they will not grow (known as the tree line), they become stunted and eventually prostrate.

Below: Most of the conifers found in mountainous regions are members of the Pinaceae family – pines, spruces, hemlocks and firs. Such trees have adapted to cope with the harsh and extreme conditions of the weather, from freezing snow to fierce winds, driving rain, and the blistering heat of the summer sun.

the whole clump moves slowly downwind. Research has shown that the average movement of these clumps is 2–7m/6½–23ft per century.

Often the branches at the bottom of mountain trees grow much better than those at the top, giving a skirted effect around the tree's base. This is because in the depths of winter these lower branches are protected from the ravages of the wind by snowdrifts.

Mountain species

The dwarf mountain pine, *Pinus mugo*, is native to the mountains of central Europe, the Carpathians, the Balkans and the Italian Apennines. It is a low-growing, shrubby tree with twisting, snake-like stems and branches that form dense, impenetrable entanglements (known in Germany as *krummholz*).

Brewer's spruce, *Picea breweriana*, is a tree that originates from the Siskiyou Mountains of California and Oregon, where it grows at elevations of up to 2,100m/7,000ft. In Scotland the rowan or mountain ash, *Sorbus aucuparia*, will grow at altitudes in excess of 700m/2,300ft.

and slowly die. The tree compensates for the lack of leaves and shoots on the windward side of the crown by producing more on the leeward side.

In exposed mountain regions, young trees can only grow in the shelter of other trees. This leads to clumps of trees scattered across the mountainsides. As trees die on the windward side and new ones grow on the leeward side,

COASTAL TREES

The coast is one of the most difficult environments of all for trees to grow in. Those that survive have adapted to the strong winds and salt-laden water by growing additional roots on their windward sides to improve anchorage, and their habit becomes low and squat, thus offering less resistance to the wind.

Only the toughest tree species can survive a combination of strong winds and salt spray. Exposure to ocean storms, with winds in excess of 160km/h/100mph, is only part of the problem. Strong wind alone is something that many trees are able to withstand. However, if those winds are laden with huge quantities of sea salt, most trees will simply die.

Salt damage

Trees can be damaged by salt in two ways: through direct contact with the foliage and by absorption from the soil through the roots. Direct and prolonged contact with salt will cause leaf-burn, branch die-back and defoliation. This in turn will reduce the ability of the tree to photosynthesize and produce its own food, so eventually it dies.

Salt can also dramatically reduce the amount of seed and fruit produced.

The most common cause of tree death by salt is through its uptake from the soil. When salt-laden winds that have travelled across the ocean reach land they condense, producing rain or dense sea mists. The salt precipitation from these mists and rain soaks into the soil. The highest salt concentrations are deposited closest to the coast.

Salt causes the soil structure to deteriorate, leading to a decrease in soil fertility. Natural calcium in the soil is replaced by sodium chloride. This increases soil alkalinity, making it dramatically harder for trees to survive. Salt also makes the soil less permeable and reduces the moisture content, causing its root systems to dehydrate and die back. The moisture

that is absorbed by the roots can literally poison the tree. It takes only half a per cent of a tree's living tissue to contain salt before the tree starts to die. This process is also what damages trees planted on roadsides, where the road is regularly covered with salt to clear it of ice.

Mangroves

One genus of trees has adapted so well to life alongside the coast that its members can actually grow with their roots in salt water. Called mangroves, they are found throughout the tropics,

Below: New Zealand is home to a diverse collection of trees. The kanuka and puriri trees and the nikau palms all thrive here. The kanuka tree is a pioneer tree, endemic to the area. The nikau palm is New Zealand's only native palm tree and thrives in coastal areas and warmer, inland regions.

1 Nikau palm
2 Puriri tree
3 Kanuka tree

particularly in shallow, muddy estuarine and coastal situations. They have to cope not only with waterlogging but also with the high salinity of seawater.

The most notable feature of mangroves is their roots. Many species are anchored in the soft mud by prop roots, which grow from the trunk, or drop roots, which grow from the branches. Oxygen is piped from the roots above ground to those below the water line. This aeration is particularly important to mangroves because they need oxygen to carry out the process of ultra-filtration, which they use to exclude salt from the tree. Each root cell works like a mini desalination plant, screening out the salt and allowing only fresh water to flow into the root system and on through the rest of the tree.

Mangroves display several other adaptations to their situation. They have leathery, evergreen leaves, which are able to conserve the fresh water within them but keep out salt-laden water that lands on

Above: Mangroves have developed their curious root system to cope with continual immersion in water.

them. They also have wind-pollinated flowers, which are able to take full advantage of sea breezes, and spear-shaped seed pods, which can stab into the mud or float away from the mother tree, coming to rest elsewhere.

Monterey cypress
At the Monterey Peninsula in San Francisco, clinging to life and the cliff edge, are two groves of Monterey Cypress, *Cupressus macrocarpa*.

The trees grow on the shore cliffs and, being undermined by the waves, occasionally fall into the sea. There are fewer than 300 trees left, ancestors of a species that covered great swathes of the temperate world at the start of the glacial cool-down a million years ago. Monterey cypress, along with other American giants, such as the Douglas fir and the giant redwood, retreated to the Pacific coast to escape the worst of the cold. When the climate warmed up 12,000 years ago and the glaciers withdrew, the trees moved back to the land they had occupied before the ice ages – all, that is, except the Monterey cypress, which remained on the Californian coast, where it has been growing in decreasing numbers since.

The trees that are left are stunted and knarled, seldom reaching more than 15m/50ft tall. Collect seed from any of them and sow it anywhere else in the temperate world however and it grows into a magnificent giant. Wherever there is the need for shelter from the wind and salt spray off the sea, this is the tree to plant.

ISLAND TREES

Islands often contain a diversity of plant life that is very different to that of the nearest mainland. This is because evolution on islands occurs in isolation. Some islands, such as New Caledonia in the Pacific Ocean, still have a range of tree which evolved during the Jurassic period.

The reason for the often unique plant life on individual islands lies in the history of the earth and particularly how each island was first formed. Islands are normally formed as a result of continental drift or volcanic activity on the seabed.

About 200 million years ago, most of the world's land was clumped

Below: Islands have unique eco-systems. The weather they receive, their landmass and the vegetation that thrives on them can differ dramatically to that of the nearest mainland.

together in a single supercontinent, known as Pangaea. Pangaea began to break up about 190 million years ago. First it split in two. The northern part, Laurasia, contained what are now North America, Europe and Asia, while the southern part, Gondwanaland, consisted of present-day South America, Africa, India, Antarctica and Australasia. Gradually Laurasia and Gondwanaland also broke up to form the continents we recognize today.

This fragmentation process not only created the major continents, but also thousands of islands. When these islands broke away from the continents, they carried with them a collection of the flora and fauna that existed on the larger land-masses at that time. Over the following millions of years, plants and animals on these isolated fragments of land adapted to their new environments,

❷

and often evolved in different directions from those on the mainland.

In some cases, evolution has continued on the continents, while little has changed on some of the islands. The island of New Caledonia, off the east coast of Australia is home to an amazing collection of ancient trees no longer found anywhere else on earth. So primeval is its landscape that it has been used as a backdrop for films on dinosaurs. In other cases it was the island life forms that changed more dramatically.

Not all of the world's islands were created by the break-up of the continents. Many were formed more recently by undersea volcanic activity and have never been physically attached to the continents at all. At first these islands had no plants of their own. Archipelagos such as the Hawaiian Islands began as barren outcrops of rock. Hawaii's native trees are all descendants of the few plants whose seeds washed up on its shores or were carried there by birds.

Tarweed is a daisy-like plant from California. Fragments of this plant floated across the ocean to Hawaii millions of years ago. Tarweed gradually colonized the island and then began to evolve into new plants, filling the empty niches. Today Hawaii has 28 species whose ancestry can

1 Coco-de-mer
2 Palm tree

be traced back to tarweed. One, *Dubautia reticulata*, is a tree that can grow to more than 10m/33ft tall.

The Galapagos Islands
Like the Hawaiian Islands, the Galapagos Islands formed in volcanic activity after the break-up of the continents. Mangroves were among the first and most successful tree colonizers of the Galapagos Islands. Four species exist there today: the black mangrove, *Avicennia germinans*; the red mangrove, *Rhizophora mangle*; the button mangrove, *Conocarpus erecta*; and the white mangrove, *Laguncularia racemosa*. Mangroves are able to live in shallow seawater and grow on the shores of almost all the islands. They are a vital part of the coastal ecosystem, as fallen leaves and branches provide nutrients and shelter for a wide variety of sea creatures, and their tangled roots protect the coastline from erosion and storm damage. The Galapagos Islands' mangroves are thought to have established themselves from plants and seeds that floated from the Far East across the Pacific Ocean.

Above: Palm trees have large seeds that can float for hundreds of miles across the ocean.

The Virgin Islands
The warm, moist climate on the northern coasts of the Virgin Islands in the West Indies supports an amazing array of tree species. Growing wild here are West Indian locust, bay rum, sandbox, kapok and hog plum. To the south and east the climate becomes much drier, creating ideal growing conditions for the turpentine tree, acacia, white cedar and the poisonous manchineel tree.

The Seychelles
More than 80 species of tree grow on the Seychelles in the Indian Ocean that grow nowhere else on earth. Among them is the record-breaking coco de mer palm with its 20kg/45lb nut. This is the largest seed of any plant in the world and it has been found washed ashore in places as far away as

Africa, India and Indonesia. Before the islands were discovered the coco-de-mer seed was thought to have grown on the seabed, hence its name.

New Caledonia
Situated off Australia's east coast, this island has been described as having 'one of the richest and most beautiful flora in the world'. The island is home to trees that are remnants of families that became extinct elsewhere millions of years ago, some as far back as the Jurassic period. *Araucaria columnaris* is a rocket-shaped relative of the monkey puzzle tree which grows wild in Chile and Argentina. Of the 19 living species of *Araucaria*, 13 are found in New Caledonia and nowhere else. The island also has unique members of the podocarp family, to which most of New Zealand conifers belong, and proteas, which only occur otherwise in South Africa.

New Caledonia is also home to some of the tallest tree ferns in the world, many of them over 30m/98ft tall. The island's rarest tree is a small evergreen called *Xeronema moorei*; this unique tree grows in isolated pockets high in the mountains and is found nowhere else on earth.

URBAN TREES

Trees have become a vital part of urban areas around the world. From the leafy avenues of downtown Manhattan to the cherry-covered walkways of Tokyo, they bring beauty and environmental benefits right to the heart of our cities.

Trees have been planted in large numbers in our towns and cities ever since the 18th century. Before that time, urban trees were the privilege of royal palaces, cathedrals, churches, monasteries and universities. Some of the earliest town plantings were in specially landscaped town gardens, squares and crescents, such as Berkeley Square in London, which was planted with London plane trees in 1789. These trees still exist today, tall spreading giants bringing shade and cool in summer.

Quite often these early plantings only took place in the more affluent areas of towns and were for the private enjoyment of those who lived there. The poorer residential and industrial areas were left largely devoid of trees.

Below: The London plane tree, a member of the sycamore family, is a popular tree for urban settings throughout the temperate world. It grows quickly, is hardy and tolerates the pollution of modern cities.

It wasn't until the Victorian era that municipal parks were laid out for the benefit of all town dwellers. At this time, the idea of parks as the 'green lungs' of towns and cities developed, improving citizens' health as well as giving them opportunities to walk, meet and relax. Public parks began to appear in North America and all over the British Empire, and trees were seen as an integral part of them. Today some of the finest tree collections in the world are found in city parks.

Urban street planting also became prevalent during this time, although the planting of trees along roadsides between towns had been going on for centuries. Plane and poplar trees were planted by the Romans to provide shade and shelter for their legions as they marched back and forth across southern Europe. This tradition was repeated by Napoleon for his armies and many Napoleonic roadside trees can still be seen today in France, Germany and Spain.

The environmental benefits of trees in towns and cities were recognized towards the end of the Victorian era by Ebenezer Howard, whose book, *Garden Cities of Tomorrow* inspired the early landscaping of suburbs and new towns that were being built outside the cities to house rapidly increasing populations. These new towns were built on 'green field' sites and the inclusion of street trees, park trees and areas of woodland between housing were drawn into landscape plans long before the houses were even built. Howard's ideas quickly spread and were used by town planners across Europe and the Americas.

Urban trees today

Trees have become an integral part of cities around the world. In terms of planning, they have almost become as important a feature of the urban landscape as the buildings themselves. Trees have a higher priority in our towns and cities now than at any time previously.

Above: Urban trees provide shade in summer and shelter in winter.

The architectural value of trees and the health benefits they offer are now well-recognized and some cities have instigated massive tree-planting campaigns.

Benefits of urban trees

Trees reduce air pollution. They help to trap particle pollutants such as dust, ash and smoke, which can damage human lungs, and they absorb carbon dioxide and other dangerous gases, releasing vital oxygen in their place. In a year, 0.4ha/1 acre of trees in a city park absorbs the same amount of carbon dioxide as is produced by 41,850km/ 26,000 miles of car driving.

Urban trees conserve water and reduce flooding. They lessen surface runoff from storms as their roots increase soil permeability. Reduced overloading of drainage systems, the main cause of localized flooding, occurs in towns with a high tree population.

Trees modify local climates as they help to cool the 'heat island' effect in inner cities caused by the storage of thermal energy in concrete, steel and tarmac. They also provide a more pleasant living and working environment. They reduce wind speed around high-rise buildings, increase humidity in dry climates and offer cooling shade on hot, sunny days.

Without trees, towns and cities are sterile landscapes. Trees add natural character; they provide colour, flowers, fragrance, and beautiful shapes and textures. They screen unsightly buildings and soften the outline of masonry, mortar and glass.

Trees for urban environments

One of the finest large trees for planting in towns and cities is the London plane, *Platanus acerifolia*. Most trees suffer in urban areas as their bark's 'breathing pores', known as lenticels, get clogged with soot and grime. The London plane frequently sheds its old bark, revealing fresh, clean bark beneath.

The maidenhair tree, *Ginkgo biloba*, native to China, is also tolerant of air pollution. Its slow growth and narrow habit make it an ideal tree for street planting. Other trees suitable for the urban environment include laburnum, *Laburnum* x *watereri* 'Vossii'; black locust, *Robinia pseudoacacia*; hawthorn, *Crataegus laevigata* 'Paul's Scarlet'; Indian bean tree, *Catalpa bignonioides*; and cherry, *Prunus* species.

ENDANGERED TREES

Trees are one of the most successful groups of plants on earth, but despite their proliferation, some trees are increasingly under threat. Ten per cent of the world's tree species are currently threatened with extinction. Across the world more than 40 hectares (100 acres) of forest are felled every minute.

One third of the land on earth is covered by trees. But that figure is set to decrease. As the human population continues to expand, so ever larger areas of the natural world are changed to meet peoples' needs. One of the first things to go is forest.

Ten per cent threatened with extinction

There are more than 80,000 different species of tree in the world. At the moment around 8,750 of them are threatened with extinction. Almost 1,000 of those are critically endangered and some species are literally down to just one or two trees.

The threats to tree species are many and varied. They include felling of woodlands and forests for timber and fuel, agricultural development, expansion of human settlements, uncontrolled forest fires and the introduction of invasive alien tree species. Across the world we are losing at least 40ha/100 acres of forest every minute. At the same time we are planting only 4 ha/10 acres.

Can we live in a world without trees?

The simple answer is no. Trees are essential to all life and incredibly important to the planet as a whole. They provide services of incalculable value to humans, including climate control, production of oxygen, pollution control and flood prevention. They also prevent soil erosion and provide food, medicine, shelter and timber. Forests are also extremely important from an ecological point of view – tropical forests contain almost 90 per cent of the worlds land-based plant species, for example.

Trees in danger

The monkey puzzle tree, *Araucaria araucana*, has become one of the most familiar trees in the temperate world. As an ornamental species, it is grown in virtually every botanical garden in Europe and North America. Yet, in its native homeland, high in the Andes Mountains of Chile and southern Argentina, the monkey puzzle is threatened with extinction. Thanks to its tall, straight trunk, its timber is highly sought after and the land it once stood on claimed for new uses. Monkey puzzle forests have been felled on a massive scale and it is thought there are now more monkey puzzles trees growing in Britain than there are in South America.

Another native of Chile and Argentina, the alerce tree, *Fitzroya cupressoides*, is a magnificent slow-growing conifer. Its Latin name was given in honour of Captain Robert Fitzroy, who captained HMS *Beagle* on Charles Darwin's epic voyage around the world in the 1830s. Even back then alerce was being felled for timber. Today it is one of the world's rarest

Below: Destruction of woodland and unsustainable forestry have contributed to the rarity of some of the world's trees.

conifers, with only 15 per cent of the original trees remaining. Although international trade in alerce timber is banned, illegal felling still continues.

Wilmott's whitebeam, *Sorbus wilmottiana*, grows in only one place in the entire world and that is the Avon Gorge, which passes through the west of the city of Bristol in England. This beautiful little tree, which produces clusters of attractive creamy white flowers in June and bunches of red berries in September, is critically endangered. There are only about 20 trees now remaining in the wild.

The Australian wollemi pine, *Wollemia nobilis*, was thought to be extinct until 40 survivors were found in a remote canyon in the Blue Mountains of New South Wales in 1994. A distant relative of the monkey puzzle tree, the wollemi pine has existed unchanged for almost 200 million years.

The Pacific yew, *Taxus brevifolia*, hit the headlines in the 1990s when it was found to contain a toxin called

Above: Lawson cypress has become an endangered species since felling for timber and disease have taken their toll on the world's population.

Below: Fitzroya cupressoides is one of the world's rarest conifers.

taxol, which, when administered to humans, helped in the treatment of breast, ovarian and lung cancer. The greatest concentrations of taxol were found to exist in the tree's bark and for a while wholesale bark stripping took place, threatening the survival of what was already a rare species of tree. Bark from ten trees is needed to produce enough taxol to treat a single patient but steps have now been taken to protect the tree in the wild. Pacific yew plantations have been established and this, together with the recent chemical synthesis of taxol, has taken the pressure off the species in the wild.

Madagascar has some of the world's most extraordinary flora, including six different species of baobab, three of which are found nowhere else in the world. *Adansonia grandidieri* is, as the name suggests, the grandest of them all. It is also the rarest. Although recognized by botanists the world over as a tree that must be conserved, numbers continue to dwindle. The problem here is not logging but human overpopulation. As Madagascar's people continue to increase in number more and more of the island's wilderness is turned into agricultural land.

A bleak future?

The problem with man's exploitation of trees is that it is very often done in an unsustainable way. Areas of forest are felled and cleared, often with little regard to replanting. Once the tree cover is removed, the animals, insects and birds that populated the area move away or die and soil erosion occurs, making it very difficult for trees to recolonize the felled area.

In some parts of the world, notably western Europe, sustainable silviculture is now practised with excellent results. Large areas of forest or woodland are never felled; trees are selectively thinned and removed one at a time, or in small clearings. These trees are then replaced by young seedlings that thrive naturally in the gaps once the light is allowed in. If this sustainable method of management could be adopted in other parts of the world then the future for some of the world's endangered trees might not be so bleak.

Below: Due to over-exploitation for timber, the monkey puzzle tree is now threatened with extinction in the wild.

TREES OF THE WORLD

Identifying trees can be an absorbing, rewarding and fascinating pastime to involve the whole family. Recognizing trees in their natural habitat helps create a stronger sense of familiarity with the area in which you live. In each locality, certain trees will thrive. This is because the soil conditions, weather and geography of the area are beneficial to the survival of the tree.

Each tree has specific characteristics making exact identification possible. It may be the overall profile, the flowers, fruit, shape of the cones, size of the leaves or even the bark that helps identify each tree with the family to which it belongs.

This section of the book will help you to identify the most popular and best-known trees in different locations, locally and internationally. The associated descriptions will clarify how each tree can be identified at all times of the year, even in winter when deciduous trees have only bare branches, bark and twigs to show. Other information in fact boxes provides general information of interest about each tree. Not every tree species is included, but those that feature on the following pages are a good representative sample of some of the most beautiful, culturally significant and ecologically important trees in the world today.

Left: Horse chestnut trees are instantly recognizable in the temperate world, by their magnificent flowers, which appear in late spring.

HOW TO IDENTIFY A TREE

Looking at and identifying trees can be an immensely enjoyable and fascinating pastime, but, unless you know what to look for, it can be confusing. The following information should help to reduce the confusion and provide a clear route to tree identification.

Whether growing in a woodland or forest, lining the hedgerows of our fields, bringing green to our city streets or standing in defiant isolation on some windswept hillside, trees form an integral part of the landscape. They are the most diverse group of plants on the planet, providing variation in shape, size, colour and texture, and in the detail of their leaves, flowers, fruit and bark.

What to look for

There are many clues to a tree's identity, primarily built around seven main features. These features will generally not all be visible at the same time, flowers and berries are normally only present during certain seasons, for example, but some features are constant. The colour and texture of bark changes little throughout the lives of most trees.

Shape and size – Is the tree tall and spire-like or low and wide spreading?

Evergreen or deciduous – Are there leaves on the tree all year round or do they fall in autumn?

Leaves – Are they long and needle-like or broad and flat?

Below: It is quite often possible to identify a tree from a distance by its overall shape.

Flowers – Are flowers (or flower buds) present? If so, what colour and shape are they?

Fruit – Does the tree have any fruit, berries, seeds, nuts or cones on it, and if so what are they like?

Bark – Does the bark have distinctive colouring or patterning?

Buds – In winter, buds can be a tremendous help in identifying temperate trees. What colour and shape are they, and how are they positioned on the twig?

By working through these features step by step, it should be possible to identify any tree.

There are other points to consider that relate to the tree's location and the environment surrounding the tree, which may yield some clues. The acidity of the soil will dictate what species will grow successfully, for example. Some trees, such as red oak, *Quercus rubra*, will only grow well on acidic soil (low pH), while others, such as whitebeam, *Sorbus aria*, prefer chalky, alkaline soil (high pH). The position of wild trees should also be taken into account. Some trees grow well alongside, or even in, water, for instance. Willow or alder enjoy damp conditions and grow naturally next to

Above: In winter the buds and bark are important clues to identification.

rivers; hawthorn on the other hand does not. Some trees, such as beech, will grow well in dense shade, others, such as the Judas tree, will only thrive in full sun.

It is generally easier to identify trees in the wild than in a park or arboretum. This is simply because the pool of species is likely to be greater in a park or arboretum than in a natural setting. Most hedgerows in Europe will contain fewer than ten tree species, for example, and the majority of those will be common native species. At the other extreme, an arboretum may contain up to 4,000 trees, brought together from various habitats in different countries all over the world.

Shape and size

Some trees have such a distinctive shape that it becomes almost unnecessary to continue down the identification trail, other than to

confirm the initial assumption. The Lombardy poplar, *Populus nigra* 'Italica', is particularly distinctive with its remarkable narrow shape and upright habit. This shape is known as 'fastigiate'. Another very distinctive tree is the monkey puzzle, *Araucaria araucana*. No other tree has such sharply toothed evergreen foliage and stiff branching. Once a tree has been identified, stand well back from it and try to commit its overall shape to memory. Then look for other trees with similar shape and confirm their identity. After a while you will find as you walk or drive around the countryside that certain species become instantly recognizable.

Evergreen or deciduous

In winter, in temperate regions, this is a fairly obvious feature to substantiate; at other times of year, or in the tropics, it may require a little more detective work. Most evergreen leaves fall into two categories. They will either be long, thin and needle-like, which will suggest that they belong to a conifer, or they will be thick and leathery, quite often with a shiny surface. In most temperate countries the latter are few and far between, making identification relatively easy. A non-conifer evergreen in Britain is almost certain to be either holly, *Ilex aquifolium*, or holm oak, *Quercus ilex*, for example. In the

Spherical   *Coniferous spreading*   *Deciduous spreading*

Ovoid   *Conical*   *Weeping*   *Columnar*

Above: Tree shape or form is the first step in identifying trees.

tropics, you may well need to look at the leaves more closely and take other features of the tree into account before its identity becomes clear.

Leaves

For most trees, the leaves are probably the most important aid to identification. There are many different leaf shapes but almost all of them fall into the following six categories. Leaves may be 'entire', which means that they

are undivided and have no serrations around the edge, such as those of magnolia. They may be 'serrated' with sharp serrations around the edge, as with the leaves of sweet chestnut, or be 'lobed', curving in towards the centre of the leaf and then back out again, as in oak. They may be 'palmate' which means hand or palm-like – sycamore

Below: Palm trees are clearly identifiable by their frond-like leaves and single trunk.

Below: Deciduous trees are easier to identify when in full leaf in summer.

Below: Evergreen trees can be identified by their cones or flowers.

entire   serrated   lobed

palmate   compound palmate   pinnate

leaf scale   needles in clusters   needles in bunches

and maple leaves are palmate. On some leaves the indentations may go right down to the petiole (leaf-stalk) as with horse chestnut, then the leaf is called a 'compound palmate' leaf. Sometimes the leaf is sub-divided into smaller leaflets, the leaf is then called 'pinnate'. Temperate trees with pinnate leaves include ash and rowan. Many tropical trees have pinnate leaves.

Flowers

Most trees produce flowers in spring, although some, such as the Indian bean tree, *Catalpa bignonioides*, wait for summer. Relatively few temperate trees flower in autumn or winter although some tropical trees flower all year round. Tree identification can be much easier when flowers are evident. Cherries are instantly recognizable by their flowers, as are magnolias. The difficulty arises when individual species or varieties of cherry or magnolia are required. Here again the flower can help. Ask yourself the following questions. What colour is it? Does it have double or single petals? How

Below: Indian bean tree flower clusters help identify the tree in spring.

long are the flower stalks? Close examination of flowers will always enable trees to be separated. The way that flowers are held on the tree is also important. Where do they appear, on the ends of twigs or in the leaf axils? Are they individual or do they appear in clusters? If they are held in clusters, what are those clusters like?

Fruit

Late summer to autumn is the best time to identify trees by their fruit. Some fruit or seeds are instantly recognizable – acorns will immediately identify an oak tree and conkers a horse chestnut. Fallen fruit are

Below: Fruit and seeds appear in a variety of forms to attract a wide range of pollinators.

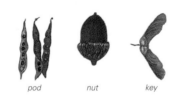
pod   nut   key

Below: Simpoh air has distinctive yellow flowers that form in racemes.

Above: There are hundreds of different leaf shapes, colours and arrangements to help identify trees. Needles too are quite distinct, and like leaves, are arranged differently on different trees.

particularly useful indicators for tropical trees, which may be too tall for flowers or leaves to be visible. Some fruit are particularly distinctive, such as those of spindle trees, *Euonymus* species. The casing is normally bright pink and opens very much like a parasol to reveal orange seeds, which hang on tiny threads.

Bark

Some trees are probably better known by their bark than any other feature. Silver birch, for example, has striking silvery white bark, while the Tibetan cherry, *Prunus serrula*, has bark that is polished, peeling and mahogany red. Other trees may not have such striking bark colour but bark may still be a useful feature to aid identification. For instance, beech has smooth light grey bark, cherry has distinctive horizontal banding and plane trees have buff-

Below: Buds can help identify a tree that is not in leaf.

Above: Breadfruit are instantly recognizable in their native West Indies.

Above: The cones of the Likiang spruce age to become almost purple in colour.

Above: The sweet chestnut tree can be identified by its distinctive fruit in autumn.

coloured bark which is constantly 'flaking' to reveal fresh, light fawn bark beneath.

Buds

Winter is the time when tree identification can be most difficult. However, close inspection of the buds can be of considerable help. Ash has very distinctive black buds, for example, while those of magnolias tend to be large and covered with a dense coating of light-grey hairs. Horse chestnut buds are large and sticky, sycamore buds lime-green in colour. The positioning of buds can also help identify a tree. They may be in pairs on opposite sides of the twig, or they may be alternately positioned with one on the left followed by one on the right. Some buds hug the twig, such as those of willow, while others, such as oak buds, appear in clusters.

Equipment

When identifying trees in the field it is worth having one or two pieces of equipment with you. A good field guide is essential. It is worth getting one that fits inside your pocket and

preferably has a waterproof cover. A pair of binoculars can be useful to get a closer look at leaves, flowers or buds, which may be at the top of the tree. A notepad and pencil will allow you to sketch relevant features and make notes on locations. Finally, sealable plastic bags are particularly useful. They enable you to collect specimen leaves, fruit or seeds and take them home for closer examination.

How to use the encyclopedia

The trees in the encyclopedia are arranged according to two major groups of trees: trees of the temperate world and trees of the tropical world; both groups include conifers and broad leaves. Within each chapter the trees are subdivided using the Cronquist system for classification of flowering plants, as developed by Arthur Cronquist in 1981.

Each main group of trees is divided into families, then genus and finally species. For each species the botanical name and common name is given. Under the common name of each tree, is first any other common name the tree is known by, the Latin name, then the abbreviated name of the authority who named the tree.

Right: In winter the overall shape of a tree and its bark, twigs and buds will all help towards identification. Quite often, in managed woodlands, the task of identification will be made simpler by the fact that many trees of the same species will be planted together.

TREES OF THE
TEMPERATE WORLD

Most variations between temperate and tropical trees are caused by the dramatic differences in climate between temperate and tropical regions of the world. Temperate trees have to deal with fluctuations in temperature and long periods of cold which inhibit tree growth. Consequently they go into a state of dormancy during the coldest months.

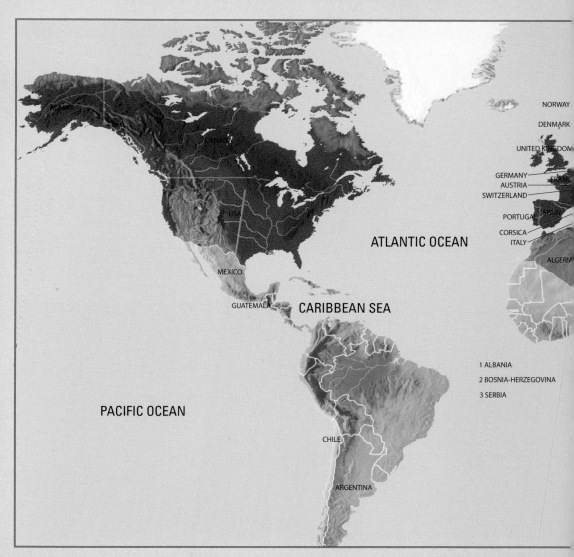

ALASKA

CANADA

USA

MEXICO

GUATEMALA

ATLANTIC OCEAN

CARIBBEAN SEA

PACIFIC OCEAN

CHILE

ARGENTINA

NORWAY

DENMARK

UNITED KINGDOM

GERMANY
AUSTRIA
SWITZERLAND

FRANCE

PORTUGAL   SPAIN

CORSICA
ITALY

ALGERIA

1 ALBANIA

2 BOSNIA-HERZEGOVINA

3 SERBIA

During this period they do not need to produce food, so they do not need their leaves. Most temperate trees are therefore deciduous – they shed their leaves in autumn, producing new leaves as the temperature rises in spring. Those that are not deciduous, such as many conifers, survive by producing thin needle-like leaves which are able to withstand long periods of severe cold. Although temperate trees grow more slowly than tropical trees they tend to live much longer, if allowed to do so. There are many examples of temperate deciduous broad-leaved and evergreen trees living for more than 1,000 years.

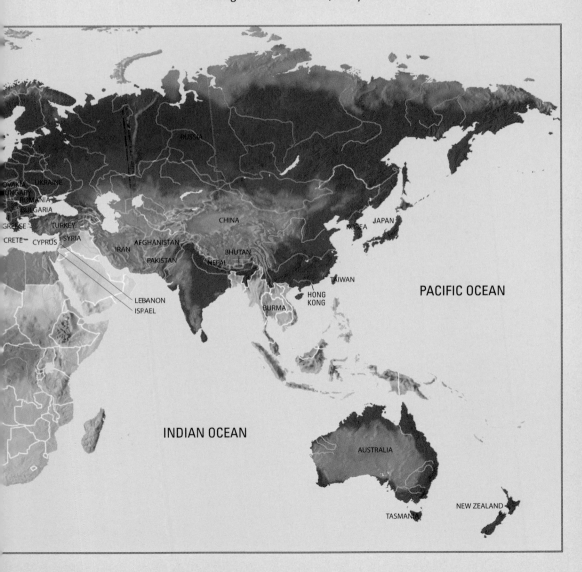

PODOCARPS

The podocarps are predominantly forest tree species from the Southern Hemisphere. They are all coniferous evergreens with linear or scale-like leaves. The most extensive genus is Podocarpus, *with over 70 species that range from southern temperate regions through the tropics to the West Indies and Japan. Many can be grown in a temperate environment and are a major component of temperate rainforests.*

Kahitkatea

New Zealand dacryberry *Dacrycarpus dacrydioides* (Rich.) Laubenf.

Having been measured at a height of over 60m/200ft, the kahitkatea is the tallest recorded endemic tree of New Zealand. It is also referred to as the New Zealand dacryberry because of the bright red, berry-like receptacles produced by the female tree. Felling for timber has reduced the frequency of its distribution throughout New Zealand to areas of scattered trees, forming groves only on less accessible or swampy ground, particularly along the west coast. It can be found growing at an altitude of up to 600m/2,000ft.

Right: The needles, which are arranged opposite each other on the shoot, are up to 2.5cm/1in long.

Above: Bright red kahitkatea berries are produced in profusion in autumn.

Identification: At maturity this is an elegant tree, developing a broad, rounded evergreen canopy in good proportion to the long and ridged buttressed trunk. Male and female flowers are produced on separate trees. The male cones are bright orange when mature.

Distribution: New Zealand.
Height: 60m/200ft
Shape: Broadly conical
Evergreen
Pollinated: Wind
Leaf shape: Linear

Right: The seed is contained in a bright red berry-like fruit.

Miro

Prumnopitys ferruginea (D. Don) Laubenf.

The miro develops to form a tall tree up to 25m/80ft with a trunk of 1m/3ft across. It is valued for its hard, durable and sometimes beautifully figured wood used for cabinet-making. Fruit from this tree takes over one year to develop, turning from red to purple when mature. A native species of wood pigeon has been recorded as playing a vital role in distributing the fruit of the miro throughout the forests, because this forms part of its natural diet.

Right: The male flowers are upright cream-coloured catkins 3cm/1¼in long and are produced in early spring.

Identification: The evergreen foliage is juvenile at seedling stage, forming a graceful specimen tree. Adult leaves are longer and broader and the habit of the tree at maturity more rounded. A related species is Matai, *Prumnopitys taxifolia*, the seed from which is blue-black.

Above: The flattened needles are up to 2.5cm/1in long.

Above right: The seed of the miro is contained in a purple berry.

Distribution: Throughout New Zealand in shady situations. It forms a component of lowland forests up to an altitude of 1,000m/3,280ft.
Height: 25m/80ft
Shape: Broadly conical
Evergreen
Pollinated: Wind
Leaf shape: Linear

Totara

Podocarpus totara D. Don

The totara is a slow-growing evergreen tree from New Zealand that is noted for its longevity (it usually lives between 800–1,000 years). Growing up to 30m/100ft it has a straight, deeply grooved trunk that often reaches nearly two-thirds of its overall height. The bark peels off in long strips to reveal a beautiful golden brown hue. Its timber is valued for general construction. Montane totara, *P. cunninghamii*, is a similar species, which has a much thinner, papery bark.

Above right: The cherry-like fruit contains two round seeds.

Identification: The crown develops from conical to a more broadly ovoid shape as it matures. It is noted for its massive trunk, which can be up to 2m/6½ft in diameter and for the huge strips of bark that peel away in a curtain-like fashion until finally falling from the tree's trunk.

Distribution: Throughout the North Island of New Zealand and into the north-eastern regions of the South Island.
Height: 30m/100ft
Shape: Broadly conical
Evergreen
Pollinated: Wind
Leaf shape: Linear

Left: The dull green needles are stiff and leathery with a sharp point at the tip.

Plum-fruited Yew *Prumnopitys andina* (Poep. ex. Endl.) Laubenf.
This tree has foliage similar to the common yew. It produces fruit 2cm/¾in long, which is yellow in colour and similar to a plum with an edible fleshy covering. The seed is noted for not having a resinous odour. The tree is cultivated throughout the warmer temperate regions as an ornamental tree. Canelo, a yellow hardwood obtained from this podocarp, is used in the production of furniture.

Below: The foliage of the plum-fruited yew is similar to the common yew.

Manio *Podocarpus salignus*
D. Don ex. Lamb.
Native to Chile, this tree is commonly referred to as the willowleaf podocarp as its leaves are linear and sickle-shaped, resembling those of a willow. It can grow to 20m/66ft tall, forming an attractive tree with gently pendulous branching and graceful foliage.

Prince Albert's Yew

Saxegothaea conspicua Lindley

The genus *Saxegothaea* is a monotypic, meaning there is only one tree in the genus. *S. conspicua* is an evergreen tree forming part of the temperate rainforests of southern Chile and adjacent Argentina. It is found growing in association with other forest species, such as *Nothofagus dombeyi*, *Drimys winteri* and *Podocarpus nubigena*, all prized for timber. It is cultivated throughout warmer regions of the Northern Hemisphere as an ornamental tree. The generic and common names are in commemoration of the husband of Queen Victoria of England.

Above: Needles of the Prince Albert's yew are slightly curved with a sharp tip and are up to 3cm/1¼in long.

Distibution: Along lowland areas at the base of the west Andean slopes, from Chile (Biobio to the Chiloé province), and into south-west Argentina.
Height: 15m/50ft
Shape: Broadly conical
Evergreen
Pollinated: Wind
Leaf shape: Linear

Identification: Grows to a height of 15m/50ft or more, developing a slender, conical crown in its native environment and a more bushy habit in cultivation. The foliage is similar in appearance to the genus *Taxus*. The fruit is thick, round and composed of fleshy scales.

Right: The leaf on the right shows the topside view and that on the left shows the underside colouring.

PLUM YEWS AND CHILE PINE

The plum yews or Cephalotaxus are very similar to the podocarps, in that they produce cones or fruit that are drupe-like. This is a characteristic also shared by the false nutmegs, or Torreya species. Of much greater difference is the Chile pine, belonging to the unique Southern-Hemisphere family Araucariaceae. It shares the characteristics of this family, being an evergreen, long-lived coniferous tree.

Plum Yew

Cephalotaxus harringtonia K.Koch var. *drupacea* (Sieb. & Zucc.) Koid.

The genus *Cephalotaxus* consists of four species, distributed from the eastern Himalayas to Japan. The plum yew is the most widely cultivated. It forms a small evergreen tree up to 10m/33ft tall with foliage similar to that of yew, but with much broader and drupe-like fruit that resembles a plum. When crushed, the foliage is pungent. In cultivation it is useful for tolerating shade, where it can develop an impressive mound-like appearance.

Identification: Leaves are broader and longer than yew. The upper surface is pale green and glossy, and the underside is slightly grey in colour with two distinctive green bands. The leaf apex is acute and often spine-tipped.

Above: Needles are up to 5cm/2in long, glossy dark green above with two light bands of stomata beneath.

Distribution: Japan and Korea.
Height: 10m/33ft
Shape: Spreading
Evergreen
Pollinated: Wind
Leaf shape: Linear

Left: Plum yew fruit has distinctive pale banding and turns brown in colour when mature.

Chile Pine

Monkey puzzle *Araucaria araucana* (Molina) K. Koch

This is a uniquely bizarre tree for its triangular shaped, very sharp, pointed leaves and distinctive whorls of long branches. It was introduced into cultivation in the late 18th century. It is widely admired for its architectural habit, but often looks misplaced. Even in its native Andean forest it is an impressive oddity. Female trees of the Chile pine produce cones 15cm/6in in length, which take over two years to ripen. The seed is edible.

Identification: As a young tree it has a slightly rounded conical outline, with foliage to ground level. As it matures, the crown broadens and the lower branches fall away. This reveals an impressive trunk with horizontal folds of grey bark, similar in appearance to elephant hide.

Above: The distinctive bark of the Chile pine.

Right: Male cones are borne in clusters at the tips of each shoot.

Distribution: Forms groves in the Andean forests of Chile and south-western Argentina.
Height: 50m/164ft
Shape: Broadly conical, becoming domed in maturity
Evergreen
Pollinated: Wind
Leaf shape: Linear to triangular

Left: The female cone is an ovoid brown cone up to 15cm/6in long.

Stinking Cedar

Torreya taxifolia Arnott

This tree is very similar in foliage to the yew, *Taxus*, but differs in having incredibly sharp, spine-like tips to the needles. When crushed, the needles release a pungent, disagreeable odour, hence the common name. In outline this tree forms a broad-based pyramid, rarely growing taller than 15m/50ft in height. As is the case with other *Torreya* species, it is commonly found in moist woodland areas. Its timber has been used for fencing, but it is not an abundant tree in its native Florida and is now considered to be under threat in the wild. It has been widely planted in ornamental collections worldwide.

Right: The fruit is a purple-green berry containing one seed.

Far right: Needles are sharply pointed, glossy dark green above and light green beneath.

Identification: This evergreen tree differs from the Californian nutmeg in having much shorter, convex needles which can be up to 4cm/1¼in long and sharply pointed. The needles are simple and linear in shape and arranged alternately. The bark is grey-brown in colour and furrows as the tree ages. The fleshy seed is poisonous if eaten. This tree is cultivated as an ornamental tree.

Distribution: USA: The distribution is restricted to the Apalichicola River in north-west Florida, and then moves northwards into Georgia.
Height: 15m/50ft
Shape: Broadly conical
Evergreen
Pollinated: Wind
Leaf shape: Linear

Kaya Nut *Torreya nucifera* (L.) Siebold. & Zucc.
This *Torreya* originates from the lowland valley areas of Honshu, Shikoku and Kyushu in Japan. A similar species to the Californian nutmeg, it develops a more open crown and much shorter leaves.

Below: Kaya nut needles are about 3cm/1¼in long and when crushed emit an unpleasant odour.

Fortune Plum Yew *Cephalotaxus fortunii* Hook. f.
Native of eastern and central China, where it forms a tree up to 15m/50ft tall. It develops an open habit, largely as a result of its long needles, which can be as much as 15cm/6in in length.

Californian Nutmeg

Torreya californica Toll.

The Californian nutmeg is very similar to some of the podocarps and plum yews in having drupe-like fruit and linear foliage. It is distinctive in producing very sharp spines at the tips of its leaves. Beneath the resinous, fleshy fruit the seed is grooved and resembles commercial nutmeg, but has no similarity in use. It is largely grown as an ornamental tree in gardens and arboreta, as the crown forms a very attractive conical outline and the branching develops in open whorls.

Identification: An evergreen tree to 20m/66ft tall. The leaves are thin and relatively short (up to 5cm/2in). They are a deep yellowish green colour and have a very shiny upper surface. Their underside has two distinctive ranks of white stomatal bands. The bark is reddish brown and flaky.

Above: There is no botanical connection between the fruit of the Californian nutmeg and the spice nutmeg Myristica fragrans.

Distribution: USA: Restricted to forested areas of California.
Height: 30m/100ft
Shape: Broadly conical
Evergreen
Pollinated: Wind
Leaf shape: Linear

Below: Needles are reminiscent of some of the silver fir species, Abies. *They are up to 5cm/2in long and sharply pointed.*

MAIDENHAIR TREE, YEW AND INCENSE CEDAR

The maidenhair tree is the only surviving representative of the Ginkgoaceae family, the other members being known solely from fossil records. The genus Taxus *is present in three continents across the Northern Hemisphere and has related characteristics to the Torreya species. Incense cedar is one of only three species belonging to the genus* Calocedrus.

Maidenhair Tree

Ginkgo biloba L.

Distribution: Originating from China, thought to be from the provinces of Anhwei and Kiangsu. It is widely cultivated throughout the Northern Hemisphere including Japan.
Height: 40m/130ft
Shape: Broadly conical
Deciduous
Pollinated: Wind
Leaf shape: Fan

Fossil records show that *Gingko biloba* existed over 200 million years ago. It was introduced into general cultivation in 1754. It produces male and female flowers on separate trees. When ripe, the fruit has a rancid odour; the seed beneath this pungent flesh is edible if roasted. *Ginkgo* has an attractive outline.

Identification: A deciduous tree, unique in producing fan-shaped leaves which resemble that of the maidenhair fern (*Adiantum*), hence its common name. The foliage is produced on characteristic short shoots, most apparent in winter. The bark is a pale grey.

Above left: The foliage turns golden yellow in autumn.

Above right: The fruit is orange-brown when ripe and has a single edible kernel.

Common Yew

Taxus baccata L.

The common yew develops a very dense, evergreen canopy, which gives this tree a sombre feel, heightened by its association over recent centuries as a tree of churchyards. Yew wood is extremely durable and is valued in the production of furniture and highly decorative veneers used in cabinet-making. It was commonly used for making bowstaves. A number of cultivars have been created. One of the most striking is 'Standishii', which has an upright habit and golden yellow foliage.

Identification: Develops a broad and loosely conical outline. Leaves are glossy above with a central groove. Bark is rich brown with a purple hue. Male cones shed pollen with cloud-like abundance in spring. The fruit is a fleshy aril, turning red at maturity, around an olive-green seed.

Below: Yew leaves are needle-like in appearance.

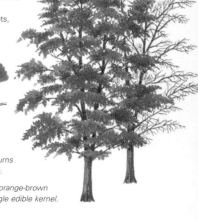

Distribution: Europe, including Britain, eastwards to northern Iran and the Atlas mountains of North Africa.
Height: 20m/66ft
Shape: Broadly conical
Evergreen
Pollinated: Wind
Leaf shape: Linear

Right: Poisonous yew berries are eaten, but not digested by birds.

Incense Cedar

Calocedrus decurrens (Torr.) Florin

Incense cedar is native to western North America. The natural habit of this tree is unusual in that it develops a columnar, almost fastigiate form. Shiny, mid-green leaves develop in flattened sprays produced on branches that are almost horizontal to the main stem. It has a very attractive, exfoliating grey to reddish brown bark. There are only two other species of tree in this genus, *C. macrolepis* from China and *C. formosana* from Taiwan.

Identification: The foliage of the incense cedar is dense, dark green and usually present to the base of the tree with only a short exposed bole. The male and female flowers are produced on the same tree. Often, abundant quantities of oblong cones are produced and become pendulous with their own weight.

Above: The red-brown bark of the incense cedar is similar to that of the giant redwood.

Far left: The yellow-brown cones have six overlapping scales.

Distribution: Western North America from mid-Oregon southwards to Baja California in northern Mexico.
Height: 40m/130ft
Shape: Narrowly columnar
Evergreen
Pollinated: Wind
Leaf shape: Linear scale-like

Above: Japanese yew is a wide-spreading, open growing tree.

Japanese Yew *Taxus cuspidata* Sieb. & Zucc. Occurring naturally throughout Japan and most of north-east Asia, it was introduced to Europe by Robert Fortune in 1855. Reaching a height of 20m/66ft in the wild, but more shrub-like in cultivation, it has spine-tipped leaf apices. This is one of the parents, together with the common yew, of a hybrid *Taxus* x *media*, the most common form of which is the fastigiate 'Hicksii'.

Chinese Yew *Taxus sumahtrana* (Miq.) Laubenf. Preferred in North America to the common yew for its ability to cope with a range of climatic conditions. Used in hedging, or as a specimen tree. This species has much longer foliage and forms a broadly conical tree in habit.

Pahautea

Libocedrus bidwillii Hook. f.

This tree from New Zealand displays a great diversity in form in relation to its surroundings. It can vary from a tall columnar-like tree at a height of over 20m/66ft when growing in moist lowland ravines, to a more shrub-like habit on mountainous slopes at an altitude of 1,200m/3,937ft. With a clean, straight trunk the papery thin, long sections of grey to reddish brown bark are clearly visible. A similar New Zealand species is the kawaka, *Libocedrus plumosa*.

Identification: The foliage consists of small triangular leaves, 2mm/¹⁄₁₆in long. These are arranged in rows of four. Male and female cones are produced on the same tree. On a mature specimen the canopy has a definite conical outline and develops gaps as the sprays of dense foliage weigh heavily on the branch ends.

Distribution: New Zealand: From Te Aroha Mountain in the Coromandel Range southwards, and in the lowland western coastal areas of the South Island.
Height: 20m/66ft
Shape: Broadly columnar
Evergreen
Pollinated: Wind
Leaf shape: Broadly linear

Below: Both the male (left) and female (middle) cones are up to 1cm/½in long.

Below right: The triangular needles are pointed and closely pressed to the shoot.

FALSE CYPRESSES

Trees belonging to the genus Chamaecyparis, *or false cypress, have a number of obvious characteristics in common. All are evergreen, and their leaves are arranged in flattened sprays and have a pungent aroma when crushed. The habitats from which they originate are generally wet and they all produce very durable timber. The genus is present in western North America, Taiwan and Japan.*

Sawara Cypress

Chamaecyparis pisifera (Sieb. & Zucc.) Endl.

A native to the islands of Japan, where it is planted for use as a forest tree and as an ornamental. This tree can reach a height of over 20m/66ft in the wild. The branches are arranged in two opposite, horizontally spreading rows, which gives the tree a rather uniform appearance. The foliage is produced in flattened sprays, the under surface of which has two distinctive white bands of stomata. A number of cultivars have been created. The most impressive is 'Fillifera'. This differs from the original in having more pendulous, thread-like foliage.

Left: The foliage is produced in flattened sprays which, when crushed, are acridly resin-scented.

Identification: The Sawara cypress has a conical habit with a branching system that is fairly open. The bark is an attractive, deep reddish brown. When crushed, the foliage has a pungent and resinous scent. Small cones the size of a pea are produced in dense clusters. Each cone has up to 12 scales and is hollow towards the centre.

Distribution: Found throughout the Honshu and Kyushu islands of Japan.
Height: 20m/66ft
Shape: Conical
Evergreen
Pollinated: Wind
Leaf shape: Linear scale-like

Nootka Cypress

Chamaecyparis nootkatensis (D. Don) Spach.

The nootka cypress is common throughout the coastal forests of western North America, where there are living examples many thousands of years old. It is distinctively conical in outline; the branches are flexible and develop a weeping appearance that distinguishes it from other *Chamaecyparis* species. There is an elegant naturally occurring form called 'Pendula', which produces elongated sprays of foliage that hang from pendulous branches. Referred to as yellow cedar, the wood is noted for being fine textured, straight grained and yellow in colour.

Identification: Up to 30m/100ft tall. The bark resembles the western red cedar in that it produces thin strips when peeled. It is brown in colour with a pinkish hue. Both male and female flowers are produced on the same tree. The cones, which take two years to develop, are about 1cm/½in across and a deep plum colour.

Below: The foliage has pale green margins.

Right: Each cone scale has a sharp spike.

Below: The branches have a graceful upward sweep towards the tip.

Distribution: USA: From Alaska, south towards northern California. At varying altitudes, from sea level to above the tree line, where competition is reduced. Found in the Olympic Mountains, the Cascades of Washington and Oregon, and east to the Blue Mountains.
Height: 30m/100ft
Shape: Narrowly conical
Evergreen
Pollinated: Wind
Leaf shape: Linear scale-like

Taiwan Cypress

Chamaecyparis formosensis Matsu.

Restricted in distribution to the island of Taiwan, this is a similar species to the Sawara cypress. An impressive tree in stature, which in its native habitat grows to a height of over 60m/200ft, with a trunk of 20m/66ft or more in girth. First introduced into cultivation in the early part of the 20th century and has yet to be recorded at the great size of its wild form. As with many of the false cypresses, its timber is noted for being durable and resistant to moisture.

Identification: Has a reddish bark with regular and shallow fissuring. The leaves are flat and produced in broad sprays; singularly they are scale-like. Cones are angular and similar to those of Sawara cypress, but are larger and carried above the foliage.

Left: The lower branches are level and sweep up towards the tip.

Distribution: Mountainous regions of central and northern Taiwan.
Height: 60m/200ft
Shape: Broadly conical
Evergreen
Pollinated: Wind
Leaf shape: Linear scale-like

Left: The scale-like needles are a light yellow-green colour and when crushed have the aroma of seaweed.

Hinoki Cypress *Chamaecyparis obtusa* (Sieb. & Zucc.) Endl.

Hinoki cypress is native to the southern Honshu, Shikoku and Kyushu islands of Japan, where it is cultivated as an ornamental tree and is highly prized for its beauty. It produces a valuable timber that is used for making a range of products that include furniture, wood panelling and veneers. The crown develops to a medium broad conical shape. Bark is soft, stringy and more grey than other *Chamaecyparis* species. Bright stomatal banding on the underside of the leaves gives the foliage an almost variegated appearance.

Southern White Cedar *Chamaecyparis thyoides* (L.) Britton, Sterns. & Pogg.

Height 15m/50ft. The southern white cedar originates from eastern North America along the Atlantic coast of New England south towards Georgia. Its fine foliage has white undersides hence its common name. A hardy tree of which there are a number of cultivars including 'Ericoides', 'Glauca' and 'Variegata'.

Leyland Cypress x *Cupressocyparis leylandii* Dallim. & Jacks.

The fastest growing conifer in the British Isles. Widely used for hedging and screening, it needs regular pruning. It is a hybrid of *Cupressus macrocarpa* and *Chamaecyparis nootkatensis* which originated at Leighton Hall, Powys, Wales, in 1888.

Lawson Cypress

Port Orford cedar, Oregon cedar *Chamaecyparis lawsoniana* (A. Murray) Pal.

Originates from North America. It develops into a tall, columnar tree to 40m/130ft with reddish-brown fibrous bark and scented foliage that has distinctive stomatal markings on the underside of the leaves. In the Pacific north-western America it is a very important source of timber with many uses, from boat-building to cabinet-making. An incredible diversity of cultivars has been produced, which vary in form, foliage and colour.

Identification: Young trees have smooth, brown-green and shiny bark, with a pendulous dominant shoot that is distinct from the mature trees. It produces globular cones on the foliage tips, which begin fleshy with a bluish purple bloom and become woody and wrinkled.

Below: The cones are globular, 7mm/⅓ in in diameter, purple-brown in colour and remain on the tree long after the seed has been shed.

Distribution: North-western USA from south-west Oregon to north-west California. Present in the Klamath and Siskiyou Mountains to an altitude that approaches 2,000m/6,561ft.
Height: 40m/130ft
Shape: Narrowly conical
Evergreen
Pollinated: Wind
Leaf shape: Linear scale-like

Below: The top side of the foliage is dark green to blue and when crushed smells of parsley.

TRUE CYPRESSES

These trees are closely related to the genus Chamaecyparis, *in that their leaves are scale-like and produced in sprays. Unlike the false cypresses the foliage is not flattened. Their cones are composed of fewer scales, between six and eight, and are twice the diameter, but contain less seed. True cypresses are distributed throughout regions of North America, Europe and Asia.*

Kashmir Cypress

Cupressus cashmeriana (Royle) Carriere

The origin of this tree is yet to be decided. It is noted as being closely related to the Himalayan cypress, *C. torulosa,* and is suspected to be native to this region. In cultivation it is a very attractive tree. The branches ascend, which extenuates the absolute pendulous nature displayed by the sprays of glaucous blue foliage. In colder regions of the Northern Hemisphere this tree is grown as a conservatory plant.

Identification: Grows to a height of 20m/66ft. It develops from a conical to a wide spreading crown with maturity. The cones are produced from an early age and turn from greenish yellow to red-brown when ripe.

Above: The seed is contained in a globular cone, each scale of which, has a hooked point.

Left: The vivid blue-white scale-like needles are 1–2mm/¹⁄₁₆in long.

Distribution: Unknown.
Height: 20m/66ft
Shape: Narrowly weeping
Evergreen
Pollinated: Wind
Leaf shape: Linear scale-like

Arizona Cypress

Cupressus arizonica Greene

The Arizona cypress belongs to a group of cypresses that are found in south-western USA along the northern border with Mexico. They are distinguished from each other largely by their geographical distribution through this region. All have blue-grey glaucous foliage composed of scale-like leaves, and tolerate the dry, sun-drenched conditions. Other cypresses in this group include the smooth cypress, *C. glabra*; San Pedro cypress, *C. montana*; pinute cypress, *C. nevadensis*; and the Cayamaca cypress, *C. stephensonii*.

Identification: Develops a conical habit to a height of 20m/66ft. Has a more textured, finely fissured bark. The foliage is a dull grey-green colour, often lacking the white, resin-secreting glands common to other cypresses in this group.

Above and right: The rounded cones are 2.5cm/1in across with six large scales and a short stalk.

Right: The scale-like needles closely overlap, and are pale to grey-green with a sharp point.

Right: The scales are arranged irregularly along the shoot.

Distribution: USA: From the central region of Arizona south towards the northern border of Mexico.
Height: 20m/66ft
Shape: Narrowly conical
Evergreen
Pollinated: Wind
Leaf shape: Linear scale-like

Monterey Cypress

Cupressus macrocarpa Gord.

With an incredible ability to withstand exposure to salt-laden winds, this tree has become as common a sight along the exposed coastal habitats of Europe as in its native California. It can attain a height of 40m/130ft, but individual trees are often stunted by the extreme conditions. In cultivation it is best known for being the female parent of the leyland cypress, × *Cupressocyparis leylandii*. Cypress timber is strong and durable so it is often used for structural work.

Right: Juvenile trees are pyramidal to columnar in shape.
Left: Mature trees become flat-topped with widespread horizontal branches.

Identification: Mature trees display a great variability in habit, from a dense crown of ascending branches to a more horizontal cedar-like form. Leaves are arranged in loose, circular sprays around the shoots. When crushed its foliage releases an aromatic odour.

Distribution: USA: Known from two sites along the coastline near Monterey, California: at Cypress Point and Point Lobos.
Height: 40m/130ft
Shape: Broadly conical
Evergreen
Pollinated: Wind
Leaf shape: Linear scale-like

Left: Cones are up to 4cm/1½ in across.

Guadelupe Cypress *Cupressus guadelupensis* S. Wats.
Grows to a height of 20m/66ft in the wild. This cypress is restricted in natural distribution to the island of Guadelupe off the coast of Baja California. The island is part of a series of ridges once connected to the mainland. The tree is seldom seen in cultivation.

Mexican Cypress *Cupressus lusitanica* Mill.
Height 20m/66ft. The Mexican cypress was first named in Portugal, having been brought over from Mexico and cultivated there. It was also believed to have been of Asiatic origin, hence its other common name, cedar of Goa.

West Himalayan Cypress *Cupressus torulosa* D. Don
Grows to a height of 20m/66ft. This is a particularly attractive tree when mature for its interesting bark that peels off in long strips. It is an important timber tree, classified as cypress along with *C. macrocarpa* and *C. sempervirens*. It is also referred to as Bhutan cypress, although its distribution suggests this is more likely to be the form *C. torulosa* var. *cornayana*.

Chinese Weeping Cypress *Cupressus funebris* Endl.
This species is native to China, where it grows with restricted distribution along the Yangtse valley. It is similar to the false cypresses in having foliage produced in flattened sprays. The habit is attractive and often pendulous. Immature plants have a fine, soft foliage that is retained for a number of years.

Italian Cypress

Cupressus sempervirens L.

This is a fascinating tree because of its ability to retain a tight columnar form throughout its life. There is no other conifer, except the Chile pine, that has such a strong sense of architecture. It is the space between the plantings of these trees that characterizes the hills and roadside verges of Tuscany in Italy, and the western Mediterranean. The foliage is a dull grey-green and, unusually for cypress, has no noticeable scent when crushed.

Identification: The Italian cypress can attain a height of 18m/60ft or more in its natural habitat. The bark is predominantly grey with some brown colouring. Cones are larger than most trees in this genus, growing to 3.5cm/1⅜in; similar to those of the Monterey cypress. They are retained on the tree for many years.

Distribution: Predominantly a Mediterranean tree with a distribution northwards to Switzerland and east to northern Iran.
Height: 18m/60ft
Shape: Very narrowly columnar
Evergreen
Pollinated: Wind
Leaf shape: Linear scale-like

Below: The cones are a grey-brown, smooth and shiny.

PATAGONIAN CYPRESS AND ARBORVITAE

A common characteristic of Fitzroya *is the three-whorled arrangements of the leaves, which distinguish it from the closely related* Cupressus. *The arborvitae, or* Thuja *species, are similar to Lawson cypress, but have much larger and broader leaves, and* Thujopsis, *or hiba, differs from* Thuja *in having thick white markings on the underside of its leaves.*

Patagonian Cypress

Fitzroya cupressoides (Mol.) I. M. Johnston

This unique genus of tree has a restricted distribution and is recorded as one of the world's oldest trees, verified at over 3,500 years. It is often referred to as the redwood of South America. Its reddish, lightweight and straight-grained timber, commonly used for shingles, furniture and masts, has been highly prized for centuries.

Identification: It has reddish brown, deeply ridged bark that peels off in strips. The foliage is produced in pendulous sprays and is blue-green with distinctive white markings on both surfaces. In cultivation it is slow-growing and forms a multi-branched, shrub-like habit.

Above: The cones develop at the end of each spiky shoot.

Left: Needles are bright blue-green with two white stomatal bands.

Distribution: South America: From southern Chile to Argentina. It is now restricted to higher altitude rainforests along the coastal ranges from south of Valdira, including Chiloe Island, to the Andean slopes.
Height: 50m/165ft
Shape: Broadly columnar
Evergreen
Pollinated: Wind
Leaf shape: Linear scale-like

Left: The angular cones have nine woody scales.

White Cedar

Thuja occidentalis L.

This slow-growing evergreen tree's origins are in eastern Canada and south-eastern USA, where it is predominantly a tree of upper forest levels, surviving in rocky outcrops as well as sites with high moisture content. Similar to its more westerly cousin, it is valued commercially as a timber that has good resistance to decay and tolerates contact with moisture. Many cultivars have been developed, mostly from dwarf forms. 'Rheingold' has attractive golden yellow foliage.

Identification: Twisted sprays of foliage give this tree a distinctive outline. During autumn and winter the foliage has attractive hints of orange and brown. The bark is brown with a golden orange hue and shreds with age. Yellow cones develop from as early as six years.

Right: Needle scales are dark green above, yellow-green below.
Below: When crushed, the foliage smells of green apples.

Left: The upright cones are 1cm/⅜in across. Yellow-green at first, they ripen to brown.

Distribution: South-eastern Canada and USA. From Nova Scotia and New Brunswick, west to Quebec and northern Ontario; through Michigan, Illinois and Indiana to the states of New England.
Height: 20m/66ft
Shape: Narrowly conical
Evergreen
Pollinated: Wind
Leaf shape: Linear scale-like

Western Red Cedar

Thuja plicata D. Don

Also known as giant arborvitae, this evergreen tree originates from the north-western Pacific coastline of America, where it is a major component of the moist, lowland coniferous forests. Individual living trees have been recorded at over 1,000 years old, and its timber has been utilized for centuries. Native American Indians used to burn out the trunks to make canoes. It has become an economically important timber, being straight grained, soft and easily worked. It has been widely used to make roofing shingles. Many cultivars have been produced, including a distinctive variegated form called 'Zebrina'.

Identification: A very tall, narrow, conical evergreen tree up to 50m/164ft. Individual specimen trees with low branching can layer to form a secondary ring of vigorous, upright trunks. The foliage is dark green and glossy above, with a sweetly aromatic scent when crushed. The bark is reddish brown, forming plates with maturity. It is fibrous and ridged.

Left: The shoots are coppery brown with sprays of deep glossy green, scale-like needles that are flattened in one plane.

Distribution: USA: Originating from the Pacific coastline of North America, it grows from southern Alaska, through British Columbia, westwards to Washington and Oregon to the giant coastal redwood forests of California.
Height: 50m/165ft
Shape: Narrowly conical
Evergreen
Pollinated: Wind
Leaf shape: Linear scale-like

Hiba

Thujopsis dolabrata (L., Sieb. & Zucc.

A monotypic genus and single species of evergreen tree originating from Japan, this is distinguished from *Thuja* in having broad leaves with striking and distinctive white undersides. In cultivation it is characteristically slow in growth and often develops no further in form than that of a dense, evergreen shrub for the first ten years. As a mature tree, the habit of *Thujopsis* can vary from tall, upright and columnar to low branching, multi-stemmed and broadly conical.

Identification: Foliage is yellow-green, glossy and hard. The white undersides of the needles are bordered by a dark green margin. The ovoid cones are 1.25cm/½in long, green becoming brown. Bark is red-brown to grey, peeling off at maturity into fine strips.

Distribution: Japan: From the southern islands of central Honshu, northwards to Shikoku and Kyhshu. A distinctive form, *T. dolabrata* var. *hondae* 'Makino', is unique to northern Honshu and southern Hokkaido.
Height: 20m/66ft
Shape: Broadly conical
Evergreen
Pollinated: Wind
Leaf shape: Linear scale-like

Right: Needles are scale-like, 6mm/¼in long, in flattened sprays.

Japanese Thuja *Thuja standishii* (Gord.) Carr.
Native of Japan, from Honshu and Shikoku. An evergreen tree to 20m/66ft. Very deep, rich red-brown bark that peels off in square plates. Similar in form to hiba, in having branches that curve sharply upwards and foliage that is hard and irregular in outline. Young growing leaf tips are blue-grey in colour. When crushed, the foliage has a lemon-like scent.

Chinese Thuja *Thuja orientalis* L.
A species from Korea, northern and southern China, this differs from other *Thuja* in having foliage that is arranged in vertical sprays, giving it a distinct character as a specimen tree. Other cultivars include 'Aurea Nana', a golden, slow-growing form, and 'Elegantissima', which has a less broadly pyramidal habit than the species.

Korean Thuja *Thuja koraiensis* Nakai
Native to Korea and the Jilin province of China, this is a small tree (10m/33ft). A similar species to the Japanese thuja, it differs in having blue-green foliage and is unique in having almost completely silvery undersides to the leaves.

Right: In spring, the new growth on each spray of the Korean thuja is a vivid lime-green colour, becoming progressively darker with age.

JUNIPERS AND KING WILLIAM PINE

The junipers are similar to the true cypresses, Cupressus, *in that they have two types of leaves on the same plant, both juvenile and scale-like. Unlike cypresses, the fruit consists of a cone in which the scales have fused together to give a berry-like appearance. King William pine is unique in the Taxodiaceae family for having foliage that closely resembles a juniper.*

Syrian Juniper

Juniperus drupacea Labill.

With the longest needles and largest fruit of the junipers, the Syrian juniper has a distinctive and fine outline developing into a tall columnar tree to 15m/50ft high. It has a similar distribution to *J. excelsa*, the Grecian juniper, which grows to a height of 20m/66ft and develops a more spreading crown of dark green-blue foliage with purple-brown, irregularly scaled bark. Between the two in distribution and heading more northwards is *J. foetidissima*, the stinking juniper.

Identification: The crown is columnar to conical in shape. The trunk has orange-brown bark, which is shed in fine vertical strips. The leaves have two white bands of stomata on the inner surface and are shiny mid-green on the outer surface.

Above: The needles are very stiff, and can be up to 2.5cm/1in long. They are sharply pointed and are arranged in whorls of three. The cone is 2.5cm/1in across, blue-green at first, it changes colour as it matures to a blackish purple.

Distribution: Distributed through southern Europe and northern Africa. Found on rocky slopes in forest or scrub, throughout Syria into Turkey and in parts of Greece.
Height: 15m/50ft
Shape: Broadly conical
Evergreen
Pollinated: Wind
Leaf shape: Linear scale-like

Eastern Red Cedar

Juniperus virginiana L.

The most widely distributed conifer through central and eastern North America, this is tolerant of dry, exposed and elevated sites, a characteristic that has made it useful for screening and wind protection. The heartwood is a beautiful reddish brown and has a typical cedar scent which is retained through drying. The wood has moth-repellent properties and is commonly used to make blanket boxes, chests and cupboard liners. Cedarwood oil is extracted from the fruit and the leaves for use in soaps and fragrances.

Identification: An evergreen tree to 30m/98ft. Eastern red cedar develops a dense pyramidal to columnar habit, with two types of foliage. It has red-brown bark, which exfoliates in long strips. The fruit is berry-like, light green in spring and dark blue when mature.

Above: The dense scale-like foliage is 6mm/¼in long, sage-green above and grey-green beneath.

Left: The small cones have a blue-grey bloom when ripe.

Distribution: Eastern and central USA. Great Plains eastwards. South-west Maine to southern Minnesota into the Dakotas and southwards to Nebraska and central Texas. East to Florida and Georgia.
Height: 30m/100ft
Shape: Narrowly conical
Evergreen
Pollinated: Wind
Leaf shape: Linear scale-like

Chinese Juniper

Juniperus chinensis L.

A juniper from China and parts of Japan, this is the most commonly used conifer for bonsai. It has been in cultivation for centuries and many cultivars have been developed. Hybrids include 'Keteleeri', which makes a dense, regular and narrowly conical tree; 'Pfitzeriana' known as the Pfitzer juniper which is an old and widely planted hybrid; and 'Hetzii', a very vigorous hybrid, which has an upright and spreading form.

Identification: A dioecious tree, the Chinese juniper has an erect, narrow and conical growing habit. The bark is grey through to reddish brown, peeling off in strips. Leaves are dark green on the outer surface and have a broad green stripe on the inner, separated by two white stomatal bands. The cones are rather lumpy in appearance and measure approximately 6–7mm/¼in across.

Above: Mature foliage has dark green scale-like needles with paler banding.

Right: When ripe, cones are dark purple with a pale grey bloom.

Distribution: Widely distributed through north and east China. Also present in Inner Mongolia and around Japan, restricted to the coastal areas of Honshu, Kyushu and Shikoku.
Height: 25m/80ft
Shape: Narrowly conical
Evergreen
Pollinated: Wind
Leaf shape:
Linear scale-like

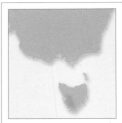

Right: Needles.

Common Juniper
Juniperus communis L.
Distributed throughout northern Europe, including Britain, south-western Asia and North America, it is generally a spreading or prostrate shrub, but occasionally a columnar tree. It has given rise to a number of cultivars, which include the Irish juniper 'Hibernica', which is narrow and grows to 8m/26ft high, and 'Suecica', with a broad, upright habit. The berry-like fruit is used to flavour gin.

Western Juniper *Juniperus occidentalis* Hook. The natural distribution of the western juniper is along the mountainous regions of the Pacific coast of North America. It has given rise to a silver grey-leaved hybrid, 'Sierra Silver', which is noted for its merit as a garden plant.

Mexican Juniper *Juniperus flaccida* Schlech. The Mexican juniper has a weeping habit that resembles the false cypress. It is found throughout northern and central Mexico.

Himalayan Juniper *Juniperus recurva* Buch.-Ham. ex. D. Don
The attractive weeping habit of the foliage from this tree gives rise to its name. It originates from the Himalayas, from Afghanistan to south-western China and northern Burma. The foliage is bluish grey, is dry to the touch and makes a rasping sound in the wind.

King William Pine

Athrotaxis selaginoides D. Don

A native of the Tasmanian temperate rainforests, this tree has red-brown bark which builds up in layers like that of *Sequoiadendron giganteum*. The timber is prized for its durability, smooth texture and straight grain. There are only two other species in this genus: the smooth Tasmanian cedar *Athrotaxis cupressoides*, and the Tasmanian cedar *Athrotaxis laxiflora*. The former is less common in the wild, and differs in having rounded shoots and closely pressed leaf scales.

Identification: A conical tree to 30m/100ft tall. It often develops a long clear trunk and small tufted crown. Leaves are spirally arranged, shiny green and spreading. The lower surface has two bright, bluish white bands.

Below: The leaves are similar in shape to those of Juniperus.

Distribution: South-western Tasmania in the mountainous regions of the central plateau, extending almost to the West coast.
Height: 30m/100ft
Shape: Broadly conical
Evergreen
Pollinated: Wind
Leaf shape: Linear

Below: Cones are orange-brown, 2.5cm/1in across and remain on the tree after the seeds are shed.

REDWOODS

This group of conifers are all members of the Taxodiaceae *family and are found in the Northern Hemisphere. The group includes some of the biggest, tallest and oldest trees in the world. The coast and giant redwood are evergreens originating from California, USA. The dawn redwood and swamp cypress are deciduous conifers. All have distinctive, fibrous, reddish-brown bark.*

Coast Redwood

Sequoia sempervirens (D. Don) Endl.

The *Sequoia* takes its name from a native American Cherokee called Sequoiah. This majestic tree attains heights in excess of 100m/328ft. The current champion, known as the 'Stratosphere Giant', is 114m/374ft. The trunk is quite often branchless for two-thirds of the height.

Left: The cones are 2–3cm/¾–1¼ in long.

Identification: Young trees have a cone-like form with widely-spaced, level slender branches, up-curved at the tips. Old trees become columnar with flat tops and branches that sweep down. Leading shoots have small pinkish green needles arranged spirally. Needles on main and side shoots are arranged in two flat rows, 1–2cm/½–¾ in long, dark green above, and speckled with two bands of white stomata on the underside. Male flowers are yellowish brown; female flowers are green, in separate clusters on same tree.

Distribution: USA: Found in a narrow coastal band running for approximately 800km/500 miles from Monterey, California to the Oregon border.
Height: 100m/328ft
Shape: Narrowly conical
Evergreen
Pollinated: Wind
Leaf shape: Linear

Left: The fissured, reddish-brown thick, spongy bark is fire resistant; protecting the tree from forest fire.

Giant Redwood

Sequoiadendron giganteum (Lindl.) Decne

The largest living thing in the world is a giant redwood called the 'General Sherman', which is estimated to weigh 6,000 tonnes. Some giant redwoods live up to 3,500 years. They thrive in any soil, site or exposure with a moderate supply of moisture but do not grow well in heavy shade. The bark is red brown, soft, thick and fibrous.

Left: Needles and cones.

Distribution: USA: Restricted to 72 groves on the western slopes of the Sierra Nevada, California.
Height: 80m/262ft
Shape: Narrowly conical
Evergreen
Pollinated: Wind
Leaf shape: Linear

Right: The trunk of a redwood may grow to more than 3m/10ft in diameter.

Identification: The crown of the tree is conical, becoming broad in old age. The leaves grow to 8mm/⅓ in, and are sharp-pointed with spreading tips. They are matt grey-green at first, covered with stomata, and turn a dark, shiny green after three years. When crushed, the foliage emits a fragrance of aniseed. The male flowers are yellowish-white ovoid, held at the end of minor shoots, and shed pollen in early spring. The female flowers are green, and develop into bunches of green ovoid cones, which ripen to brown in their second year.

Swamp Cypress

Bald cypress *Taxodium distichum* (L.) Richards

Also known as the bald cypress because of its deciduous habit, this tree grows naturally in wet conditions and can tolerate having its roots submerged for several months. In these conditions it will produce aerial roots known as 'knees' or 'pneumatophores' which provide oxygen to the roots. An excellent tree for colour; the leaves turn from old gold to brick red in early to mid-autumn.

Right: Autumn needles.

Left: Cones are borne on the same trees as male flowers.

Identification: Bark is a dull reddish brown and frequently fluted. The crown is typically conical, although some trees develop a rather domed appearance in maturity, with heavy, low, upswept branches. Shoots are pale green, up to 10cm/4in long, with soft, flattened 2cm/¾in-long leaves arranged alternately along the shoot, emerging late in the season. The male flowers, to 5–6cm/2–2½in, are prominent throughout the winter as three or four catkins held at the end of each shoot. These lengthen to 10–30cm/4–12in when pollen is shed in early spring. Female cones are on a short stalk, globular and light green until ripe.

Right: The deciduous, needle-like foliage turns red in autumn.

Distribution: South-eastern USA: Delaware to Texas and Missouri.
Height: 40m/130ft
Shape: Broadly conical
Deciduous
Pollinated: Wind
Leaf shape: Linear

Pond Cypress *Taxodium ascendens* Brongniart
This broadly conical tree from the south-eastern USA reaches 40m/130ft tall. It has linear leaves 1cm/½in long, which are closely pressed around upright, deciduous shoots. The bark is red-brown, thick and heavily fluted. The male flowers are yellow-green, and held in catkins up to 20cm/8in long. The female flowers are green and appear in clusters at the base of the male catkins. The fruit is a green globule cone, 3cm/1¼in across.

Chinese Swamp Cypress
Glyptostrobus pensilis (Staunton) K. Koch
This small tree seldom reaches heights in excess of 10m/33ft. It originates from south-east China and grows wild in swamps and along riverbanks. It is now very rare in the wild. It has linear, scale-like leaves, 1.5cm/¾in long, arranged spirally on deciduous side shoots. The bark is grey-brown and the flowers insignificant. The fruit is an egg-shaped green cone up to 2.5cm/1in long. This fairly tender tree does not thrive in northern Europe.

Dawn Redwood

Metasequoia glyptostroboides (Hu & Cheng)

Until this beautiful tree was discovered growing in east Szechwan by Chinese botanist T. Kan in 1941, it had only been seen as a fossil and was deemed extinct. It was first introduced to the West in 1948. Since then it has become a popular species for ornamental planting. It has bright orange-brown stringy bark and the trunk is quite often fluted.

Identification: The crown is conical in most trees, although some are broad with upswept branches. When grown in the open, the crown is dense, but in shade it becomes sparse. The leaves are down-curved at the tips, 2cm/¾ in long, bright green above with a pale band each side of the midrib below. Male flowers are ovoid, set on panicles, which are up to 25cm/10in long. The female cone is green ripening to brown, and 2cm/¾in across with stalks 2cm/¾in long.

Distribution China: The Shui-sha valley, in the north-west part of Hueph Province and into Szechwan Province.
Height: 40m/130ft
Shape: Narrowly conical
Deciduous
Pollinated: Wind
Leaf shape: Linear

Below: The leaves are positioned opposite each other on the shoot, which is bright green.

FALSE CEDARS, FIRS AND PINES

A group of ancient conifers belonging to the Pinaceae and Taxodiaceae families. The origins of all lay in the Jurassic period, 208–144 million years ago. Today, the Douglas fir and the Japanese red cedar are planted in their millions around the world for timber production. The others are scarcely seen outside botanical collections.

Japanese Red Cedar

Cryptomeria Japonica (L. F.) Don

This stately conifer produces a large, straight trunk which tapers quickly from a broad base above the roots. It has reddish brown bark which is soft, fibrous and peels off, hanging in long strips from the trunk. This tree has been extensively planted throughout Japan and China for its timber, which is strong, light and pink-brown.

Above: Branches occasionally touch the ground, causing layering.

Distribution: Found in Japan in Honshu, Shikuka and Kyushu. It is also found in Chekiang and Fukien provinces in China.
Height: 30m/100ft
Shape: Broadly conical
Evergreen
Pollinated: Wind
Leaf shape: Linear

Identification: The crown is narrow when young, broadening with age. Often the heavy branches sweep downwards before ascending at the tips. The foliage is a system of bright green branchlets covered with hard, forward-facing needles 1.5cm/⅝in long. Male flowers are yellowish brown, ovoid, clustered along the final 1cm/½in of each branchlet. They are bright yellow when ripe, and shed pollen in early spring. Female flowers are green rosettes and are found on the same tree as male flowers. Cones are globular, 2cm/¾in across, and held on upright, stiff stalks.

Right: At the base of each needle is a long protruding keel which runs down the branchlet.

Chinese Fir

Cunninghamia lanceolata (Lambert) Hooker fil.

The Chinese fir is a handsome tree with a domed crown of short, drooping branches. At first glance there is a similarity with the Chile pine. It has prickly, lance-shaped needles, which are glossy, dark green. It grows in pure stands on Chinese mountainsides up to an elevation of 1,520m/5,000ft, enduring hot summers and high humidity.

Right: A male flower.

Right: Female flowers.

Identification: The bark is chestnut-brown, with parallel, vertical shallow fissures running down the trunk. It has a columnar or conic shape with a domed top. Branches are widespread giving a sparse appearance, often concealed by the drooping foliage. The needles are strap-shaped, to 6cm/2½in long, spirally set on the shoots, but twisting to lie in just two planes on each side of the shoot. They are deep, glossy green on top, with two striking white bands underneath. Male flowers are yellow-brown, borne in clusters at the shoot tips. Female flowers are yellow-green and held singularly on terminal branchlets. The fruit is a rounded cone, 4cm/1½in across, bright green, maturing to brown.

Distribution: Central and southern China south of a west-east line from Szechwan, Hupph and Honan to Kwangsi, Kwangtong, Fukien and Hong Kong.
Height: 25m/80ft
Shape: Broadly columnar
Evergreen
Pollinated: Wind
Leaf shape: Lanceolate

Left: The distinctive glossy, dark green foliage of the Chinese fir makes it an excellent ornamental species.

Japanese Umbrella Pine

Sciadopitys verticillata (Thesis.) Sieb. & Zucc.

The Japanese umbrella pine grows at elevations between 180–1,520m/590–5,000ft on rocky slopes and ridges. It has been widely planted in other parts of the world, including North America, as an ornamental species due to its unusual leaf formation and its regular shape. In Japan its timber, which is pure white, springy and very durable is used for making bathtubs, casks and boats.

Identification: A very distinctive tree with widely spaced whorls (spirals) of shiny green needles which are deeply grooved and grow up to 12cm/4¾in long. Each whorl sits about 3.5cm/1½in apart from its neighbour on buff-brown shoots. Male flowers are globular, yellow and green and bunched in clusters of 12. Female flowers appear on the same tree; they are green and held at the end of each shoot.

Below: The fruit is an egg-shaped cone up to 7.5cm/3in across.

Distribution: Exclusive to Japan – mountains of central and southern Honshu.
Height: 33m/110ft
Shape: Narrowly conical
Evergreen
Pollinated: Wind
Leaf shape: Linear

Right and left: The arrangement of the needles within each whorl resembles the ribs of an umbrella – hence the common name.

Douglas Fir

Pseudotsuga menziesii (Michel) Franco.

Distribution: North-west Pacific Seaboard, from Mexico through USA to Canada including Vancouver Island.
Height: 75m/250ft
Shape: Narrowly conical
Evergreen
Pollinated: Wind
Leaf shape: Linear

Below: Cones have bracts that project from each scale.

Douglas fir is commercially one of the most important timber-producing trees in the world. It has been planted throughout North America, Europe, Australia and New Zealand. It is a huge tree, attaining heights in excess of 75m/250ft. Quite often there is no branching for the first 33m/110ft. The bark is corky and deeply fissured in maturity; young trees have smooth, shiny grey-brown bark that is pock-marked with resin blisters.

Identification: When young this majestic tree is slender, regularly conical, with whorls of light ascending branches. In old age it becomes flat-topped with heavy branches high up in the crown. Needles are linear to 3cm/1¼in long, rounded at the tip. They are a rich green colour with distinctive white banding beneath, and arranged spirally on the shoot. When crushed the foliage emits a sweet citrus aroma. Male flowers are yellow, and grow on the underside of the shoot. Female flowers are green, flushed pink to purple at the tip, and grow in separate clusters on the same tree. The fruit is a hanging cone up to 10cm/4in long, green, ripening to orange-brown, with distinctive three-pronged bracts.

Large-coned Fir (above)
Pseudotsuga macrocarpa Mayr.
Native to south-western California, this rare tree has dull grey bark with wide, vertical orange-coloured fissures. Its crown is broadly conical and branches are level. Needles are up to 5cm/2in long, stiff, pointed and widely spaced all around the shoot. The cone is ovoid-cylindrical, up to 18cm/7in long, with a bract which only just protrudes from beneath each scale.

Japanese Fir *Pseudotsuga japonica* (Shirasawa) Beissner
This tree, found only in south-east Japan, is rare in the wild and uncommon in cultivation. It has a flattened crown and seldom reaches heights half that of Douglas fir. The leaves are soft, light green, 2.5cm/1in long, blunt and notched at the tip. No fragrance is emitted when the foliage is crushed. The cone is 5cm/2in long, few scaled, smooth, with a spreading bract which is slightly deflexed.

ASIAN PINES

Some of the most beautiful pines in the world originate from Asia, principally China, Japan and the Himalayas. No self-respecting Japanese garden is complete without its pine tree. Part of the Pinaceae family, Asian pines combine graceful foliage, interesting form and stunning bark colour in a way that instantly distinguishes them from their European and American cousins.

Bhutan Pine

Pinus wallichiana A. B. Jackson

The soft, slender, pendulous appearance of this pine belies its resilience and ruggedness. In the Himalayas it is able to grow at altitudes higher than 2,440–3,800m/ 8,000–12,470ft. It has also proved more resistant to air pollution than virtually any other conifer.

Although the tree is sometimes confused with the Weymouth pine, *P. strobus*, its appearance has far more in common with the Mexican white pine, *P. ayacahuite*. The bark of young trees is grey with resin blistering. On older trees the bark becomes pinkish orange and lined with tiny fissures.

Identification: The crown is strongly whorled and relatively open. Young trees have a conical appearance; older trees become more broad and columnar. Lower branches descend gracefully from the trunk, curving upwards at their tips. Upper branches sweep skywards. The shoots are long, strong and pale grey with a purple bloom. Needles are light green, 18–20cm/7–8in long, produced in groups of five and cupped in a red-brown basal sheath. They curve forwards along the shoot, then droop at each side. Male flowers are pale yellow, ovoid, positioned at the bottom of new shoots and shed their pollen in early summer. Female flowers also appear in early summer; they are dull purple in colour and grow towards the tips of new shoots. The fruit is a long, up to 30cm/12in, drooping, green, banana-shaped cone covered in sticky white resin. It ripens to pale brown in the second year.

Right: After hanging for more than a year on the tree, cones open to drop their seeds.

Distribution: The Himalayas, from Afghanistan to eastern Nepal and Bhutan.
Height: 40m/130ft
Shape: Broadly conical
Evergreen
Pollinated: Wind
Leaf shape: Linear

Japanese Black Pine

Pinus thunbergii Parlatore

Distribution: East coast of Japan, from Kyushu northwards to central Honshu.
Height: 40m/130ft
Shape: Broadly conical
Evergreen
Pollinated: Wind
Leaf shape: Linear

This pine is primarily a species that likes to grow along the coastline. However, over the centuries it has been widely planted throughout Japan to the extent that it is now one of the most common trees in the centre and south of the country. It has been widely planted to help stabilize sand dunes and reduce the effects of mountain erosion. Because of its irregular shape, it has become a popular tree for Japanese gardens and bonsai.

Identification: The bark of Japanese black pine is a purple or pink-grey colour, with deep, irregular, vertical fissures. The whole tree often has a somewhat crooked appearance, with a crooked trunk and horizontal spreading branches. The shoots are golden brown, with rough scales in between the whorls of needles. The needles are in pairs, thick, stiff and sharply pointed, giving a spiky appearance. They are grey-green in colour, 10cm/4in long and slightly twisted. Buds are cylindrical and covered with white hairs, giving them a silky appearance. Cones are prolific; sometimes as many as 100 can be found clustered along 30cm/12in of stem. They are flat-based, reddish grey and 6cm/2½in in length.

Right: Cones are often bunched together and occur in large numbers.

Lace-bark Pine

Pinus bungeana Zuccarini

This very slow-growing tree is one of the most beautiful of all pines. It has smooth, grey-green bark, which the tree gradually sheds in round scales to reveal patches of pale yellow, which turn olive-brown, red and purple on exposure to light. It was originally introduced to the West in 1846, but surprisingly, considering its beauty, it is still relatively uncommon and only found growing in the most comprehensive tree collections.

Identification: Lace-bark pines usually produce a broad, somewhat bushy tree. The branches are long and sweep sharply upwards. New shoots tend to be pale olive-green with dark red-brown ovoid buds; second-year shoots are dull grey-brown. Needles are held in threes, spread widely apart on the shoots and face forwards. They are dark yellow-green, shiny, stiff and 6–8cm/2½–3in long. The cone is ovoid, 4cm/1½in across and dark brown with few scales.

Distribution: Eastern and central China.
Height: 20m/66ft
Shape: Broadly conical
Evergreen
Pollinated: Wind
Leaf shape: Linear

Left: Lace-bark pine cone, needles and flower. The needles are relatively stiff.

Long-leaved Indian Pine *Pinus roxburghii* Sargent
Sometimes known as the Chir pine, this tender species is found in the Himalayas, from north-west Pakistan to Bhutan, where it grows up to elevations of 2,300m/7,545ft, and reaches 55m/180ft in height. Needles are held in threes, are light green, and up to 40cm/16in long.

Japanese Mountain Pine *Pinus parviflora* Siebold & Zuccarini
More often known as the Japanese white pine, this small, graceful tree is native to the mountains of southern Japan, on Honshu, Kyushu and Shikoku. It has long been grown as a Japanese garden species and many dwarf cultivars have originated from it. It has scaly purple bark and deep blue-green needles, 5–7cm/2–2¾in long and held in fives.

Korean Pine *Pinus koraiensis* Siebold & Zuccarini
Native to north-east Asia from Korea, Manchuria, the Japanese islands of Honshu and Shikoku, and through to the Pacific coast of Russia. In these areas it provides valuable timber and the cone seeds are eaten as nuts. Korean pine grows to 50m/165ft in height. It has a smooth reddish grey bark, and the young shoots are covered in rust-coloured hairs. The needles are held in threes and are up to 12cm/5in long. Cones are cylindrical, purple when young and up to 16cm/6¼in long.

Chinese Red Pine

Pinus tabuliformis Carriere

This pine was introduced to the West in 1862. It is relatively rare in cultivation but where it is grown, it produces a small to medium-sized flat-headed tree. Young trees grow fast when first planted, but over a longer period it grows slowly.

Identification: The orange-grey bark becomes heavily fissured from an early age. Young trees are conical in shape but in maturity the crown becomes dense and domed. Branches are long and level, with smooth pink-brown shoots standing out from them at right angles, giving a 'table-effect', hence the botanical name *tabuliformis*. Male flowers are yellow and borne at the shoot base. Female flowers are red-purple and grow at the shoot tip on the same tree.

Distribution: North-east China from Hopei in the north to Shensi in the south and on into Korea.
Height: 25m/82ft
Shape: Broadly spreading
Evergreen
Pollinated: Wind
Leaf shape: Linear

Above: Ripe cones persist on the branches for several years.

Right: Needles are up to 15cm/6in long, usually in pairs but may be in threes. They are thick, shiny and grey-green in colour.

EUROPEAN PINES

The pines of Europe, of the family Pinaceae, are as diverse as the landscapes they inhabit. From the sprawling shrub-like pines of the Alps to the stately giants of the Mediterannean coastline, there are pines for every location. Perhaps the most widespread and easily recognizable is the Scots pine, Pinus sylvestris. It has a natural range from Scotland to Siberia and occurs south as far as the Mediterranean.

Bosnian Pine

Pinus leucodermis Antoine

A medium-sized, neat, distinctive tree, this grows particularly well on dry and shallow soils overlying chalk or limestone, where it can live for more than 1,000 years. The needles are a deep black-green colour which gives the whole tree a sombre, dark appearance, making it instantly recognizable.

Left: Fallen cone.

Identification: The bark is greenish grey and smooth, becoming finely fissured in maturity. The overall tree shape is ovoid to conical, rather narrow, regular and dense. The branches ascend slightly from the trunk. Shoots are pale brown, slightly hairy and have a glaucous bloom. The male flowers are yellow and females purple-red. Both are held at the tips of the shoots on the same plant. Clouds of pollen are often seen blowing in the breeze around the tree in late spring.

Above and below: The needles, which are in pairs, are prolific on the shoot; they are up to 9cm/ 3½in long and all point neatly forward at a 45-degree angle. They have a sharp point and are very rigid.

Distribution: Balkans, Bosnia-Herzegovina, Bulgaria, Albania into northern Greece and south-western Italy.
Height: 25m/82ft
Shape: Narrowly conical
Evergreen
Pollinated: Wind
Leaf shape: Linear

Corsican Pine

Pinus nigra subsp. *laricio* (Poiret) Maire

A large tree, this differs from the straight species, *P. nigra*, Austrian pine, by having a more open crown with fewer, shorter branches, which are level rather than ascending. Corsican pine is grown throughout Europe, including Great Britain, for its timber, which is strong and relatively knot free.

Identification: Shoots are pale yellow-brown, stiff and stout, with buds which are narrowly conical, sharply pointed and commonly covered with white resin. Needles are in pairs, sparsely positioned on the shoot. They are pale grey-green, up to 18cm/7in long and twisted. Male flowers are golden yellow and abundant at the shoot base, shedding pollen from late spring until early summer. Female flowers are dull pink and positioned on the tips of growing shoots. The cone is ovoid to conical with a slight sweep and up to 8cm/3in long.

Distribution: Southern Italy and Corsica.
Height: 40m/130ft
Shape: Broadly columnar
Evergreen
Pollinated: Wind
Leaf shape: Linear

Right: Needles are long, measuring up to 18cm/7in.

Above: The bark is light grey to pink and fissured from an early age.

Left: Flowers appear from spring to early summer.

Aleppo Pine *Pinus halepensis* Miller
Native to Mediterranean regions through to south-west Asia and Afghanistan, the Aleppo pine is very tolerant of drought and has been widely planted in arid countries in afforestation schemes to help stabilize sandy soils. It reaches a height of around 20m/66ft and has a conical crown, which becomes rounded in old age. Needles are held in pairs, bright fresh green and up to 10cm/4in long.

Maritime Pine *Pinus pinaster* Aiton
Native to central and western Mediterranean regions, including North Africa. Loves growing alongside the coast and is very tolerant of salt spray. It has been extensively planted along the coast of France, Spain and Portugal. It reaches heights in excess of 40m/130ft and typically has a long, clean trunk and a domed top. Needles are in pairs and are up to 20cm/8in long.

Identification: The bark is grey, with orange fissure lines running vertically down the trunk. The tree has a short main trunk and has branching relatively low down. The shoot is a pale green colour, smooth and curved, with a bright chestnut-red bud, fringed with white hairs, at the shoot tip. The needles are forward pointing, in pairs, grey-green in colour, stout and up to 12cm/4½in long. The cone is flat-based but almost round, up to 10cm/4in across, glossy brown, smooth. The cone is relatively heavy and can weigh up to 375g/12oz. After forming, the cones remain tightly closed for three years before opening to reveal up to 100 edible seeds.

Stone Pine

Umbrella pine *Pinus pinea* Linnaeus

Widely planted throughout the Mediterranean for its seeds, which are eaten as nuts, it is also known as the umbrella pine because of its flat-topped, umbrella-like shape in maturity. With its long, horizontal branches and dense foliage, it is a tree of distinct and aesthetically pleasing habit, that has become a distinctive part of the Mediterranean landscape.

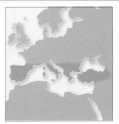

Distribution: Mediterranean from Portugal to Turkey.
Height: 20m/66ft
Shape: Broadly spreading
Evergreen
Pollinated: Wind
Leaf shape: Linear

Above: Female cone (left) and male cone (right).

Above: The needles are long and occur in pairs.

Right: The closed cone is almost egg-shaped.

Scots Pine

Pinus sylvestris Linnaeus

This is one of the temperate world's most prolific and popular trees, which most Americans would instantly recognize as their Christmas tree. The Scots pine flourishes on dry, sandy soils but will grow in wet conditions, although more slowly. It is a prolific seed producer and is able to colonize new territory quickly. It is well known as a pioneer species, establishing itself long before other trees begin to move in.

Identification: The bark of Scots pine is one of its most distinguishing features. It ranges from grey-green as a juvenile to a stunning orange-red in maturity. On branches this red bark peels and flakes away. On the main stem it becomes cracked and fissured with age. Old trees have a distinctive low, broadly domed crown and large, level but snaking branches. The paired needles are stiff, twisted, bluish green, set in an orange-brown basal sheath and up to 7cm/2¾in long. Male flowers are yellow and female are red; both are held in separate clusters on young shoots in late spring and early summer. The cone is egg-shaped, up to 7cm/2¾in long, and green, ripening to brown.

Distribution: From Scotland right across northern Europe to the Pacific coast and southwards to the Mediterranean and Turkey.
Height: 35m/115ft
Shape: Broadly spreading
Evergreen
Pollinated: Wind
Leaf shape: Linear

Left: The trunk is often branchless.

Right: Cones may occur in pairs.

NORTH AMERICAN PINES

There are over 100 different pine species in the world and almost half are native to North America and Mexico. They naturally divide into west-coast pines, central and east-coast pines and southern pines. North American pines include the oldest and some of the biggest trees in the world. Many are important timber-producing trees, and some have provided food for Native Americans for centuries.

Monterey Pine

Pinus radiata D. Don

Distribution: USA: Californian coast around the Monterey Peninsula.
Height: 30m/100ft
Shape: Broadly conical
Evergreen
Pollinated: Wind
Leaf shape: Linear

Right: Needles are held in threes, are shining dark green and are 10–15cm/4–6in long.

The Monterey pine is a Californian coastal species with a very limited range. It is seldom found growing wild more than 9km/6 miles from the coast. Originally discovered by the plant collector David Douglas in 1833, it has become one of the most widely planted trees for timber production in the world. In New Zealand it makes up more than 60 per cent of all conifers growing there and covers more than 400,000ha/1 million acres.

Above: Cones may persist on the tree for up to 30 years.

Identification: The bark is dark grey and deeply fissured in old age. Young trees are conical with sharply ascending branches. Older trees develop a large domed crown, which looks black from a distance. The male flowers are bright yellow and shed copious amounts of pollen in early spring. The cone is reddish brown with dark grey scale centres. It is roughly ovoid in shape, up to 10cm/4in across and held on a curved stalk 1cm/½in long. Large, irregular scales tend to distort its overall shape.

Western Yellow Pine

Pinus ponderosa Lawson

The natural range of this pine is vast, stretching from the Pacific coast to elevations of 2,750m/9,000ft in the Rocky Mountains in Colorado. It is planted as an ornamental species in large parks and gardens because of its attractive bark, fast growth and yellow leading shoots.

Identification: The bark is pale purple-grey, flaking to reveal attractive yellow, red and cinnamon-coloured bark beneath. As a young tree, it is narrow in shape with strongly ascending branches. Older trees develop an irregular crown with several large, horizontal branches and dense foliage. The shoot is stout, bright yellow-brown in colour and has clusters of needles, held in threes, along its length. The needles are up to 25cm/10in long, dark grey-green and all face forward. Male flowers are dark purple and female flowers red. Both occur on the same tree. The cone is egg-shaped, up to 10cm/4in long, glossy reddish brown and has a hard spiny tip to each scale.

Above: Older trees often have an irregular clumped crown.

Distribution: North America, from British Columbia to Mexico.
Height: 50m/165ft
Shape: Broadly conical
Evergreen
Pollinated: Wind
Leaf shape: Linear

Left: The needles are extremely long, each measuring up to 25cm/10in from base to tip.

Montezuma Pine

Pinus montezumae A. B. Lambert

This pine is named after the early 16th century Aztec emperor, Montezuma II. It is a very variable tree with several different forms, all extremely attractive, mainly because of its long, distinctive foliage. It is a fairly tender species, only surviving in the mildest regions of North America and Great Britain.

Identification: The Montezuma pine has pinkish grey, rough bark with wide, brownish, vertical fissures, leaving ridges, which are cracked horizontally. The juvenile crown is gaunt, with a few ascending branches; however, as it matures, it develops a huge low dome, with upturned shoots covered with long, lax, brush-like foliage. Male flowers are purple, ripening to yellow; female flowers are red. The cone is conical and up to 15cm/6in long.

Distribution: North-east Mexico and south into Guatemala.
Height: 20m/66ft
Shape: Broadly spreading
Evergreen
Pollinated: Wind
Leaf shape: Linear

Left: The blue-green needles are up to 30cm/12in long.

Ancient Pine

Pinus longaeva Bailey

This species, allied to the bristlecone pine, *P. aristata*, contains some of the oldest living trees on earth. The oldest tree is reliably recorded at being more than 4,700 years old and is affectionately known as Methuselah. It is to be found growing 3,475m/11,400ft up in the White Mountains of California, USA.

Left: Both needles and cones have a scuffy, feather-like appearance.

Distribution: USA: From the White Mountains of eastern California through central Utah and southern Nevada.
Height: 15m/50ft
Shape: Broadly conical
Evergreen
Pollinated: Wind
Leaf shape: Linear

Identification: This species has scaly black-grey bark. Young trees are conical in habit, but old trees become gnarled and spreading. The shoot is red-brown and hairy, with needles tightly clustered in fives along its length. Needles are approximately 3cm/1¼in long and shiny grey-green on top with white stomata and resin canals visible as two grooves on the underside. They persist on the tree for anything up to 30 years. Cones are ovoid, rounded at the base, up to 10cm/4in long and a rich chestnut-red colour. This species is particularly hardy, being able to withstand prolonged winter periods with temperatures well below freezing, and long summer periods of drought.

Big-cone Pine *Pinus Coulteri* D. Don
Native to Southern California and north-western Mexico. Mainly known, and planted, because of the massive cone it produces. The cone is shaped like a flat-bottomed, honey-brown coloured rugby ball up to 35cm/14in long. It can weigh up to 2.3kg/5lb when fresh. On ripening, the cone scales open with an explosive crack.

Mexican White Pine *Pinus ayacahuite* Ehrenberg
This beautiful tree attains heights of up to 35m/115ft in its native Mexico and northern Guatemala. It is extremely hardy and grows high on mountain slopes. It has graceful, drooping foliage with blue-green, slender, lax needles up to 15cm/6in long and held in fives. The cone can grow up to 45cm/18in long and is normally covered with sticky white resin.

Lodgepole Pine *Pinus contorta* Loudon
This pine originates from the Rocky Mountains in North America, occurring from the Yukon to southern Colorado. It can grow up to 30m/98ft tall, with a straight trunk regularly interspersed with whorls of stiff, ascending branches. Needles are 5cm/2in long, twisted, held in pairs and dark green in colour. The name derives from the fact that this species was commonly used by Native Americans as the centre pole for their lodges or tepees.

Sugar Pine *Pinus lambertiana* Douglas
The sugar pine grows from western Oregon south to northern Mexico. It grows to heights of 25m/82ft in the wild. Needles point forward along the shoot, are rich green in colour, twisted and up to 10cm/4in long. The cones are large, cylindrical and can be up to 65cm/26in long. The common name refers to the fact that if the bark is damaged, a sweet, edible resin is exuded.

NORTH AMERICAN SILVER FIRS

The term 'fir' has become a general description for anything vaguely coniferous-looking. In reality this is erroneous; the true, or silver, firs are a select band of conifers botanically linked within the genus Abies. *They include some of the finest conifers and nine of the best are found in North America. They range across the continent, from the balsam firs of Canada to the Santa Lucia firs of California.*

Noble Fir

Abies procera Rehder

This is a superb species which truly deserves its name. It has a stately, noble appearance with a long, straight stem and large cones that stand proudly above the surrounding foliage. It is particularly hardy, growing at up to 1,500m/4,921ft in the Cascade Mountains, USA. Noble fir has been planted widely outside its natural range for its timber, which is light brown, close-grained and very strong.

Identification: The bark is silvery grey, smooth and has occasional resin blisters. Young trees are conical, with widely spaced whorls of branches. Older trees become flat-topped, with characteristic twisted, dead branches. Needles are grey-green above with two distinct white stomata bands on the underside. They are strongly parted on the shoot, curving upwards and then down. Needles on top of the shoot are 1cm/½in long; beneath the shoot, they are 3.5cm/1½in long. When crushed, they emit a pungent smell, like cat's urine. Cones are broad cylinders up to 25cm/10in long, and are held erect from the branch.

Above: Cones are normally confined to the topmost branches.

Below: Male flowers are clustered beneath the shoot in spring.

Right: Female flowers are upright on the shoot.

Distribution: USA: Cascade Mountains of Oregon, Washington State and northern California.
Height: 80m/262ft
Shape: Narrowly conical
Evergreen
Pollinated: Wind
Leaf shape: Linear

Santa Lucia Fir

Bristlecone fir *Abies bracteata* (D. Don) Nuttall

Sometimes known as the bristlecone fir because of the long bristle attached to each cone scale, this west coast species is the rarest native North American fir. It is only found growing naturally in the bottom of a few rocky canyons. It is rare in the wild and in cultivation. Although relatively hardy, it has not been widely planted. In 1852 it was introduced to Europe by William Lobb.

Identification: Bark on young trees is dark grey with wrinkles and black lines around branch knots. Older trees develop black or purple-black bark with deep cracks. The shape is broad at the base, narrowing rapidly to a long, conical crown. Branches tend to fan out and droop towards their tips. Needles are strongly parted each side of the shoot. They are forward pointing, up to 5cm/2in long with a sharp tip, dull green above and have two bright white bands beneath. Cones are found on the topmost branches, like candles. Each cone scale has a long bristle, giving it a very distinct appearance. Cones normally disintegrate on the tree.

Above: New needles often have a purple tinge to them.

Distribution: USA: Santa Lucia Mountains, southern California.
Height: 35m/115ft
Shape: Narrowly conical
Evergreen
Pollinated: Wind
Leaf shape: Linear

Left: The cone has hair-like protrusions, giving it a very scruffy appearance.

Grand Fir *Abies grandis* Lindley Found from northern Vancouver Island, south to Navarro River, California, this is one of the giants of North American coniferous forests, frequently exceeding 60m/200ft in height. It has graceful, downward-sweeping branches with upturned tips, the lower boughs reaching to the ground. Needles are glossy green on top, silvery below and up to 5cm/2in long.

Alpine Fir *Abies lasiocarpa* (Hooker) Nuttall Native to mountain terrain from Alaska to northern Arizona, the Alpine fir is now rare in the wild. It is a tall, slender tree, which looks at home on the snow-covered mountain slopes. The alpine fir has a dense covering of needles, all pointing forwards on the shoot. They are 2.5cm/1in long, shiny grey-green above, with two narrow white stomatal bands beneath.

Pacific Fir *Abies amabilis* (Douglas) Forbes Found along the Pacific coast from California to Alaska, this is a luxuriant-looking, tall, spire-like tree with dense foliage. Needles sweep flat on each side of the shoot and are dusty grey-blue when young, maturing to a glossy rich green. When crushed they emit a strong fragrance of tangerines. The upright cone is cylindrical and up to 15cm/6in long.

Low's Fir

Pacific white fir *Abies concolor var. lowiana* (Gordon) Lemmon

This fast-growing tree is an intermediate between grand fir, *A. grandis*, and the Colorado white fir, *A. concolor*, taking characteristics from both trees. It is a fine ornamental tree and was widely distributed in Europe by Messrs Low, the English nurserymen from about 1862 – hence the name.

Identification: The bark ranges in colour and texture from black with shallow fissures to deep-brown with large cracks which are reddish brown in colour. The crown is conical, becoming rather broad in old age. There is a tendency for multiple leading shoots to grow at the top of the tree. Needles are parted on the shoot and rise at 45 degrees or more, creating a V-shaped gap along the top of the shoot. The needles are pale blue-grey and up to 4cm/1½in long. Cones are upright columnar cylinders, 8–12cm/3–4½in long and only occur on the very topmost branches.

Distribution: USA: Mid-Oregon to the southern end of the Sierra Nevada, California.
Height: 50m/165ft
Shape: Narrowly conical
Evergreen
Pollinated: Wind
Leaf shape: Linear

Left: Cones are long and slender.

Below: Needles may appear a lush green in bright sunlight.

Red Fir

Abies magnifica A. Murray

This is a tree of the high mountains, where snow lies for months on end before being followed by long periods of summer drought. It is named after the red colour of its bark, but the botanical name *magnifica* is more representative, because this truly is a magnificent species. Its short, regularly spaced, horizontal branches provide for perfect symmetry.

Identification: Bark, even on relatively young trees, is thick, corky and has deep fissures. Overall, red fir has a very regular shape, keeping its neat, conical appearance into old age. The needles are almost round in cross-section, 3.5cm/1¾in long, wide-spreading, and curving back in towards the shoot at the tips. They are dark grey-green in colour with two lighter bands of stomata on both the upper and lower surfaces. The upright cones are seldom seen, growing right at the top of the tree and disintegrating in situ. They grow up to 20cm/8in long, are barrel-shaped, smooth and golden green.

Above: Upright cones are borne at the top of the tree.

Distribution: USA: Cascade Mountains of Oregon, Mount Shasta and Sierra Nevada, California.
Height: 40m/130ft
Shape: Narrowly conical
Evergreen
Pollinated: Wind
Leaf shape: Linear

Left: Male cones are purple-red and appear in spring.

EUROPEAN AND ASIAN FIRS

The diversity among European and Asian firs is quite remarkable. They include some of the tallest firs in the world and some of the smallest. They can be found growing wild from China to Spain. Several have been adopted as ornamental species and planted just about everywhere, from large arboreta to small town gardens. All are handsome trees, producing lush foliage, good symmetry and attractive cones.

European Silver Fir

Abies alba Miller

Distribution: Pyrenees, France, Corsica, the Alps, and the Black Forest south to the Balkans.
Height: 50m/165ft
Shape: Narrowly conical
Evergreen
Pollinated: Wind
Leaf shape: Linear

This species is long-lived for a conifer – some specimens are known to be over 300 years old. Although widely planted for timber, it is very susceptible to aphid damage, which can be fatal in close-grown plantation conditions. It is widely used as a Christmas tree in many parts of Europe. Prolific natural regeneration from seed is a characteristic of this species.

Identification: In young trees the bark is smooth and dull grey. Older trees have a paler bark with shallow pink-brown fissures. Young trees are symmetrical, with regular, slightly ascending branches. In maturity the stubs of dead branches cover the trunk and the leading stem becomes heavily forked. Needles are 1–2cm/½–¾in long, shiny green above, with noticeable linear grooves and white stomatal banding below. They have rounded tips and are flattened each side of the shoot. Cones are clustered on just a few branches at the top of the tree. They are red-brown, cylindrical, up to 15cm/6in long and disintegrate on the tree. In spring, new growth is an attractive bright lime-green colour but quite often gets burnt by the sun melting late frost.

Right: The long cones stand upright from the finger-like shoots.

Korean Fir

Abies koreana Wilson

The Korean fir is an alpine species and the smallest of all firs. It originates from the volcanic island of Quelpeart, where it grows in vast forests on mountain slopes up to 1,000m/3,280ft. It has become a firm favourite for planting in gardens because of its manageable size and profusion of purple-blue cones on even the youngest of trees.

Identification: The Korean fir forms a broad, tall shrub or small tree. It has dark olive-green to black bark, which is pock-marked with light freckle-like lenticels. The shoot is a pale fawn colour and slightly hairy. It is covered in a profusion of short, stubby, dark-green needles, 1–1.5cm/½–⅝in long, which curve upwards from the shoot, almost obscuring it from view. On the underside of the needles are two bright white stomatal bands. The male flowers are red-brown, normally covered in resin and clustered all around the side shoots. Female flowers are dark red to purple, ripening to attractive, dark blue-purple cones up to 7cm/2¾in long. These are normally covered with a sticky white resin.

Above: The female flowers ripen to cones covered with sticky, white resin.

Below: The male flowers.

Distribution: South Korea.
Height: 15m/50ft
Shape: Broadly conical
Evergreen
Pollinated: Wind
Leaf shape: Linear

Right: The cones stand upright from the shoots.

Forrest's Silver Fir

Abies delavayi var. *forrestii* (Rogers) Jackson

Forrest's silver fir is named after Scottish plant collector George Forrest (1873–1932), who discovered it in 1910. It grows at high altitudes on thin, dry chalky soils. It is a vigorous tree and differs from *A. delavayi* in the height it can attain, the size of its cone and the colour of its foliage.

Identification: The bark is grey and smooth, with fissures towards the base of the trunk. In a few trees the bark becomes very cracked and scaly. The tree is compact, straight and conical-shaped, with bright orange-brown young shoots, which dull to deep maroon in the second year. The needles are spread all around the shoot. They are 2–4cm/¾–1½in long, dark glossy green above with a central groove and banded silver-white beneath. The cone is up to 10cm/4in long and stands erect from the branch. Attached to each cone scale is a short bract, 5mm/¼in long, which curves out and down from the cone, giving it a whiskery appearance.

Above: Cones are a distinctive purple-blue colour.

Distribution: Yunnan and Szechwan Province, China and into Tibet.
Height: 20m/66ft
Shape: Narrowly conical
Evergreen
Pollinated: Wind
Leaf shape: Linear

Left: The flower develops into a barrel-shaped cone. Forrest's silver fir needles are dark green above and silvery below.

Caucasian Fir *Abies nordmanniana* (Steven) Spach
Native to the western Caucasus and north-east Turkey, this attractive, uniform-looking tree reaches 50m/165ft in height. Needles are dense, luxuriant, up to 4cm/1½in long and blunt tipped and glossy rich green. This is the 'non-drop' tree sold at Christmas time. When the foliage is crushed, it emits a fruity, citrus aroma.

Momi Fir *Abies firma* Siebold & Zuccarini
Native to the southern Japanese islands of Honshu, Kyushu and Shikoku, this wide-spreading, large tree, to 30m/100ft tall, has pink-grey bark and distinctive yellow-green, stiff leathery needles, each up to 5cm/2in long and rounded at the tips. It has a rather open appearance with well-spaced, long branching. Cones are yellow-brown and 12cm/4½in long.

Algerian Fir *Abies numidica* De Lannoy
Native to Mount Babor in north-eastern Algeria, where it grows up to 1,850m/6,070ft above sea level, this large tree, up to 25m/82ft tall, is extremely tolerant of high pH lime soils. It has blue-green needles 1–2cm/½–¾in long, which are arranged all over the upper half of the shoot, creating an attractive, spray-like appearance.

Himalayan Fir *Abies spectabilis* (D. Don) Spach.
Native to the eastern Himalayas from Bhutan to Afghanistan, this tree has a broad, columnar, gaunt appearance. It is flat-topped from an early age with large, level branching. It produces dense epicormic growth from the main stem. Needles are heavily grooved, deep green, yellowing towards the tip and up to 6cm/2½in long.

Greek Fir

Abies cephalonica Loudon

This large, ungainly tree thrives on well-drained, rocky limestone slopes. In its native land, it will grow up to elevations of 1,000m/3,280ft. However, it is prone to frost damage because it is one of the first conifers to come into leaf in spring. Old trees have an untidy, rough appearance.

Identification: The bark in young trees is smooth and pink-brown or grey. In old age it becomes slate-grey and fissured. The tree is broadly conical when young but as it matures it becomes flat-topped and very irregular with huge, low, meandering branches and multiple stems high in the crown. Needles are 2–3cm/¾–1¼in long, stiff, leathery and have a sharp point. They are glossy green above with two narrow white bands beneath and are densely clustered around the shoot, which is stout, pale brown and shiny. The cones are 10–15cm/4–6in long, cylindrical and narrow towards the ends.

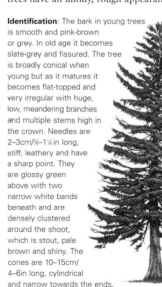

Distribution: Mountain regions of Greece, including the island of Cephalonia.
Height: 35m/115ft
Shape: Broadly conical
Evergreen
Pollinated: Wind
Leaf shape: Linear

Above: Male flower.

Right: Female flowers are yellow-brown.

Right: Most cones grow at the tree's crown.

NORTH AMERICAN SPRUCES

The spruces, Picea, *are a group of hardy evergreen conifers that grow throughout much of the colder regions of the Northern Hemisphere. There is one significant difference with firs,* Abies, *which allows for quick genus identification. On all spruces there is a peg-like stump at the base of every needle. When the needles fall this peg remains, creating a rough texture to the shoot. Firs have smooth shoots.*

Brewer Spruce

Picea breweriana Watson

Although relatively rare in the wild, the Brewer spruce has been widely cultivated in parks, gardens and arboreta. Trusses of ribbon-like foliage hang from downward-arching, evenly-spaced, slender branches. This tree comes from a region of high snowfall and has adapted this weeping habit so that snow can be easily shed, thus protecting the branches from breakage.

Above: The cone is a narrow cylinder, 10–12cm/4–4¾in long and light red-brown in colour.

Identification: Dull, dark grey-pink bark when young, maturing to purple-grey with prominent roughly circular plates of bark, which curl away from the trunk at the edges. Male flowers are yellow and red, positioned on the ends of hanging shoots. Female flowers are dark red, cylindrical and only found on topmost shoots. Needles are soft, positioned all around the shoot, point forwards, and up to 3cm/1¼in long. Their upper surface is glossy dark green and dulls with age. The lower surface has prominent, bright white, linear stomatal bands.

Distribution: USA: The Siskiyou and Shasta Mountains bordering Oregon and California.
Height: 35m/115ft
Shape: Narrowly weeping
Evergreen
Pollinated: Wind
Leaf shape: Linear

Left: Brewer spruce is one of the most beautiful conifers. It has a very graceful, weeping habit.

Sitka Spruce

Picea sitchensis (Bongard) Carriere

Distribution: USA: Narrow coastal strip from Kodiak Island, Alaska, to Mendocino County, California.
Height: 50m/165ft
Shape: Narrowly conical
Evergreen
Pollinated: Wind
Leaf shape: Linear

The largest of the North American spruces, this is a major species within north-west American forests. Valued for its timber, Sitka spruce has been widely planted across the Northern Hemisphere in forestry plantations. The timber is pale pinkish brown and very strong for its light weight. Originally used for aircraft framing, it is now the major species used in pulp for paper manufacture.

Far left: Male flower.

Left: Female flower.

Right: Cones are pale buff, 10cm/4in long, have thin papery scales and are pendulous in habit.

Identification: Bark in young trees is a deep purple-brown colour. Older trees have large, curving cracks, which develop into plates of lifting bark. The overall shape is an open, narrow cone, with widely spaced, slender, ascending branches. Sitka spruce can easily grow more than 1m/3ft a year when young. Needles are stiff with a sharp point, blue-green above with two white stomatal bands beneath, and up to 3cm/1¼in long. They are arranged all around the pale, buff-coloured shoot. Male flowers are reddish and occur in small quantities on each tree, shedding pollen in late spring. Female's are greenish red and only present on the topmost shoots.

Engelmann's Spruce *Picea engelmannii* (Parry)
This tall tree grows up to 40m/130ft in height
and is native to the Rocky Mountains from
Alberta to New Mexico. It is very hardy, growing
on exposed sites in impoverished soils. It has
red-brown bark and a narrow crown with dense,
level branching. Needles are bluish-green,
2cm/¾in long and when crushed give off a
strong menthol fragrance.

Blue Engelmann's Spruce *Picea engelmannii*
'Glauca' (Parry)
This is a slender, attractive cultivar, which has
orange flaking bark and bright glaucous blue-
grey, soft needles, with vibrant white stomatal
banding. It has a pendulous cone, which is up to
6cm/2½in long, thin, papery and found mostly in
clusters at the top of the tree. Engelmann, the
discoverer of the tree, was a German botanist
and doctor who practised in the US city of
St Louis, Missouri.

Black Spruce *Picea mariana* (Miller) Brittan,
Sterns & Poggenberg
Black spruce occurs right across the north of
North America from Alaska to Newfoundland,
where it grows in subarctic, almost Tundra,
conditions. It is a very dense-looking tree,
which from a distance, has a bluish-black
appearance. Lower branches have the unusual
habit of layering. Needles are 1.5cm/⅝in long,
dark, dull green and when crushed emit a
lemon-balm scent.

Colorado Spruce

Blue spruce *Picea pungens*, Engelmann

Otherwise known as the blue spruce
(because of its blue-green needles), the
Colorado spruce grows in the Rocky
Mountains at altitudes up to
3,050m/10,000ft. It is often
found growing as a solitary
specimen on dry slopes and
alongside dried-up stream
beds. It was first discovered
in 1862 on Pike's Peak,
Colorado, by Dr C. C.
Parry, who sent seeds to
Harvard University.

*Above: The cone is a
pale brown to cream
pendulous cylinder, up to
10cm/4in long, with thin scales
wrinkled at the margins.*

Distribution: USA: Montana,
Colorado, Utah, Arizona,
New Mexico.
Height: 35m/115ft
Shape: Narrowly conical
Evergreen
Pollinated: Wind
Leaf shape: Linear

Identification: The dark red-
brown bark is rough with scales.
The tree has a narrow conical
form with short, level branches.
It has shiny, pale yellow-brown
shoots that are slightly hairy, but
it is best identified by its foliage.
The needles are an attractive
blue-grey to grey-green, with a
slight glaucous bloom, up to
3cm/1¼in long and arranged all
around the shoot. Male flowers
are red and the female's green.
They appear in separate clusters
on the same tree in late spring.

Red Spruce

Picea rubens Sargent

This widespread tree is found in north-eastern
North America from Newfoundland down
the Appalachian Mountains to northern
Georgia, where it thrives on wet acid soils.
The red spruce is a long-lived species,
easily reaching 150 years old. It is able to
tolerate low light levels and will grow in
shady forest conditions.

Identification: When young the bark is a rich
purplish red colour, peeling away in flakes. In
older trees the bark is a dark purple-grey,
cracking into irregular concave plates. The
crown remains narrowly conical throughout
the life of the tree. It has a rather dense
form that tapers to a clear spire. The
needles are thin, wiry, up to 1.5cm/⅝in long
and lie forwards on the shoot but curve
inwards. They are a glossy, grassy green
colour and when crushed emit a fragrance
reminiscent of apples or camphor. Male
flowers are bright crimson. The cones are
4–5cm/1½–2in long, pale orange-brown with
convex scales, which are crinkled and finely toothed.

*Above: Young needles are a rich
light green.*

*Below: The cones hang
from the shoots.*

Distribution: USA: Nova
Scotia to North Carolina.
Height: 25m/82ft
Shape: Narrowly conical
Evergreen
Pollinated: Wind
Leaf shape: Linear

Left: A female flower.

*Right: The distinctive
red male flowers gave
rise to this tree's
common name.*

EUROPEAN AND ASIAN SPRUCES

There are 37 different species of spruce in the world and almost half of these are native to China.
Europe has two, with the rest split fairly evenly between North America and the rest of temperate Asia.
The spruces of Europe and Asia include some of the most graceful conifers. Their natural range extends
from the Pyrenees in the west to the eastern Himalayas and on into China and Japan.

Likiang Spruce

Picea likiangensis (Franchet) Pritzel

This Chinese spruce was discovered by
French missionary Delavay in the Likiang
range of Yunnan in 1884. Since then it has
been widely cultivated as an ornamental
species in gardens and arboreta in
Europe and North America. Although
its broad form is interesting, its most
attractive feature is its flowers. Both
male and female flowers are bright red,
and in spring are produced in such
profusion that from a distance it
looks like the tree is covered with
burning embers.

*Above and below: The cone is up
to 12cm/4½in long, pale
purple-brown and becomes
almost purple
with age.*

Identification: The bark is pale grey with
dark vertical fissures. The crown is broad
and open with widely spaced
horizontal branches, which turn
upwards at their tip. New shoots are pale
buff and covered with soft hairs. Needles are rounded
at the tip and up to 1.5cm/⅝in long.

*Above and right: The
needles are blue-green above and
white below. Flowers are bunched.*

*Right: Male
and female
flowers.*

Tiger-tail Spruce

Picea polita (Siebold & Zuccarini) Carriere

*Left: The hanging
cones are large,
growing up to
12cm/4½in long.*

*Right: This tree has
the sharpest needle
of any spruce,
easily capable of
puncturing skin.*

This attractive pyramidal shaped tree has a
very stiff habit. In Japan it grows extremely
well on sites of previous volcanic activity.
Although not widely
planted, it makes a
good specimen for
a large lawn.

Identification:
The bark is
grey-brown, rough
and scaly with
irregular fissures. It is prone to
epicormic growth on the lower part of
the trunk. The shoot is stout and rigid
and a pale buff to creamy white colour.
Needles are dark, shiny green, up to 2cm/¾in
long, very stiff and have a vicious point. The
cone is a curving banana shape, glossy Yellow-
brown in colour, maturing to purple brown. The
cone scales are leathery and rounded, with a lighter
coloured wavy margin.

*Right: Needles are arranged all
round the shoot. Those on the
upper side curve forwards.*

Norway Spruce

Picea abies (L.) Karsten

Norway spruce is the Christmas tree of Europe. It has a regular, symmetrical form with horizontal branching at low levels, which gradually becomes upswept towards the top of the tree. It grows naturally throughout northern Europe (except for the UK) up to altitudes of around 1,500m/4,921ft. Elsewhere it has been widely cultivated for its timber. Norway spruce is traditionally used to make the bellies of violins and other stringed instruments.

Left: Cones hang down.

Identification: The bark in young trees is a deep coppery pink colour; on older trees it becomes a dark purple, with shallow round or oval plates which lift away from the trunk. Needles are a rich dark green colour with a faint sheen and are up to 2cm/¾in long. When crushed they emit a citrus fragrance, which has become synonymous with Christmas. Male flowers are a golden colour, shedding copious amounts of pollen in late spring. Female flowers are purple-red and frequently confined to the top of the tree. Cones are pendulous, cylindrical, slightly curved and up to 15cm/6in long.

Left: Male flowers occur in groups at shoot tips.

Right: A female flower.

Distribution: Most of northern Europe (excluding UK), from the Pyrenees to western Russia.
Height: 50m/165ft
Shape: Narrowly conical
Evergreen
Pollinated: Wind
Leaf shape: Linear

Oriental Spruce *Picea orientalis* (L.) Link.
Sometimes called the Caucasian spruce, this attractive tree originates from the Caucasus Mountains and on into Turkey, where it grows on mountainsides up to 2,140m/7,021ft. In maturity it has a dense, columnar form with short, shiny, fresh green needles 8mm/⅓in long. Cones have a distinct ash-brown colour.

Dragon Spruce *Picea asperata* Masters
This variable tree has a wide range on the mountains of western China, where it attains heights up to 20m/66ft. It is a hardy tree, with chocolate-brown bark that flakes easily. Dragon spruce has a broad habit with large level branching. Needles are a dark bluish green colour, 2cm/¾in long, and radiate all around a stout, yellow-brown shoot.

West Himalayan Spruce *Picea smithiana* (Wallich) Boissier
The west Himalayan spruce (which is also known as morinda spruce) has weeping foliage, which allows it to shed snow easily. It is native to Afghanistan, Kashmir and Nepal, where it grows at altitudes in excess of 3,500m/11,500ft. Needles are slender, up to 4cm/1½in long and shiny dark green.

Hondo Spruce *Picea jezoensis* var. *hondoensis* (Siebold & Zuccarini) Carriere
This is a variety of the Jezo spruce, a native of Japan and the Pacific coast of Asia. The Hondo spruce grows specifically on the Japanese island of Honshu, which was previously called Hondo. It is a taller, more vigorous tree than the true species, reaching heights in excess of 50m/164ft. It is also hardier. The Hondo spruce has a reddish brown cone and upswept needles, which are deep green above, with two bright white stomatal bands beneath.

Serbian Spruce

Picea omorika (Pancic) Purkyne

The Serbian spruce has a very small natural population and because of this is considered to be endangered in the wild. It is a beautiful slender spire-like tree with branches that sweep elegantly downwards only to arch upwards at their tip. This habit means that it is able to resist damage by efficiently shedding snow rather than collecting it. It is also the most resistant spruce to atmospheric pollution.

Identification: Bark is orange-brown to copper and broken into irregular to square plates. The shoot is a similar colour to the bark and quite hairy. Needles are short with a blunt tip, less than 2cm/¾in long, glossy dark green above and with two broad white stomatal bands underneath. Male flowers are crimson and held below new shoots; female flowers are also red but confined to the topmost branches. This tree's most distinctive characteristic is its spire-like form.

Right: The cone is pendulous, held on a thick curved stalk, tear-shaped, 6cm/2½in long and purple-brown in colour.

Distribution: Europe: Confined to the Drina Valley in south-west Serbia.
Height: 30m/100ft
Shape: Very narrowly conical
Evergreen
Pollinated: Wind
Leaf shape: Linear

TRUE CEDARS AND HEMLOCKS

Although there are only four true cedars, they are without doubt the real stars of the coniferous world. Nothing can touch them for sheer majesty and dignity. Three are clustered around the Mediterranean and the fourth makes it a little further east into the Himalayas. The hemlocks, on the other hand, are all to be found in either North America or Asia.

Deodar

Cedrus deodara G. Don

In the days of the British Empire, when the Indian Imperial Forest Service carried out surveys of the region, huge deodars 75m/246ft tall were found, some of them over 900 years old. Sadly most of these have been felled for their timber. Deodar has light brown, very durable timber, which is highly prized.

Below: The barrel-shaped cones are 12cm/4¾in long, ripen to dull brown.

Identification: In young trees the bark is smooth and dark grey. The bark on older trees becomes cracked and covered with pink-grey fissures. Juvenile foliage is blue-grey, becoming dark green with age. Deodar is narrowly conical when young, and broadens as it matures. It is easily distinguished from other cedars by the drooping ends to its branches. Needles are arranged in whorls around the shoot and are 4cm/1½in long. Male flowers are very prominent, erect, purple ripening to yellow, up to 8cm/3in long, and shed copious amounts of pollen in late autumn.

Distribution: Western Himalayas, Kuram Valley to Kumaon and on to Afghanistan.
Height: 50m/165ft
Shape: Broadly conical
Evergreen
Pollinated: Wind
Leaf shape: Linear

Right: The needles are sparse.

Cedar of Lebanon

Cedrus libanii A. Richard

This large stately tree is probably the best known of all the cedars. It has been revered for thousands of years. In biblical times it stood as a symbol for fertility. King Solomon is believed to have built his temple out of its timber. On Mount Lebanon it grows at altitudes up to 2,140m/7,021ft. Although in the wild, numbers are decreasing, it has been widely planted as an ornamental tree in parks, gardens and arboreta in Britain and North America.

Identification: The bark is a dull brown with even, shallow fissures. For the first 40 years of its life, cedar of Lebanon is a narrow, conical-shaped tree; thereafter it broadens rapidly with long level branches which seem, in some cases, to defy gravity: such is their length. The needles are grey-blue to dark green (depending on the provenance of the individual tree), 3cm/1¼in long and grow in dense whorls on side shoots and singly on fast-growing main shoots. The cone is barrel-shaped, erect, grey-green and matures to purplish brown.

Distribution: Mount Lebanon, Syria and the Taurus Mountains in south-east Turkey.
Height: 40m/130ft
Shape: Broadly columnar
Evergreen
Pollinated: Wind
Leaf shape: Linear

Right: Cones are 12cm/ 4¾in long.

Atlantic Cedar

Cedrus atlantica (Endlicher)
This tree is also known as the Atlas cedar after the mountain range it originates from. The Atlantic cedar is the fastest growing of all the cedars reaching 3m/10ft in less than seven years. It is also the straightest, maintaining its leading stem into old age. The form 'Glauca' is far more widely planted than the true species because of its strikingly beautiful silvery blue foliage.

Cyprus Cedar *Cedrus brevifolia* (Hooker fil.) Henry
The tree is confined to forests surrounding Mount Paphos in Cyprus. At one time considered a form of Lebanon cedar, it is now treated as a separate species. It does not look much like Lebanon cedar as it maintains a single stem, has shorter needles, a more open habit and from a distance has a yellow-green crown.

Himalayan Hemlock *Tsuga dumosa* D. Don) Eichler
The Himalayan hemlock is found growing wild from north-west India to northern Burma and on into China, where it attains heights in excess of 50m/165ft. However in cultivation elsewhere it seldom reaches 20m/66ft. Bark is pink-brown and scaly, rather like larch. Needles are relatively long for a hemlock, 3cm/1¼ in, hard and rigid, green-blue above and have two silver stomatal bands beneath.

Western Hemlock

Tsuga heterophylla (Rafinesque) Sargent

This tall, elegant tree has weeping branches and soft pendulous foliage. However, this softness is deceptive; western hemlock is as hardy as any conifer. It thrives in the Rockies up to 1,830m/6,000ft above sea level and is extremely shade-tolerant, out-growing its competitors in the thickest forest.

Identification: Bark is reddish purple in young trees, becoming dark purple-brown with age. The tree has a narrow conical shape, with ascending branches that arch gently downwards towards the tip. The leading shoot is always lax. Needles are 2cm/¾ in long, deep dark green above with two broad blue-white stomatal bands beneath. New growth is bright lime green in spring, contrasting dramatically against the rather sombre mature foliage. Male and female flowers are red. Much pollen is shed in late spring. Cones are pendulous, egg-shaped, 2.5cm/1in long, with few scales, and are a pale green ripening to deep brown.

Distribution: West coast of USA from Alaska to California.
Height: 60m/200ft
Shape: Narrowly conical
Evergreen
Pollinated: Wind
Leaf shape: Linear

Left and below: Small egg-shaped cones appear in late summer at the tips of branches.

Mountain Hemlock

Tsuga mertensiana (Bongard) Carriere

Native to the west coast of America from Alaska to California, this handsome tree has a columnar crown of grey pendulous foliage. The mountain hemlock is sometimes mistaken for *Cedrus atlantica* 'Glauca', as it has thick blue-grey needles, which radiate all around the shoot.

Identification: The bark is a dark orange-brown in colour becoming vertically fissured into rectangular flakes in maturity. The branches are slightly drooping with weeping branchlets hanging from them. The shoot is a shiny pale brown colour. The needles are similar to cedar, 1.5–2cm/¾ in long, dark grey-green to blue-grey and borne radially all over the shoot. The cone is spruce-like, 7cm/2¾ in long, cyclindrical and buff pink maturing to brown.

Below: Cones before and after opening.

Distribution: Alaska to California, USA.
Height: 30m/100ft
Shape: Columnar
Evergreen
Pollinated: Wind
Leaf shape: Linear

Left: The needles have a definite bluish tinge to them and radiate out from the twigs. From their ends, shoots appear star-like.

DECIDUOUS LARCHES

This small genus of fewer than a dozen species is confined to temperate regions of the Northern Hemisphere. Deciduous larches are fast-growing conifers – several species have been widely planted for forestry purposes. Larches are some of the most seasonally attractive of all conifers. Their needles turn gold and fall in autumn, to be renewed every spring with a flush of lime-green foliage.

European Larch

Larix decidua Miller

This attractive, hardy tree grows naturally at altitudes up to 2,500m/8,200ft above sea level. It is a long-lived conifer, with some trees in the Alps recorded at over 700 years old. European larch has been widely planted throughout Europe and North America for both forestry and ornamental reasons.

Identification: Bark on young trees is pale grey and smooth. Old trees have heavily fissured, dark pink bark. Whorls of upswept branches are well spaced. Needles are soft, 4cm/1½in long and bright green, becoming yellow before falling in autumn. They are carried singly on main shoots and in dense whorls on side shoots. The shoots are pendulous and straw coloured. Male flowers are pink-yellow rounded discs, normally on the underside of the shoots. Female flowers appear before the leaves in early spring. They are purple-pink, upright and develop quickly into an immature cone.

Right and left: Cones are 4.5cm/1¾in long.

Distribution: From the southern Alps through Switzerland, Austria and Germany to the Carpathian Mountains of Slovakia and Romania.
Height: 40m/130ft
Shape: Narrowly conical
Deciduous
Pollinated: Wind
Leaf shape: Linear

Japanese Larch

Larix kaempferi (Lambert) Carriere

In the wild, Japanese larch is confined to the volcanic mountains of the Japanese island of Honshu, where it grows at altitudes exceeding 2,750m/9,000ft. It is extensively planted throughout Japan for forestry and is one of the country's most important timber-producing trees. It is also grown as an ornamental species in Japanese temple gardens, where it is quite often trained as a bonsai.

Above: Cones are borne intermittently along the shoot among the foliage.

Identification: Bark is reddish brown and scaly. The form is broader than European larch. Branches sweep upwards when young, becoming level or even slightly descending in older trees. Young shoots are a distinctive purple-red colour, sometimes covered with a slight silver bloom. Needles are 5cm/2in long, and flatter and broader than those of European larch. They dull to grey-green in summer, then become orange before falling in autumn. Male flowers are yellow globules clustered on pendulous shoots. Female flowers, which occur all over the tree, have a pink centre and creamy yellow margins. Cones are bun-shaped and 3cm/1¼in long.

Distribution: Central Honshu, Japan.
Height: 30m/100ft
Shape: Broadly conical
Deciduous
Pollinated: Wind
Leaf shape: Linear

Left: Japanese larch cones have scales that turn outwards. Needles are soft, bright green when they sprout in early spring, then they fade to grey-green in summer, and turn orange in autumn.

Golden Larch

Pseudolarix amabilis (Nelson) Rehder

The golden larch is a slow-growing, deciduous conifer but not actually a true larch. It differs in having cones that disintegrate on the tree and spur-shoots that lengthen annually. Golden larch is relatively rare in the wild, growing in deciduous forests comprised of Chinese tulip trees, *Liriodendron chinensis*, and sweet gums, *Liquidambar formosana*.

Identification: The bark is grey-brown, deeply fissured into thick, square plates. The overall shape is broadly conical with level branches that sometimes curve upwards at the tips. The shoot is pale yellow to pink-buff. Needles are 5cm/2in long, soft, set spirally around the shoot. They occur in dense whorls on side shoots and singly on leading shoots, where they face forwards. They are bright grass-green on emerging in spring and a glorious bright orange-gold in autumn just before falling. Both male and female flowers are yellow and are borne in clusters at the ends of shoots on the same tree. Cones only appear after long, hot summers; they are 6cm/2½in long, with curious, triangular-shaped scales, reminiscent of a green globe artichoke. They ripen golden brown in autumn before breaking apart on the tree.

Distribution: Provinces of Chekiang, Anhwei and Kiangsi in eastern China.
Height: 40m/130ft
Shape: Broadly conical
Deciduous
Pollinated: Wind
Leaf shape: Linear

Left: Bright, new needles appear in spring. The cones ripen in autumn, then open to release their seeds.

Dahurian Larch *Larix gmelini* (Ruprecht)
Native to eastern Siberia and north-eastern China, this broad, rather squat tree will, in good growing conditions reach 20m/66ft tall, elsewhere it may resemble a spreading bush. Needles emerge bright green in mid-winter. They are 4cm/1½in long and turn a butter yellow in autumn before falling. Cones are produced prolifically. They are 2.5cm/1in long, ovoid, shiny pale brown and have broad scales that curve slightly outwards at the margins.

Dunkeld Larch *Larix x eurolepis* Henry
The Dunkeld larch is a hybrid between the European larch, *L. decidua*, and the Japanese larch, *L. Kaempferi*. Both species were planted in close proximity to each other at Dunkeld House, Scotland. In 1897 seed was collected from these trees and propagated; the resulting seedlings were identified as hybrids in 1904. They differ from each parent in being more vigorous and having a deep orange-brown shoot.

Sikkim Larch *Larix griffithiana* Carriere
Sometimes known as the Himalayan larch, this tree is native to eastern Nepal, Sikkim, Bhutan and Tibet. A narrow, conical tree up to 20m/66ft tall, it is rare both in the wild and in cultivation. The Sikkim larch has bark like a Corsican pine – grey-purple fissured into rough, scaly ridges. A graceful tree, it has pendulous red-brown shoots, bright green needles 5cm/2in long, and large erect cylindrical cones, 7–10cm/2¾–4in long.

Tamarack

American Larch, Hackmatack *Larix laricina* (Du Roi) Koch.

This hardy tree is just as much at home on an exposed mountainside as in a boggy swamp. Although widespread in the wild, it is rare in cultivation. A short-lived tree, it is very slow growing but pioneering, and colonizes inhospitable ground long before other trees.

Identification: Tamarack is a narrow, thin tree with short, level branches. The branches have a characteristic curled tip, which curls upwards and inwards back towards the crown. Young shoots are pink, turning brown as they mature. Needles are soft, blue-green, 2.5cm/1in long and have two grey stomatal bands beneath. Male flowers are numerous, small and yellow, growing beneath the shoot. Female flowers are red and held upright on the shoot.

Distribution: North America: Alaska and Canada south to New Jersey and Maryland.
Height: 20m/66ft
Shape: Narrowly conical
Deciduous
Pollinated: Wind
Leaf shape: Linear

Above: The bark is a pinkish orange colour, flaking into small circular scales.

Left: Cones have few scales and are pale brown, ovoid, erect and up to 2cm/¾in long.

TULIP TREE AND NORTH AMERICAN MAGNOLIAS

The Magnoliaceae family contains 12 genera and just over 200 species. The majority of species are native to North America or Asia. They include some of the most beautiful of all flowering trees. Magnolias are planted in gardens the world over and countless cultivars have been developed from true species. There are magnolias to suit all locations – some are giant, others little more than large shrubs.

Tulip Tree

Yellow poplar *Liriodendron tuliperfera* Linnaeus

This magnificent tree is one of the largest and fastest growing deciduous trees in North America. It stands out from the crowd for several reasons, including its size, its flower, its leaf shape and its ability to withstand atmospheric pollution. It is an adaptable tree, growing in extreme climatic conditions, from severe Canadian winters to subtropical Florida summers.

Identification: The bark is grey-brown and smooth, becoming fissured with age. In maturity, tulip trees have clear, straight stems with broad crowns. The dark green leaves are up to 15cm/6in long and lobed on each side with a cut-off indented leaf tip. The underside of the leaf is almost bluish white. In autumn the leaves turn a butter-yellow colour before falling. Flowers are produced in summer when the tree reaches 12–15 years old. They are upright, 6cm/2½in long, tulip-shaped and have nine petals: some are green; some are light green to yellowy orange at the base. Inside each flower is a bright cluster of orange yellow stamen. Unfortunately, because of the branchless stem of older trees, the flowers are very often positioned at the top of the tree, so it is very difficult to admire their beauty.

Distribution: Eastern North America from Ontario to New York in the north to Florida in the south.
Height: 50m/165ft
Shape: Broadly columnar
Deciduous
Pollinated: Bee
Leaf shape: Simple

Left: As the flowers fade on the tree, the leaves change colour giving the tulip tree a second flourish of beauty.

Cucumber Tree

Mountain magnolia *Magnolia acuminata* Linnaeus

The cucumber tree is sometimes called the mountain magnolia because of its ability to grow at altitudes up to 1,220m/4,000ft in the Smoky Mountains. This is the largest of the seven magnolias native to North America. The name 'cucumber' comes from the unripe seed pods, which are up to 18cm/7in long, green and fleshy.

Identification: The brown-grey bark is unlike that of any other North American magnolia; it is rough and divided into narrow ridges with vertical fissures. Overall form is of a tall, broad tree with a conical crown of mainly upswept branches. The leaf is elliptical to ovate, 25cm/10in long and 15cm/6in across, rich green above, blue-green and slightly hairy below. Flowers appear in early to midsummer; they are blue-green to yellow-green in colour, bell-shaped, 9cm/3½in long and quite often lost among the foliage. The seed pod ripens from a cucumber-like fruit into an erect, bright red cylinder 7.5cm/3in long, containing as many as 50 seeds.

Left: The flowers appear in summer but are often difficult to see among the leaves.

Distribution: Eastern North America from Ontario to Alabama.
Height: 30m/100ft
Shape: Broadly conical
Deciduous
Pollinated: Insect
Leaf shape: Simple ovate

Left: Red cylindrical seed pods appear from the middle of summer onwards.

Bull Bay

Magnolia grandiflora Linnaeus

This magnificent evergreen flowering tree is more often than not grown as a wall shrub. However, given a warm, sheltered, sunny position it will develop into a broad-canopied, short-stemmed tree. The bull bay grows best close to the coast and at low altitudes; it rarely thrives above 150m/500ft. The combination of glossy, dark green, leathery leaves and creamy white flowers makes it a very popular garden tree.

Identification: The bark is grey-brown, cracking into irregular small plates. The leaves, which grow up to 25cm/10in long and 10cm/4in across, are thick, rigid, glossy dark green above and either pale green, or covered in copper-coloured hairs beneath. Flowers will begin to appear when the tree is only ten years old; they are a wide-brimmed and cup-shaped, creamy white to pale lemon and deliciously scented. They can be up to 30cm/12in across and stand out splendidly against the dark foliage.

Above: The spectacular flowers are like dinner plates, measuring up to 30cm/12in across.

Left: In the wild, flowers are produced in spring.

Distribution: North American south-east coastal strip from north Carolina to Florida and west along the gulf to south-east Texas.
Height: 25m/82ft
Shape: Broadly conical
Evergreen
Pollinated: Insect
Leaf shape: Elliptic to ovate

Right: These red seed pods will first appear in midsummer.

Magnolia 'Charles Raffill'
This is a hybrid between *M. campbellii* and the subspecies *M. campbellii mollicomata*. It is a very vigorous deciduous tree, easily reaching 25m/82ft in height and, once established, grows up to 60cm/24in a year. It produces large, deep pink, goblet-shaped flowers in early spring.

Magnolia 'Elizabeth'
This hybrid between the cucumber magnolia, *M. acuminata* and *M. denudata* is a small, deciduous, conical-shaped tree. It produces pale primrose-yellow, fragrant, cup-shaped flowers in early to mid-spring before the leaves emerge from their winter bud. It was raised at the Brooklyn Botanic Garden by Eva Maria Sperbes in 1978 and named after Elizabeth Scholtz who was Director of the Brooklyn Botanic Garden at the time.

Magnolia 'Samuel Somner'
This magnificent form of *M. grandiflora* produces probably the largest flowers of any magnolia. They are creamy white, very fragrant, saucer-shaped and up to 35cm/14in across. The leaves are evergreen, thick, leathery, glossy dark green on the top-side and deep brown and hairy beneath. This form is very hardy and wind-resistant and can be grown in the open.

Magnolia 'Wada's Memory'
This lovely deciduous hybrid between *M. kobus* and *M. salicifolia* is broadly conical and grows up to about 10m/33ft tall. It produces white, fragrant flowers, which are cylinder-like as they emerge from the bud in early spring, opening to a lax, saucer shape, approximately 15cm/6in across. The flowers are held horizontally on the branch.

Sweet Bay

Swampbay *Magnolia virginiana* Linnaeus

This large shrub or small tree thrives on coastal plains and in wet swampy conditions. It was the earliest North American magnolia to be introduced into Europe, arriving in Great Britain in 1688. In the wild, the tallest trees tend to grow in the Carolinas and Florida, where heights of 25m/82ft have been recorded. Elsewhere it seldom achieves 10m/33ft.

Identification: The bark of sweet bay is smooth and grey. The overall form is normally shrubby, with branching low on the stem. Leaves are ovate in shape, up to 12cm/4¾in long and 6cm/2½in wide. They are deep lustrous green above and blue-white and downy beneath, especially when young. Flowers are creamy white, maturing quickly to pale yellow. They are cup-shaped at first opening to a broad saucer. The flowers are short-lived but produced over a long period from early to late summer and are highly scented. The sweet bay rarely sets seed in Europe.

Distribution: Eastern United States from Massachusetts to Florida.
Height: 25m/82ft
Shape: Broadly spreading
Semi-evergreen
Pollinated: Insect
Leaf shape: Ovate

Left: Flowers are produced throughout the summer.

ASIAN MAGNOLIAS

Some of the most beautiful trees in the world are Asian magnolias. Originating mainly from China and Japan, this group includes some of the tallest and smallest magnolias. Some flower on bare branches before winter has properly passed; others are summer-flowering. Some are evergreen; others deciduous. All are planted throughout the world for the colour, interest and fragrance they bring to our gardens.

Yulan Magnolia

Lily tree *Magnolia denudata* Desrouss

Distribution: Central and eastern China.
Height: 15m/50ft
Shape: Broadly spreading
Deciduous
Pollinated: Insect
Leaf shape: Ovate

Right: The beautiful, white flowers are unfortunately prone to browning if subjected to frost.

Sometimes known as the lily tree, this beautiful small- to medium-sized tree has been cultivated in Chinese Buddhist temple gardens since 600AD. Its pure white, cup-shaped fragrant flowers were regarded as a symbol of purity in the Tang Dynasty and it was planted in the grounds of the Emperor's palace.

Identification: The Yulan magnolia is a rather low, rounded, thickly branched tree. It has thick, bright green leaves which, once fallen, decompose to leave just a skeletal form. The leaves are ovate, 15cm/6in long and 8cm/3in wide. The pure white flowers are heavily scented, with a citrus-lemon fragrance. They open from early to late spring; erect and goblet-shaped at first, then gradually spreading to water-lily shape, as each thick petal curls outwards.

Japanese Big-leaved Magnolia

Magnolia hypoleuca Siebold & Zuccarini

Sometimes known as *M. obovata*, this is one of the largest of all magnolias, not only in height but also in girth. In the forests of Hokkaido, Japan, where it is highly prized for its light, but strong, easily worked timber, girths in excess of 3m/10ft have been recorded. In some parts of Japan, the large leaves that earn this tree its name are used for wrapping food.

Identification: The bark in young trees is smooth and a dark purple-brown colour. In maturity it becomes slate grey. Leaves are up to 45cm/18in long, 20cm/8in wide, thick and leathery, sage green above, silvery blue and pubescent beneath. They are held in whorls of five to eight positioned at the end of each shoot. Large, cup-shaped, creamy pink flowers are produced in early summer. Each up to 20cm/8in across, they are strongly scented and have bright purple-red stamens, which create a distinctive central 'eye' to each flower. Seeds are produced on a conspicuous red cylindrical pod, up to 20cm/8in long.

Distribution: Japan and the Pacific coast of Russia.
Height: 30m/100ft
Shape: Broadly columnar
Deciduous
Pollinated: Insect
Leaf shape: Obovate

Left: The flowers of this tree, although large, are dwarfed by its massive leaves.

Hybrid Magnolia *Magnolia x soulangeana*
Soulange-Bodir
A hybrid between *M. denudata* and *M. liliiflora*, this has become the most widely planted ornamental magnolia in gardens across the world. The deciduous, obovate leaves are up to 20cm/8in long and 12cm/4¾in wide. The flowers are goblet-shaped, slowly opening to cup-and-saucer-shaped. They are generally creamy white, with a pink blush tinge to the base of each thick petal.

Star Magnolia *Magnolia stellata*
(Sieb. & Zucc.) Maxim.
This slow-growing, compact Japanese tree, or large shrub, seldom reaches more than 3m/10ft in height. It flowers on bare branches in late winter and early spring. The flowers are fragrant, pure white, maturing to pale pink, star-shaped, and have 12–18 petals.

Goddess Magnolia *Magnolia sprengeri* 'Diva'
Pampan
M. sprengeri is a large Chinese magnolia, discovered in western Hubei Province in 1900. The cultivar 'Diva' derives from a Chinese form planted at Caerhays Castle in Cornwall. It is much more vigorous than the species and has rose-pink flowers, similar in shape to, but smaller than, those of *M. campbellii*. A specimen of 'Diva' planted at south-west England's Westonbirt Arboretum in 1960 is already 28m/92ft tall.

Wilson's Magnolia

Magnolia wilsonii (Fin. & Gagnep.) Rehd.

One of the loveliest of all magnolias, this was named after the British plant collector Ernest Wilson (1876–1930), who first discovered the species in western China in 1908. It is distinctive for having drooping flowerheads, which can only be seen at their best when standing directly beneath the tree.

Identification: A large spreading shrub, or small tree, which is primarily grown for its delightful flowers. The flowers are cup-shaped, pure white, up to 10cm/4in across and have a brilliant crimson centre. The flower bud is covered in dense grey, soft down, which is obvious from mid-winter onwards. After flowering, a purple-pink, cylindrical-ovoid seed pod is produced, which is 5–8cm/2–3in long and contains scarlet-coated seed. The leaf is almost spear-shaped, dull green above and covered in pale-brown pubescence beneath. This magnolia is most often found growing in shade.

Distribution: Western Szechwan and Yunnan, China.
Height: 8m/26ft
Shape: Broadly spreading
Deciduous
　　Pollinated: Insect
　　　Leaf shape: Elliptic-lanceolate

Above: The flowers appear in great quantities in spring.

Campbell's Magnolia

Magnolia campbellii J. D. Hooker & Thomson

This majestic tree is capable of attaining heights up to 30m/100ft in less than 60 years. It is a hardy tree, growing up to 3,000m/9,850ft above sea level in the Himalayas.

M. campbellii is grown widely for its dramatic flowers, which only appear on seedlings after 20 years. Flowers appear as early as mid-winter and are prone to frost damage.

Below: The flowers are very big, up to 30cm/12in across.

Identification: Bark is smooth and grey, even in old age. Leaves are up to 30cm/12in long, with a pronounced point, medium green above, sometimes faintly hairy beneath. Flower buds are large, ovoid and covered in grey hairs. They stand out dramatically on the bare branches in late winter. The flowers are even more dramatic, beginning goblet-shaped but opening to a lax cup-and-saucer shape, up to 30cm/12in across. Colour can vary from deep pink to pale pinkish white. There is a slight fragrance to the flower. Each flower is held upright on a smooth green stalk. The fruit is a cylindrical, cone-like pod up to 15cm/6in long, containing bright red seed.

Right: Flowers often appear in profusion, both on cultivated and wild trees.

Distribution: Himalayas from Nepal to Assam and on into south-west China.
Height: 30m/100ft
Shape: Broadly conical
Deciduous
Pollinated: Insect
Leaf shape: Obovate

EVERGREEN LAURELS

The Lauraceae family contains more than 40 genera and 2,000 different species, most of which are tropical, originating from Asia and South America. Those that are hardier, and can survive in temperate regions of the world, tend to have several things in common, including aromatic foliage or bark and evergreen leaves.

Sassafras

Sassafras albidum (Nuttall) Nees.

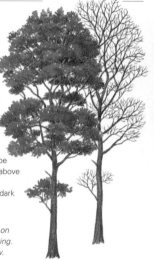

Both the leaves and bark of sassafras are pleasingly aromatic. In the past, both have been used for medicinal purposes. The bark of the root is often used to make a drink not dissimilar to beer. Although fairly widespread in the wild, sassafras has never been widely cultivated in parks and gardens. The leaves, which can be heavily lobed, are similar in outline to those of the common fig.

Identification: A medium-sized suckering tree with wavy or zig-zag branching, which is particularly noticeable when the leaves have fallen in winter. Leaves are 15cm/6in long, 10cm/4in across, variable in shape, sometimes having a pronounced lobe on one or both sides. They are grass-green above and blue-green below. In autumn they turn orange-yellow before falling. The fruit is a dark blue, egg-shaped berry, 1cm/½in across.

Distribution: Eastern North America from Canada to Florida and westwards to Kansas and Texas.
Height: 25m/82ft
Shape: Broadly columnar
Deciduous
Pollinated: Insect
Leaf shape: Ovate to elliptic

Left: Male and female flowers are held on separate trees and produced in late spring. Both are inconspicuous and greenish yellow.

Sorrel Tree

California bay, California olive, Oregon myrtle *Umbellularia californica*

(W. J. Hooker & Arnott) Nuttall

This tree resembles the bay tree in everything but size, being extremely vigorous and capable of reaching 30m/100ft in height in sheltered, moist valley bottoms. It has a dense leafy habit and foliage which, when crushed, emits a very powerful odour, which can induce nausea, headaches and in some cases unconsciousness. It may also cause skin allergies in some people.

Identification: The bark is dark grey and smooth when young, cracking into regular plates as the tree matures. The leaves are up to 12cm/5in long, alternately placed on sage-green shoots, elliptic in shape but tapering at both ends, leathery, glossy dark green above and pale beneath. The flowers are inconspicuous, 5mm/¼in across and yellowy green in colour. They are produced on sage-green upright stalks, 2.5cm/1in long, in late winter and early spring. The fruit is a pear-shaped berry, 2.5cm/1in long, green at first, then changing to purple. The timber of Californian laurel is highly prized for veneers and cabinet-making; known as 'pepperwood' it has pale brown figuring and can be polished to a fine finish.

Distribution: North America, California north to Oregon.
Height: 30m/100ft
Shape: Broadly spreading
Evergreen
Pollinated: Insect
Leaf shape: Elliptic to oblanceolate

Left: Flowers appear in winter and early spring.

Right: The leaves resemble those of bay.

Bay Laurel

Sweet bay *Laurus nobilis* Linnaeus

This is the laurel used by the Greeks and Romans as a ceremonial symbol of victory; it was usually woven into crowns to be worn by champions. Fruiting sprays were also made into wreaths and given to acclaimed poets, hence the term 'poet laureate'. The term 'bachelor', as awarded to those with university degrees, is derived from the French word *bachelier* which means 'laurel berry'.

Identification: A dense, evergreen small tree or shrub with aromatic leaves, which are commonly used as food flavouring. The bark is dark grey and smooth, even in old age. Leaves are leathery, alternate, dark glossy green above with a central lighter vein, and pale green beneath. They are 10cm/4in long, 4cm/1½in across and pointed at the tip. Male flowers appear in late winter; they are greenish yellow, 1cm/⅓in across, with many yellow stamens, positioned in the axils of the previous year's leaves.

Above: The small, male flowers open during late winter. Bay leaves are commonly harvested for use in cooking.

Distribution: Throughout Mediterranean regions.
Height: 15m/50ft
Shape: Broadly conical
Evergreen
Pollinated: Insect
Leaf shape: Elliptic

Left: The fruit is a rounded berry, 1cm/⅓in across, green ripening to a glossy black.

Wheel Tree *Trochodendron aralioides* Siebold & Zuccarini
This attractive, evergreen, Japanese tree is the sole species in the only genus within the family Trochodendraceae. Its nearest relative is believed to be *Drimys winteri*. It has dark green, shiny, narrow, elliptical, leathery leaves and aromatic bark. Its most interesting feature by far is its wheel-like flowers, which are bright green, 2cm/¾in across and have exposed stamens radiating outwards from a central disc, rather like the spokes on a cartwheel. They appear on upright slender stalks from early spring to early summer.

Gutta Percha *Eucommia ulmoides* Oliver
This Chinese tree is the only member of the Eucommiaceae family. It is believed to be most closely related to the elms, hence its species name *ulmoides*. It is the only temperate tree that produces rubber. If the leaf is gently torn in half, the two halves will still hang together, held

by thin strands of sticky latex. In China, gutta percha has been cultivated for hundreds of years and used for medicinal purposes. It has never been found growing wild, so its actual origins are not known.

Camphor

Cinnamomum camphora (Linnaeus) Sieb.

This tender, small tree reaches 15m/50ft in tropical Asia but elsewhere is more often a tall shrub. It will only survive in the mildest locations but is worth persevering because it is a handsome plant, with dark green, lush foliage. The wood produces camphor oil, which is used for medicinal purposes and in the production of celluloid film.

Identification: Bark is smooth and grey-brown when young, becoming finely cracked in old age. Camphor has oval to obovate slender-pointed leaves (which are tapered at the base) alternately arranged on dull-green smooth shoots. The leaves are up to 15cm/6in long and 7.5cm/3in wide. They are firm and leathery and very fragrant when crushed. Each leaf has a deep glossy green upper surface, with very pronounced veining, which appears to segment the leaf. The underside of the leaf is pale glaucous green. The flowers are greenish white, only 2.5mm/⅛in across and held on long-stalked, drooping panicles.

Distribution: Tropical Asia: Malaysia to China and Japan.
Height: 15m/50ft
Shape: Broadly spreading
Evergreen
Pollinated: Insect
Leaf shape: Obovate

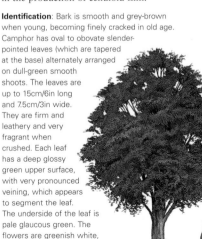

Above: The small flowers appear from early to mid-spring.

Left: The berry-like fruit is almost black in colour.

AUTUMN COLOUR

Although the trees under this heading all belong to different families, they have two things in common. They are all deciduous, dropping their leaves in autumn and producing replacements the following spring. And, before they lose their leaves, they all produce spectacular autumn leaf colour. Because of their beauty, many are planted as ornamental trees.

Katsura Tree

Cercidphyllum japonicum Siebold & Zuccarini

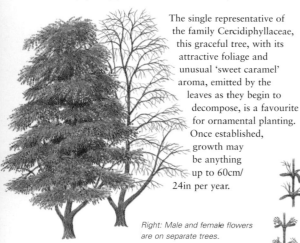

The single representative of the family Cercidiphyllaceae, this graceful tree, with its attractive foliage and unusual 'sweet caramel' aroma, emitted by the leaves as they begin to decompose, is a favourite for ornamental planting. Once established, growth may be anything up to 60cm/24in per year.

Identification: The bark is grey-brown, freckled with lenticels and becomes fissured and flaking in maturity. The thin leaves are heart-shaped, slightly toothed around the margin, up to 8cm/3in long and wide, emerging a bronzy pink in autumn. The male flowers are bright red, appearing on side shoots before the leaves appear in early spring. Female flowers develop in late spring in clusters of four to six.

Distribution: Western China and Hokkaido and Honshu in Japan.
Height: 30m/100ft
Shape: Broadly spreading
Deciduous
Pollinated: Insect
Leaf shape: Cordate

Right: Male and female flowers are on separate trees.

Left: Leaves fade to blue-green in summer and then vibrant shades of butter-yellow to purple-pink in spring.

Oriental Plane

Platanus orientalis Linnaeus

The Oriental plane is a majestic tree. Hippocrates, the ancient Greek 'father of medicine', is said to have taught his medical scholars under the great Oriental plane tree that still exists on the island of Cos. Another large Oriental plane on the Bosporus near Buyukdere is known as 'the plane of Godfrey de Bouillon', because tradition states that he and his knights camped under it during the first crusade in 1096.

Identification: One of the largest of all deciduous temperate trees. It can reach heights in excess of 30m/100ft tall, with a great spreading canopy and a trunk girth of 6m/20ft. It has attractive buff-grey bark, which flakes to reveal cream-pink patches. The leaves are palmate, 20cm/8in long and 25cm/10in across, deeply cut into five narrow lobes, shiny green above, pale green below and have brown tufts of hair along the veins. Leaves are attached alternately to the shoot by a yellow-green petiole up to 7.5cm/3in long. In autumn the leaves turn from clear yellow to old gold. The fruit is globular and mace-like, 2.5cm/1in across, attached in clusters of two to six on a pendulous stalk.

Right: Fruit remains on the tree through the winter.

Distribution: Albania, Greece, Crete, Cyprus, Lebanon, Syria and Israel.
Height: 30m/100ft
Shape: Broadly spreading
Deciduous
Pollinated: Insect
Leaf shape: Palmate lobed

Sweet Gum

Liquidamber styraciflua Linnaeus

This giant of a tree is known to have reached 45m/150ft in height and is one of the main constituents of the deciduous hardwood forests of eastern North America. In autumn its leaves turn every shade from orange through red to purple.

Identification: The bark is a dark brown-grey colour becoming fissured into long vertical ridges with age. The leaves are up to 15cm/6in long and broad, normally with five tapering lobes (sometimes seven), the centre one of which is normally largest. The margin of the leaf is slightly toothed. The leaf shape sometimes leads to identification confusion with maples; however maple leaves are in opposite pairs on a smooth shoot, whereas *Liquidamber* leaves are alternately positioned on a corky shoot.

Above: Male and female flowers are both small and round, greeny yellow in colour and appear in late spring.

Distribution: North America from Connecticut in the north to Florida and Texas in the south. Also found in Central America.
Height: 40m/130ft
Shape: Broadly conical
Deciduous
Pollinated: Insect
Leaf shape: Palmate lobed

Left: The seed is contained in clusters of round, brown hanging pods approximately 4cm/1½in across.

Persian Ironwood

Parrotia persica (Candolle) C. A. Meyer

A member of the Hamamelidaceae family, this is one of the finest trees for autumn colour, turning from copper to burgundy in mid-autumn. In the wild it tends to be a broad upright tree, but in cultivation it becomes a sprawling mass, seldom attaining a height in excess of 15m/50ft. The botanical name is derived from the German climber F. W. Parrot, who made the first ascent of Mount Ararat in 1829.

Identification: Quite often seen in large gardens and arboreta as a dense low-spreading mound, which is quite difficult to penetrate because of criss-cross branching. The bark is a dark brown, flaking to reveal light brown patches. Leaves are obovate, sometimes elliptic, 12cm/4¾in long and 6cm/2½in wide, becoming progressively shallow toothed and wavy towards the top of each leaf. They are bright glossy green above and dull green with slight pubescence beneath. Flowers are tiny, clothed in soft velvet-brown casing but emerging a startling ruby-red colour, which stands out dramatically upon the bare branches in mid-winter. The fruit is a nut-like brown capsule, 1cm/½in across.

Below: Leaves are darker and glossier on the tops and lighter beneath.

Small ruby-red flowers appear in winter.

Distribution: Mount Ararat, Eastern Caucasus to northern Iran.
Height: 20m/66ft
Shape: Broadly spreading
Deciduous
Pollinated: Insect
Leaf shape: Obovate

Buttonwood *Platanus occidentalis*, Linnaeus
Sometimes called the American sycamore, this large tree occurs right across eastern North America. The leaf is heart-shaped at the base, with more, but shallower, lobing than either the London plane or the Oriental plane. The bark is grey-brown and has the same flaking characteristic as the other planes.

London Plane *Platanus* x *hispanica* Miller ex Munchhausen
This tree is a hybrid between the Oriental plane, *Platanus orientalis* and the American buttonwood, *P. occidentalis*. It is widely planted in cities across the world (including London) because of its ability to withstand atmospheric pollution and severe pruning. The London plane differs from each parent in being more vigorous, and having leaves with shallower lobes and a lighter coloured bark, which peels to reveal cream patches.

Below: London plane is a common sight in cities around the world.

ELMS

This Ulmaceae family contains about 15 genera and 140 different species of mainly deciduous trees. They thrive in all but the poorest of soils and are widespread throughout most temperate regions of the Northern Hemisphere, including Europe, North America and Asia, except that is, where they have been affected by the fungus Ophiostoma novo-ulmi, *which causes Dutch elm disease.*

Wych Elm

Ulmus glabra Hudson

This tough medium-sized tree survives particularly well in exposed coastal areas and on mountain slopes. It has strong, dense timber, which is very resistant to decay when immersed in water. For centuries, hollowed-out elm branches were used for water pipes, water-wheel paddles and boat building.

Identification: The bark is grey-brown and in maturity uniformly lined with vertical fissures. The overall shape is of a short, stocky stem surmounted by a wide-spreading, open crown. Leaves are up to 20cm/8in long and 10cm/4in broad. They are coarsely and doubly toothed, with unequal sides at the base of the leaf where it joins the petiole. The upper surface of the leaf is dull green and rough textured; the lower surface is lighter in colour and heavily furred. Flowers appear in late winter before the leaves. The seed is carried in the centre of a flat, papery, hairy disc, known as a samara. Samaras are 5mm/¼in across and borne in clusters.

Distribution: Europe from Spain to Russia including western Scandinavia.
Height: 30m/100ft
Shape: Broadly spreading
Deciduous
Pollinated: Wind
Leaf shape: Oval to obovate

Right: Male flowers have bright red anthers and are very conspicuous in early spring, when copious amounts of pollen are released.

Nettle Tree

Hackberry *Celtis occidentalis* Linnaeus

Distribution: North America.
Height: 25m/82ft
Shape: Broadly columnar
Deciduous
Pollinated: Wind
Leaf shape: Ovate

Right: The nettle tree is named for its leaves, which resemble those of the stinging nettle.

This medium-sized tree, which is closely related to elm, grows naturally right across North America from the Atlantic seaboard to the Rocky Mountains and north into Canada. It is also known as hackberry and produces a profusion of purple, edible, sweet-tasting berries, that are an important food source for birds.

Identification: The bark is light grey, smooth when the tree is young, becoming rough and corky with warty blemishes in maturity. Leaves are ovate, up to 12cm/4¾in long and 5cm/2in across, pointed, toothed at the tip and rounded at the base, where there are three pronounced veins. They are glossy rich green and smooth on top; lighter green and slightly hairy on the veining underneath. Both the male and female flowers are held separately on the same tree in spring – they are small and green, without petals and appear in the leaf axils. The fruit is a purple-black, rounded berry, approximately 1cm/½in across and borne on a thin green stalk, 2.5cm/1in long.

Keaki

Zelkova serrata (Thunberg) Makino

A large, elm-like Asian tree, in its native lands this grows best in low-lying river valleys where the soil is deep and rich. However, it is also found growing naturally in the Japanese mountains of Kyushu and Honshu up to altitudes of 1,220m/4,000ft. Many of the oldest Japanese temples are built of its timber, which is strong and extremely durable.

Identification: The bark is pale grey and smooth, like beech. In maturity it peels or flakes, leaving light, fawn-grey patches. Lower branching is light and sweeps upwards, ending in thin, straight twigs. Leaves are ovate, 12cm/4¾in long and 5cm/2in broad, with 6–13 sharp teeth on each side. Small, green male and female flowers appear on each tree in spring. The fruit is round and small, 5mm/¼in diameter.

Distribution: China, Japan and Korea.
Height: 40m/130ft
Shape: Broadly spreading
Deciduous
Pollinated: Wind
Leaf shape: Ovate

Right and far right: The leaves are dark green and slightly rough above; pale green with pubescence beneath. In autumn they turn an orange-red colour.

Huntingdon Elm *Ulmus* x *hollandica* 'Vegeta' Miller
Huntingdon elm is one of the most resistant 'British' elms to Dutch elm disease. It is a hybrid between wych elm, *U. glabra*, and smooth-leaved elm, *U. minor*. It was first produced from seed collected from elm trees growing at Huntingdon, England in 1750. Leaves are similar in shape and size to wych elm, but the overall form is more upright and vigorous.

American Elm *Ulmus americana* Linnaeus
More usually known as white elm, this wide-spread tree grows from Saskatchewan to Florida and west to Texas. It is a magnificent tree, attaining heights in excess of 35m/115ft, with a wide-spreading crown of graceful, pendulous branching. It has been planted widely as an ornamental shade tree since colonial times, although since 1930 the population has been drastically reduced through Dutch elm disease.

English Elm *Ulmus minor* var. *vulgaris* (Ait.) Richens
This large tree, formerly known as *U. procera*, was probably introduced to England from Spain by Neolithic travellers. For centuries it was one of the most characteristic features of the English countryside; but in the 1960s, Dutch elm disease wiped out almost the entire population.

Chinese Elm *Ulmus parvifolia* Jacquin
This small tree, native to China, Japan, Taiwan and Korea, inhabits lower rocky slopes of mountains. It appears resistant to Dutch elm disease but does not have the stature of either the English or American elm, so has not been widely planted.

Caucasian Elm

Zelkova carpinifolia (Pallas) K. Koch

This slow-growing, long-lived forest tree has a very distinctive and pleasing shape. It is similar to hornbeam, having a short trunk and a large, almost mop-head of dense, upright branching. The overall impression is of a tree that was once pollarded but has long since been neglected.

Identification: Bark is a smooth, grey-buff colour that flakes in maturity; the trunk has pronounced fluting and a buttressed base. The flowers are small, green and are borne in the leaf axils each spring. The fruit is an insignificant looking, small, rounded pea-like capsule with pronounced ridging.

Distribution: Caucasus Mountains and northern Iran.
Height: 30m/100ft
Shape: Broadly columnar
Deciduous
Pollinated: Wind
Leaf shape: Elliptic to oblong

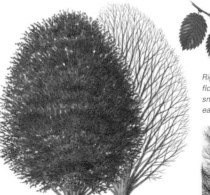

Left: the leaves are 10cm/4in long and have parallel veining.

Right: The flowers are small and easily missed.

MULBERRIES AND WALNUTS

One of the main characteristics of these two families is that they both contain trees that produce edible fruits. The mulberry or Moraceae family includes both mulberries and figs, while the walnut, or Juglandaceae family includes the common walnut. There are about 800 different species of fig; the majority of them are found in tropical and subtropical regions.

Common Walnut

Juglans regia Linnaeus

Although walnut is naturally widespread, it has been distributed farther by man, who has cultivated the tree for its nuts since Roman times. The Romans introduced it to Britain and it was introduced into the USA during colonial times.

Above: Flowers hang from the twigs.

Above: Individual leaflets have smooth edges and are up to 2cm/5in long.

Distribution: From Greece in the west to central China and Japan in the east.
Height: 30m/100ft
Shape: Broadly spreading
Deciduous
Pollinated: Wind
Leaf shape: Pinnate

Identification: The bark is light grey with black fissures, creating narrow, rough ridges. Leaves are pinnate with up to nine leaflets on each leaf stalk. Each leaflet is bronze-pink when young, becoming deep green with a dull sheen in maturity. When the shoot is cut lengthways, a compartmentalized pith is revealed. Male and female flowers are green catkins, which appear on the tree in late spring. The fruit is a round green husk, 5cm/2in across, not unlike a spineless horse-chestnut husk. Inside is the familiar, brown walnut.

Japanese Walnut

Juglans ailantifolia Carriere

This attractive ornamental tree has the largest of all walnut leaves. The sticky fruit husk is poisonous but the nut inside is edible and has been a valuable food source in Japan for centuries. The timber is light and strong and has been used in the manufacture of aircraft.

Identification: The grey-brown bark is fissured, segmenting into irregular plates in maturity. The leaves are pinnate and large, each with up to 17 slightly toothed leaflets 15cm/6in long. They are rich green and slightly hairy above; the undersides are very furry. The stout brown shoot is also hairy and very sticky. Male flowers are green, pendulous catkins, up to 30cm/12in long. Both male and female flowers appear on the same tree but are borne separately in late spring. The brown nut is contained in a green, hairy, sticky, rounded husk up to 5cm/2in across.

Distribution: Japan.
Height: 25m/82ft
Shape: Broadly spreading
Deciduous
Pollinated: Wind
Leaf shape: Pinnate

Above: The nuts are borne on the tree in clusters of up to 20 in autumn.

Right: Female flowers are red upright catkins up to 10cm/4in long.

Mulberry

Morus nigra Linnaeus

King James I of England decreed in 1608 that 'every Englishman should cultivate a mulberry tree' as a way of establishing a native silk industry. Many took him at his word and dutifully planted mulberries. Unfortunately they planted the black mulberry, *M. nigra*, rather than the Chinese white mulberry, *M. alba*, and silkworms will only flourish on the white. Although not a good start for the silk industry, it did result in a land full of delicious black mulberry fruits.

Identification: Black mulberry trees often look older than they are. The orange bark takes on an ancient look early in life and trees often start to lean, or even fall over, at a young age, often growing in a prostrate position for many years. Leaves are bright green, broadly ovate, over 12cm/4¾in long and 10cm/4in wide, rough and hairy, with coarsely serrated margins. Both male and female flowers are small, green, soft, cone-like structures. They appear in early summer and are followed by raspberry-like fruits, which ripen from green to red to dark purple.

Distribution: Western Asia.
Height: 10m/33ft
Shape: Broadly spreading
Deciduous
Pollinated: Insect
Leaf shape: Ovate

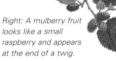

Right: A mulberry fruit looks like a small raspberry and appears at the end of a twig.

Common Fig *Ficus carica* Linnaeus
Originally from south-western Asia, this large shrub or small spreading tree is now cultivated for its fruit throughout the temperate world. It has smooth, grey bark and distinctive heavily lobed leaves. The male and female flowers, which are fertilized by wasps, are small and green and borne on separate trees. The delicious fruit is heart-shaped and green, becoming purple-brown when ripe.

Manchurian Walnut *Juglans mandshurica* Maxim.
This medium-sized tree grows wild in south-eastern Russia, north-eastern China and Korea. It can grow to heights of 20m/65ft in the wild and is occasionally seen in cultivation elsewhere in the temperate world. It has a broad spreading habit with pinnate leaves up to 60cm/24in long. The leaves are made up of as many as 17 leaflets, and each leaf can be up to 15cm/6in long. The angular nut is protected on the tree within a green pointed husk 5cm/2in long.

Paper Mulberry *Broussonetia papyrifera* (Linnaeus) Ventenat
This medium-sized, broadly spreading tree is a close relative of the true mulberries and comes from eastern Asia. The paper mulberry has attractive, coarsely-toothed, hairy, purple-green leaves, which vary in shape from ovate to rounded and are deeply lobed. The name derives from Japan, where the tree's inner bark was traditionally used to make paper.

Osage Orange

Maclura pomifera (Rafinesque) Schneider

Found primarily in wet areas alongside rivers, this tree is best known for its showy orange-like fruit. The fruit is in fact inedible and, when fresh, full of a sour milky juice. Fruits are not always present because the tree is dioecious (male and female flowers are on separate trees) and therefore both sexes are required to be in close proximity for pollination to occur.

Identification: The bark is an orange-brown colour. Branches are often twisted and when broken exude a milky sap. Leaves are a glossy rich green above and pale green beneath. They are ovate, pointed at both ends, untoothed, 10cm/4in long and 5cm/2in wide. Sometimes a sharp green spine is present at the base of the petiole. Male and female flowers are yellow-green, 1cm/½in long and produced in clusters on separate trees in early summer. The fruit is orange-like, green, ripening to yellow and up to 10cm/4in across. It is actually a cluster of smaller fruits that have fused together.

Below: The fruit of the osage orange looks remarkably like a real orange.

Distribution: Central and southern America.
Height: 15m/50ft
Shape: Broadly spreading
Deciduous
Pollinated: Insect
Leaf shape: Ovate

WING NUTS AND HICKORIES

The Juglandaceae family contains seven genera and over sixty species of tree, which grow throughout temperate regions of North America, Europe and Asia. They include some of the fastest-growing of all deciduous trees. The leaves of all species are pinnate and the flowers are all catkins. Many of these trees produce edible fruit in the form of a nut.

Caucasian Wing Nut

Pterocarya fraxinifolia (Lamarck) Spach.

The natural habitat of the Caucasian wing nut is damp woodland adjacent to rivers and marshland. It is a very fast-growing species, quite regularly achieving 3m/10ft growth in one year. Re-growth from coppiced stumps has been known to reach twice that height in a season. This tree has a habit of producing a profusion of sucker shoots around its base.

Above: The nut-like fruit has a pair of semi-circular wings.

Identification: The bark is a light grey colour, smooth in young trees and turning fissured in maturity. Leaves are pinnate, up to 60cm/24in long and made of up to 23 slightly toothed, ovate to oblong dark green leaflets, up to 15cm/6in long. Winter buds are naked, with brown hairy bud leaves, not unlike those of the wayfaring tree, *Viburnum lantana*. The flowers are small, green with red stigma, and carried in pendulous catkins up to 15cm/6in long in spring.

Distribution: Caucasus Mountains, the eastern shore of the Black Sea, southern shore of the Caspian Sea and into the northern provinces of Iran.
Height: 30m/100ft
Shape: Broadly spreading
Deciduous
Pollinated: Wind
Leaf shape: Pinnate

Left: The nuts are borne in hanging 'necklaces' (far left) up to 50cm/20in long. The flower is a pendulous catkin.

Chinese Wing Nut

Pterocarya stenoptera C. de Candolle

Native to damp woodland and riverbanks throughout China, the Chinese wing nut was first identified by the French missionary Joseph Callery in 1844 and introduced into Europe in 1860. It is easily distinguished from the Caucasian wing nut by its serrated wings on the leaf stalk in the spaces between each pair of leaflets.

Identification: This fast-growing tree has grey-brown bark, which becomes deeply fissured as it matures. The bright green, smooth leaves are pinnate, with up to 21 slightly toothed leaflets, from 10–20cm/4–8in long. The flowers are small, green and held in separate pendulous catkins, each up to 5cm/2in long. They appear on the same tree in spring. The seed is a nut, flanked by two green-pink, narrow erect wings. Seeds occur in long pendulous catkins up to 30cm/12in long, throughout the summer.

Right: The nut-like seed is winged.

Distribution: China.
Height: 25m/82ft
Shape: Broadly spreading
Deciduous
Pollinated: Wind
Leaf shape: Pinnate

Left: Flowers are hanging catkins.

Right: Nuts occur in necklace-like structures.

Pecan

Carya illinoinensis (Wangenheim) K. Koch

This tall tree is known around the world for the delicious nuts it produces. In southern USA it is extensively cultivated within orchards and is of great commercial value. The pecan grows naturally in damp soils in forests and river valleys, such as that of the Mississippi.

Identification: The bark is grey, corky and deeply fissured and ridged. The leaves are pinnate with up to 17 dark green leaflets, 15cm/ 6in long. Each leaflet has a serrated margin and curves slightly backwards at the tip. In autumn the foliage can turn a butter-yellow colour. Male flowers are yellow-green, small and clustered on pendulous catkins hanging in threes. They appear in late spring and early summer. The nut is thin-shelled and brown.

Distribution: South-east and central North America.
Height: 30m/100ft
Shape: Broadly columnar
Deciduous
Pollinated: Wind
Leaf shape: Pinnate

Left: The pecan nut grows inside a husk 5cm/2in long. Nuts are harvested in autumn.

Hybrid Wing Nut *Pterocarya* x *rehderiana* Schneider
This hybrid, raised at the Arnold Arboretum of Havard University in 1879, is more vigorous than either of its parents, *P. fraxinifolia* and *P. stenoptera*. It has pinnate leaves, with up to 21 leaflets; purple-brown, obliquely fissured bark and pendulous catkins 45cm/18in long, which contain winged seeds in summer.

Mockernut *Carya tomentosa* (Poir.) Nutt
This North American hickory, sometimes called 'big-bud hickory', is highly valued for its timber, which has several uses. Its strength and ability to withstand impact has meant it has been used for tool handles the world over. It is also used to make sports equipment, such as hockey sticks. When the wood is burnt, the fragrance it emits is used to smoke meats. The pinnate leaves give off a pleasing aroma when crushed.

Bitternut *Carya cordiformis* (Wangenheim) K. Koch
The bitternut is native to eastern North America from Canada to Florida. As the name indicates, the nuts are not eaten but were traditionally crushed to produce lamp oil. The name 'hickory' comes from the Native American word *pawcohiccora* meaning 'nut oil'.

Pignut *Carya glabra* (Mill.) Sweet
This medium-sized, North American hickory has smooth grey bark, which gradually becomes vertically fissured in old age. It has pinnate leaves comprised of five to seven smooth, sharply toothed, taper-pointed leaflets. The name comes from the fact that the nut was traditionally used as a foodstuff for pigs.

Shagbark Hickory

Carya ovata (Miller) K. Koch

Distribution: Eastern North America from Quebec to Texas.
Height: 30m/100ft
Shape: Broadly columnar
Deciduous
Pollinated: Wind
Leaf shape: Pinnate

Right: Fruit occurs at twig ends.

Below: The husk has four ridges.

Right: Leaves appear finger-like before they fill out.

This large, vigorous tree differs from other hickories in having flaking, grey-brown bark, which curls away from the trunk in long thin strips up to 30cm/12in long, but stays attached to the tree at the centre point. This gives the whole trunk a shaggy, untidy but attractive appearance.

Identification: The leaves are pinnate, with five to seven leaflets on each leaf. Each leaflet is up to 25cm/10in long, yellowish green and has a serrated edge for the top two-thirds. In autumn the leaves turn brilliant yellow. In winter, the bud scales curve away from the bud at the tip. Both the male and female flowers are small, yellowish green and borne on pendulous catkins clustered in threes in late spring. In North America, the tree produces a profusion of nuts most years. Elsewhere, crops are not so prolific. The white, sweet-tasting, kernel is contained in a green husk.

BEECHES

The Fagaceae family contains ten species of true beech, which all occur in temperate regions of the world. They can be found in Asia, North America and Europe, including Great Britain. Beeches are some of the most majestic of all deciduous trees. They typically have smooth, thin, silver-grey bark and can attain heights in excess of 40m/130ft.

Common Beech

Fagus sylvatica Linnaeus

The name 'beech' comes from the Anglo-Saxon *boc* and the Germanic word *buche*, both of which gave rise to the English word 'book'. In northern Europe early manuscripts were written on thin tablets of beech wood and bound in beech boards. Beech is widely used for hedging because it retains its dead leaves in winter, providing extra wind protection. In summer, the leaves provide good browse for livestock.

Distribution: Europe from the Pyrenees to the Caucasus and north to Russia and Denmark.
Height: 40m/130ft
Shape: Broadly spreading
Deciduous
Pollinated: Wind
Leaf shape: Ovate to obovate

Identification: The bark is silver-grey and remains smooth even in maturity. The leaves are up to 10cm/4in long and 5cm/2in wide. They have a wavy, but normally untoothed, margin and a rather blunt point at the tip. In spring, juvenile leaves have a covering of hairs and are edible, having a nutty flavour. Older leaves become tough and bitter. Beech flowers are small; female flowers are green and the male's are yellow. Both are borne in separate clusters on the same tree in spring. The fruit is an edible nut. Up to three nuts are contained within a woody husk, covered in coarse bristles.

Right: The husks open in early autumn.

Far right: Mature leaves are smooth and have a rich colour.

Dawyck Beech

Fagus sylvatica 'Dawyck'

This tree was discovered by a Mr Naesmith on the Dawyck Estate in the Tweed valley, southern Scotland, in 1860. It stood out from the rest of the beech woodland because it was shaped more like a Lombardy poplar, being tall and thin. It became an 'overnight success' with many gardeners, providing the perfect solution for those who wanted a beech tree but did not have the room.

Identification: The bark is thin and grey and looks similar to that of common beech. The tree's overall shape is very formal, appearing tall and upright, particularly when young. As Dawyck beech matures, the crown begins to take on an oval appearance. The branches and shoots are held in dense upward-thrusting sprays. The leaves are similar to those of common beech in shape but tend to be a brighter green. The winter buds are cigar-shaped and a rich red-brown colour, which, from a distance, gives the tree a distinctive red-purple hue.

Right: Dawyck beech is a variety of common beech. Its leaves are very similar to those of the species but brighter green.

Distribution: Originated in Scotland, and has been widely planted in Europe and North America.
Height: 25m/82ft
Shape: Narrowly columnar
Deciduous
Pollinated: Wind
Leaf shape: Ovate to obovate

American Beech

Fagus grandiflora Ehrhart

This tree is prolific in North America but has never been much of a success elsewhere. In Britain it never really thrives, developing into a rather shrubby-looking tree. Its one distinctive feature is that it can regenerate very easily from root suckers, particularly when coppiced, or badly damaged.

Identification: The bark is slate-grey, thin and smooth, even in old age. The glossy leaves are ovate to elliptic, up to 12cm/4¾in long and 5cm/2in wide. They are sharply toothed and taper to a pointed tip. On the underside, they are pale green with tufts of white hair along the midrib and in the vein axils beneath. Young shoots are also covered with fine hair.

There are up to 15 pairs of leaf veins as opposed to up to 10 on common beech. Male flowers are yellow; female are green. Both are small and borne in clusters on the same tree in late spring. Fruits are 2cm/¾in long bristly husks with up to three angular nuts.

Right: American beech nuts (or mast) are held in bristly husks. The leaves are a dark green colour.

Distribution: North America from Nova Scotia to Florida.
Height: 25m/82ft
Shape: Broadly spreading
Deciduous
Pollinated: Wind
Leaf shape: Ovate to elliptic

Copper Beech *Fagus sylvatica* 'Purpurea'
Neither true species, nor of garden origin, copper or purple beeches are 'sports' or 'quirks' of nature. They were first seen growing naturally near the village of Buchs, Switzerland, and in the Darney Forest in the Vosges of eastern France in the 1600s. Seed collected from common beech trees may produce one in a thousand seedlings with purple leaves. There are few finer sights than a copper beech coming into leaf in spring. The leaves are a deep vibrant purple-pink, quickly dulling to deep purple.

Oriental Beech *Fagus orientalis* Lipsky
The Oriental beech is native to the forests of the Caspian Sea, the Caucasus, Asia Minor, Bulgaria and Iran. It is similar to common beech and there is without doubt some hybridization between the two species on its western boundary. Oriental beech has larger leaves with more pairs of veining than common beech and will, in good growing conditions, develop into a larger tree.

Pendulous Beech *Fagus sylvatica* 'Pendula'
Several cultivars of common beech have weeping foliage, but 'Pendula' has to be the best. It grows into a large tree with enormous pendulous branches, which droop from the main stem rather like elephants' trunks. Where they touch the ground they sometimes take root, sending up another stem that will in turn begin to weep. Over time a large tent-like canopy can develop around the original tree. Probably the best example of this is in the grounds of the old Knap Hill nursery near Woking in Surrey, England.

Japanese Beech

Siebold's beech *Fagus crenata* Blume

This species is sometimes called Siebold's beech after the German doctor Phillip Franz von Siebold (1796–1866), who was physician to the Governor of the Dutch East India Company's Deshima trading post. It was Siebold who first identified the tree in Japan, where it forms considerable forests from sea level to 1,500m/4,921ft. It was first introduced to the West in 1892.

Identification: Similar to common beech, it differs mainly in its more obovate leaf shape and a small leaf-like structure found at the base of each seed husk in early autumn. Bark is silver-grey and smooth, even in older trees. Leaves are up to 10cm/4in long and 5cm/2in wide with a wavy, finely pubescent margin and blunt teeth. Leaf veins occur in seven to eleven pairs. The leaf stalk is 1cm/½in long. Leaves turn an 'old-gold' colour in autumn. The seed husk is 1.5cm/⅔in long and covered in long bristles.

Right: A Japanese beech leaf and mast.

Distribution: Japan.
Height: 30m/100ft
Shape: Broadly spreading
Deciduous
Pollinated: Wind
Leaf shape: Ovate to obovate

FALSE BEECHES

This relatively little known group of trees is from temperate regions of the Southern Hemisphere, and is known by the botanical genus Nothofagus. Nothos *comes from the ancient Greek for 'spurious' or 'false' and* fagus *means 'beech'; so the name can be translated as 'false beeches'. Although these trees are similar to beech there are some differences. Many* Nothofagus *are evergreen and have smaller leaves.*

Antarctic Beech

Nothofagus Antarctica (J. G. Forster) Oersted

A fast growing small to medium-sized tree that is extremely elegant, especially when young. It has leaves that, when crushed, or on hot days, emit a sweet, honey-like fragrance. Also known as *nirre* in Chile, it inhabits mountainsides from Cape Horn to northern Chile. In autumn, the leaves turn into a range of glorious colours from scarlet, through orange to butter yellow.

Identification: The bark is dark grey, becoming scaly in maturity. The leaves are up to 4cm/1½in long, broadly ovate, rounded at the tip and finely toothed around the margin. They are set in two neat rows along the shoot and have a crinkly, shell-like appearance. Flowers are small and pendulous, produced in late spring, the male borne singly or in twos or threes in the leaf axils. The fruit is a four-valved husk approximately 5mm/¼in long, each valve containing three nuts.

Distribution: South America: southern Argentina and Chile.
Height: 15m/50ft
Shape: Broadly columnar
Deciduous
Pollinated: Insect
Leaf shape: Ovate

*Left: A flower and fruit.
Right: Leaves are finely toothed.*

Rauli

Raoul *Nothofagus nervosa* (Poeppig & Endlicher) Oersted

Also known as *N. procera*, this large, deciduous forest tree has upswept branching and heavily veined leaves. The name was given by early Spanish settlers who saw its grey, smooth bark and called it after the Spanish word for beech. It is a fast-growing tree, which produces quality timber and is being planted in temperate regions of the Northern Hemisphere for forestry.

Identification: The bark is dark grey and becomes heavily fissured as the tree matures. The leaves are ovate to oblong, up to 10cm/4in long and 5cm/2in across. They are easily distinguished from other *Nothofagus* because they have 14–18 pairs of deep veins, but could at first glance be mistaken for hornbeam. Leaves are positioned alternately along the shoot; they are bronze-green above and paler beneath, with some pubescence on the midrib and veins. The fruit is a four-valved husk about 1cm/½in long, containing three small nuts.

Distribution: Central Chile and western Argentina.
Height: 25m/82ft
Shape: Broadly conical
Deciduous
Pollinated: Insect
Leaf shape: Oblong to ovate

Left and right: The long, elegant leaves hang heavily. Unlike those of other members of this genus, they have up to 18 pairs of deep veins.

Myrtle Tree

Nothofagus cunninghamii (Hooker f.) Oersted

This Australasian tree, thousands of miles away from the majority of the *Nothofagus* genus in South America, shows how at one time the continents of Australasia and South America were all part of the vast supercontinent of Gondwanaland. It is a rare, medium-sized tree which takes its scientific name from James Cunningham, a Scottish surgeon and amateur botanist who worked for the English East India Company.

Distribution: Tasmania and Victoria, Australia.
Height: 30m/100ft
Shape: Broadly columnar
Evergreen
Pollinated: Insect
Leaf shape: Deltoid

Identification: The bark is dark grey, smooth when young, becoming scaly and developing vertical fissures in old age. The leaves are dark, glossy green, only 5mm/¼in long, bluntly toothed around the upper margin with a short pubescent petiole. They are densely borne on wiry shoots, which are covered in short, dark hair. The male flowers are green and tiny and borne singly in the leaf axils. The fruit is a four-valve husk covered in dense bristles and containing three nuts, the centre one being virtually flat.

Right: Myrtle has numerous, tiny leaves, each triangular to almost diamond shaped.

Dombey's Southern Beech
Nothofagus dombeyi (Mirbel) Blume
Native of Chile and Argentina and introduced into Europe in 1916, this vigorous, evergreen tree is one of the most elegant of all South American temperate trees. In maturity it resembles the form of an old cedar and as a juvenile its dark, glossy green leaves in combination with bright red male flowers make it a real show-stopper.

Roble Beech *Nothofagus obliqua* (Mirbel) Blume
Roble is Spanish for 'oak' and in some respects this large Chilean tree does resemble a European deciduous oak. It has grey bark, which becomes cracked and fissured with age, is broadly columnar, attaining heights around 30m/100ft and has dark green, lobed leaves up to 7.5cm/3in long. The leaves are arranged alternately on the shoot.

Black Beech *Nothofagus solandri*
(J. D. Hooker) Oersted
Black beech is native to lowland and mountain regions in both the North and South Islands of New Zealand. It is a tall, slender, evergreen tree growing to 25m/82ft in the wild. It has small, elliptic, dark green leaves, heavily pubescent beneath, which are densely borne on wiry shoots, which develop into ascending fan-like branches.

Silver Beech *Nothofagus menziesii*
(Hooker f.) Oersted
Native to both islands of New Zealand, where it grows up to 1,000m/3,280ft above sea level, this evergreen tree reaches 30m/100ft in height. It has a silvery white trunk, which dulls to grey in maturity. Leaves are ovate to diamond shaped, doubly round toothed and 1cm/½in long. Both the petiole and the shoot are covered in a yellowish brown pubescence.

Red Beech

Nothofagus fusca (Hooker f.) Oersted

This beautiful evergreen tree is native to both islands of New Zealand from 37 degrees latitude southwards. It reaches large proportions in the wild but in cultivation, in the Northern Hemisphere, seldom attains more than 25m/82ft in height. It is quite tender when young, being prone to frost damage, but becomes hardier with age.

Distribution: North and South Island, New Zealand.
Height: 30m/100ft
Shape: Broadly spreading
Evergreen
Pollinated: Insect
Leaf shape: Ovate to round

Identification: The bark of red beech is smooth and dark grey when young, becoming flaky with lighter patches in maturity. The leaves are very distinctive because of their deep, sharply toothed margin. At 4cm/1½in long they are also bigger than those of any other evergreen *Nothofagus*. They have long leaf veins, normally in three to four pairs. Although evergreen, before the old leaves eventually fall, they turn a coppery red colour, hence the common name. The leaf-stalk is covered in grey-brown pubescence. The fruit is a four-lobed husk containing three nuts.

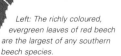

Left: The richly coloured, evergreen leaves of red beech are the largest of any southern beech species.

CHESTNUTS

The chestnut genus Castanea *contains just twelve deciduous trees, all of which grow wild in temperate regions of the Northern Hemisphere. They are closely related to both the beech,* Fagus, *and oak,* Quercus, *genera. The majority are long-lived, large trees, which are drought resistant and thrive on dry, shallow soils. They all have strongly serrated leaves and edible fruit in the form of a nut.*

American Chestnut

Castanea dentata (Marshall) Borkhausen

This majestic tree was once widespread throughout North America, but since the 1930s its population has been devastated by the effects of chestnut blight, *Endothia parasitca*. Today it is rare in the wild, with the species likely to become endangered in the next 20 years. The disease entered North America from East Asia at the end of the 19th century.

Distribution: Eastern North America.
Height: 30m/100ft
Shape: Broadly columnar
Deciduous
Pollinated: Insect
Leaf shape: Oblong

Identification: The trunk and form of American chestnut is similar to that of sweet chestnut; it has dark grey-brown bark, which becomes spirally fissured with age. Both male and female flowers are found in the same yellow, upright catkin. Catkins are up to 20cm/8in long and ripen in early summer. Fruit is a spiny green (ripening to yellow) husk, up to 6cm/2½in across.

Right: The oblong leaves are up to 25cm/10in long and have a margin that is edged with sharp-toothed serrations. The nuts can be eaten.

Sweet Chestnut

Spanish chestnut *Castanea sativa* Miller

This fast-growing ornamental tree is native to warm, temperate regions around the Mediterranean and on into south-western Asia. It has been widely cultivated elsewhere, often introduced by the Romans, who valued the tree as a source of food for themselves and their animal stock.

Identification: As a young tree the bark is smooth and grey. Older trees develop spiral fissures, which immediately distinguish the tree from oak. The leaves are oblong, up to 20cm/8in long, sharply pointed at the tip and rounded at the base. The leaf margin is edged with coarse teeth, each tooth linking to a strong vein running back to the midrib. Each catkin may be up to 25cm/10in long. The fruit is a spiny greenish yellow husk, up to 6cm/2½in across, with up to three edible brown nuts.

Distribution: Southern Europe, North Africa and south-west Asia.
Height: 30m/100ft
Shape: Broadly columnar
Deciduous
Pollinated: Insect
Leaf shape: Oblong

Above left: The male and female flowers are borne on the same upright yellow catkin in summer, making it one of the last trees to come into flower.

Left and right: The chestnuts ripen in autumn.

Chinquapin *Castanea pumila* (Linnaeus) Miller
This deciduous small tree, or large shrub, is native to the eastern and southern United States and very rare in cultivation elsewhere. It is distinguished from other chestnuts because it throws up suckers from the root system. Quite often these will result in a dense thicket around the base of the tree. Both the shoots and the underside of the leaves are covered with a white-grey pubescence. Leaves are oblong, coarsely toothed and up to 12cm/4¾in long. Fruit is an egg-shaped nut up to 2.5cm/1in long.

Castanopsis cuspidata (Thunb.) Schottky
This is a large, elegant evergreen tree in its native homeland of southern Japan, China and Korea. In cultivation elsewhere, it seldom becomes more than a small, bushy tree. Leaves are oval in shape, glossy, dark green and leathery. The fruit is an acorn, borne on a stalk with up to ten others, all encased within rows of downy scales.

Japanese Chestnut *Castanea crenata*
Siebold & Zuccarini
This small tree is native only to Japan but is cultivated elsewhere in botanic gardens and arboreta. It was first introduced into Europe in

1895. In Japan it is a valuable food source and the tree is grown in orchards for its edible nuts, which are slightly smaller than those of *C. sativa*, but produced in greater profusion.

Golden Chestnut

Golden chinkapin *Chrysolepis chrysophylla* (W. J. Hooker) Hjelmqvist

This evergreen tree is quite often referred to as the golden chinkapin and botanically as *Castanopsis chrysophylla* – this is incorrect because the flowers on *Castanopsis* are borne on separate catkins, whereas on this tree they are on the same catkin. The name 'golden' refers to the underside of the leaf, which is covered with a bright golden pubescence, a feature that quickly distinguishes it from just about any other member of the Fagaceae family.

Identification: The bark is grey, smooth when young, becoming fissured in old age. Leaves are evergreen, lanceolate to oblong, broad in the centre tapering to a point at each end, up to 10cm/4in long and 2.5cm/1in wide. Glossy dark, almost black-green above and with a rich golden pubescence beneath, they are held on a green petiole 1cm/½in long. Both male and female flowers are fragrant, creamy-yellow and borne on the same erect, 4cm/1½in-long catkin in summer.

Distribution: USA: Oregon and California.
Height: 30m/100ft
Shape: Broadly conical
Evergreen
Pollinated: Insect
Leaf shape: Lanceolate to oblong

Below: The fruit is a spiny husk, very similar to sweet chestnut, containing up to three glossy brown nuts.

Tanbark Oak

Lithocarpus densiflorus (Hooker & Arnold) Rehd.

This evergreen tree is closely related to an oak, but several of the characteristics relating to its flowers are very different from oak. It is native to California and Oregon, where it grows into a pyramidal-shaped tree up to 25m/82ft tall. The leaves are sharply toothed, dark glossy green above and covered with white pubescence beneath. Fruit is an acorn, 2.5cm/1in long, set in a shallow, pubescent cup with reflexed scales.

Identification: This tender, small tree has smooth grey-brown bark which becomes uniformly fissured with age. The bark is an excellent source of tannin. It has stiff leathery leaves. Both the underside of the leaf and the young shoots are covered with thick grey-white wool. Both the male and female flowers are creamy yellow and small. They are held in erect, thin spikes, up to 10cm/4in long, in May.

Distribution: USA: Oregon and California.
Height: 25m/82ft
Shape: Broadly pyramidal
Evergreen
Pollinated: Insect
Leaf shape: Oval to oblong

Left: Both male and female flowers are long, upright spikes.

Right: The fruit is a small pointed acorn, in a shallow cup.

AMERICAN OAKS

There are almost 600 different species of oak, Quercus, *in the world, the majority of which grow in the Northern Hemisphere. Almost 80 of these grow in North America and at least 60 are large trees. There are oaks native to every region of the North American continent from Alaska to New Mexico. Some play an integral part in the leaf-colour spectacle every autumn in New England.*

Swamp White Oak

Quercus bicolor Willd

Distribution: Eastern North America from Quebec to Missouri.
Height: 25m/82ft
Shape: Broadly columnar
Deciduous
Pollinated: Wind
Leaf shape: Obovate

The swamp white oak is a medium-sized deciduous tree. It has loose, scaly bark, particularly when young, which gives the trunk a shaggy appearance. As its common name suggests, swamp white oak grows best in deep, damp soils and alongside rivers. The species name *bicolor* refers to the fact that the leaf has two different colours.

Identification: The overall shape of swamp white oak varies from rounded to narrowly columnar. The lower branches tend to hang, producing a weeping effect. The leaves are obovate, becoming broader towards the tip, up to 15cm/6in long and 8cm/3in wide. They are tapered at the base, with six to eight shallow lobes on each side. The upper surface of the leaf is glossy dark green, the underside is silvery grey and covered in soft down. Leaf veins, midrib and petiole are all greeny yellow. In autumn the leaves turn red and gold before falling. The fruit is an oval-shaped acorn, up to 2.5cm/1in long, half enclosed in a scaly cup.

Right: The leaves and fruit give the tree away as an oak immediately.

Red Oak *Quercus rubra* Linnaeus
The red oak is one of the largest and most widespread deciduous trees in eastern North America. It is found growing naturally from Nova Scotia to North Carolina and, like scarlet oak, *Q. coccinia*, is an important player in the autumn leaf-colour scene of New England. It has similar deeply cut leaves to scarlet oak, but they are not so glossy on the upper leaf surface.

Pin Oak *Quercus palustris* Munchhausen
Native to eastern and central North America, this is one of the tallest American oaks; some specimens are known to have exceeded 50m/165ft in height. Pin oak grows naturally in wet, swampy ground and can withstand flooding better than any other oak. The name 'pin' refers to the profusion of short side shoots that cover the lower part of the crown. The leaves are even more deeply cut than those of scarlet oak, *Q. coccinea*.

Swamp Chestnut Oak *Quercus michauxii* Munchhausen
This wetland oak has several other names including 'cow oak', because the acorns were used by early colonial settlers as food for

their cattle, and 'basket oak', because thin strips of its wood were used to make baskets for transporting cotton from the cotton fields. It is native to eastern American river valleys and flood plains from New Jersey to Florida. The deciduous leaves are shaped like chestnut leaves but are more elliptical with softer serrations.

Shingle Oak *Quercus imbricaria* A. Michaux
Shingle oak is native to central and eastern USA from Pennsylvania to North Carolina. The name refers to the fact that early colonial settlers made roofing shingles from its wood. Shingle oak has deciduous oblong to lanceolate, untoothed leaves, up to 15cm/6in long with a wavy margin. The flat acorn cup is covered with overlapping woody scales.

White Oak *Quercus alba* Linnaeus
One of the most popular and commercially important US trees, the white oak is the state tree of Maryland, Illinois and Connecticut. Its timber has long been regarded as one of the stalwarts of the United States Forest Service. It was traditionally called the 'stave oak' because its timber was used to make the staves of barrels.

Scarlet Oak

Quercus coccinea Munchhausen

Scarlet oak is one of the most ornamental trees of eastern North America, contributing greatly to the autumn leaf-colour spectacular. The leaves stay on the trees far longer than those of any of the other autumn-colour trees. It grows on poor sandy soils up to elevations of 1,520m/5,000ft in the Appalachian Mountains. It does not grow well in shade.

Distribution: Eastern North America from Ontario to Missouri, but not Florida.
Height: 25m/82ft
Shape: Broadly spreading
Deciduous
Pollinated: Wind
Leaf shape: Elliptic

Identification: The bark is slate grey and smooth, becoming slightly fissured in maturity. Although the leaves are roughly elliptical in shape they are eaten into by several angular lobes, some cutting almost to the midrib. Each lobe point is tipped with a sharp bristle. The upper leaf surface is dark green and glossy, the underside is pale green with tufts of pubescence in the vein axils. Male flowers are borne in yellow, drooping catkins in late spring, the female flowers are inconspicuous, but borne on the same tree. The acorn is 2–3cm/1in long. Half of it enclosed in a deep, shiny cup. Although very often confused with red oak, *Q. rubra*, scarlet oak is altogether a narrower and more open tree, with a rounder and deeper acorn cup.

Left: The leaves, which have a very ragged appearance for an oak, stay on the tree later than its relatives.

Willow Oak

Quercus phellos Linnaeus

This oak is easily recognized by its willow-like leaves. It prefers to grow in moist, swampy soils but will tolerate drier conditions. It is widely planted throughout America as a street tree in urban areas. It was first introduced into Europe in the year 1723, although it has never been widely cultivated outside America. Willow oak grows into a broad, open tree.

Identification: The bark is smooth light grey when young, maturing to a rather ridged bark, which cracks into irregular plates. The deciduous leaves are narrow and willow-like, up to 10cm/4in long and 2.5cm/1in across. They are sage green above and paler beneath, untoothed but with a wavy margin ending in a fine point. New leaves are yellow as they emerge from the bud. The male flowers are borne on greeny yellow weeping catkins; the female flowers are inconspicuous but borne separately on the same tree in spring. The acorns are small, the size of a large redcurrant, almost round and held in a shallow, flat cup, which encloses only a quarter of the acorn.

Distribution: Eastern USA to northern Florida.
Height: 30m/100ft
Shape: Broadly spreading
Deciduous
Pollinated: Wind
Leaf shape: Narrowly oblong to lanceolate

Below: The long, hanging leaves look more like those of willow than oak, hence the tree's name. The acorn, however, is typically oak-like in appearance.

EUROPEAN AND ASIAN OAKS

The oaks of Europe and Asia are on the whole slower growing and have less dazzling autumn leaf colour than their American cousins, but what they lose in terms of vibrancy and vigour, they more than make up for in diversity and longevity. Several important European oaks are evergreen and some have clearly hybridized, as with the two British oaks, Quercus robur *and* Q. petraea.

English Oak

Common oak *Quercus robur* Linnaeus

Distribution: All of Europe from Ireland to the Caucasus and north to Scandinavia.
Height: 35m/115ft
Shape: Broadly spreading
Deciduous
Pollinated: Wind
Leaf shape: Elliptic to obovate

This majestic tree is one of the most familiar arboreal sights across Europe. It is usually a lowland species, growing best on damp, rich, well-drained soils. It is a long-lived tree, with many recorded veterans over 1,000 years old. In the United Kingdom it has hybridized with the sessile oak, *Q. petraea*, which is dominant in upland areas.

Identification: The bark is pale grey and smooth when young, quickly developing regular vertical fissures. The leaves are mainly obovate, up to 10cm/4in long and 8cm/3in wide and either have no stalk or are on short stalks. The leaf margin is cut into three to six rounded lobes on each side, tapering towards the base where there are normally two smaller lobes. The upper surface is dark green, the underside glaucous. An acorn is up to 4cm/1½in long, one-third of which is in a cup which is attached to the shoot by a long, slender stalk up to 10cm/4in long.

Right: The male flowers are long catkins and appear in late spring.

Chestnut-leaved Oak

Quercus castaneifolia C. A. Meyer

Distribution: Caucasus Mountains into northern Iran.
Height: 30m/100ft
Shape: Broadly spreading
Deciduous
Pollinated: Wind
Leaf shape: Oblong

This wide-spreading, handsome tree resembles the Turkey oak, *Q. cerris*, in general appearance. Given its beauty, it is surprisingly rare in cultivation outside its native region. It was introduced into western Europe in 1846, and a splendid specimen can be seen at the Royal Botanic Gardens at Kew in London.

Identification: The bark is grey and smooth, similar to sweet chestnut, *Castanea sativa*, when young, becoming fissured into irregular small plates in maturity. The main stem is to branch low down and to continue to fork after this. Leaves are chestnut-like, oblong, up to 20cm/8in long with six to twelve prominent leaf veins ending in sharp, forward-pointing teeth. They are glossy dark green above and pale green-blue and slightly pubescent beneath. Male flowers appear in spring on long, drooping greeny yellow catkins. The acorn is 2.5cm/1in long, one half of which is enclosed within a 'bristly' cup with recurved woody scales.

Right: The slender catkins appear in spring, when the long, pointed leaves are still fresh and light green in colour.

Right: Acorns mature on the tree in autumn, before the leaves fall.

Cork Oak

Quercus suber Linnaeus

This medium-sized evergreen tree has thick, corky bark and for centuries it has been used to make cork products such as stoppers for wine bottles. Cork oak is cultivated in orchards, particularly in Portugal and Spain, and the outer bark is stripped from the tree on a rotation of 8–10 years. Removed carefully, this does no damage to the living tissue beneath the bark and some trees are known to be over 300 years old.

Identification: The obvious distinguishing feature of this tree is its pale grey, prominently creviced, corky bark. The leaves are similar to those of holm oak, *Q. ilex*, although far more variable. They may be anything from oblong to oval in shape, up to 8cm/3in long, normally with an entire margin or with occasional serration. They are dark, glossy green on top and covered with a grey pubescence underneath. Although the tree is evergreen, the older leaves are shed and replaced in early summer. Acorns are up to 3cm/1¼in long, glossy brown and half encased in the cup.

Distribution: Western Mediterranean and southern European Atlantic coast.
Height: 20m/66ft
Shape: Broadly spreading
Evergreen
Pollinated: Wind
Leaf shape: Ovate to oblong

Right: The distinctive thick bark.

Below: The male flower is carried on a weeping yellow catkin in spring.

Above: The leaves are up to 8cm/3in long. Acorns are quite slender and pointed at the tip.

Turkey Oak *Quercus cerris* Linnaeus
Turkey oak is a tall, vigorous, deciduous tree with a straight stem and deeply fissured, grey-brown bark. It is native to central and southern Europe, although its exact range is unknown because it has been planted across the rest of Europe for centuries and naturalizes easily. The elliptic leaves are up to 10cm/4in long, with irregular lobing, particularly on young trees. Acorn cups are covered in whiskers.

Hungarian Oak *Quercus frainetto* Tenore
This large, distinctive deciduous tree is native to south-eastern Europe. It has beautiful, deep green, shiny, but slightly rough, irregular shaped leaves with many forward-pointing lobes. The leaves can be up to 20cm/8in long and 10cm/4in across, tapering towards the base.

Algerian Oak *Quercus canariensis* Willdenow
Also known as Mirbeck oak, this handsome tree is native to North Africa and south-western Europe. It also survives well further north, where it is regularly planted in gardens. Although not strictly evergreen, most of its neatly lobed leaves stay on the tree in winter.

Holm Oak *Quercus ilex* Linnaeus
This domed, densely branched oak tree is one of the most important trees for shelter in coastal areas throughout Europe. In the wild it grows from sea level to altitudes above 1,520m/5,000ft in Italy, France and Spain. The bark is charcoal grey, smooth at first but quickly developing shallow fissures, which crack into small and irregular plates. In more mature trees the narrow evergreen leaf normally has an entire margin with no serrations.

Caucasian Oak *Quercus macranthera* Fischer & C. A. Meyer
This handsome, medium-sized to large, rounded, deciduous tree is native to the Caucasus Mountains and northern Iran, south of the Caspian Sea. It has strongly ascending branches and verdant foliage. The leaves are large, and can be up to 15cm/6in long and 10cm/4in wide. They taper towards the base, with up to eleven rounded, forward-pointing lobes on each side.

BIRCHES

The birches, Betula, *are a group of catkin-bearing, alternate-leaved, deciduous trees, native to northern temperate regions of the world. There are more than 60 species in total, spread right across the region, from Japan to Spain and across North America. They are particularly well known for their attractive bark, which, depending on species, can vary from pure white to red.*

Yellow Birch

Betula alleghaniensis Britton

Distribution: Eastern North America.
Height: 30m/100ft
Shape: Broadly columnar
Deciduous
Pollinated: Wind
Leaf shape: Ovate to oblong

Previously known as *B. lutea*, this large, handsome birch has long been a valued timber tree to the US Forest Service. The name is well chosen, for this tree has several yellow characteristics, including the bark. It has been widely planted as an ornamental species elsewhere in the temperate world.

Identification: The bark is yellowish brown, peeling in horizontal flakes to reveal more vibrant, yellow-coloured bark beneath. The leaves are ovate-oblong, up to 10cm/4in long and 5cm/2in across, finely toothed along the margin, tapering to a point, grass green above, paler beneath. In autumn they turn a golden yellow colour. The male flowers are borne in drooping yellow catkins, 10cm/4in long; female flowers are borne in shorter, red-brown erect catkins.

Above: Male and female flowers occur on the same tree.

Below: Fruit.

Silver Birch

Betula pendula Roth.

Silver birch is one of the toughest of all trees, able to withstand intense cold and long periods of drought. It seeds prolifically and will quickly establish on cleared ground. Birch was one of the first trees to colonize northern Europe after the last ice age 12,000 years ago. It is just as much at home in semi-tundra regions of northern Scandinavia as it is in temperate southern France.

Distribution: All Europe from the Atlantic to the Pacific and south into northern Asia.
Height: 30m/100ft
Shape: Narrowly weeping
Deciduous
Pollinated: Wind
Leaf shape: Ovate to triangular

Identification: Bark is a distinctive white to silver colour. Mature trees develop corky black fissures between white irregular plates. Leaves are almost triangular in shape, 6cm/2½in long and 4cm/1½in across. The margin is coarsely serrated, tapering to a fine point. The leaves are glossy grass green above and paler beneath, normally turning butter-yellow before falling in autumn. The leaf stalk is normally red-brown, 2.5cm/1in long and attached to a slim, hairless, rather warty weeping shoot. Both male and female flowers are catkins, appearing separately on the same tree in early spring. The male flower is yellow and drooping, up to 6cm/2½in long; the female flower is green, erect and much smaller.

Above: Silver birch is often planted ornamentally for its distinctive bark.

Right: The catkins are thick and the leaves strongly serrated.

Himalayan Birch

Betula utilis D. Don

The exact distribution of the Himalayan birch is difficult to define because several other Asiatic birches occur in the same region and cross-pollination and hybridization do occur. At one stage Chinese red-barked birch, *B. albo-sinensis*, was considered to be a form of Himalayan birch and not a separate species. The colour of Himalayan birch bark varies from white in the west of its natural range to pink-brown or orange-red in the east. The tree grows up to elevations in excess of 4,250m/14,000ft in the Himalayan foothills.

Distribution: Himalayas from Kashmir to Sikkim and on into western and central China.
Height: 25m/82ft
Shape: Broadly conical
Deciduous
Pollinated: Wind
Leaf shape: Ovate

Identification: The variable coloured bark is paper thin and peels off in long ribbon-like, horizontal strips. The taper-pointed, serrated leaves are ovate, up to 10cm/4in long and 6cm/2½in wide. They have strong veining with up to 12 pairs of parallel veins, each vein ending in a sharp tooth. Leaf colour is dark shiny green above and paler beneath, with some pubescence on the midrib. Leaves are attached to pubescent shoots by a short leaf stalk, 1.25cm/½in long. Flowers are catkins: male long, yellow and drooping, up to 12cm/5in; female smaller, green and upright. Both flowers are borne on the same tree in early spring.

Right: Male catkins are long and yellow. Left: Leaves are almost teardrop shaped.

River Birch *Betula nigra* Linnaeus
Native to North America from New Hampshire to Florida, where it grows on river banks and low-lying swampy ground, this tree has ovate, toothed leaves up to 10cm/4in long and peeling, pink-brown bark, which becomes fissured in maturity. River birch regenerates well from the stump and is often coppiced to encourage multiple stems, displaying this peeling effect.

Canoe Birch *Betula papyrifera* Marshall
Known as the paper birch, this creamy white-barked large birch occurs right across northern North America from coast to coast. Native Americans used the timber for canoes. It is an extremely hardy tree growing as far north as Alaska and Labrador. It has ovate, toothed leaves that turn orange-yellow in autumn.

Cherry Birch *Betula lenta* Linnaeus
Native to North America from Quebec to Alabama, this large birch has deep red-brown bark marked by distinctive horizontal bands of pale lenticels. It is also known as black birch or sweet birch. The latter name refers to the sweet fragrance given off by the leaves when crushed. Wintergreen oil was once distilled from the wood.

Dwarf Birch *Betula nana* Linnaeus
This smallest of all birches is native to northern temperate regions, from Alaska and through Scandinavia to Siberia. It is extremely hardy and able to withstand low temperatures and prolonged periods of frozen ground. It seldom reaches more than 5m/16½ft tall and has small, sage-green, almost round leaves, up to 1.5cm/⅔in across.

Chinese Red-barked Birch

Betula albo-sinensis Burkill

This beautiful, medium-sized birch is best known for its attractive coppery to orange-red bark on both the trunk and branches, which peels to reveal cream-pink bark beneath. It grows high in the mountains in mixed woodland on relatively impoverished, shallow soils. It was first introduced into Europe in 1901 by the English plant collector Ernest Wilson and has been a favourite for planting in gardens and arboreta ever since.

Distribution: Western China.
Height: 25m/82ft
Shape: Broadly conical
Deciduous
Pollinated: Wind
Leaf shape: Ovate

Identification: The leaves are ovate, 8cm/3in long and 4cm/1½in across. The margin is cut by forward pointing, sharp serrations and the leaf ends in a long, fine, slightly curved tip. When the leaves emerge from a small, slightly sticky bud, they are covered with a soft down. This quickly disappears to reveal a glossy grass-green leaf, which turns a golden yellow colour in autumn before falling. Both male and female flowers are catkins, very similar to those of Himalayan birch. Fertilized female flowers develop into brown papery catkins containing hundreds of winged seeds.

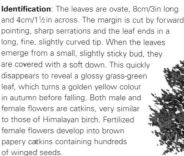

Right: Male and female flowers are produced in catkins on the same tree.

ALDERS, HAZELS AND HORNBEAMS

Alders are a group of 36 species of deciduous trees within the Betulaceae family. They are native primarily to northern temperate regions of the world, where they grow in damp conditions, quite often alongside rivers and watercourses. Hornbeams are also members of the Betulaceae family, as are the hazels. All of these trees produce male and female flowers in the form of catkins.

Common Alder

Alnus glutinosa (Linnaeus) Gaertner

Since the dawn of history this tree has been associated with water. It thrives in damp, waterlogged conditions close to rivers and marshy ground, where it creates its own oxygen supply. Alder timber is waterproof and has been used to make everything from boats to water pipes. It also forms the foundations of many of the buildings in Venice and is used to make wooden clogs.

Identification: The bark is dark grey-brown and fissured from an early age. The leaves are obovate to orbicular, finely toothed with up to ten pairs of pronounced leaf veins and a strong central midrib. Up to 10cm/4in long and 8cm/3in wide, they are dark green and shiny above and pale grey-green beneath, with tufts of pubescence in the leaf axils. Both male and female flowers are catkins: the male is greenish yellow, drooping and up to 10cm/4in long; the female is a much smaller, red, upright catkin which, after fertilization, ripens into a distinctive small brown cone. Spent cones persist right through to the following spring.

Distribution: Whole of Europe into western Asia and south to North Africa.
Height: 25m/82ft
Shape: Broadly conical
Deciduous
Pollinated: Wind
Leaf shape: Obovate

Left: Catkins appear in early spring, before the leaves open. Alder cones begin to grow in summer, by which time the rounded leaves are thick on the branches.

Hornbeam

Carpinus betulus Linnaeus

Distribution: Central Europe, including southern Britain to south-west Asia.
Height: 30m/100ft
Shape: Broadly spreading
Deciduous
Pollinated: Wind
Leaf shape: Ovate

Left: The fruit is a ribbed nut which is held in a three-lobed bract.

Hornbeam is sometimes confused with beech because of its silver-grey bark and similar leaf. However, hornbeam bark is far more angular than beech bark. Hornbeam leaves also have obvious serrations around the margin, which are not present on beech. Hornbeam timber is dense and hard and has a clean white, crisp appearance. It was traditionally used for ox yokes and butchers' chopping blocks.

Identification: The leaves are oval to ovate, up to 10cm/4in long and 5cm/2in across, double-toothed around the margin and tapering to a long point. There are normally between 10 and 13 pairs of leaf veins. The upper leaf surface of the leaves is dark green, the underside a paler green. In autumn the leaf turns a rich yellow colour before falling. Both catkins are borne separately in spring on the same tree. The fruit is a distinctive three-lobed bract with a small, ribbed, brown nut at the base of the centre bract. The bract is green in summer, ripening to fawn in autumn and persisting on the tree through to the following spring.

Right: Male catkins are up to 5cm/2in long. Female catkins (not shown) are much smaller.

Hop Hornbeam

Ostrya carpinifolia Scopoli

This distinctive ornamental tree is primarily known for its hop-like fruit which, when ripe, hangs in clusters of buff-coloured, overlapping papery scales, enclosing a small brown nut. Mature trees have long, low, horizontal branches, which seem to defy gravity.

Identification: The bark of hop hornbeam is smooth and brown-grey when young, becoming flaky, rather like Persian ironwood, in maturity. The ovate to oblong leaves are up to 10cm/4in long and 5cm/2in across. They are sharply pointed and have forward-pointing double teeth around the margin. They are dark green above and paler beneath, with slight pubescence on both sides. Each leaf has between 12 and 15 pairs of parallel leaf veins and a pronounced midrib. Flowers are catkins: the male yellow, drooping and up to 10cm/4in long; the female much smaller and green. The overall shape in maturity is broadly spreading, the width quite often exceeding the height.

Distribution: Southern Europe to Iran.
Height: 20m/66ft
Shape: Broadly spreading
Deciduous
Pollinated: Wind
Leaf shape: Ovate

Left and above: The hop-like fruit develops in summer from long, drooping catkins.

Red Alder *Alnus rubra* Bongard
This pioneer species is native to the west coast of North America, where it grows on just about every available space not already colonized by other species. Although not a big tree, it grows particularly fast until it reaches its optimum height of 15m/50ft. Red alder has light brown-grey bark, which is rough and warty, and an ovate leaf up to 10cm/4in long with rusty-red pubescence on the underside.

Grey Alder *Alnus incana* (Linnaeus) Moench
Native to the Caucasus Mountains of central Europe, this medium-sized tree grows up to elevations of 1,000m/3,280ft. It gets its name from the dense covering of grey hairs on the underside of the leaf. The leaves are ovate, up to 10cm/4in long, double toothed and have a pointed tip. The bark is dark grey and smooth even in maturity.

Sitka Alder *Alnus sinuate* (Reg.) Rydb.
This small, hardy tree is native to western North America from Alaska to California. It grows well at high altitudes and can withstand intense cold and frost. Sitka alder has distinctive yellow male catkins, which can be up to 15cm/6in long and are borne in great profusion in early spring.

Italian Alder *Alnus cordata* Desfontaines
This handsome, broadly conical tree originates from southern Italy and Corsica, where it grows at up to 1,000m/3,280ft on dry mountain slopes. It is by far the largest of the alders, easily reaching heights in excess of 30m/100ft. Italian alder has large obovate, glossy, dark green leaves, each up to 10cm/4in across.

Common Hazel

Corylus avellana Linnaeus

There is much discussion as to whether hazel is a tree or a shrub. In theory a tree should have 1m/3ft of clear stem before it branches or forks and have the potential to grow to more than 6m/20ft in height. Hazel can certainly achieve the latter, but has a tendency to fork low down. This impression is not helped by the fact that for centuries, right across Europe, hazel has been regularly coppiced to ground level. Its ability to regrow after harsh pruning has made it a popular plant for agricultural hedging.

Identification: The bark is smooth and silver-grey to pale brown, even in maturity. The trunk seldom exceeds 20cm/8in in diameter. The leaves are up to 10cm/4in across, with double teeth around the margin. They are thick and rough to the touch, with coarse pubescence on the leaf, bud and shoot. The male flower is a long, yellow catkin, up to 10cm/4in long, which ripens in early spring to release copious amounts of pollen to the wind. The female flower is a tiny red floret borne on the end of what are seemingly leaf buds. The fruit is a round to ovoid, matt light brown, edible nut that is half encased in a green calyx.

Right: Hazel catkins are a familiar sight across Britain and Europe in early spring.

Distribution: Europe into western Asia and North Africa.
Height: 15m/50ft
Shape: Broadly spreading
Deciduous
Pollinated: Wind
Leaf shape: Orbicular

Left: Hazel leaves are almost round in shape. This plant produces the popular hazelnut.

LIMES

There are about 45 different species of lime within the Tilia genus. They are all deciduous and all found in northern temperate regions. Limes are handsome trees, many growing into large, ornamental specimens. Several have been used for urban tree planting, as they respond well to pollarding and hard pruning in street situations. Limes look good planted in avenues and within formal vistas.

Oliver's Lime

Chinese white lime *Tilia oliveri* Szysz

This splendid tree with beautiful foliage grows naturally in the moist lowland woodlands of central China. It was first discovered by the Irish physician Augustine Henry in 1888 and was introduced into Europe by the English plantsman Ernest Wilson in 1900. It is rare in cultivation.

Identification: The bark is similar to beech, being light silver-grey and smooth even in maturity. The overall shape of the tree tends to be spreading, owing to large horizontal lower branches. By far the most attractive feature of Oliver's lime is the leaves, which are smooth above and covered with pure white hairs beneath. A slight breeze will cause the leaves to flutter in the wind, creating a shimmering display of white and green.

Distribution: North-west Hupeh Province, central China.
Height: 25m/82ft
Shape: Broadly spreading
Deciduous
Pollinated: Bees
Leaf shape: Broadly ovate

Right: The leaves are 10–15cm/4–6in long. Flowers ripen into pea-like fruit, each held on a long stalk.

Henry's Lime

Tilia henryana Szysz

Distribution: Western Hueph Province, central China.
Height: 25m/82ft
Shape: Broadly columnar
Deciduous
Pollinated: Insect
Leaf shape: Broadly ovate

This rare, medium-sized tree grows at elevations in excess of 1,200m/3,937ft in central China. It is named after the Irish physician Augustine Henry, who discovered it in 1888 while working as medical officer for the Chinese customs service. Henry discovered Oliver's lime the same year. Although it is cultivated in the West, Henry's lime never grows as vigorously as it does in the wild.

Identification: The bark is silver and smooth even in maturity. The leaves are very distinctive, having a strongly serrated leaf margin with a pronounced bristle at the end of every tooth. They are 5–12cm/2–4¾in long, bright green above with fawn-coloured pubescence beneath. The flowers are pale cream to white, borne in fragrant pendulous clusters of up to 20 in summer. Each cluster is accompanied by a hairy, narrow, pale green floral bract up to 10cm/4in long. The fruit is a rounded, grey-green woody 'pea', borne on a long stalk.

Left: The ragged edges to the leaves make Henry's lime quite unmistakable.

Right: The small, green fruit start to appear in late summer. They are produced in clusters but each is held on an individual stalk.

European Lime

Common lime *Tilia* x *europaea* Linnaeus

European lime is a hybrid between small-leaved lime and large-leaved lime, and occurs naturally throughout Europe wherever the natural ranges of the two parents overlap. It does not have the elegance of either parent, producing unsightly suckering around the base. It is also prone to aphid attack in summer, which results in a coating of sticky aphid excrement appearing on anything that lingers for long beneath its boughs. Surprisingly, despite all this, European lime is regularly planted in towns, cities and avenues in preference to its parents.

Distribution: Most of Europe.
Height: 40m/130ft
Shape: Broadly columnar
Deciduous
Pollinated: Insect
Leaf shape: Broadly ovate

Identification: The bark is grey to grey-brown, smooth when young and develops shallow vertical fissures in maturity. The leaves are broadly ovate, and up to 10cm/4in both in length and across. They are cordate (heart-shaped) at the base with a sharply toothed margin and end in a tapering point at the tip. The leaves are a rather flat, green colour above and slightly paler beneath, with hairy tufts in the main vein axils. The flowers are yellow, fragrant and borne in drooping clusters of up to ten in summer.

Right: The clusters of flowers hang down beneath the leaves in summer.

Left: Like that of other limes, the fruit is small and pea-like.

Large-leaved Lime

Tilia platyphyllos Scopoli

This splendid, large, domed-top tree has a clean straight trunk and graceful arching branches. Unlike European lime, it does not produce suckers, nor does it suffer from aphid attack in summer, so does not shed sticky honeydew on cars parked beneath.

Left: The leaves have a pointed tip.

Distribution: Europe into South-west Asia.
Height: 30m/100ft
Shape: Broadly columnar
Deciduous
Pollinated: Insect
Leaf shape: Broadly ovate

Identification: Bark is light grey with shallow fissures in maturity. The large leaves are rounded, up to 15cm/6in across and deep green above with some pubescence. They are light green on the underside, with dense pubescence along the midrib and in the vein axils. The leaf stalk, which can be up to 5cm/2in long, is also covered in soft white down.

Flowers are pale yellow, very fragrant and produced in weeping clusters of up to six in early summer. Each flower cluster is accompanied by a pubescent floral bract up to 13cm/5in long and 1.5cm/⅗in wide. The fruit is a pale green, downy 'pea', borne on a stalk in late summer and early autumn.

Small-leaved Lime
Tilia cordata Miller
Native to most of Europe from Portugal to the Caucasus Mountains, this tall, column-like tree has small, cordate leaves. In Britain its presence in woodland indicates the woodland is ancient. The inner bark or 'bast' was traditionally used to make rope. Some coppiced trees are believed to be over 2,000 years old.

American Basswood *Tilia americana* Linnaeus
Commonly known as American lime, this attractive tree has a natural range from Maine to North Carolina and west to Missouri. It has two distinguishing features: first, rough, almost corky bark in maturity; and second, the largest leaf of any lime. Each leaf may be up to 20cm/ 8in long and almost as broad.

Silver Lime *Tilia tomentosa* Moench
Sometimes known as European white lime, this handsome pyramidal-shaped tree is native to the

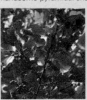

Balkans, Hungary, Russia and into western Asia. It has erect branches with striking two-coloured leaves, dark green above and covered in silver-white hair beneath.

POPLARS

The poplars, Salicaceae, are a genus of over 35 species of deciduous trees found throughout northern temperate regions of the world. They produce small male and female flowers, which are borne in catkins on separate trees and pollinated by wind. Poplars are fast-growing trees, many of which can withstand atmospheric pollution and salt spray from the ocean.

Chinese Necklace Poplar

Populus lasiocarpa Oliver

Distribution: Central China.
Height: 20m/66ft
Shape: Broadly spreading
Deciduous
Pollinated: Wind
Leaf shape: Broadly ovate

Right: The large leaves have toothed margins.

This striking, medium-sized tree has one of the largest and thickest leaves of any poplar. The word 'necklace' in the name refers to the long, hanging, green seed capsules that appear in midsummer. By late summer these ripen and burst, shedding phenomenal amounts of seed, wrapped in a white cotton wool-like material, over a wide area.

Identification: The bark is grey-brown and fissured in maturity. The overall shape of the tree tends to be open and gangly; it tends to look particularly dishevelled in winter. The leaves are large and broadly ovate to heart-shaped; on some trees they are up to 35cm/14in long and 20cm/8in across. The leaves have a leathery feel and are each attached to chunky shoots by a red leaf stalk up to 10cm/4in long. The leaf-stalk colouring appears to 'bleed' into the midrib and main veins. In autumn the leaves turn light brown and crisp, making a distinctive sound on windy days. Male and female flowers are stiff, yellow-green catkins borne on separate trees in spring.

Right: The green 'necklaces' of seed capsules are what give this poplar its name.

Western Balsam Poplar

Black cotton wood *Populus trichocarpa* Hooker

This large, vigorous North American tree is the fastest growing of all the balsam poplars. The first western balsam poplar to be planted at the Royal Botanic Gardens in London in 1896 reached 17m/56ft tall in just 13 years. Many fast-growing clones and hybrids of this species have been developed for forestry purposes and are now quite widely planted.

Identification: The bark is smooth and yellow-grey, becoming vertically fissured with age. The young shoots and winter buds are golden yellow and covered in a sticky, fragrant balsamic gum. In spring, as the buds open and the leaves unfurl, they emit a delicious balsam fragrance. The leaves are ovate and slightly heart-shaped at the base, up to 25cm/10in long and 13cm/5in wide, dark, glossy green above and light sage-green beneath, displaying a network of tiny leaf veins. The male catkins are 5cm/2in long and the female catkins 15cm/6in long. Both are carried on separate trees in early spring.

Left: The elegant leaves have a glossy upper surface.

Distribution: Western North America from Alaska to California.
Height: 40m/130ft
Shape: Broadly columnar
Deciduous
Pollinated: Wind
Leaf shape: Ovate

Right: Male and (far right) female catkins are produced in early spring on separate trees. Female catkins are three times as long as the male ones.

Cottonwood *Populus deltoides* Marsh.
Also known as eastern cottonwood and
American black poplar, this wide-spreading tree
has a short trunk and large horizontal branches.
It is native to eastern North America, from Texas
in the south to Quebec in the north. The
botanical name *deltoides* refers to the fact that
the leaves are deltoid or triangular in shape.

Black Poplar *Populus nigra* Linnaeus
Native to western Asia and Europe, the western
European subspecies of black poplar is called
P. betulifolia and differs from the species in
having a pubescent covering to the petiole,
shoot, leaf midrib and flower stalk. It is an
endangered tree in the wild, mainly because
much of the remaining population is male.

Grey Poplar *Populus* x *canescens*
(Aiton) P. Smith
This large tree is a fertile hybrid between the
white poplar and aspen, which has become
widespread throughout Europe and western Asia.
It has striking leaves, deep sage-green above and
grey-green with heavy pubescence beneath. The
pale grey to cream bark develops distinctive
diamond-shaped dark plates in maturity.

White Poplar *Populus alba* Linnaeus
Native to Europe, western Asia and parts of
North Africa, this tree has become a favourite for
planting alongside motorways, where it is able
to withstand localized atmospheric pollution. It
has light grey bark and distinctive white
pubescence to both the shoot and underside of
the leaf.

Lombardy Poplar

Populus nigra 'Italica' Linnaeus

The Lombardy poplar is probably one of the
most easily recognizable of all trees because
of its slender, columnar outline and upright
branching. It is not a true species but a
distinctive variety of black poplar, *Populus
nigra*, which is believed to
have originated on the
banks of the River Po
in northern Italy in the
early 1700s. Since then
Lombardy poplar
has been propagated
by cuttings and
planted as an
ornamental tree
around the world.

*Below: Leaves may be
10cm/4in wide. Catkins
have an orange tinge.*

Distribution: Originated as a
'sport' (variety) of black poplar
in northern Italy.
Height: 30m/100ft
Shape: Narrowly columnar
Deciduous
Pollinated: Wind
Leaf shape: Ovate

Identification: Immediately
recognizable by its upright form.
Strongly ascending branches
grow virtually from ground level.
The trunk, with its dark grey bark,
is normally fluted and buttressed
at the base. Each deciduous leaf
is ovate to diamond-shaped and
bright glossy green. Lombardy
poplars are predominantly male
trees, hence the need to
propagate from cuttings. Male
catkins are up to 8cm/3in long
and borne in mid-spring. The
Lombardy poplar is not long-lived
and is susceptible to bacterial
canker and fungal diseases.

Aspen

European aspen *Populus tremula* Linnaeus

This tree is properly known as European aspen, so as not
to confuse it with its American cousin, *P. tremuloides*.
The botanical name *tremula* is derived from the fact
that the leaves, which are borne on slender flattened
petioles (leaf stalks), tremble and quiver in even the
slightest breeze. 'To tremble like an aspen leaf' is a
phrase that goes back to the time of the English
poet, Edmund Spenser (1522–1599).

Identification: This medium-sized suckering tree has grey,
smooth bark, becoming ridged at the base in maturity. The
leaves are 8cm/3in long and equally wide. The leaf margin is
edged with rounded teeth and there are three distinct, light-
coloured veins at the base of each leaf. Leaves
emerge a pink-bronze colour from the bud in
spring, gradually turning a dull green by
early summer. Both male and female flowers
are catkins, up to 5cm/2in long, borne in early
spring before the leaves emerge. Tiny seeds carried
in white, cotton wool-like hairs are released from
green catkin-like capsules in late spring.

Distribution: Europe from
the Atlantic to the Pacific,
south to North Africa.
Height: 20m/66ft
Shape: Broadly spreading
Deciduous
Pollinated: Wind
Leaf shape: Broadly ovate

*Right: Male and female
catkins appear on
separate trees.*

*Left: Leaves
are rounded.*

WILLOWS

There are more than 300 different species of willows in the world, varying from large spreading ornamental specimens to diminutive, creeping, tundra-based alpines. The majority are native to northern temperate regions of the world. Willows are mainly deciduous, although one or two subtropical species have leaves that persist into winter. Male and female flowers are normally borne on separate trees.

Weeping Willow

Salix x sepulcralis 'Chrysocoma' Simonkai

Weeping willow is a hybrid between white willow and Chinese weeping willow, and developed naturally where the ranges of these two species met in western Asia. The form 'Chrysocoma' has been selected and cultivated from the hybrid for its golden shoot and more graceful weeping habit. It is the familiar weeping form seen alongside European riverbanks.

Identification: A large, spreading tree with ascending primary branches, supporting long secondary branches, which reach to the ground. The bark is pale grey-brown with shallow, corky fissures. The shoot and young wood is a glorious golden yellow colour, as is the long, slender winter bud that hugs the shoot. The leaves are up to 13cm/5in long and up to 2.5cm/1in wide. Male and female flowers appear as the leaves emerge in early spring.

> **Distribution**: A hybrid, so not native to anywhere, but widely cultivated throughout temperate regions of the world as an ornamental.
> **Height**: 20m/66ft
> **Shape**: Broadly weeping
> **Deciduous**
> **Pollinated**: Insect, and occasionally wind
> **Leaf shape**: Narrowly lanceolate

Below: The hanging branches make for an unmistakable form.

Left: Catkins grow upwards.

Right: Leaves are long and slender.

White Willow

Salix alba Linnaeus

White willow thrives in damp soils and grows naturally alongside rivers and in watermeadows. A variety of white willow known as S. *caerulea* has been cultivated since the early 1700s for the manufacture of cricket bats.

Identification: The bark is brown-grey, becoming deeply fissured in maturity. The leaves are lanceolate, tapering at both ends, and are up to 10cm/4in long and 1.25cm/½in wide. Young leaves are covered in silver hairs on both sides; mature leaves retain this pubescence on the underside but the top side becomes smooth and bright green. Both male and female flowers are catkins borne on separate trees in spring as the leaves emerge. The fruit is a green capsule, ripening to release numerous white-haired seeds, which are dispersed by the wind.

Right: The long, slender leaves hang from the tree and move easily in the wind.

> **Distribution**: Europe and western Asia.
> **Height**: 25m/82ft
> **Shape**: Broadly columnar
> **Deciduous**
> **Pollinated**: Insect, and occasionally wind
> **Leaf shape**: Lanceolate

Right: Male catkins are 5cm/2in long and have yellow anthers; female catkins are green and smaller.

Common Osier

Salix viminalis Linnaeus

The common osier is one of the most important willows to the basket-making industry. Over the centuries, hundreds of clones have been developed for varying basketry uses. The common osier is a vigorous small tree, easily growing up to 2m/6½ ft from the cut stump in one season. It grows naturally beside rivers, lakes and floodplains and can survive being immersed in water for several months.

Right: The small catkins stand upright.

Distribution: Europe (not Mediterranean), through to the Himalayas and north-east Asia.
Height: 6m/20ft
Shape: Broadly spreading
Deciduous
Pollinated: Insect and wind
Leaf shape: Linear to lanceolate

Identification: An erect large shrub or multi-stemmed small tree with smooth, grey-brown bark. The leaves are rather stiff, long and narrow, up to 25cm/ 10in long and taper to a fine point. They are a dull, dark green above and covered with silver-grey hairs beneath. Shoots are also covered with fine hair when young. Flowers are upright grey-green catkins, up to 2.5cm/1in long, borne in early spring before the leaves emerge. Fruit is a green capsule, ripening to release hundreds of white-haired seeds, which are dispersed by the wind.

Left: Leaves are long and have smooth edges.

Contorted Willow *Salix babylonica* 'Tortuosa' Linnaeus
A peculiar, deformed-looking tree, otherwise known as the dragon's claw willow or corkscrew willow, this has twisted and contorted branches and shoots, and has become widely cultivated as a garden ornamental. It forms a tangled tree up to 10m/33ft tall.

Goat Willow *Salix caprea* Linnaeus
This rounded small tree, to 10m/33ft tall, also known as sallow or pussy willow, is rather different from most other willows in several ways. First, it does not thrive in wet conditions, preferring drier, free-draining soils. Second, it has a broad, oval leaf rather than a narrow lanceolate one. Third, it does not propagate naturally from cuttings, relying on generous amounts of wind-borne seed to regenerate.

Crack Willow *Salix fragilis* Linnaeus
This tree is native to most of Europe and northern Asia, where it lines watercourses. It reaches heights in excess of 15m/50ft and has long lanceolate leaves up to 15cm/6in long, which are rich green above and glaucous beneath. Crack willow has brittle shoots that make a distinctive 'cracking' sound when broken.

Bay Willow *Salix pentrandra* Linnaeus
This handsome, medium-sized willow, native to northern Europe and northern Asia, has ovate deep green, glossy, aromatic leaves reminiscent of bay laurel, *Laurus noblis*. When crushed, they emit a sweet fragrance and in Scandinavia they have been used as a culinary flavouring. The male flowers are erect, yellow catkins, which are an attractive contrast with the leaves in early summer.

Violet Willow

Salix daphnoides Villars

The name 'violet willow' refers to the fact that the young shoots of this tree are a striking plum colour, covered with a silver bloom, which wears off as the shoot matures. In cultivation the tree is quite often coppiced to encourage the growth of these striking stems. In the wild this hardy tree inhabits upland slopes.

Identification: The bark is grey and smooth. The young shoots are plum coloured with a whitish bloom. The leaves are narrowly elliptic, up to 13cm/5in long and 3cm/1¼in across and have a wavy, slightly toothed margin. They are shiny dark green above and glaucous beneath with some pubescence on both surfaces of juvenile leaves. Both the male and female flowers are small, silky grey catkins up to 4cm/1½in long, borne in early spring before the tree comes into leaf. The fruit is a small, green capsule, which ripens to release copious amounts of fluffy, white seeds to be dispersed by the wind.

Below: The catkins are silky grey.

Distribution: Central Europe from Scandinavia to the Alps, through to the Himalayas and the Urals.
Height: 10m/33ft
Shape: Broadly conical
Deciduous
Pollinated: Insect and wind
Leaf shape: Narrowly elliptic

STRAWBERRIES, PERSIMMONS AND SNOWBELLS

Strawberries, persimmons and snowbells form part of the camellia subclass known as Dilleniidae. *They are a mixture of deciduous and evergreen, acid-loving and lime-tolerant species. They have an ornamental appeal, which has secured their place in gardens and arboreta across the temperate world.*

Hybrid Strawberry Tree

Arbutus x *andrachnoides* Link

Distribution: Greece.
Height: 10m/33ft
Shape: Broadly spreading
Evergreen
Pollinated: Insect
Leaf shape: Ovate to elliptic

Right: Fruit is strawberry-like drupes, 1.5cm/⅔in across, enclosing countless seeds. Produced on the tree in autumn it ripens from green to red.

Above and below right: Small white, slightly fragrant, urn-shaped, pendulous clusters of flowers are borne on the ends of the shoots in autumn and spring.

This natural hybrid between the Irish strawberry tree and the Grecian strawberry tree occurs in Greece, where both parents grow wild. It was brought into cultivation as early as 1800 and has been widely planted, primarily for its attractive foliage and bark. The tree takes its hardiness from *A. unedo*, allowing it to be grown further north than *A. andrachne*.

Identification: The bark is a cinnamon-brown colour and peels from the trunk in long, vertical strands. The shoots are also this colour with some pubescence that carries on right through to the leaf petiole. The leaves are up to 10cm/4in long, 5cm/2in wide, thick and rigid, shiny dark green above and glaucous beneath. They have a pronounced bright yellow-green midrib.

Persimmon

Possum wood *Diospyrus virginiana* Linnaeus

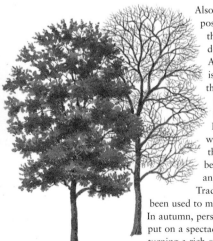

Also known as possum wood, this large deciduous North American tree is one of only three truly hardy members of the ebony family, Ebenaceae. The wood resembles that of ebony, being black, dense and very tough. Traditionally it has been used to make golf clubs. In autumn, persimmon leaves put on a spectacular display, turning a rich orange-yellow colour before falling from the branches.

Identification: A wide-spreading tree with black-brown rugged bark, cracking in maturity into rough square plates. The leaves are commonly ovate, up to 13cm/5in long and 8cm/3in across, deep glossy green above and light sage-green beneath with an untoothed margin. By far the most distinctive feature of this tree is the fruit, which is quite often described as orange-like but is more akin in looks and size to a small orange tomato. Measuring 4cm/1½in across, it ripens on the tree in late summer to early autumn and contains up to eight brown seeds. The fruit is edible but too sharp for most palates.

Right: Both male and female flowers are pale yellow, bell-shaped and borne on separate trees in summer.

Distribution: Central-southern United States from Connecticut to Texas.
Height: 30m/100ft
Shape: Broadly spreading
Deciduous
Pollinated: Insect
Leaf shape: Ovate to oblong

Japanese Snowbell Tree

Styrax japonica Siebold & Zuccarini

This beautiful, small, spreading tree deserves to be much better known and more widely planted than it is. It was first introduced to the West in 1862 when Richard Oldham collected a plant from Japan, which was then planted at the Royal Botanic Gardens, Kew, London. Since then the tree has been planted in various botanic collections and arboreta, but is comparatively rare as a garden tree. It is an ideal tree for a small garden seldom reaching more than 7m/25ft tall and perfectly hardy even in cooler regions, although late frosts may injure the flower buds.

Identification: The bark is orange-brown, smooth at first and becoming fissured in maturity. The leaves are oval to elliptical, tapering at both ends, to 10cm/4in long and 5cm/2in across. The leaf margin is set with small, shallow teeth. Leaves are a rich shiny green above and a paler green beneath, and are normally arranged in groups of three on the shoot. The slightly fragrant, creamy white, open bell-shaped flowers with yellow anthers hang, either on their own or in small clusters, all along the branches on long slender stalks in early summer. The overall effect is delightful. The fruit is an egg-shaped green-grey berry containing a single seed.

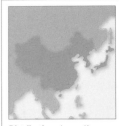

Distribution: Japan, Korea and China.
Height: 10m/33ft
Shape: Broadly spreading
Deciduous
Pollinated: Insect
Leaf shape: Oval to elliptic

Below: The leaves are reminiscent of bay. Once pollinated, the hanging flowers form green berries.

Karo *Pittosporum crassifolium* A. Cunn.
This small evergreen tree is native to the Kermadec islands in the Pacific Ocean and the North Island of New Zealand. One of the hardiest *Pittosporum* in cultivation, it has thick, leathery, oval-shaped and lustrous leaves. These are grass-green above and covered with white pubescence beneath. Karo grows particularly well in coastal locations.

Snowdrop Tree *Halesia Carolina* Linnaeus
This beautiful, small, spreading tree, growing up to 10m/33ft, is native to south-eastern states of the USA. It has ovate to elliptic, deep green leaves, each up to 8cm/3in long. In spring the whole tree is covered with clusters of creamy white, nodding bell-shaped flowers. The flowers look more like white bluebells than snowdrops and this is reflected in the species' other common name – the silverbell tree.

Kohuhu

Pittosporum tenuifolium Gaertner

This tree is native to both the North and South Islands of New Zealand, where it grows from sea level to 1,000m/3,280ft and may reach 30m/98ft tall. In cultivation elsewhere it is never as hardy or vigorous, rarely exceeding 10m/33ft in height, and is liable to damage by frost in all but the most sheltered locations.

Identification: This bright-leaved evergreen tree has dark grey to black bark on the trunk, branches and shoots. The contrast of black twigs and shoots against the lustrous light-green leaves is extremely attractive and much in demand by florists and flower arrangers. The leaves are 8cm/3in long, oblong to elliptic and have a wavy but entire margin. The flowers are deep purple, tubular and very small – only 1cm/½in long. However, what they lack in size they make up for in honey-sweet fragrance, which can fill a garden on a warm, late spring evening. The fruit is a brown-black round capsule, 1.25cm/½in across.

Distribution: New Zealand.
Height: 10m/33ft
Shape: Broadly columnar
Evergreen
Pollinated: Insect
Leaf shape: Oblong to elliptic

Below: Kohuhu leaves have rounded ends and wavy edges. The flowers are small but highly scented.

CHERRIES

The cherry genus, Prunus, contains over 400 different species of tree, the majority of which are deciduous and native to northern temperate regions of the world. They include some of the most beautiful spring-flowering trees, many of which have been cultivated in parks, gardens and arboreta for centuries. The genus is distinguished by having fruit that is always a drupe surrounding a single seed.

Sargent's Cherry

Prunus sargentii Rehder.

Sargent's cherry is one of the loveliest of all cherries, producing a profusion of rich pink, single flowers coupled with bronze-coloured emerging leaves in spring, and brilliant orange-red leaf colours in autumn. It is named after Professor Charles Sargent, one-time Director of the Arnold Arboretum, Boston, Massachusetts, USA, who obtained a supply of the tree's seed from Japan in 1892.

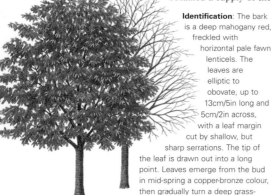

Identification: The bark is a deep mahogany red, freckled with horizontal pale fawn lenticels. The leaves are elliptic to obovate, up to 13cm/5in long and 5cm/2in across, with a leaf margin cut by shallow, but sharp serrations. The tip of the leaf is drawn out into a long point. Leaves emerge from the bud in mid-spring a copper-bronze colour, then gradually turn a deep grass-green. The single pink flowers, which are normally produced in profusion, have five petals and are up to 4cm/1½in across. They appear just before the leaves emerge. The fruit is a black, egg-shaped drupe.

Distribution: Northern Japan, Korea and the island of Sakhalin.
Height: 20m/66ft
Shape: Broadly spreading
Deciduous
Pollinated: Insect
Leaf shape: Elliptic to obovate

Above left: The blossom of Sargent's cherry is a rich pink colour.

Right: Autumn leaves turn glorious shades of orange.

Tibetan Cherry

Prunus serrula Franchet

The Tibetan cherry tree is worth growing simply for its bark, which is like highly polished, deep-red, mahogany timber, segmented into sections by light brown, horizontal banding. This small, slow-growing tree is ideal for a small garden and its bark makes it a wonderful tree for winter colour. Ernest Wilson introduced it to the West from western Szechwan, China, in 1908.

Distribution: Western China.
Height: 15m/50ft
Shape: Broadly spreading
Deciduous
Pollinated: Insect
Leaf shape: Lanceolate

Right: Pointed leaves and polished red bark make the Tibetan cherry easy to identify.

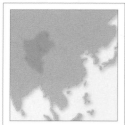

Identification: The bark alone is enough to identify this tree; however, it also has willow-like leaves which are up to 10cm/4in long, finely serrated around the leaf margin and drawn out into a long pointed tip. The white flowers are relatively inconspicuous, 2cm/¾in across with orange-tipped stamens, borne singly or in small clusters, after the leaves emerge in spring. There are red stipules, or leaf glands, at the base of the petiole. The fruit is egg-shaped, crimson and borne in pairs on long stalks.

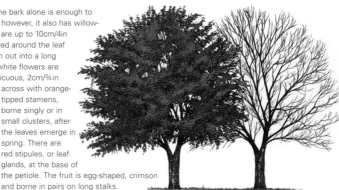

Plum

Prunus domestica Linnaeus

> **Distribution**: Unknown but probably a hybrid of garden origin.
> **Height**: 10m/33ft
> **Shape**: Broadly spreading
> **Deciduous**
> **Pollinated**: Insect
> **Leaf shape**: Elliptic to obovate

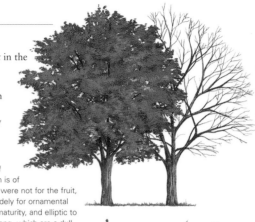

The origins of the garden plum are lost in the mists of time. It is probably a hybrid, possibly between the sloe, *P. spinosa*, and the cherry plum, *P. cerasifera*. Both species are native to the Caucasus and known hybrids have occurred naturally here. In the future, DNA examination may be able to unravel the mystery.

Identification: There are countless cultivars of plum, all developed to enhance the fruit, which is of course not just edible, but quite delicious. If it were not for the fruit, it is unlikely that this tree would be planted widely for ornamental purposes. It has brown-grey bark, fissured in maturity, and elliptic to obovate bluntly serrated leaves, up to 8in/3in long, which are a dull grass-green colour. Flowers are white, slightly fragrant and about 2.5cm/1in across, and are borne in spring before the leaves emerge.

Above: The plum fruit is a succulent drupe with a single large seed, or stone (pit).

Right: There are various plum cultivars, which produce egg-shaped fruit in a variety of different colours. Plum leaves and flowers are always the same, however.

The Great White Cherry *Prunus* 'Tai Haku'
Hundreds of ornamental garden cherries have been cultivated in Japan. Most are either forms or hybrids of two native Japanese cherries: the Oshima cherry and the mountain cherry. The great white cherry is one of the finest hybrids. It has large, pure white, single flowers, which open at the same time as its bronze-pink leaves emerge from the bud.

Mount Fuji Cherry *Prunus* 'Shirotae'
Shirotae is Japanese for 'snow white' and that is exactly the colour of the semi-double (sometimes single) flowers that cluster upon this tree's graceful, low-spreading branches in spring. At the same time, bright grass-green leaves are emerging from their winter buds, providing a wonderful contrast to the flowers.

Japanese Apricot *Prunus mume* 'Beni-shirdare'
This small, rounded form of the Japanese apricot has stunning, deep pink, goblet-shaped flowers and a superb fragrance. The flowers appear before the leaves emerge and stand out dramatically against the almost black branches.

***Prunus* 'Accolade'**
This hybrid between Sargent's cherry and the spring cherry, *Prunus subhirtella*, is a small tree. Its pink, semi-double flowers hang in clusters from the wide-spreading branches in spring.

Hawthorn

May *Crataegus monogyna* Jacquin

Native throughout Europe, the hawthorn is a slow-growing, hardy tree, which will withstand exposure, strong winds and cold better than most northern temperate trees. For centuries, hawthorn has been used to both shelter animal stock and enclose it, particularly in upland areas. A regularly clipped hawthorn hedge is a very effective windbreak and virtually impenetrable. The other name for hawthorn is may, which refers to the timing of flowering when the tree is at its most conspicuous.

> **Distribution**: Europe.
> **Height**: 10m/33ft
> **Shape**: Broadly spreading
> **Deciduous**
> **Pollinated**: Insect
> **Leaf shape**: Obovate

Identification: The bark is dull brown with vertical orange cracks. Leaves are deeply cut, almost to the midrib in some cases, so the outline is not obvious. They are dark green above and paler with some pubescence in the vein axils beneath. The creamy white, slightly pungent-smelling flowers are produced in profusion in mid-spring.

Above: Fruit is deep red.

Right: Twigs have vicious thorns.

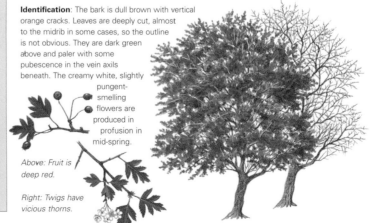

FLOWERING CRABS

The flowering crab genus, Malus, contains over 25 species, native mainly to northern temperate regions. They are hardy, small to medium-sized deciduous trees, widely grown as garden ornamentals for their profusion of spring flowers and late summer fruit. The flowers are similar to cherry, except that crab apple flowers have five styles presenting the female stigma for pollination instead of just one.

Crab Apple

Malus sylvestris (Linnaeus) Miller

Distribution: Europe
Height: 10m/33ft
Shape: Broadly spreading
Deciduous
Pollinated: Insect
Leaf shape: Elliptic

Far right: Crab apples produce a mass of white flowers in spring. The crab apples themselves develop through the summer.

This tree is known to many as the 'sour little apple', for its profusion of small green, but inedible, apples in late summer. The wild crab apple is not regarded as an important ornamental species; however, it is one of the parents of the domestic orchard apple, *M. domestica* and of some very attractive ornamental flowering crabs.

Identification: The bark is brown and fissured even when relatively young. The overall appearance is of an uneven, low-domed tree with a head of dense twisting branches, normally weighted to one side. The leaves are elliptic to ovate, 4cm/1½in long, slightly rounded at the base, deep green above and grey-green beneath with some pubescence on the leaf veins. The leaf margin is finely, but bluntly, toothed. Flowers are white, flushed with pink, 2.5cm/1in across and carried on short spurs. The fruit is apple-like, up to 4cm/1½in across, green to yellow and sometimes flushed with red.

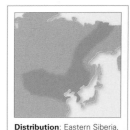

Siberian Crab

Malus baccata (Linnaeus) Borkhausen

This small to medium-sized very hardy, eastern Asian tree has a rounded habit when young, becoming spreading with age. The botanical name *baccata* means a fruit with a fleshy or pulpy coat. In Siberia the fruits are collected and made into wine and jelly. Although itself not widely planted, this tree is the origin of several attractive cultivars including 'Gracilis'.

Identification: Siberian crab has brown flaking bark, which sheds in irregular to square plates, revealing fresh reddish brown bark beneath. The leaves are up to 8cm/3in long, ovate to elliptic and have very fine teeth around the margin. They are dark green above, paler beneath with no pubescence. The flowers are held on single stalks but borne in clusters. They are white flushed with pink, up to 5cm/2in across with yellow stamens. They open in spring at the same time as the leaves emerge. The fruit is a small rounded 'apple', 1cm/½in across.

Right: The leaves have very fine serration around the edges. Siberian crab apple fruit start out yellow and gradually turn red.

Distribution: Eastern Siberia, Mongolia, northern China and Korea.
Height: 15m/50ft
Shape: Broadly spreading
Deciduous
Pollinated: Insect
Leaf shape: Ovate to elliptic

Hupeh Crab

Malus hupehensis (Pampanini) Rehder.

This is one of the most beautiful of all small deciduous trees. The Hupeh crab is a hardy tree growing in the mountainous region of central China, where local people use the leaves to make a drink called 'red tea'. It was introduced to the West in 1900 by the plant collector Ernest Wilson.

Identification: The bark is a lilac-brown colour with irregular shaped plates flaking from the trunk to reveal orange-brown fresh bark beneath. The leaves are 10cm/4in long, elliptic to ovate and finely toothed around the leaf margin. They are grass-green above and pale beneath, with some pubescence along the midrib and main veins. The flowers are pink in bud, opening white with a rose flush. They are 5cm/2in across and slightly fragrant. The fruit is greenish yellow ripening to red and normally stays on the tree long after the leaves have fallen.

Distribution: Central and western China.
Height: 12m/40ft
Shape: Broadly spreading
Deciduous
Pollinated: Insect
Leaf shape: Ovate to elliptic

Left: The fruit is a rounded 'apple' 1cm/½in across.

Left: The leaf tapers to a fine point.

Right: Flowers open in early spring.

Sweet Crab Apple *Malus coronaria* 'Charlottae'
This delightful cultivar of the North American sweet crab apple was discovered growing wild in Illinois in 1902. 'Charlottae' has semi-double, light pink flowers, 5cm/2in across, which appear in mid-spring in profusion. They have a strong fragrance similar to violets. The ovate, 10cm/4in-long leaves turn marmalade-orange in autumn.

Malus 'Golden Hornet'
This crab apple hybrid has become one of the most planted of all garden crab apples. In autumn, it produces deep yellow, rounded to egg-shaped fruits up to 2.5cm/1in long, which stay on the tree long after the leaves have fallen. The fruits shine brightly like little lanterns in winter sun. The parentage is unknown but it was developed in England in the 1940s.

Malus 'Liset'
This third generation hybrid has the Japanese *M. Sieboldii* as one of its parents. It was raised in Holland. It has blood-red flower buds, which open bright red before paling. The flowers contrast against the dark green leaves and deep brown branching freckled with fawn lenticels.

Malus 'Dartmouth'
This North American cultivar was raised in New Hampshire before 1883. It bears pure white single flowers, 2.5cm/1in across, in profusion in mid-spring against a backdrop of fresh green leaves. These are followed in autumn by deep crimson, slightly angular fruits, up to 5cm/2in across, which are covered in a purple bloom and persist long after the leaves have fallen.

Weeping Silver-leaved Pear

Willow-leaved pear *Pyrus salicifolia* Pallas

This tree is the most ornamental of all the pears. It was discovered in 1780 by the German botanist and explorer P. S. Pallas who first introduced it to Western cultivation. It is a firm favourite for planting where a small tree with silver foliage is required. Unfortunately, it is not a long-lived species.

Above left: Blossom appears in clusters.

Left: Mature leaves are sage-green and smooth.

Distribution: Russia, Caucasus, from the Steppes south into Turkey and northern Iraq.
Height: 10m/33ft
Shape: Broadly weeping
Deciduous
Pollinated: Insect
Leaf shape: Lanceolate

Identification: The bark is pale grey, becoming vertically fissured in maturity. The leaves are narrowly lanceolate, up to 10cm/4in long and tapering at both ends. They have a characteristic twist along their length. When young, the leaves are covered with a silvery white pubescence, which gradually wears off. They are borne on thin, horizontal branches, which become pendulous towards the tip. When young, these are also covered in silvery hairs. The flowers are 2.5cm/1in across, creamy white with purple anthers. The fruit is green, hard, pear-shaped and up to 3cm/1¼in long.

MEDLARS, QUINCES AND ROWANS

The rose family, Rosaceae, is one of the largest of all plant families. It encompasses an incredibly diverse range of plants, including cherries, apples, quinces, loquats, cotoneasters, rowans and of course roses. It is also one of the most commonly represented families within cultivation, simply because of the flowering and fruiting beauty of its members. They include this diverse and beautiful group of trees.

Medlar

Mespilus germanica Linnaeus

This small, spreading tree has rather angular branching. It is grown mainly for its fruit, which is an acquired taste. When ripe, the dumpy, pear-shaped fruits have an extremely disagreeable taste and are not edible until they have been exposed to frost and then 'bletted' (allowed to reach the first stages of decay). Even then the taste is rather acidic. Medlars were popular in the past and widely cultivated in orchards.

Distribution: South-west Asia and south-east Europe.
Height: 6m/20ft
Shape: Broadly spreading
Deciduous
Pollinated: Insect
Leaf shape: Elliptic to lanceolate

Identification: The bark is dull brown, smooth at first, developing fissures in maturity. The bright green, almost stalkless, elliptic leaves are up to 15cm/6in long, minutely toothed around the margin and slightly hairy on both sides. The flowers, borne singly at the end of leaf branches, are up to 5cm/2in across, white with five well-spaced petals and appear in early summer. The fruits are russet-brown and like a flattened pear in shape. They grow to 3cm/1¼in across and have a slightly open brown top surrounded by a persistent calyx, which gives them a tasselled look.

Left: The flowers open in summer, later than those of many fruit trees. The fruit itself is small and brown.

Quince

Cydonia oblonga Miller

Like many trees long cultivated for their fruit, the exact origins of the common quince are unknown. It has certainly been grown around the Mediterranean for at least 1,000 years. In the wild it commonly inhabits shallow, limestone soils on mountain slopes. The golden yellow fruit is pear-shaped.

Identification: The bark is brownish purple, smooth at first but maturing into irregular plates that flake to reveal orange-brown fresh bark beneath. The leaves are ovate to elliptic, up to 10cm/4in long, dark green and smooth above with cinnamon-grey-coloured hairs beneath. Leaves persist on the branches into early winter. The flowers are white flushed with pink and up to 5cm/2in across. They are borne singly at the end of hairy leaf shoots in mid-spring. The fragrant, golden yellow, pear-shaped fruit grows up to 10cm/4in long and is quite waxy to the touch.

Right: Quince fruit is fragrant and quite bitter. The tree's leaf has smooth, unserrated edges and stays on the tree until the beginning of winter.

Distribution: South-west Asia.
Height: 5m/16½ft
Shape: Broadly spreading
Deciduous
Pollinated: Insect
Leaf shape: Ovate to elliptic

Snowy Mespilus

June berry, Serviceberry, *Amelanchier lamarckii* Schroeder

This beautiful little tree is hardy, easy to grow and provides colour from early spring to mid-autumn. Although cultivated in Europe for at least 300 years, some botanists believe it originally came from Canada.

Below: The small, black fruit is sweet to taste.

Identification: This multi-stemmed tree has smooth grey bark when young, developing vertical fissures in maturity. The leaves emerge from bud in early spring a copper-khaki colour with a covering of silky, white hairs on the underside. Gradually, as the days get warmer, they turn dark green above and glaucous beneath. They are elliptic to ovate, up to 8cm/3in long and 4cm/1½in across, slightly toothed and attached to the shoot by a 2.5cm/1in-long leaf stalk. White, narrow-petalled flowers are borne in erect clusters of between eight and ten in early spring as the leaves emerge. In autumn the leaves turn red and orange before falling.

Distribution: Naturalized in western Europe. Some schools of thought suggest that it originates from North America.
Height: 12m/40ft
Shape: Broadly spreading
Deciduous
Pollinated: Insect
Leaf shape: Elliptic or ovate

Rowan *Sorbus aucuparia* Linnaeus
This small, hardy tree is native right across Europe and temperate Asia. It is also known as the mountain ash, which is probably a more suitable name, because it does have bright green, ash-like leaves and is regularly found growing high up on mountainsides: sometimes, it seems to be growing out of bare rock. The flowers, which are creamy white and slightly pungent, emerge in mid-spring and clusters of bright red berries appear in late summer.

Chinese Rowan *Sorbus hupehensis* Schneider
This is a beautiful small tree, native to much of temperate China and cultivated throughout the temperate world as a garden ornamental. It has ash-like, deep green leaves and delightful white berries, slightly flushed with pink.

Service Tree *Sorbus domestica* Linnaeus
This tree is very like rowan except much bigger. Native to southern and central Europe and North Africa, it has large, brown-red, rounded or slightly pear-shaped fruit and rough, dark brown, scaly bark. The fruit was at one time used to make a beer-type drink.

Wild Service Tree *Sorbus torminalis* (Linnaeus) Crantz
This distinctive tree is native to Europe, North Africa and south-western Asia but fairly rare in cultivation. It has broadly ovate, stiff leaves up to 10cm/4in long and wide, which are deeply cut into three to five sharply pointed lobes on each side. The berry is russet-coloured and oval.

Whitebeam

Sorbus aria (Linnaeus) Crantz

Whitebeam is a tree of calcareous uplands, thriving on thin limestone and chalk soils. Its edible red fruit is collected and made into jam, jelly and wine in some parts of Europe. The timber is dense and hard and at one time was used to make wheels and cogs. In the past it was sometimes referred to as the 'weather tree', for when the white underside of the leaf became visible, rain was believed to be on the way.

Identification: The bark is smooth silver-grey-brown even in maturity. By far the most distinguishing feature of this tree is its two-coloured leaves. They are up to 13cm/5in long and 6cm/2½in wide, pale green when emerging from the bud, turning a shiny deep green above and white with hairs beneath. When the wind catches the leaves, the effect of flickering green and white over the whole tree is quite remarkable. The flowers are borne in flattened clusters in mid-spring. The fruit is slightly speckled and rough, due to surface lenticels. Although the leaves do not produce good autumn colour they do persist beneath the tree as a grey, crisp covering right through winter.

Distribution: North, west and central Europe.
Height: 15m/50ft
Shape: Broadly columnar
Deciduous
Pollinated: Insect
Leaf shape: Ovate

Above: The flowers are 1cm/½in across.

Below: The fruit is a red, round berry.

LABURNUMS AND MIMOSAS

The pea family, Leguminosae, contains over 15,000 species of trees, shrubs and herbaceous plants in 700 genera. They are found growing wild throughout the world in both temperate and tropical conditions. Most have compound leaves, pea-like flowers and seed pods, and root systems which have the ability to use bacteria to absorb nitrogen from the soil.

Pagoda Tree

Sophora japonica Linnaeus

Despite its botanical name, *japonica*, the pagoda tree is thought not to be a native of Japan. However, it has been widely cultivated there for centuries, particularly in temple gardens and places of learning. In China the flower buds were used to make a yellow dye and all parts of the tree, if taken internally, create a strong purgative effect. Flowers on trees grown from seed take anything up to 30 years to appear.

Identification: The bark is greenish brown, becoming vertically fissured and ridged in maturity. The overall shape is rounded, with branching starting low on the stem. The leaves are pinnate and up to 25cm/10in long, with up to 15 opposite, untoothed, ovate, pointed leaflets, which are dark green above and glaucous with some pubescence beneath. The flowers are white, pea-like, fragrant and borne in terminal panicles in summer. The fruit is a seed pod up to 8cm/3in long, containing up to six seeds. It ripens from green to brown.

Distribution: Northern China but could be more widespread.
Height: 20m/66ft
Shape: Broadly spreading
Deciduous
Pollinated: Insect
Leaf shape: Pinnate

Left: The white flowers of the pagoda tree are produced in summer in open sprays.

Chinese Yellow Wood
Cladrastis sinensis Hemsl.
This slow-growing, beautiful, small- to medium-sized tree (to 12.5m/40ft in height) is native to western and central China. It was introduced to the West in 1901 by the plant collector Ernest Wilson. Chinese yellow wood has white fragrant flowers flushed with pink. These are borne in profusion on terminal erect panicles up to 30cm/12in long in midsummer. The flowers are quickly followed by seed pods. In maturity this deciduous tree becomes pyramid shaped. It thrives in sunny sites, in well-drained soil.

Honey Locust *Gleditsia triacanthos* Linnaeus
This large, spreading tree with frond-like leaves and sharp spines is native to eastern and central North America, from Ontario to Florida. It is sometimes known as sweet locust, because of the sweet, edible flesh that surrounds the seeds in its long (up to 45cm/18in) glossy brown pods. Honey locust is extremely tolerant of atmospheric pollution and widely planted in urban areas.

Kentucky Coffee Tree *Gymnocladus dioica* (Linnaeus) K. Koch
This elegant tree is native to eastern and central USA, where the seeds were used as a substitute for coffee by early colonial settlers. It is a medium-sized, slow-growing tree, which has extremely large compound, bipinnate leaves. These can be up to 1m/3ft long. They emerge bronze-pink from the bud in spring, gradually turn dark green in summer and finally become butter-yellow before falling in autumn.

Black Locust *False acacia Robinia pseudoacacia* Linnaeus
In the wild, black locust grows in moist humid conditions on river banks and on the edges of forests. In the Appalachian Mountains it grows up to 1,000m/3,280ft above sea-level. It is a fast growing, short-lived tree with brittle branches that have a tendency to break in exposed conditions. It throws up a profusion of root suckers from an early age which may appear a considerable distance from the main tree. The bark is grey-brown and smooth when young, becoming deeply fissured and ridged in maturity. Old stems tend to become rotten and hollow. Young branches and shoots have two ferocious spines at the base of each bud. The leaves are pinnate, to 30cm/12in long, with up to 19 pairs of opposite, ovate to elliptic slightly pubescent grey-green soft leaflets. The pea-like fragrant flowers are white with a yellow blotch, 2.5cm/1in long, clustered upon pendulous racemes, 20cm/8in long, in early summer. The fruit is a brown pea-like pod, 10cm/4in long, containing four to ten seeds.

Mimosa

Silver wattle *Acacia dealbata* Link

This tender temperate tree is prized by florists and flower arrangers the world over for its delicate, feathery foliage and fragrant yellow flowers. It has been known to reach 30m/98ft in height in the wild but seldom attains this in cultivation. It is extremely popular for planting as an ornamental street tree in Mediterranean countries but does not grow as well in cooler climates farther north.

Identification: The bark is green-grey to almost glaucous with pale vertical striations. It becomes darker in maturity. The lax leaves are double pinnate, up to 12cm/4¾in long and have countless small, linear, blue-green hairy leaflets, giving the whole tree a soft, feathery effect. The small, rounded flowers are sulphur-yellow and fragrant. They are clustered upon rounded panicles up to 10cm/4in across. In the Southern Hemisphere flowers appear in summer; in Europe they bloom from late winter into early spring. The fruit is a flat, blue-white seed pod, ripening to brown. It contains several round brown seeds.

Right: The flat seed pod measures up to 8cm/ 3in long.

Distribution: South-east Australia and Tasmania.
Height: 25m/82ft
Shape: Broadly conical
Evergreen
Pollinated: Insect
Leaf shape: Bipinnate

Left: The scented flowers open in summer in the Southern Hemisphere. North of the Equator they appear earlier.

Common Laburnum

Laburnum anagyroides Medikus

This beautiful tree occurs in mountainous regions of central Europe at elevations up to 2,000m/6,561ft. A small, spreading, short-lived tree, it grows particularly well on lime-rich soils and is best known for its profusion of pendulous golden yellow flowers in late spring. All parts of the tree contain an alkaloid that is poisonous if eaten; the green, unripe seed pods are particularly toxic.

Above: The bright yellow flowers appear in spring.

Distribution: Central and southern Europe from France to Hungary and Bulgaria.
Height: 9m/30ft
Shape: Broadly spreading
Deciduous
Pollinated: Insect
Leaf shape: Trifoliate

Above: Laburnum leaves grow in threes. The seed pods turn from green to brown as they ripen.

Identification: Bark is dark brown-grey and smooth, becoming shallowly fissured in maturity. New shoots are olive green and winter buds are covered with silver hairs. The elliptic leaflets, borne in threes, are up to 10cm/4in long, rich green above, grey-green beneath and covered with silver hairs when young. Flowers are golden yellow, pea-like, 2.5cm/1in long, in dense, hanging sprays up to 30cm/12in long. Flowers are followed by green, hairy, pea-like seed pods, which ripen brown and contain several small round black seeds.

EUCALYPTUS

There are over 400 species of eucalyptus, or gum tree, all native to the Southern Hemisphere. They are particularly abundant in Australia, Tasmania, New Guinea, the Philippines and Java. Most eucalyptus are evergreen and fast-growing, with attractive bark, luxuriant foliage and white flowers. They have been widely cultivated for their ornamental qualities and timber in other warm temperate regions of the world.

Cider Gum

Eucalyptus gunnii, J. D. Hooker

The cider gum is native to the island of Tasmania, where it grows in moist mountain forests up to 1,300m/4,265ft above sea level. It is one of the hardiest of all eucalyptus species and one of the most widely planted around the world. Cider gum has attractive glaucous-coloured, round, juvenile foliage, which is prized by flower arrangers and florists. Trees that are regularly coppiced maintain juvenile foliage. Wild trees grow up to 30m/98ft tall.

Right: If left to mature, cider gum leaves become long and slender, and hang from the branches.

Identification: This potentially large, fast-growing tree has smooth, grey-green to orange bark, peeling to reveal creamy fawn patches. The juvenile leaves are round, 4cm/1½in across, glaucous to silver-blue in colour and borne opposite in pairs. Mature leaves are lanceolate, up to 10cm/4in long, sage-green to silver-coloured and borne alternately on the twig. Flowers are white with numerous yellow stamens, borne in clusters of three in the leaf axils during summer. The fruit is a green, woody capsule, open at one end and contains several seeds.

Right: After pollination in summer, the flowers develop into woody fruit.

Distribution: Tasmania.
Height: 30m/100ft
Shape: Broadly columnar
Evergreen
Pollinated: Insect
Leaf shape: Juvenile leaves are rounded, and the mature leaves are lanceolate

Small-leaved Gum

Eucalyptus parviflora Cambage

This extremely hardy, rare, small to medium-sized tree grows wild in just one location in New South Wales at elevations in excess of 1,500m/4,921ft. Unlike many eucalyptus, the small-leaved gum will grow well on limestone soil. It was first introduced into Europe in the 1930s and has established itself as far north as Great Britain, where one tree, at Windsor, is already over 21m/69ft tall.

Below: The mature leaves are lanceolate in shape.

Identification: A handsome, medium-sized, densely leaved tree with attractive smooth, grey, peeling bark. The ovate, juvenile grey-green leaves are borne opposite, in pairs, on short leaf stalks up to 2cm/¾in long. Mature leaves are carried alternately on longer leaf stalks. They are blue-green to glaucous, up to 5cm/2in long and 5mm/¼in wide. The flowers are white and borne in clusters of four to seven on a short, common stalk in summer. The seed is contained in a woody, grey-green cylinder, which is closed at the base. The hanging seed pods are long and woody.

Left and right: The creamy-white, brush-like flowers are often obscured by leaves.

Distribution: Australia.
Height: 10m/33ft
Shape: Broadly columnar
Evergreen
Pollinated: Insect
Leaf shape: Juvenile ovate, adult lanceolate

Alpine Ash

Eucalyptus delegatensis R. T. Baker

This is one of the tallest of all eucalyptus, regularly attaining heights in excess of 60m/197ft in the wild. It is native to the mountains of Tasmania, where it grows at elevations of up to 1,000m/3,280ft. It also occurs in south-eastern Australia. In the state of Victoria it grows at up to 1,300m/4,265ft above sea level. Alpine ash is widely cultivated by foresters.

It yields a tough, hard timber that is sold as Australian or Tasmanian oak.

Distribution: Tasmania and mainland Australia.
Height: 60m/200ft
Shape: Broadly columnar
Evergreen
Pollinated: Insect
Leaf shape: Lanceolate

Identification: This tall tree has a straight, clean trunk and sparse, airy crown. The juvenile bark is smooth, bluish grey and shed in narrow, vertical ribbons; in maturity it becomes rough and fibrous. Young shoots are a glaucous, blue-red colour. The juvenile leaves are round to lanceolate, opposite and held in pairs. The adult leaves are alternate, stalked, lanceolate, up to 15cm/6in long and a dull sage-green colour with conspicuous veining. Flowers are white and held in clusters of 7–15 on a common stalk in the leaf axils. The fruit is a slightly pear-shaped woody tube, 1cm/½in long, with holes known as valves at one end. It contains several brown seeds.

Right: When they first appear, the leaves are dull and rounded.

Left: Mature alpine ash leaves are long and slender. The small, woody fruit has a conspicuous hole at one end.

Cabbage Gum *Eucalyptus pauciflora* Sieber
Also known as snow gum, this broadly spreading, hardy tree is native to Tasmania, Victoria and New South Wales in Australia. It has grey and white peeling bark, and lanceolate, glossy bright green adult leaves that grow to 15cm/6in long.

Tasmanian Blue Gum *Eucalyptus globulus* Labill. Native to Tasmania and Victoria in Australia, this fast-growing species can reach 55m/180ft tall. Elsewhere, particularly in Europe, it rarely reaches large proportions. However, one specimen on Jersey in the Channel Islands is supposed to have reached 35m/115ft in just 30 years.

Lemon-scented Gum *Eucalyptus citriodora* Hooker.
This tender species is native to Queensland, Australia, where it reaches heights in excess of 20m/66ft. Elsewhere, particularly in northern temperate regions of the world, it is unlikely to survive outside, although it does well in cool conservatories. It has smooth, white bark and when the juvenile foliage is crushed it emits a pleasant citrus-like fragrance.

Mountain Gum *Eucalyptus dalrympleana* Maiden
This handsome tree is native to Tasmania, New South Wales and Victoria in Australia. It is also known as the broad-leaved kindling bark because it sheds large, dry patches of pale cream bark. It grows on steep, rocky slopes at elevations of up to 1,500m/4,921ft above sea level. It has grey-green lanceolate leaves that are bronze-coloured when juvenile.

Urn Gum

Eucalyptus urnigera J. D. Hooker

This hardy species is native to the rocky slopes of Mount Wellington in the mountains of south-eastern Tasmania. It is to be found at elevations of up to 1,000m/3,280ft. Outside Tasmania it has been widely planted as an ornamental species and also for wind protection. It is, in many respects, very similar to the cider gum, *E. gunnii*, but can be distinguished by its smaller fruit and smaller overall size.

Distribution: South-east Tasmania.
Height: 12m/40ft
Shape: Broadly columnar
Evergreen
Pollinated: Insect
Leaf shape: Juvenile leaves rounded, adult leaves lanceolate

Identification: This is a small tree or large shrub with horizontal branches that droop at the ends. The bark is pale grey to orange-yellow, shedding vertically in long strips. The juvenile leaves are rounded, up to 5cm/2in in length and width, and are silver-blue with a white bloom. The adult leaves are ovate to lanceolate, waxy to the touch, glossy green and up to 15cm/6in long. The flowers are white with several golden yellow stamens. They grow in clusters of three in the leaf axils in spring. The fruit is urn-shaped (hence the name), about 1.5cm/⅔in long, woody, and tapers sharply below the rim. It is similar in appearance to a poppy seed capsule.

Above: The flowers and urn-shaped seed capsules grow from the leaf axils.

Left: The brush-like flowers are held together in clusters of three.

HOLLIES AND HANDKERCHIEF TREE

There are over 400 species of temperate and tropical evergreen and deciduous trees and shrubs in the
Aquifoliaceae family; the vast majority belong to the holly, or Ilex, genus. Hollies are dioecious (either
male or female). The leaves occur alternately on the shoot and the fruit is a berry. Within the Nyssaceae
family are two of the most attractive of all temperate trees: the tupelo and the handkerchief tree.

Common Holly

Ilex aquifolium Linnaeus

Holly is one of the most useful and ornamental trees of the temperate world. It is extremely
hardy and its dense foliage provides better shelter in exposed coastal and mountainous
localities than just about any other tree. Holly has long been considered an integral part of
Christmas celebrations and its bright berries cheer up the dullest of winter
days. Holly timber is dense and hard and has been used for making
just about everything, from piano keys to billiard cues. The common
holly has given rise to numerous attractive garden cultivars.

Distribution: Whole of
Europe, western Asia and
North Africa.
Height: 20m/66ft
Shape: Broadly columnar
Evergreen
Pollinated: Insect
Leaf shape: Elliptic to ovate

Identification: The bark is silver-grey and smooth even in maturity. The leaves
are elliptic to ovate, up to 10cm/4in long, glossy dark green and waxy above,
and pale green beneath. They are extremely variable: some leaves have
strong spines around the margin; others are spineless. Both the male
and female flowers are small and
white with a slight fragrance; they
appear on separate trees clustered
into the leaf axils in late spring and
early summer. The fruit is a round,
shiny, red berry up to 1cm/½in
across, borne in clusters along
the shoot in winter.

*Right: The dense foliage of holly
makes it a useful hedging plant.*

*Right: Holly flowers are
scented and
appear from
spring into
summer.*

Tupelo

Black gum, Sour gum *Nyssa sylvatica Linnaeus*

This slow-growing, medium-sized tree has a huge range in
North America, stretching from Ontario in the north to
Mexico in the south. It has been extensively cultivated
elsewhere, primarily for its spectacular autumn leaf
colouring, which ranges from yellow and orange
through to red and burgundy. Tupelo was introduced
into Europe in 1750.

Identification: The bark is dark grey and smooth when young,
becoming cracked and fissured into square plates in maturity.
The leaves are obovate to elliptic, up to 15cm/6in long and
8cm/3in across, and have an entire margin and a blunt tip. They
are lustrous grass-green above and glaucous beneath. Both the
male and female flowers are small, green and
inconspicuous. They are borne
in long stalked clusters on
the same tree in summer.
The fruit is a blueberry-
coloured, egg-shaped glossy berry, up to
1.5cm/⅔in long. It is edible but not
particularly palatable, being rather sour.

Distribution: Eastern North
America
Height: 25m/82ft
Shape: Broadly columnar
Deciduous
Pollinated: Insect
Leaf shape: Obovate

*Right: Tupelo flowers are green
and hard to see against the leaves.
The fruit usually appears in pairs.*

American Holly *Ilex opaca* Aiton
The American holly, native to eastern North America from Massachusetts to Florida, grows wild on coastal sandy soils. It is an evergreen tree up to 20m/66ft tall, similar to common holly except that the leaf is less glossy above and a yellowish green colour beneath. It also has a more regular leaf shape with less variability in the number of spines on the leaf margin.

Japanese Holly *Ilex crenata* Thunb.
Native to both Japan and Korea, this attractive evergreen plant is more a tall shrub than a tree, seldom attaining heights in excess of 4m/13ft. It has stiff, deep green, glossy, small leaves, which are 1cm/½in long and more akin to those of common box than holly. These are densely borne on reddish brown shoots, which also carry globular, glossy black berries in winter.

Chinese Holly *Ilex cornuta* Lindl.
Also known as horned holly because of its horn-like spines, this small evergreen tree is native to China and Korea, and rare in cultivation. It has slightly larger red berries than common holly and a rectangular-shaped leaf with a large spine at each corner, plus smaller intermediate spines. It is slow-growing with a neat compact habit.

Highclere Holly *Ilex* x *altaclarensis* Dallim.
The term Highclere holly has come to represent a whole group of ornamental holly cultivars developed from the original *Ilex* x *altaclarensis* hybrid between the common holly, *I. aquifolium*, and the Madeira holly, *I. perado*. The original hybrid was developed at Highclere Castle, Berkshire, England in the late 1800s. Most of the cultivars have broad, rounded, glossy leaves. One of the most popular cultivars is 'Golden King', which has leaves with deep green centres and golden margins.

Handkerchief Tree

Dove tree, Ghost tree *Davidia involucrata* Baillon

This beautiful tree was first introduced into the West from China in 1904 by the English plant collector Ernest Wilson, who had been commissioned by Veitch's nursery to collect propagation material from 'this most wondrous of species'. All of the tree's common names refer to the white hanging leaf bracts that appear in late spring.

Identification: The bark is orange-brown with vertical fissures, creating flaking, irregular plates. The leaves, up to 15cm/6in long and 10cm/4in wide, are sharply toothed with a drawn-out, pointed tip. They are glossy bright green above and paler with some hairs beneath. In times of drought they tend to roll into a cigar shape in an effort to reduce water loss by transpiration. The flowers appear in late spring. They are small, numerous, clustered into a ball and have conspicuous lilac-coloured anthers. The fruit is a green-purple husk containing a single, hard nut, inside which are up to five seeds.

Below: Surrounding the flowers are two large white bracts of unequal size, up to 20cm/8in long, which flutter in the breeze.

Distribution: Western China.
Height: 25m/82ft
Shape: Broadly conical
Deciduous
Pollinated: Insect
Leaf shape: Heart-shaped

Common Box

Buxus sempervirens Linnaeus

This small tree or spreading shrub has dense foliage and has been grown for centuries in gardens for hedging, screening and topiary. It is a favourite for use in defining knot gardens and parterres, and clips well. It withstands dense shade and will happily grow beneath the branches of other trees. It has hard, cream-coloured wood, which has been extensively used for wood engraving and turnery.

Identification: The bark is fawn or buff-coloured, smooth at first, then fissuring into tiny plates. The leaves are ovate to oblong, 2.5cm/1in long, rounded at the tip with a distinctive notch, glossy dark green above, pale green below and borne on angular shoots. Both male and female flowers are produced in mid-spring; they are small, pale green with yellow anthers and carried separately in the same clusters on the same trees.

Left: The fruit is a small woody capsule holding up to six seeds.

Right: Male and female flowers are produced separately in the leaf axils.

Distribution: Europe, North Africa and western Asia.
Height: 6m/20ft
Shape: Broadly conical to spreading
Evergreen
Pollinated: Insect
Leaf shape: Ovate

HORSE CHESTNUTS

The horse chestnut genus, Aesculus, contains some of the most popular and easily recognizable ornamental trees in the world. There are just 15 species, all native to northern temperate regions, where they are widely grown in parks, gardens and arboreta for their stately habit, and attractive flowers and fruit. All horse chestnuts have compound, palmate leaves and large flowers borne in upright panicles.

Indian Horse Chestnut

Aesculus Indica (Cambessedes) J. D. Hooker

Distribution: North-western Himalayas into northern India.
Height: 30m/100ft
Shape: Broadly columnar
Deciduous
Pollinated: Insect
Leaf shape: Compound palmate

Right: The leaflets spread like fingers from the leaf stalk. Indian horse chestnut seeds are contained in a smooth husk.

This magnificent tree is not as widely known as the common horse chestnut, but equals it in stature and beauty. In the forests of the Himalayas, where it grows wild, Indian horse chestnut regularly exceeds 30m/98ft. Tall flower spikes appear in midsummer. For many years the white, light timber was used to make tea boxes.

Identification: The bark is grey-brown and smooth even in maturity. The leaves are compound and palmate with either five or seven leaflets all joining the leaf stalk at a common point. Each leaflet is obovate to broadly lanceolate and up to 25cm/10in long. They emerge bronze-coloured, gradually turning glossy grass-green in summer and then golden yellow in autumn. The white to pale pink flowers are borne in midsummer on erect, cylindrical panicles, up to 30cm/12in long. Each flower has a yellow or red blotch at the base. The fruit is a rough (but not spiny), green, slightly pear-shaped husk containing up to three dark brown nuts known commonly as 'conkers'.

Right: The flowers appear on long spikes in the middle of summer and poke through the foliage like candles.

Yellow Buckeye

Sweet buckeye *Aesculus flava* Solander

Sometimes referred to *A. octandra* or sweet buckeye, this handsome, round-headed tree was introduced from North America into Europe as early as 1764. *Flava* means yellow and refers to the yellow flowers that appear in early summer. This is one of the best horse chestnuts for autumn colour because the leaves turn a stunning orange-red in early autumn.

Identification: The bark is brown-grey, flaking in maturity into large irregular-shaped scales. Branches tend to be horizontal or even drooping with a characteristic sweep upwards towards the tip. The leaves are compound and palmate, with five sharply toothed dark-green leaflets, each up to 15cm/6in long, all joining a pea-green leaf stalk at a common point. The flowers are yellow with a pink blotch and borne on upright panicles up to 15cm/6in long in late spring and early summer. The fruit, two brown nuts or 'conkers', are encased in a smooth, round husk, up to 5cm/2in across.

Distribution: USA: From Pennsylvania to Tennessee and Georgia, and west into Ohio and Illinois.
Height: 30m/100ft
Shape: Broadly conical
Deciduous
Pollinated: Insect
Leaf shape: Compound palmate

Left: Leaf and flower stalk.

Right: Smooth fruit.

Common Horse Chestnut

Aesculus hippocastanum Linnaeus

This tree is often wrongly thought to be native to a much larger area than just Albania and Greece because of its popularity and widespread planting as an ornamental tree. It extended its range as early as 1650, having been first introduced into Vienna.

Identification: The bark is orange-brown to grey, smooth at first, turning shallowly fissured and scaly in maturity. The large winter buds are a rich red-brown colour and covered in a sticky resin. The leaves are compound, palmate and large – each leaflet can be up to 30cm/12in long. There are normally five to seven strongly-veined, obovate leaflets on each compound leaf, all leaving the leaf stalk at a common point. The nuts or 'conkers' are grouped in twos or threes in a husk that is 5cm/2in across.

Left: Horse chestnut leaf buds are covered by brown scales. The seed husks have sharp spines.

Distribution: Albania and Greece.
Height: 30m/100ft
Shape: Broadly columnar
Deciduous
Pollinated: Insect
Leaf shape: Compound palmate

Left: The flowers are creamy white, blotched with yellow and pink, and borne in large upright, conical panicles, up to 25cm/10in long, in mid-spring.

Red Horse Chestnut *Aesculus x carnea* Hayne
This popular tree is a hybrid between *A. hippocastanum* and *A. pavia*. It is not known where this hybrid first originated, but it is likely that it occurred naturally in Germany in the early 1800s. It is a round-headed, spreading tree, seldom reaching heights in excess of 20m/66ft. The flowers are deep pink to red and borne in upright panicles in late spring.

Californian Buckeye *Aesculus californica* (Spach) Nuttall
A low-spreading, small tree, up to 10m/33ft and native to California, USA. It has small, compound, palmate leaves made up of five to seven broadly lanceolate leaflets; each one is 15cm/6in long, deep green above and sage-green below. The fragrant, white flowers, flushed with pink, appear in summer in dense, upright panicles, each up to 15cm/6in long.

Japanese Horse Chestnut

Aesculus turbinata Blume

In many ways this large tree is similar in appearance to the common horse chestnut, *A. hippocastanum*. It is widely planted in Japan as an ornamental species but is slower growing than the common horse chestnut and its flowers are not so large or carried in such profusion. Its leaves are much larger, however, and turn bright orange in autumn.

Identification: The bark is brown and flaky in maturity. The winter buds are glossy, red-brown and sticky. The leaves are compound and palmate, with five to seven obovate, stalkless, toothed leaflets all attached at the same point to a common leaf stalk. Each rich green leaflet can be up to 40cm/16in long and is heavily veined. The flowers are creamy white with a red blotch and borne on upright panicles up to 25cm/10in tall in late spring. The fruit is an egg-shaped, virtually spineless yellow-green husk, ripening brown to reveal two to three shiny brown seeds, or 'conkers', inside.

Distribution: Japan.
Height: 30m/100ft
Shape: Broadly columnar
Deciduous
Pollinated: Insect
Leaf shape: Compound palmate

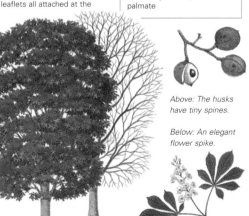

Above: The husks have tiny spines.

Below: An elegant flower spike.

MAPLES

There are more than 100 species of maples, Acer, in the world and countless cultivars, particularly of the Japanese maples. They are mainly deciduous and predominantly found throughout northern temperate regions, with a few extending into subtropical Asia. They range in size from mighty American giants to slow-growing Japanese bonsai. Many are cultivated for their attractive foliage and graceful habit.

Ash-leaved Maple

Box elder *Acer negundo* Linnaeus

This variable small to medium-sized maple is found growing wild across North America, particularly alongside rivers and in moist soils. The leaves do not resemble those on the Canadian flag, but are pinnate with up to seven leaflets that individually resemble the leaves of elder, *Sambucus*. The name 'box' comes from the fact that the timber is white and dense, like boxwood.

Identification: The bark is brown to silver-grey, thin and smooth. The leaves are pinnate with each leaflet approximately 10cm/4in long and sometimes lobed. Leaflets are arranged opposite in pairs, with a terminal leaflet that is usually slightly bigger than the rest. They are rich green above and lighter green with some hair beneath. Both male and female flowers are small, yellow-green and borne on separate trees in spring, just as the leaves are emerging. The male flowers are tassel-like with long drooping stamens; the females soon develop the familiar seed wings. The fruit is the classic, downward-pointing, two-winged seed.

Distribution: North America.
Height: 20m/66ft
Shape: Broadly columnar
Deciduous
Pollinated: Insect
Leaf shape: Pinnate

Left: Flowers hang, tassel-like, from the outer twigs. The seeds each have two wings to catch the wind and spin as they fall from the tree. The leaves are different from those of most maples.

Sycamore

Acer pseudoplatanus Linnaeus

Sycamore is one of the most common northern temperate trees. It has an extensive natural range and has been widely planted and subsequently naturalized in North America and the UK. It is hardy, and resistant to strong winds and exposure to salt-laden air in coastal areas.

Identification: The bark is grey and smooth when young becoming a delightful greyish pink in maturity with irregular-sized flaking plates. The leaf buds are lime green. They open in spring to release a bronzy yellow leaf, which turns deep green within two weeks of emergence. Leaves are up to 20cm/8in across, palmate and have five coarsely toothed lobes. The small flowers are borne in dense, yellow-green, pendulous clusters as the leaves emerge in spring. The fruit is the familiar two-winged seed. Each wing is 2.5cm/1in long. Seeds are grouped in pendulous clusters from early summer; they are red-green in colour, ripening to brown in mid-autumn.

Right: Sycamore seeds are easily recognized by their paired wings. The leaves are typically maple-shaped.

Distribution: Europe from the Pyrenees in Spain to the Carpathians in the Ukraine.
Height: 30m/100ft
Shape: Broadly columnar
Deciduous
Pollinated: Insect
Leaf shape: Palmate

Silver Maple

Acer saccharinum Linnaeus

This is one of the fastest-growing North American maples and is widely planted as an ornamental specimen for parks and gardens. It is altogether more refined than sycamore, having a light, open crown with bi-coloured leaves, which catch the light as they flutter in the breeze. It does have rather brittle wood, which means that it has a tendency to drop its branches – sometimes with no warning.

Identification: The bark is grey and smooth when young, becoming flaky with epicormic growth in maturity. The leaves are palmate, up to 15cm/6in long and wide, and have five sharply toothed lobes, each ending in a sharp point. They are light green above and glaucous with some hair beneath. The leaves are borne on lax stalks up to 15cm/6in long, allowing them to flutter in even the lightest breeze. Both male and female flowers are small and greenish yellow. They are clustered on the young shoots as the leaves emerge. The fruit is winged seeds carried in pairs; each wing is up to 2.5cm/1in long.

Distribution: Eastern North America from Ontario to Florida.
Height: 30m/100ft
Shape: Broadly columnar
Deciduous
Pollinated: Insect
Leaf shape: Palmate

Left: In mid-autumn the leaves turn yellow before falling.

Red Maple *Acer rubrum* Linnaeus
Native to eastern North America from Quebec and Ontario to Florida and Texas, red maple is one of the first trees to flower in spring. Long before the leaves emerge, clusters of bright red drooping flowers stand out like tiny burning embers on the bare branches. Red maple is a handsome large tree. Its leaves have three or five lobes, each up to 12.5cm/5in long and irregularly toothed. The leaf colour in autumn is bright red.

Sugar Maple *Acer saccharum* Marshall
This North American species has palmate, lobed leaves, up to 12.5cm/5in wide. Each lobe is heart-shaped at the base and pointed at the tip. Also known as rock maple, this is the species that produces the sweet sap that is sold throughout the world as maple syrup.

Cappadocian Maple *Acer cappadocicum* Gleditsch
Native to the Caucasus Mountains, this round-headed, large tree has palmate leaves with five to seven, taper-pointed, untoothed lobes. The leaves are borne on long stalks which, when cut, exude a milky white sap. In autumn the leaves turn a brilliant butter-yellow colour before falling.

Nikko Maple *Acer maximowiczianum* Miquel
A delightful, round-headed, medium-sized Japanese tree with trifoliate leaves, the undersides of which are covered with soft blue-white hairs. It is one of the finest maples for autumn colour. Leaflets gradually change from green through yellow and orange to red, before falling. Sometimes wrongly referred to as *A. nikoense*.

Paperbark Maple

Acer griseum (Franchet) Pax

This beautiful small tree was discovered in 1901 and almost immediately became a garden favourite. It has striking, cinnamon-coloured, wafer-thin, peeling bark, which flakes away to reveal fresh orange bark. The distinctive trifoliate leaves turn rich orange, red and burgundy in autumn.

Identification: The flaking, cinnamon-coloured bark is almost the only identifying characteristic required; this distinctive colouring being evident from an early age. The trifoliate leaves have three elliptic leaflets, each up to 10cm/4in long and with several large blunt teeth on each side. They are dark green above and glaucous beneath, with some pubescence. Drooping clusters of small greenish yellow flowers are borne on hairy stalks in spring, as the leaves unfurl. The fruit is a pair of winged seeds. They are normally pale green and covered in soft down; each wing is approximately 3cm/1¼in long. Although freely borne, the seed has a low germination rate with rarely more than five per cent successfully developing into seedlings.

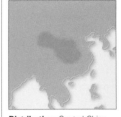

Distribution: Central China.
Height: 15m/50ft
Shape: Broadly columnar
Deciduous
Pollinated: Insect
Leaf shape: Trifoliate

Left: The red, flaking bark distinguishes this tree from other maples.

Smooth Japanese Maple

Acer palmatum Thunberg

Smooth Japanese maple was first discovered in 1783 and introduced into the West in 1820. Surprisingly though, it was almost another 80 years before it became popular and began to be widely planted. The famous Acer Glade at Westonbirt Arboretum, in Gloucestershire, England was not planted until 1875. Today there are literally hundreds of cultivars of smooth Japanese maple. In the wild the species grows within, or on the edge of, mixed broad-leaved woodland, providing dappled shade and shelter.

Identification: The bark is grey-brown and smooth, even in maturity. The overall shape of the tree is like a large natural bonsai, with horizontal, spreading, meandering branches forking from the main stem quite close to the ground. The leaves are palmate with between five and seven deep, pointed lobes that have forward-facing serrations around the margin. They are up to 10cm/4in across. The flowers are burgundy-red with yellow stamens. They are borne in upright or drooping clusters as the leaves emerge in spring. The fruit is green to red winged seeds carried in pairs; each wing is up to 1cm/½ in long and clustered together on the branch with up to 20 other seeds.

Below left: In autumn, the leaves turn red and gold before falling.

Distribution: China, Taiwan, Japan and Korea.
Height: 15m/50ft
Shape: Broadly spreading
Deciduous
Pollinated: Insect
Leaf shape: Palmate

Right: New leaves emerge a bright green colour.

Oregon Maple

Bigleaf maple *Acer macrophyllum* Pursh

The big leaves are the main characteristic of this handsome North American species, which inhabits riverbanks, moist woods and canyons. In fact everything about this tree is big; its trunk, flowers and fruit are also among the largest for the genus. The timber of Oregon maple is highly valued in America, where it is used to make furniture.

Identification: The bark is grey-brown and smooth, becoming vertically fissured in maturity. The leaves are palmate with large, coarsely toothed lobes cutting deep into the leaf centre. They are up to 25cm/10in long and 30cm/12in across, grass-green coloured and carried on long, buff-coloured leaf stalks. The flowers are green-yellow, fragrant and hang in conspicuous clusters up to 20cm/8in long as the leaves unfurl in spring. The fruit has paired wings, each up to 5cm/2in long, covered in fawn bristles and containing one seed at its base.

Distribution: Western North America from British Columbia to California.
Height: 25m/82ft
Shape: Broadly columnar
Deciduous
Pollinated: Insect
Leaf shape: Palmate

Below: The flowers appear in spring as the new leaves emerge.

Below left: The winged seeds are held on the tree in small bunches.

Fullmoon Maple *Acer japonicum* Thunberg
The fullmoon maple is native to Japan and is hardly ever seen as a species in gardens anywhere else, despite the fact that it was introduced into the West as long ago as 1864. However, it has produced some of the finest and most popular ornamental Japanese maple cultivars, including the vine-leaved Japanese maple, 'Vitifolium', the delightful 'Aconitifolium' and the golden-leaved 'Aureum', which is now considered a species in its own right under the name *A. Shirasawanum.*

Amur Maple *Acer ginnala* Maximowicz
The Amur maple is native to China and Japan, where it grows in mountain valleys, normally close to rivers. It is a small, wide-spreading tree seldom attaining more than 10m/33ft in height. The Amur maple has narrow leaves with three deep lobes on each side and ending in a coarsely toothed, central-pointed lobe. It produces striking red autumn colour which, unfortunately, does not last long – the leaves tend to fall within days of turning colour.

Van Volxem's Maple *Acer velutinum* var. *vanvolxemii* Brossier
This is a variety of the Caucasian *A. velutinum* collected by G. Van Volxem in 1873. It is superior to the species in having larger leaves and flowers. The leaves are somewhat similar to sycamore but larger, with some pubescence on the leaf veins on the underside of the leaf, which is blue-green in colour.

Moosewood

Striped maple *Acer pensylvanicum* Linnaeus

This tree got its name because in North America moose eat the bark; however, striped maple is far more descriptive because of the way the grey-brown bark is beautifully striped with vertical, wavy white lines. This species thrives in moist woodlands. There is a popular cultivated garden form of moosewood called 'Erythrocladum', which has bright crimson shoots and winter buds.

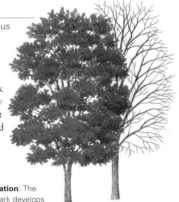

Distribution: Eastern North America.
Height: 10m/33ft
Shape: Broadly columnar
Deciduous
Pollinated: Insect
Leaf shape: Oblong

Identification: The striped bark develops at a young age; immature shoots are green, ripening to reddish brown before developing vertical white lines (within three years). The leaves are up to 15cm/6in long, oblong with three triangular, taper-pointed, toothed lobes cutting into the top half of the leaf. They are deep green and crinkly with pronounced veining above and some rust-coloured pubescence beneath. The inconspicuous green flowers are borne in weeping clusters in spring. The fruit is a small two-winged seed; each wing is 2.5cm/1in long.

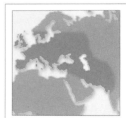

Left: The distinctive striped bark.

Right: The winged seeds.

Norway Maple

Acer platanoides Linnaeus

This fast-growing, handsome, hardy maple has been cultivated as an ornamental species for centuries. It has a large spreading crown with upswept branches and is as much at home in parkland settings as in woodland. Recently, smaller cultivars have been developed, which are being planted in great numbers alongside roads.

Identification: The bark is grey and smooth when young, becoming vertically ridged and fissured in maturity. The leaves are rather like the leaf on the Canadian flag – palmately lobed, with five lobes, each ending in several sharp teeth and a slender point. Each leaf is up to 15cm/6in in both length and width, bright green and borne on a long, slender, pink-yellow leaf stalk. The flowers are bright yellow, sometimes red, and borne in conspicuous drooping clusters in spring as the leaves emerge.

Right: Flowers may be either yellow or red.

Left: The fruit is a pair of green-yellow winged seeds borne in clusters. Each wing is up to 5cm/2in long.

Distribution: South-west Asia and Europe, north to southern Norway.
Height: 30m/100ft
Shape: Broadly columnar
Deciduous
Pollinated: Insect
Leaf shape: Palmate

Right: Fresh foliage is a light green colour.

ASHES AND CATALPAS

There are about 65 species within the ash genus, Fraxinus. All have pinnate leaves and are found within temperate regions of the world, primarily North America, Europe and Asia. They are hardy, fast-growing deciduous trees that tolerate exposure, poor soils and atmospheric pollution. The catalpas make up a genus of eleven species of beautiful flowering trees, mainly native to North America and China.

Common Ash

Fraxinus excelsior Linnaeus

One of the largest of all European deciduous trees, common ash is found growing wild from the Pyrenees to the Caucasus. Ash grows particularly well on calcareous limestone soils. It produces strong, white timber that has long been used where strength and durability are required, along with impact resistance. The wooden frames for the 1960s Morris Traveller car were made of ash.

Distribution: Europe.
Height: 40m/130ft
Shape: Broadly columnar
Deciduous
Pollinated: Insect
Leaf shape: Pinnate

Identification: Ash bark is pale fawn when young, becoming grey and fissured with age. The overall form is of a light airy crown, with a trunk that tends to be straight and long with little branching. One distinguishing characteristic of ash is its velvet-black winter buds. The fruit is a flattened, winged seed, 4cm/1½in long, borne in clusters known as 'keys' throughout the winter.

Right: The leaves are pinnate and up to 30cm/12in long. Each may have up to 12 pairs of shallow toothed, rich green leaflets.

Left: Both male and female flowers are produced in profusion in early spring.

Narrow-leaved Ash

Fraxinus angustifolia Vahl

This elegant tree has, as the name suggests, the narrowest leaves of any ash. These give the tree an open, feathery look. It is a fast-growing tree that was first introduced into Western Europe in 1800. There are several cultivars of *F. angustifolia* including 'Raywood', which has leaves that turn plum-purple in autumn.

Identification: The bark is grey-brown with vertical fissures. Older trees may have been grafted on to the rather incompatible, slower growing *F. excelsior*, which results in a prominent horizontal banding effect at the graft union. The flowers are small and inconspicuous, green or purple and borne on bare twigs in early spring. The winter buds are dark brown. The fruit is flattened, winged seeds, up to 4cm/1½in long, borne in hanging fawn clusters, which persist well into winter.

Above: Narrow-leaved ash is a graceful tree with well-spaced branches and light, airy foliage.

Distribution: Southern Europe, North Africa and western Asia.
Height: 25m/82ft
Shape: Broadly columnar
Deciduous
Pollinated: Insect
Leaf shape: Pinnate

Right: The leaves are pinnate, with up to 13 lanceolate, sharply toothed, glossy dark-green leaflets, up to 10cm/4in long.

Foxglove Tree

Paulownia tomentosa (Thunberg) Steudel

This beautiful flowering tree is native to the mountains of central China. It takes its genus name from the daughter of Czar Paul I of Russia, Anna Paulownia. The spectacular pale purple, foxglove-like flowers appear on spikes in late spring. The timber has a certain resinous quality and was used in China and Japan to make a stringed instrument similar to a lute. Quite often *Paulownia* is coppiced for its foliage, which on juvenile shoots can be up to 45cm/18in across.

Identification: The bark is rather like beech, being grey and smooth, even in maturity. The leaves are ovate, up to 45cm/18in wide and long, heart-shaped at the base and have two large, but normally shallow, lobes on each side. They are dark green, with hair on both surfaces and shoots. The shoots are soft and pithy. Each trumpet-shaped, pale purple flower, blotched inside with dark purple and yellow, is 5cm/2in long. Flowers are on upright panicles up to 45cm/18in tall.

Distribution: Central and eastern China.
Height: 20m/66ft
Shape: Broadly columnar
Deciduous
Pollinated: Insect
Leaf shape: Ovate

Left: The fruit is a green, pointed, egg-shaped, woody capsule containing several winged seeds. The purple flowers resemble foxgloves.

Manna Ash *Fraxinus ornus* Linnaeus
This flowering ash grows wild in south-western Asia and southern Europe. It has been widely cultivated elsewhere since around 1700. It produces (rather unusually for an ash) large panicles of creamy white, fragrant flowers, which hang in fluffy clusters from the branches in late spring. Manna sugar, which is used in the treatment of diabetes, is derived from the sap of this tree.

Western Catalpa *Catalpa speciosa* (Warder ex Barney) Engelmann
This large, fast-growing tree is native to the USA, where it grows wild in swamps and along riverbanks. The flowers are similar to those of the Indian bean tree, but not borne in such profusion. The timber of western catalpa is extremely water-resistant. Gate posts made from it will remain undamaged in direct contact with the soil for more than 50 years. A group of these trees that were flooded to two-thirds of their height in Missouri, USA, were still sound almost 70 years later.

Yellow Catalpa *Catalpa ovata* G. Don
This rare, small, spreading tree is native to China. It has ovate leaves, which are more distinctly lobed than either of its two North American cousins and white flowers, which are suffused with yellow. The flowers open in late summer and are followed by dark brown seed pods, each up to 30cm/12in long, in autumn. Flowers are borne in upright panicles in late summer.

Indian Bean Tree

Catalpa bignonioides Walter

The Indian referred to in the name is in fact the Native American, who used to dry and paint catalpa seeds and wear them as decoration. This is one of the last trees in its region to flower, and is normally at its best in midsummer. It tolerates atmospheric pollution well and has become a firm favourite for planting in towns and cities, despite its broadly spreading crown.

Identification: Catalpa has grey-brown bark, becoming loose and flaking in patches in maturity. The leaves are broadly ovate, up to 25cm/10in long and 15cm/6in wide, rarely lobed and heart-shaped at the base. On emerging from the bud they are bronze-coloured, gradually turning grass-green with some hair beneath. Each leaf is borne on a long, lax leaf stalk. Branches are quite brittle and prone to breakage in summer.

Distribution: South-east USA.
Height: 20m/66ft
Shape: Broadly spreading
Deciduous
Pollinated: Insect
Leaf shape: Ovate

Right: The seed pods are 40cm/16in long.

Below: Each of the trumpet-shaped flowers is up to 5cm/2in long.

TREES OF THE TROPICAL WORLD

Within the tropical and subtropical area is a range of diverse habitats.
These include ferociously hot dry deserts, humid and windless lowland
forests, cool temperate-like montane areas and coastal mangrove
swamps. Understandably, the trees that inhabit these areas vary

ATLANTIC OCEAN

AZORES

CANARY
ISLANDS

MEXICO   FLORIDA KEYS
CUBA
CARIBBEAN ISLANDS
BELIZE
HONDURAS
GUATEMALA   CARIBBEAN SEA
SENEGAL
COSTA RICA   TRINIDAD
VENEZUELA
PANAMA   GUYANA

ECUADOR

PACIFIC OCEAN

BRAZIL

PERU
BOLIVIA

CHILE   PARAGUAY

URUGUAY

ARGENTINA

enormously. Constant factors are the high light intensity and day length, which fluctuates around 12 hours throughout the year, and the resulting weak seasonality. Trees receive plenty of light, and the majority are evergreen, but if they are deciduous, it is often only fleetingly, or to advertise glamorous flowers. Numerous tropical flowers are large and intoxicatingly beautiful. Many tropical trees demonstrate cauliflory, whereby flowers and fruit emerge directly from the trunk, enabling easier access for pollination by wind, insects, bats and birds.

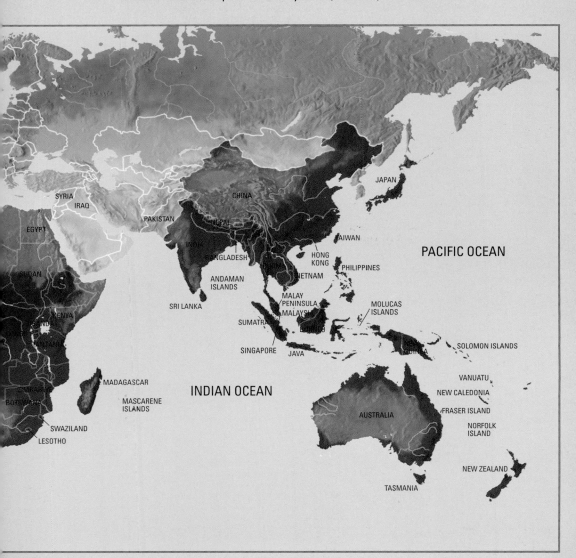

CONIFERS

Gymnosperms include all of the plants known as conifers, in which the naked seeds are held within a cone. The majority are evergreen trees with leaves reduced to needles or scales. Many of them live to a great age. Incredibly, for such a large and ancient group, they are rare in the tropics.

Hoop Pine

Araucaria cunninghamii ait. ex. D. Don.

This species occurs naturally in drier rainforests, although most wild trees have been cut down for timber. The hoop pine is incredibly slow growing and long lived, growing at only 2–3mm/⅛in a year when mature and living for up to 450 years. The tight clusters of foliage around the branches give the tree the appearance of having soft, fluffy protruding arms.

Identification: The young bark is coppery but matures to become rough and then peels horizontally, resulting in lines or 'hoops'. The short horizontal branches carry branchlets in dense tufts at their tips. The juvenile leaves are 1–2cm/⅖–¾in long, bright green and have a sharp tip. When mature, the leaves become tiny, pointed, inward-curving scales. Hoop pines may not produce cones until they are 200 years old. The male cones are spike shaped and 5–8cm/2–3in long. The female cones are 10cm/4in long x 8cm/3in wide and appear through the winter. When ripe, cones fall apart releasing winged seed.

Far left: The female cone contains naked seeds.

Left: A branchlet of tiny scale leaves.

Distribution: New South Wales and Queensland, Australia and New Guinea.
Height: 60m/200ft
Shape: Columnar
Evergreen
Pollinated: Wind
Leaf shape: Lanceolate, curved

Queensland Kauri

Agathis robusta (C. Moore ex. F. Muell.)

An emergent tree of subtropical rainforest, the Queensland kauri is also found at the bottom of valleys and in small clearings. The thick trunk, reaching 4m/13ft in girth, tapers very little and is often free of branches for two-thirds of its height. Consequently, the timber is knot free with a straight grain. It is also strong and durable, making it valuable, and this species is now under threat.

Distribution: South Queensland and Frasier Island, Australia.
Height: 45m/150ft
Shape: Conical
Evergreen
Pollinated: Wind
Leaf shape: Ovate

Far right: The unusual broad foliage of the Queensland kauri.

Right: A hard female cone.

Identification: The trunk is coated in highly resinous, thick, rough, flaky, brown bark. The whorled horizontal side branches remain short while the tree is young. They carry spirally arranged leaves, which will persist on the tree for many years. The immature leaves are a reddish colour. When mature they are ovate, 10–15cm/4–6in long, 9–10cm/3½–4in wide, dark green, thick and leathery with longitudinal lines on the upper surface, and paler green below. The male catkins emerge singly from the leaf axils and are 3–5cm/1¼–2in long. The woody female cones are ovoid, 10–13cm/4–5in long, 9–10cm/3½–4in wide and covered in 2.5cm/1in-wide scales.

Norfolk Island Pine *Araucaria heterophylla* (Salisbury) Franco.
From Norfolk Island but not a pine, this beautiful, fast-growing conifer reaches 60m/200ft and grows successfully throughout the tropics. In Hawaii, plantations provide timber for ships' masts. The Norfolk Island pine is a very symmetrical, formal looking tree. It stands upright and has a conical shape with a regular branching pattern. The soft, curved leaves are bright green and glossy. This tree will thrive in deep sand and is wind tolerant, and as a result, is often seen planted in coastal locations. Due to its tolerance of low light levels when young, it is sold as a houseplant in temperate climates.

Amboina Pine *Agathis dammara* (Lamb.) Rich.
Agathis is an ancient plant genus very closely allied to *Araucaria*. All parts of these trees spontaneously exude a resin called dammar (or damar), which is collected and used commercially in varnishes and the making of linoleum. The amboina pine grows in dense clumps in the rainforests of Sumatra and peninsular Malaysia. It grows to 55m (180ft) tall, has grey or black bark and ovate, dark green, 6–12cm/2½–5in long leaves. The male cones are 4–7cm/1½–3in long spikes, the female cones are ovoid, 6–8.5cm/2½–3in long.

Blue Kauri *Agathis atropurpurea* B. Hyland
This tree grows in the montane rainforest of northern Queensland, where it is protected from over-exploitation across large areas. It reaches 60m/200ft tall and has a purplish-brown or black bark. The leaves are oblong to elliptic with a blunt notched tip, 4cm/1½in long and tightly arranged. The male cones are 1.5cm/½in long. The female cones are olive green, round and 3.5–5.5cm/1½–2in across.

Dacrydium elatum (Roxb.) ex. Hook.
This interesting conifer has leaves of two forms, some are tiny and triangular, packed tightly together to form green stems, while others are four-sided, needle-like and up to 2cm/¾in long. The fine foliage is greyish green. The tree grows from India through to mainland Malaysia in highland forested areas. It reaches 24m/80ft and has a dark, fissured, scaly bark, and dense, domed crown. The flowers of the male tree are tiny catkins, while those of the female tree form in short spikes, producing black seeds in a shallow, fleshy cup.

Caribbean Pine

Cuban pine *Pinus caribaea* Morelet.

Also commonly called the Cuban pine, this conifer is grown commercially for its timber, which is resinous, and for the making of turpentine (white spirit). The mature, open, broad crown is rounded and consists of heavy, spreading branches.

Identification: The bark varies from grey to brown and naturally sheers off in large, flat plates. The winter buds at the branch tips are cylindrical, producing the leaves, which have adapted into thin needles. Each leaf is 30cm/12in long, deep green and glossy. Leaves occur in bundles of three to five. The male cones consist of many catkins bunched together, producing large amounts of pollen. The female cones may be oval or conical and are 10–13cm/4–5in long by 5–6cm/2–2½in wide. They are covered in glossy, reddish-brown scales with a prickle at the end of each, and contain black, triangular seeds.

Distribution: Central America, south-east United States, Honduras and Cuba.
Height: 30m/100ft
Shape: Domed
Evergreen
Pollinated: Wind
Leaf shape: Needle

Left: The foliage and cones easily identify this tropical pine.

Bunya-Bunya

Araucaria bidwillii Hook. f.

This slow-growing, distinctive tree has a symmetrical form. The long, horizontal, whorled branches and foliage are sparse low down the trunk, whereas in the crown they are dense with the foliage clustering to the ends of the twigs. The seed-bearing cones are impressive, weighing up to 8kg/18lbs and looking remarkably like large, green pineapples. The seeds are eaten by Australia's aboriginal people.

Identification: The thick, pale bark is resinous and peels off the trunk. The leaves are arranged spirally and densely clustered at the end of the branches. Each leaf is 5cm/2in long, 1cm/½in wide, lanceolate, curved, bright to dark green and leathery with a stiff, prickly point at the tip. The male cones are 15–18cm/6–7in long and 1.5cm/½in wide. The female cones are 30cm/12in long and 23cm/9in wide, and carry up to 150 seeds.

Distribution: Coastal southeast Queensland, Australia.
Height: 45m/150ft
Shape: Domed
Evergreen
Pollinated: Wind
Leaf shape: Lanceolate, curved

Right: The male cones release pollen.

Below: The foliage is spiny to the touch.

THE ANNONA FAMILY

The Annonaceae family consists mostly of tropical trees, shrubs and climbers. Annonas have a distinctive odour and smooth, simple leaves arranged alternately, or spirally in paired ranks. Flowers have both male and female organs, three sepals and two whorls of three petals. Beetles are the major pollinators. Fruit often consists of a cluster of units, sometimes fused together, and contains large, hard, smooth seeds.

Keppel Tree

Stelechocarpus burahol (Blume.) Hook. f. Thomson

This endangered tree is rare both wild and cultivated. It is grown in a small area of Java for its fruit, which hangs in masses directly from the lower trunk. The fruit has a spicy, mango-like flavour. Indonesian people once believed that eating the fruit gave one's bodily secretions a pleasant aroma.

Identification: The dark green, glossy leaves alternate on the twigs and form a dense crown. When young, the leaves are deep red. The flowers are small and appear in clusters directly from the trunk. The fruit is eye-catching with rough, pale orange to cinnamon-brown skin and a pointed tip. The flesh of the fruit is orange and contains reddish-brown seeds.

Distribution: South-east Asia.
Height: Small
Evergreen
Pollinated: Beetle
Leaf shape: Narrowly oblong

Right: Keppel fruit is 8cm/ 3in across and emerges directly from the trunk, a common characteristic of tropical fruit.

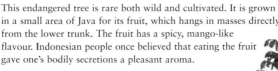

Left: Smooth surfaces and pointed tips of the leaves help excess water run off.

Ylang-Ylang

Cananga odorata L.

This well-known tree produces fragrant flowers from which an oil (ilang-ilang) is distilled for use in the perfume industry. Ylang-ylang flowers are sold locally in markets for perfuming rooms, as temple offerings, for leis (in Hawaii) and for scenting coconut oil. The tree is fast growing on moist soil and has long, pendulous, rather brittle branches.

Distribution: Tropical Asia, Pacific Islands, India.
Height: 25m/80ft
Shape: Oval crown
Evergreen
Pollinated: Beetle
Leaf shape: Oblong to elliptic

Identification: The glossy green leaves are 10–35cm/ 4–14in long, vary in shape from oblong to elliptic and may be slightly wavy along the margins. Flowers appear in clusters throughout the year and are particularly abundant in autumn. The flowers are green when they open and gradually become yellow. They are spidery with six long, twisted, hanging petals, each 4–9cm/1½–3½in long. The clusters of fruit, each 1–2cm/½–1in across, are rounded and black when ripe.

Above left: The smooth, pale grey trunk is often hidden behind awkward, drooping branches.

Left: The fragrance of the flowers is variable, and wild specimens may smell quite rank.

Indian Mast Tree

Polyalthia longifolia L.

This is a popular tree in parks and avenues throughout Asia. It thrives in monsoon areas but is also found next to rivers in drier regions. Indian mast trees vary in their width. Some grow into upright poles of greenery, while others have a somewhat looser shape. The more columnar forms have been selected for cultivation, but many lose their tight form when they mature, with their lower branches spreading wider.

Identification: The drooping branches have dark grey bark and clothe the trunk almost entirely to the ground with swathes of glossy green, wavy-edged leaves, 15cm/6in long. The small flower clusters appear in the leaf axils on older branches in summer but are often hidden on the lower part of the tree by dense foliage. Each tiny star-like flower is greenish yellow and less than 1cm/⅖in across. The round to oval fruit is 2cm/¾in long and ripens from yellow through red to black.

Above: leaves are yellowish underneath, have wavy edges and may curl under at the tip.

Distribution: Sri Lanka.
Height: 15m/50ft
Shape: Narrowly columnar
Evergreen
Pollinated: Insect
Leaf shape: Lanceolate

Left: Each flower results in a bunch of five to thirteen fruits which are eaten by bats.

Canary Beech *Polyalthia nitidissima*
Grown in gardens for its dark glossy foliage and bright red and yellow, inedible fruits, the canary beech grows wild in dry rainforests and damp riverside locations in the Australian states of New South Wales and Queensland, and in New Caledonia. The alternate leaves are glossy, smooth, and bright green, on short leaf stems. It grows to 18m/60ft tall and produces small green flowers in the summer. The clustered fruit does not ripen simultaneously, so black, red, orange, yellow and green fruit may be seen together through the summer and autumn.

Yellow Lacewood *Polyalthia oblongifolia*
Found in New Guinea, it is grown for its timber, which is used in marquetry and varies from a light cream to mid-brown. It has smooth, leathery, 25cm/10in-long, broadly oblong, alternate leaves with prominent veins. Flower clusters form opposite or between leaves. They are 3cm/1¼in long and have a rusty pubescence on the sepals. Small one-seeded fruit forms in clusters. Each is egg shaped, smooth and 1.5cm/⅗in long.

Anaxagorea javanica Bl.
Common in Malaysia's rainforests, this small evergreen tree has beautifully scented flowers similar to ylang-ylang. The tree reaches 6m/20ft, or may grow as a shrub. Leaves are elliptic to oblong, 10–25cm/4–10in long, light green, and blunt-ended. The 2.5cm/1in flowers have thick, fleshy, green or cream petals and are followed by 2.5–5cm/1–2in-long, thin, dark green fruit. Ripe fruit fires its two small, smooth, black seeds 2–3m/yd from the tree.

African Nutmeg

Monodora myristica (Gaertn.) Dunal.

This beautiful, very tropical-looking tree produces fleshy seeds high in an aromatic oil similar to nutmeg. Historically the fruit was exported from Africa to the West Indies, where the oil was extracted. The African nutmeg tree has a straight trunk and large, horizontal branches. It prefers moist ground and if grown in drier conditions may become deciduous.

Identification: The drooping leaves are bright, shining green with a prominent paler midrib and reach 60cm/24in long. The flowers hang from the branches and are 25cm/10in long x 15cm/6in wide and fragrant. They have three large, frilled petals, which are bright yellow or white and fringed with purple or red and green spots. The outsides of the flowers are downy and the insides shiny. The fruits are round, dark brown and 8–20cm/3–8in across. They have a very hard shell and hang on strong, 60cm/24in-long stems. The flesh and seeds of the fruit are very like true nutmeg.

Distribution: Tropical Africa, Senegal through Nigeria to Kenya.
Height: 23m/75ft
Evergreen
Pollinated: Beetle
Leaf shape: Elliptic to obovate

Below: These beautiful and unusual flowers are thought to trap beetles inside them before they are ready to release their pollen.

ANNONAS

Annona is a large genus of more than 100 species within the family Annonaceae. The species are all similar: they are tropical and subtropical trees, usually evergreen, with large, simple, oblong, smooth-margined and aromatic leaves. The fruit-scented flowers are fleshy, emerging directly from old wood. The fruit is made of many fused segments and is normally edible.

Custard Apple

Annona squamosa L.

The custard apple is grown for its delicious fruit, sometimes described as tasting like strawberries and cream. The fruit is eaten fresh or processed into confectionery and drinks. The tree has an open crown of zigzagging branches and needs high humidity, so is only seen in the truly humid tropics.

Distribution: North of South America and West Indies.
Height: 6m/20ft
Shape: Spreading
Semi-deciduous
Pollinated: Beetle
Leaf shape: Lanceolate to oblong

Identification: The leaves, which are fragrant when crushed, vary in shape and may be from 9–15cm/3½–6in long. They are dull, pale green and smooth with minute dots on both surfaces, and may drop in dry spells. The pleasantly scented flowers occur all year round. They have three fleshy petals 5cm/2in long, are greenish yellow and found singly or in small clusters. The fruits occur with the flowers. They are greenish yellow but with a bluish green surface bloom. Each fruit is 5–13cm/2–5in long, round or heart shaped and made up of prominent lumps which, when ripe, may be pulled apart. The white flesh has a smooth texture and is sweet.

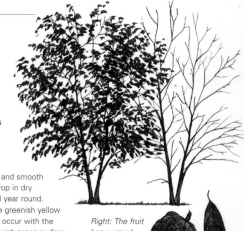

Right: The fruit has custard-like flesh, and the leaves are scented.

Soursop

Annona muricata L.

The soursop is the easiest *Annona* to grow in the tropics and carries the largest fruit, weighing up to 1kg/2lbs. The prolifically produced fruit appears throughout the year. It is not sour as the name suggests, but has ill-smelling skin and is often rather fibrous. It is rarely eaten fresh, but instead is processed into refreshing drinks and ices.

Identification: Sometimes seen as a multi-stemmed tree, the branches are sharply ascending and begin low on the trunk; young growth is covered in silky brown hairs. The leaves are 15cm/6in long, slightly curved, variable in shape, bright, glossy dark-green above and rusty below, with an unpleasant aroma if crushed. The odd flowers appear year-round from the trunk and branches. They have three very thick, cardboard-like petals, are 5cm/2in long, pale greenish-yellow and fragrant. The fruit is yellow when ripe, often oval, yet distorted in shape, 30cm/12in long and covered in short, fleshy spines. The skin of the fruit is thin. The flesh is firm, white, juicy, pleasantly fragrant and embedded with black seeds.

Distribution: West Indies and north of South America.
Height: 7m/23ft
Shape: Columnar
Evergreen
Pollinated: Beetle
Leaf shape: Ovate, obovate, elliptic to lanceolate

Right: The simple, glossy soursop foliage smells unpleasant.

Left: The flowers of the soursop are stiff and the fruit prickly.

Cherimoya

Annona cherimola Mill.

Found in mountain valleys in its native Andes, the cherimoya is suited to cooler, drier conditions than many others in this genus. It forms an attractive, low-branched, spreading tree. The cherimoya is grown in various parts of the world for its tasty, slightly acidic fruit.

Distribution: Peru and Ecuador.
Height: 8m/26ft
Shape: Spreading
Briefly deciduous
Pollinated: Beetle
Leaf shape: Ovate, elliptic or lanceolate

Right: The fruit grows slowly, ripening in mid- to late spring.

Identification: The leaves, which drop briefly in the spring, are rather variable in shape. They are a dull, deep green with velvety undersides, 25cm/10in long and strongly scented. The fragrant, hanging flowers are produced in the middle of summer. They consist of three thick, fleshy petals, are 2.5cm/1in long and vary from greenish yellow to reddish brown on the outside, and pale yellow or off-white with a purple central blotch on the inside. The ripe fruit is yellow, 15 x 10cm/6 x 4in and covered in large overlapping scales, each with a small black spot on it. The flesh is white and pulpy.

Ilama *Annona diversifolia* Safford
This spreading tree from lowland areas of western Mexico and Central America reaches 7m/23ft in height. It has tasty fruit, but may not produce it in great quantity. Although grown only on a local scale there are many varieties grown. Some have fruit with rich red flesh, in others it is white, pink or purple. The 2.5cm/1in flowers are maroon with furry petals and held on long stalks. The aromatic leaves are glossy green above, dull below and 15cm/6in long. The fruit is variable in shape and texture and may be light green, deep pink or even purple.

Pond Apple *Annona glabra* L.
Occurring in swampy and mangrove areas of southern Florida, northern South America, Peru and West Africa, the pond apple tree grows to 12m/40ft tall. Its evergreen leaves are glossy above, paler and hairy below, and vary in shape and size. The large, thick flowers grow in pairs in summer. They are maroon inside and yellow with red spots on the outside. The round, ovoid or cone-shaped fruit is greenish yellow, 8cm/3in long and inedible.

Poshte *Annona scleroderma* Safford
Reputed to be one of the tastiest of all annonas, the poshte is unfortunately rarely seen outside of its native Mexico, Belize, Guatemala and Honduras. It is grown in Guatemala on a local scale, but being a 20m/66ft-tall evergreen tree, is difficult to harvest and causes excessive shade over other crops. The leathery, lanceolate, shiny leaves are 25cm/10in long and 8cm/3in wide. The tough-skinned fruit may be green, green with brown spots or reddish. The flesh is smooth and creamy or grey in colour.

Bullock's Heart

Annona reticulata L.

The fruit of this tree takes time to develop and is less pleasantly flavoured than other annonas. Nonetheless, the bullock's heart is grown locally for its fruit in the tropics. Depending on location, it may drop its leaves for part of the year or stay evergreen.

Identification: The 20cm/8in long leaves are dark green, smooth, pointed, and dotted on the surface. If crushed they release an unpleasant odour. The fragrant flowers hang in clusters from the leaf axils on new wood. They are yellow or yellowish green with a purplish blotch or tint inside, 2.5cm/1in long and have narrow, fleshy petals. The fruit may be heart shaped, oval or conical, weighing up to 1kg/2lbs, but often less, and 8–16cm/3–6½in across. It is greenish yellow, becoming reddish brown or rosy on the side facing the sun. The surface is smooth and lined, marking where each capsule joins. The flesh is creamy white and pulpy.

Distribution: West Indies and northern South America.
Height: 10m/33ft
Shape: Spreading
Semi-evergreen
Pollinated: Beetle
Leaf shape: Oblong-lanceolate

Above: The flowers of this annona form near the growing tips.

Above: The fruit may contain hard or grainy sections within the flesh.

THE LAUREL FAMILY

The Lauraceae family is made up mostly of aromatic, evergreen, tropical and sub-tropical trees and shrubs. The leaves are often irregularly spaced and clustered at branch tips. They are simple, generally elliptical and glossy with smooth margins – typical rainforest leaves. The six-petalled flowers are small, greenish or yellow and arranged singly along stalks in racemes. The fruit is a one-seeded berry or drupe.

Avocado Pear

Persea americana Mill.

In their native homes avocados grow in wet lowlands but have been planted extensively throughout the tropics. They are grown for their tasty and highly nutritious, savoury fruit, which is rich in minerals, oils and sugars. This fast-growing tree initially forms a round head but may become spreading in maturity. As the plants need to cross-pollinate to produce fruit, two or more are usually grown together.

Identification: The trunk is short with dark fissured bark. The leaves are leathery, elliptical, heavily veined, and up to 45cm/18in long. They are dark green and glossy above and coated with bloom below. The green, branched racemes of fragrant flowers arise from the axils each autumn through to spring. Each flower measures 1cm/½in. The fruits may weigh up to 1kg/2lbs but are usually smaller, measuring about 10–15cm/4–6in long. They are pear shaped and purple to greenish brown with leathery skin.

Left: The fruit has a buttery texture and is often eaten with spices and sugar.

Distribution: Mexico and West Indies.
Height: 18m/60ft
Shape: Domed
Evergreen
Pollinated: Insect
Leaf shape: Elliptical

Right: The leaves carry a pale bloom on their undersides.

Cinnamon

Cinnamomum zeylanicum Bl.

Cinnamon spice is obtained by peeling the bark from young trunks and branches and drying it into quills. To ensure a regular supply of young bark the trees are often grown as coppiced specimens. All parts of the tree above ground are highly aromatic. Cinnamon is grown on a large scale in its native Sri Lanka but has become an invasive weed in the Seychelles, where it has spread beyond the confines of plantations.

Identification: The bark is light brown and papery when mature, and cinnamon-coloured when young. The smooth leaves are eye-catching; they are bright red and droopy for a few days when young and gradually mature to become glossy green with three distinctive white parallel veins. Pale below, they grow to 18cm/7in long. The insignificant but numerous, tiny flowers are found in loose racemes and are off-white or pale yellow. The very dark purple to black fruit is less than 1cm/½in across and equally easy to miss.

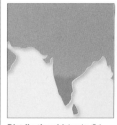

Above: Cinnamon bark is harvested at 2–3 years old and 3cm/1¼in in diameter for cinnamon production.

Right: The beautiful leaves have distinctive parallel veins.

Distribution: Malaysia, Sri Lanka and southern India.
Height: 10m/33ft
Shape: Domed
Evergreen
Pollinated: Insect
Leaf shape: Oblong

Above: Large numbers of the tiny flowers form into loose racemes.

Camphor Tree

Cinnamomum camphorum (L.) Sieb.

Some camphor trees bear camphor oil, others solid camphor. Camphor is used in the manufacture of plastics, lacquers, explosives and film. It is also used as an insect repellent and has medicinal properties. Camphor is extracted by distilling the wood, roots, twigs and leaves of the tree in water. This fast-growing species can be an invasive pest as it seeds readily in most types of ground. It has a dense crown up to 21m/70ft in diameter and low heavy branches on the short trunk. In some towns and cities, camphor is grown along streets as an ornamental or shade tree.

Identification: The bark is coppery on young wood and ages to become grey brown and heavily fissured. The young leaves are a pinkish coppery colour, maturing through pale to deep, glossy green. They are 13cm/5in long, ovate, have three distinctive veins, are leathery and smell of camphor, if crushed. The flowers are tiny and greenish yellow. The fruit is a small black berry.

Distribution: China, Taiwan and south Japan.
Height: 30m/100ft
Shape: Rounded spreading crown
Evergreen
Pollinated: Insect
Leaf shape: Ovate

Right: The heavily fissured bark of a mature camphor tree.

Right: The flowers and fruit of the camphor tree are insignificant. The leaves are distilled to extract camphor.

Persea **Cultivars**
Avocado cultivars are selected for many fruiting characteristics, including non-stringy flesh, small seeds, good storage and firm attachment to the tree. The trees must produce steady yields, remain small, and have a spreading habit. Each cultivar has different characteristics. Fruit can vary from 5cm/2in to 60cm/2ft long, and the skin can be light green, dark green, brownish, purple or red. The flesh may be fibreless, thick and creamy or watery, insipid and fibrous. The most popular are the Mexican and Guatemalan crosses: 'Fuerte' matures in winter and spring with smooth green skin, but fruits in alternate years; 'Hass' has a purple to black warty skin, and is produced in spring and summer.

Persea indica (L.) Spreng.
This lesser-known species of avocado originated in the Azores and Canary Islands. It is valued for its 25cm/10in-long blue-black fruit and its hard, well marked wood. This tree is evergreen and grows to 20m/66ft tall with a broad, domed crown. The branchlets and leaf stalks have a silky or woolly surface. The alternate, hairless leaves are elliptic-oblong to lanceolate-oblong with smooth margins, 8–20cm/3–8in long, deep green and leathery. The 5mm/¼in-long, whitish to yellowish green flowers are crowded into branched racemes 15cm/6in long.

Cassia

Cinnamomum aromaticum Nees.

Cassia is sometimes added to true cinnamon but is a much thicker, coarser product and does not coil into quills as effectively. It is cultivated in both Burma and China and is used to spice drinks and sweets. Cassia was the first known source of 'cinnamon' to Europeans, who used it to flavour wine and as an analgesic drug.

Identification: The bark is thick, highly aromatic and pale coppery brown. The leaves are 15–18cm/6–7in long and have an 8cm/3in tail. When young, the foliage is cream coloured blushed with pink or red. Mature leaves are green with three distinctive, pale, parallel veins, and have incredibly fine hair below. The flowers are tiny and yellow, and held on erect, branched racemes. The fruit is a small black berry.

Distribution: Burma and southern China.
Height: 15m/50ft
Shape: Rounded
Evergreen
Pollinated: Insect
Leaf shape: Oblong to lanceolate

Right: Young cassia leaves are a pretty cream and pink colour before they turn green. The small flowers are insignificant.

THE NUTMEG AND MAGNOLIA FAMILIES

The families Myristicaceae and Magnoliaceae are closely related to the annona family within the Magnoliales order. The nutmeg family is made up of tropical trees and shrubs throughout Asia, Africa and South America. They usually have aromatic wood and foliage, and seeds wrapped in a coloured aril. The magnolia family contains trees, shrubs and climbers of temperate and sub-tropical regions.

Nutmeg

Myristica fragrans Houtt.

Naturally found in coastal regions in the humid tropics, nutmegs are grown commercially in Indonesia, Sri Lanka and on the Caribbean island of Grenada. They are famed for their hard seed containing richly scented oil and for the bright red tissue that surrounds the seed, the spice mace. This pretty tree has a dense, formal canopy of close set whorls of branches. Both nutmegs and mace are used in cooking, while nutmeg oil is used medicinally.

Identification: This slender, slow-growing tree has smooth, grey bark. The leaves alternate on each side of the stem and are aromatic, 12cm/4½ in long, smooth and have smooth margins. When new, they are covered in small, silver scales, which persist on the lower surface throughout the life of the leaf. The flowers are produced throughout the year. They have pale yellow sepals but no petals, and are found individually, hanging like small bells 1cm/⅜ in long. Nutmeg trees are either male or female, and only female trees produce fruit. The fruit takes five to six months to develop; it is pear shaped, 8cm/3in long, pale yellow and fleshy. Each fruit contains one brown seed (the nutmeg itself) 3–4cm/1–1¼in long.

Distribution: Moluccas islands of Indonesia.
Height: 15m/50ft
Shape: Columnar
Evergreen
Pollinated: Insect
Leaf shape: Oblong-elliptic

Above: The seed has a hard brown case and a bright red laced aril.
Left: The simple leaves are silvery on their lower surface.

Orange Chempaka

Michelia champaca L.

This tree has highly scented blossoms, which appear all year round in truly tropical conditions, filling the air with their perfume. In cooler, less humid areas it flowers only in summer. Throughout its range, the blossoms are used as temple offerings. The orange chempaka is a fast-growing tree. Conical at first, it soon becomes oblong with horizontal branches.

Identification: The mature bark is pale grey and smooth, whereas the twigs are covered with short, soft, downy hair. The light green, silky smooth leaves droop from the branches. They have soft hair below and measure 28cm/11in long x 10cm/4in wide. The flowers vary in colour from white through yellow to orange. They have twelve long, narrow, twisted petals, are cup shaped and sit upright on the branch tips. Each flower is 10–13cm/4–5in wide with a very sweet scent during the day that becomes foul smelling at night.

Above: The simple leaves are little to go by when identifying this tree.

Distribution: India, Java, lower Himalayas.
Height: 30m/100ft
Shape: Oblong
Evergreen
Pollinated: Beetle
Leaf shape: Ovate-lanceolate

Left and right: The beautifully scented flowers often form out of sight, high in the canopy, but their perfume penetrates the air.

THE CECROPIA FAMILY

These plants have prominent stilt roots and sheaths or caps protecting their growing tip. They often have palmate, lobed leaves and produce brown latex in the shoot tips. The cecropia family, Cecropiaceae, is very closely related to the fig family, Moraceae, and is considered by some to be a sub-division of it. It is also related to the nettle family, Urticaceae.

Guarumo

Cecropia insignis L.

This fast-growing, softwood species inhabits wet lowland rainforest and is a pioneer species, colonizing open or recently disturbed places with plenty of light. The guarumo grows into a large, open-crowned tree with branches radiating in tiers. Its trunk and thick branches are hollow, providing a home for aggressive ants which defend it from leaf-cutting ant species. The large, umbrella-like leaves of this species are very eye-catching.

Identification: The trunk is pale in colour and produces milky sap: the twigs are reddish brown. Each of the dramatic leaves is round, up to 1m/3ft across and heavily lobed, usually with seven separate lobes. Lobes are oblong to egg shaped with the narrow end nearest the leaf stalk. The tiny flowers are densely clustered on to spikes: the male and female flower spikes are similar, 6–12cm/ 2½–4½in long by 1cm/½in wide, initially enveloped in a pink to brownish-red spathe (a modified leaf), pale green and generally erect. The tiny, green fruit is a dry, single-seeded nut, held on a spike up to 22cm/ 8½in long x 1cm/½in wide.

Left: The leaves are rough on the upper surface.

Distribution: Costa Rica.
Height: 25m/80ft
Shape: Irregularly domed
Deciduous
Pollinated: Insect
Leaf shape: Orbicular, deeply lobed

Right: Each spike carries numerous tiny seeds, which are popular with birds.

Amazon Grape *Pourouma cecropifolia* Mart.
The amazon grape is grown for its enormous, majestic leaves and for the fruit that it produces prolifically over three months in the wet season. This fast-growing tree may produce fruit from the age of three years. The fruit has a sweet, white pulp beneath an inedible skin that is easily removed. It is eaten fresh and used to make sweet wine, jams and jellies. The amazon grape grows on damp ground, exploiting the light from gaps in the forest canopy.
   This tree has a light tar-coloured trunk, characteristic stilt roots and short, very wrinkly branches, often containing brown latex. The beautiful circular leaves consist of 10–13 lobes, each broader and rounded at the tip and tapering at the base. When young, the leaves are burgundy in colour and droop, but they flatten out as they mature. Each mature leaf is 60cm/24in long x 80cm/28in wide and held on a bright green, 60cm/24in long leaf stalk. The leaf itself is wavy edged, mid-green and rough above with strongly marked veins. Sometimes there is a woolly down on the underside. The young leaf stems are covered with a dark rusty brown velvet. The flowers form in a dense branched structure 10cm/4in long. The yellowish green fruit is ovoid, 2cm/1in long and covered in a dense, velvety hair.
Each fruit contains a large seed and sweet, juicy pulp with a gummy, sticky texture.

Monkeyfruit *Myrianthus abroreus* P. Beauv.
From tropical West Africa, this 20m/66ft evergreen tree is used in numerous medicinal preparations. The leaves, sap, roots, fruit and bark are all used in many different preparations to treat disorders as varied as headaches, chest complaints, dysentery, boils, and difficulties in pregnancy. The young leaves and shoots are eaten, and are said to make good soup. The fruit pulp, which may be sweet or acidic, depending on the tree, is eaten fresh, while the seeds, which are rich in oil, are eaten once cooked. The pale, fibrous wood from this tree is of poor quality and used for burning.
   The tree grows in secondary rainforest and particularly favours damp or riverside positions. The trunk is often short, branching close to the ground, and reaches 1m/3ft in diameter with many aerial stilt roots. The bark is variable in colour, generally pale and sometimes greenish. The huge leaves can be 70cm/28in wide and are divided into seven to nine leaflets. Each leaflet has a coarsely toothed margin, and the largest may be 50cm/20in long. The flowers form towards the end of the dry season. The small, yellow male flowers form in panicles, while the female flowers are green and grow in clusters. The fruit is composed of many four- or five-sided fused fruits. It is soft and yellow when ripe, 10–15cm/4–6in across, and generally heart shaped. The fruit contains 5–15 seeds.

THE MULBERRY FAMILY

The diverse family Moraceae includes mostly tropical trees, shrubs, herbs, climbers and stranglers. All members have milky sap and distinctive conical caps that cover the growing tips of twigs. The leaves are simple and often large. Flowers are of one sex, generally small and clustered in spikes, discs or hollow receptacles. The fruits are fleshy with a single, hard stone, and often many are grouped into one body.

Paper Mulberry

Broussonetia papyrifera (L.) Vent.

Easy to grow, this tree is widely cultivated in eastern Asia and has naturalized in the Pacific Islands. It is a fast-growing, untidy, sprawling, sparse tree or large shrub with a rounded crown. The paper mulberry is grown primarily for the fine, smooth fibres of its inner bark. These silky fibres are extracted and made into paper and cloth.

Identification: The trunk is dark with an uneven surface. The shoots and leaves have a thick woolly surface. The alternate leaves are generally dull green, although they may vary in colour, and vary greatly in shape. Juvenile leaves may be 30cm/12in long with two or three lobes. Mature leaves are thin, rarely lobed and have a toothed margin. They are 8–20cm/3–8in long and nearly as wide. The male flowers are twisted catkins 4–8cm/1½–3in long, and the female flowers have globular heads 1cm/½in wide. The fruit appears in groups. It is 1cm/½in across, round, red, dry and unpalatable.

Distribution: Eastern Asia, China and Japan.
Height: 15m/50ft
Shape: Domed
Deciduous
Pollinated: Wind
Leaf shape: Ovate

Left to right: This unkempt tree has rough serrated leaves, small globular female flowers, catkins as male flowers and rounded, fuzzy fruit.

Breadfruit

Artocarpus altilis (Parkinson) Forb.

It was the lavish attention received by breadfruit saplings that caused the infamous mutiny on the Bounty. The trees now thrive in the West Indies and are grown throughout the humid tropics for their valuable and plentiful fruit. The fruit is rich in carbohydrate, and tastes and is cooked like potato. The cooked seeds are also eaten and taste like chestnuts.

Identification: These fast-growing trees have smooth bark, ascending branches and a dense bushy crown. The leaves are very dramatic looking. They are 60–90cm/24–36in long, ovate and deeply cut into six to nine lobes. Deep glossy green above, they have a rougher texture and are paler below. The minute green flowers are found on a round organ, which looks like a developing young fruit. The compound fruit is round or ovoid, 10–20cm/4–8in long, weighs up to 5kg/10lbs and is green with a bumpy surface. Breadfruit does not usually have seeds – those that do produce seeded fruit are called breadnuts.

Distribution: Malaysia, Indonesia, Pacific Islands.
Height: 20m/66ft
Shape: Columnar to domed
Evergreen
Pollinated: Wind and insect
Leaf shape: Ovate

Left: Breadfruit leaves are huge and glossy green.

Above: The compound fruit oozes white sticky latex when cut but is a popular tropical staple.

Jackfruit

Artocarpus heterophyllus Lam.

Jackfruit trees are grown for their gigantic compound fruit, which measures up to 90cm/36in long x 50cm/20in across and weighs up to 18kg/40lbs. The fruit varies enormously between trees. It is full of starches – 23 per cent of the sticky, pink to golden yellow, waxy flesh is carbohydrate. Jackfruit flesh has a strong, unpleasant smell but a sweet taste. The seeds within the flesh are also eaten. These fast-growing trees are cultivated throughout the wet tropics, particularly in South-east Asia.

Identification: The reddish brown, straight trunk carries a dense crown. Juvenile leaves are often lobed, whereas mature leaves are oblong to egg shaped with the leaf stalk at the narrow end, dark green, leathery, 10–20cm/4–8in long and downy beneath. The flowers are minute, greenish and emerge directly from the trunk and older branches. The fruit contains numerous 3cm/1¼in-long seeds with a gelatinous covering.

Distribution: India to Malaysia.
Height: 20m/66ft
Shape: Domed, columnar
Evergreen
Pollinated: Wind and insect
Leaf shape: Obovate

Left: The yellowish green fruit has short fleshy spines and hangs from the trunk.

Common Cluster Fig *Ficus sycomorus* L. This is the biblical 'Sycamore Fig' that Zacchaeus the tax collector climbed to see Jesus. This species originated in the area from Egypt to Syria and is now widespread throughout Africa. It has a huge, spreading crown held up by a very thick trunk with narrow buttresses. The large leaves are ovate and smooth or slightly rough. The young leaves and leaf stalks are slightly hairy. This species' figs are found in clusters on the trunk, branches and twigs. They are 5cm/2in wide, yellowish red, often produced abundantly. The fruits are edible and used as animal fodder.

Iroko *Milicia excelsa* (Welw.) C. Berg. Iroko wood is very valuable because it is hard, termite resistant and durable. It is used around the world for furniture, doors, panelling, flooring and outdoor products such as garden furniture. It grows quickly for a hardwood and is a popular choice for plantations, although it often proves difficult to establish. In the wild it grows in lowland and riverine forests throughout tropical Africa, reaching heights of 50m/164ft. It is a deciduous tree and has leathery leaves up to 20cm/8in long and 10cm/4in wide. The mature leaves are elliptic to oblong with a notched margin; when young, they are hairy. The male flowers are 15cm/6in spikes and hang from the branches. The female flowers are upright spikes of 5cm/2in long by 2cm/¾in wide. The fruit takes only a month to develop. It is fleshy, elliptic, 3mm/⅛in across, soft when ripe and popular with bats and squirrels.

Bo Tree

Ficus religiosa L.

It is said that the Buddha was sitting beneath a bo tree when he attained enlightenment. This type of fig is incredibly long lived, with specimens thought to be more than 2,000 years old. It is sacred to Buddhists and Hindus and is regularly seen growing in the grounds of temples. A strangling climber, it may start its life on house roofs or gutters. Despite the problems this can cause, it is rarely removed, because of its sacred status.

Identification: The great trunk has slight buttressing and dark brown bark. Most mature specimens have only a few aerial roots and some surface roots. The open crown, which is as wide as the tree is tall, consists of heart-shaped leaves with long elegant tails. Each leaf is 20cm/8in long x 15cm/6in wide and blue-green with a pale midrib. The leaves have long stalks on which they move in the slightest breeze, and drop briefly in late winter. The tiny dark purple or brown figs grow in pairs in leaf axils along the branches.

Distribution: India, Burma, Thailand and South-east Asia.
Height: 30m/100ft
Shape: Spreading
Deciduous
Pollinated: Wasp
Leaf shape: Heart (deltoid)

Left: The elegant, wispy-tailed leaves of the bo tree are used in arts and crafts in the West.

FIGS

This large genus of plants, in the mulberry family, has around 750 species growing predominantly in the tropics and subtropics. Figs are enormously varied and range from small-leafed climbers to huge trees and epiphytes (plants that grow on others). The infamous 'strangling' figs begin their lives as small epiphytes. Fig flowers are tiny and enclosed within a fleshy receptacle. This receptacle is the fig itself.

Banyan Tree

Ficus benghalensis L.

Distribution: South Asia, India, Burma, South China, Thailand.
Height: 30m/100ft
Shape: Very low and spreading
Evergreen
Pollinated: Wasp
Leaf shape: Broadly ovate to elliptic, blunt ended

Banyans are awe-inspiring trees of often grandiose proportions. They include the largest trees in the world in terms of spread, some covering many acres. Banyans may start as epiphytes, strangling their host. The pale grey or tan trunk carries immense, low, spreading branches from which grow reddish brown aerial roots. Some of these will stiffen and thicken, forming secondary trunks. In this way, the tree spreads over huge areas. Ancient writings suggest that there may be trees now living that are more than 5,000 years old. Banyans are planted widely throughout the tropics as shade and avenue trees.

Identification: The leaves are thick, leathery, blunt ended and may reach 25cm/10in long. Dark green with a pronounced pale yellow midrib and veins, they are used in some parts of Asia to hold food in place of plates. The figs grow in pairs in the leaf axils along the branches. Spherical, they are up to 2cm/¾in in diameter and turn scarlet when ripe.

Above and left: The dense foliage of the banyan casts deep shade.

Fiddleleaf Fig

Ficus lyrata L.

A small, attractive and formal-looking tree, the fiddleleaf fig is found in tropical forests, and is sometimes planted for ornamental purposes or shade. It occasionally begins life as an epiphyte but rarely produces aerial roots.

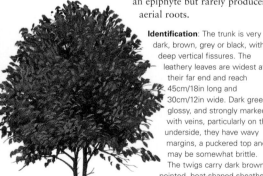

Identification: The trunk is very dark, brown, grey or black, with deep vertical fissures. The leathery leaves are widest at their far end and reach 45cm/18in long and 30cm/12in wide. Dark green, glossy, and strongly marked with veins, particularly on the underside, they have wavy margins, a puckered top and may be somewhat brittle. The twigs carry dark brown, pointed, boat-shaped sheaths at the leaf bases, and the figs grow in the leaf axils near the tips of twigs, either singly or in pairs.

Distribution: Tropical west and central Africa.
Height: 12m/40ft
Shape: Narrow
Evergreen
Pollinated: Wasp
Leaf shape: Fiddle-like

Above: The tree has an upright, stiff habit and dense canopy.

Right: The tree was named after its fiddle-shaped leaves.

Below: When ripe, the figs are round, brownish green with white specks, fleshy and 3–5cm/1–2in in diameter.

Weeping Fig

Ficus benjamina L.

A graceful tree that, when mature, is wider than it is tall, the weeping fig has strongly ascending branches that weep at the tips. It grows as an epiphyte and strangler fig in forests, rocky places and by streams. The pale grey bark of the trunk, sometimes almost white, is latticed with aerial roots, which form a dense mass around the trunk but rarely fall away from it. The invasive roots can disrupt building foundations – nevertheless this tree is often planted on streets. Various varieties with dark, variegated or twisted foliage are grown as house plants in temperate regions.

Distribution: South and South-east Asia, north Australia and south-west Pacific.
Height: 30m/100ft
Shape: Spreading and domed
Evergreen
Pollinated: Wasp
Leaf shape: Ovate-elliptic

Identification: The 10cm/4in-long alternate leaves are smooth, pale green and glossy. They are delightful shimmering in a breeze. The figs are produced throughout the year and grow in pairs in leaf axils near the end of twigs. They are attractive in their own right, changing from green through to pink, red, scarlet and deep purplish black as they ripen.

Right and left: Leaves are elegant, thin and tough.

Moreton Bay Fig *Ficus macrophylla* Desf. ex. Pers.
This strangler from tropical Australia reaches 60m/200ft high and has an even greater spread. The light brown or grey trunk is heavily buttressed, reaching up to 3m/10ft in circumference. The Moreton Bay fig produces few prop roots but does have many wide, pale surface roots. The 25cm/10in-long leaves are glossy and leathery with bright pink persistent sheaths. The 2cm/¾in-wide figs occur along the twigs and are purplish brown specked with white or yellow.

Java Fig *Ficus virens* ait.
A deciduous fig from India to the Solomon Islands and Northern Australia, this species reaches 15m/50ft in height and has ascending branches that droop at the ends. The leaves, up to 17cm/6½in long, have wavy margins and long tails. The 1cm/½in-wide figs are white with red spots when ripe. In the northern Indian state of Sikkim the young shoots are pickled and eaten.

Rusty-leaf Fig *Ficus rubiginosa* Desf. ex Vent.
This fig from tropical Australia prefers moist conditions and grows to 18m/60ft tall with a slightly wider spread. The dark grey or black trunk sometimes forms buttress roots near its base. The rusty-leaf fig gets its name from the soft, rust-coloured hairs on young cinnamon-coloured young leaves and leaf stems. Young bark is cinnamon coloured and the figs, in pairs towards twig tips, vary from yellowish green to cinnamon.

Indian Rubber Tree

Ficus elastica Roxb. ex. Hornem.

A mature specimen is an impressive sight. Curtains of aerial roots form a veritable forest of high buttressed trunks, while the surface roots swarm over the soil. The tree lives wild in tropical and subtropical forests but is grown throughout Asia for shade and ornament. In temperate countries this species is known as the rubber plant and grown in pots indoors. The milky latex tapped from the trunk was the traditional rubber of commerce until *Hevea* rubber was discovered.

Distribution: East Himalayas, north-east India, Burma, north Malay Peninsula, Java, Sumatra.
Height: 60m/200ft
Shape: Spreading
Evergreen
Pollinated: Wasp
Leaf shape: Oblong to elliptic, tip pointed

Identification: Each leaf measures over 30cm/12in long and 15cm/6in wide and has a single, prominent midrib. Young leaves are tinged pink, and a long pink or red sheath protects the growing tip. The leaves form a dense crown at the end of clear branches. The oval, 2cm/¾in-long, greenish-yellow figs are crowded in pairs in the leaf axils towards the ends of twigs on trees over 20 years old. Figs are produced all year round.

Right: The spirally arranged foliage is simple, dark green, very smooth, thick and leathery.

THE NETTLE AND CASUARINA FAMILIES

The nettle family, Urticaceae, and casuarina family, Casuarinaceae, are closely linked to the mulberry family. The nettle family is mainly tropical and includes only a few trees. Many of these plants have stinging hairs. Their small flowers are usually green, and when the pollen is ripe, it is released when the anthers suddenly uncoil. The casuarina family contains only the one genus featured below.

Upas Tree

Antiaris toxicaria (Pers.) Leschen.

The upas tree is famous for being poisonous and has an unwarranted reputation for killing anyone unlucky enough to fall asleep under it. The sap is poisonous and used on arrow-tips; the dense inner bark is also used by forest people. Once beaten to remove the sap, it is made into a thick fibrous material for clothing, ropes and sacking. This tree towers above other trees in its native evergreen forests.

Identification: The upas tree has a buttressed trunk. Its young shoots, leaf stems and midribs are velvety. The smooth, pointed leaves are 8–20cm/3–8in long, and some have toothed margins. The flowers appear in September and October. The male flowers are crowded on to flat mushroom-shaped organs in the leaf axils, while the female flowers are enclosed inside a pear-shaped receptacle. The elliptical, ripe fruit is 2–4.5cm/¾–1¾in long, velvety and red or purple.

Distribution: Sri Lanka, Malaysia, Philippines, Burma, northern India and Fiji.
Height: 75m/250ft
Shape: Domed
Evergreen
Pollinated: Wind
Leaf shape: Oblong-elliptic

Right: In Polynesia the tree is grown for its edible fruit. The leaves contain thin white poisonous latex that turns brown on contact with air.

Australian Pine

Casuarina equisetifolia Forst. & Forst.

This elegant, wispy tree looks to all intents and purposes like a pine, hence its common name. However, it is not a true pine. Fast growing, this species has the ability to fix nitrogen by its roots and is tolerant of wind and some salinity. The Australian pine is used for windbreaks, soil stabilization and dune reclamation in coastal regions. It is also grown for its timber, which is used for making boats, furniture and houses. This species may live for several hundred years.

Identification: The short trunk has thick, brown, peeling bark, while the long, weeping branches are silvery grey. From the branches arise 10–20cm/4–8in-long, extremely narrow, downy branchlets. These branchlets resemble long pine needles and are coated in minuscule triangular leaves. The flowers appear in May and June. Male flowers are red, tufted, catkin-like and measure 4cm/1½in long x 5mm/¼in wide. Female flowers are greyish brown and globular, and measure 2cm/¾in across. The cone-like fruit takes five months to develop. It is greenish grey, 2.5cm/1in long and contains winged seeds.

Distribution: Coastal regions of north-east Australia, South-east Asia and Polynesia.
Height: 35m/115ft
Shape: Columnar
Evergreen
Pollinated: Wind
Leaf shape: Reduced to tiny scales

Right and far right: The tiny scale leaves are highly adapted to coastal conditions.

Left: The compound, cone-like fruit is highly misleading as an identifying feature, as this tree is not a conifer.

THE BUCKWHEAT AND POKEWEED FAMILIES

The buckwheat family, Polygonaceae, contains mostly temperate plants from the northern hemisphere.
Their small flowers are usually held in spikes and produce one-seeded fruit. The majority of plants in the
pokeweed family, Phytolaccaceae, are tropical, from South America and Africa. Many have succulent
leaves, some are spiny and many have poisonous sap.

Sea Grape

Coccoloba uvifera (L.) L.

The beautiful sea grape is completely salt tolerant
and will grow right on the beach. It has been
planted in coastal locations throughout the
tropical and warmest temperate regions of its
range. Tree shape and size vary immensely and
are dependent on climatic factors. The sea
grape can be dense and domed, or many
stemmed, sprawling and untidy. Whatever its shape, this
tree's distinctive leaves make it easy to recognize.

Distribution: Coastal tropical
America and West Indies.
Height: 9m/30ft
Shape: Variable, domed
Evergreen
Pollinated: Insect
Leaf shape: Kidney (reniform)

Identification: The thick trunk has grey, fissured bark. The leaves are
very tough, leathery and stiff. Olive green and veined in red, pink or
white, they are 20cm/8in across. The leaves turn a rich orange or
maroon before dropping. The scented, greenish-white flowers are
produced year round but are particularly abundant in the spring and
summer. They are held in dense, erect clusters, 25cm/10in long. The
purple fruit occurs in long, hanging bunches like grapes – each
fruit is 1.5–2cm/¾in wide. The fruit has an acidic flavour and is
used to make jellies.

Right: Male and female flowers are separate. Female flowers produce
the grape-like bunches of edible fruit.

Bella Sombre

Phytolacca dioica (L.) Moq.

Bella sombre is Spanish for 'beautiful shade', and this tree is often planted for shade in
villages. The wonderfully sculptured, buttressed and spreading surface roots create natural
seating up to 2m/6½ft high and spread across an area up to 18m/60ft in diameter. The bella
sombre tree is often multi-stemmed and stores large amounts
of water in its massive trunks. It is a fast-growing
species native to grassy plains and is fire and wind
resistant. The tree is very highly revered in
Argentina, and often lives to a very great age.

Distribution: South Brazil,
Uruguay, Paraguay and
north Argentina.
Height: 20m/66ft
Shape: Domed
Semi-evergreen
Leaf shape: Elliptical

Identification: The bark of the sturdy trunks and surface
roots is white. The soft, thick leaves are smooth and
10cm/4in long with a prominent midrib that is red when
the leaves are young. Before falling, the leaves turn
yellow and then purple. The small, white flowers are held
in pendulous clusters 10cm/4in long. The fruit is a small
berry ripening through yellow and red to black.
When ripe, it is fleshy with
reddish-purple juice.

Right: Trees may drop their leaves in the autumn or
during cold or dry spells. Each tree is male or female,
with only the female trees producing berries.

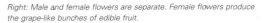

THE DIPTEROCARP FAMILY

Dipterocarpaceae are tall forest trees found predominantly in Asia, where they dominate the forest. They are mostly evergreen, resinous and buttressed. The name 'dipterocarp' means two-winged-fruit, but the seeds may actually have up to five wings, and some have none. These trees are grown and harvested from the wild for their hard timber. Many species also secrete valuable resin and camphor.

Sal

Shorea robusta Gaertner

Distribution: Northern and central-eastern India, Burma, Thailand, Indo-China.
Height: 35m/115ft
Shape: Flattened to domed
Semi-evergreen
Pollinated: Insect
Leaf shape: Broadly ovate

This tree's heavy, durable wood has been used in India for more than 2,000 years. Sal has many other uses: butter is made from its fat rich seeds; plates are fashioned from its leaves; tannins are extracted from its bark; dammar resin is taken from it for incense and torch fuel; and it produces another, more oily resin, which is used in inks, varnishes, for fixing perfume, as flavouring, and in medicine. Sal is a slow-growing, upright, dry forest tree with thick, fire resistant bark. Wherever it is found, this tree is normally the dominant species.

Identification: The bark is dark brown with longitudinal fissures. The smooth, shiny, leathery leaves are 10–25cm/4–10in long. The small flowers are pale grey and velvety on the outside and orange inside. They appear early in summer in large branched structures, which appear from the axils and the ends of twigs and branches. The hard, brown fruit has two or three wings and appears early in summer. The fruit is 5–8cm/2–3in long and often germinates while still hanging on the tree.

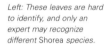

Right: Shuttlecock-like fruit spins away from the parent tree.

Left: These leaves are hard to identify, and only an expert may recognize different Shorea species.

Thingham

Hopea odorata

This highly variable species occurs in the middle layer of moist dipterocarp forests, often near to streams. Its wood is light yellowish brown with a tight, even grain. It is easy to work and used mostly for joinery. Thingham trees also produce dammar resin, and the leaves are harvested for their tannins, which are used to strengthen leather.

Identification: The trunk is straight with small buttresses. The bark is a dark grey brown but fissured with orange-brown marks. The ascending branches form a dense crown. The leaves are dark green above and bright olive green below. They measure 15cm/6in long by 6cm/2½in wide. The flowers are small and pale and have frilled petals. Fragrant, grey and velvety, they appear in spring and are borne on branched structures, growing from the leaf axils. The conical fruit appears in early summer. It measures 5cm/2in long, including the pair of brown wings.

Distribution: India, Bangladesh, Burma, Thailand, Malaysia.
Height: 37m/122ft
Shape: Conical
Evergreen
Pollinated: Insect
Leaf shape: Ovate-lanceolate

*Above: Thinghams are reminiscent of the European beech (*Fagus sylvatica*).*

Left: When fruiting, the dark green leaves are obscured by pale green fruit.

Kapur

Dryobalanops lanceolata

This extremely large tree has a very long, straight trunk with no branches for its first 15–30m/50–100ft and large buttresses up to 4m/13ft high. It is found away from wet areas in mixed dipterocarp forests, and is an emergent species with its crown above the forest canopy. The timber is reddish brown with a very straight, even grain and a camphorous odour. Fungus resistant, it polishes to a high shine and is used for flooring, joinery, construction and boatbuilding. Kapur is currently being planted in secondary (regrown) rainforest in northern Borneo as part of a forest enrichment programme.

Left: Dipterocarps have an erratic fruiting habit. In a fruiting year, trees will be smothered in flowers and yield heavily, while in other years they yield no fruit.

Identification: The bark varies from dark brown to grey with a purplish tinge and has vertical fissures. The smooth leaves have short leaf stems and measure 7–20cm/2¾–8in long. The white flowers vary in size and have 27–33 stamens. The fruit measures 2.5 x 2.5cm/1 x 1in and has four or five wings each 7–10cm/2¾–4in long x 1–2cm/½–¾in wide.

Distribution: Borneo, Malay Peninsula and East Indian Islands.
Height: 60m/200ft
Shape: Domed
Evergreen
Pollinated: Bee
Leaf shape: Ovate-lanceolate

Shorea macrophylla This tree has a long, clear trunk up to 24m/80ft in length and 1.5m/5ft wide. The wood has a cedar-like aroma and is moderately hard, although not as durable as the wood of other dipterocarps. Even so, it is grown in plantations in Malaysia. The tree flowers in early summer and bears fruit in late summer and autumn. The two winged seeds each weigh 30g/1oz.

Camphor Kapur *Dryobalanops aromaticum* This 60m/200ft-tall tree was recorded by Marco Polo in 1299 and has been used as a source of camphor in Arabia since the sixth century. In recent times the majority of camphor has been extracted from *Cinnamomum camphorum* or produced synthetically instead. The camphor kapur tree also yields aromatic, volatile, oily resins, which are used in medicine. It grows in western Malaysia and northern and eastern Sumatra. The bark is light brown and comes away in large scaly flakes. The branches are held erect and carry an elegant, light, airy, columnar crown. Once the tree reaches 20 years old it produces its first attractive, white, fragrant flowers. It continues to produce these every three or four years for the rest of its life.

Dipterocarpus alatus This tree from Bangladesh, Burma and the Andaman Islands is found scattered in mixed forest. The timber is used for making canoes and housing, while the bark is used medicinally. The tree is also a source of oily resin. The leaves are ovate to elliptic and 10–15cm/4–6in long. This species flowers in April and produces large pink flowers on short branched structures from the axils. The seeds are produced in May, measure 3 x 4cm/1¼ x 1½in and have five wings.

Nawada

Shorea stipularis

This tree grows in wet lowland evergreen rainforest. It is harvested for timber for construction, as a source of incense resin and for its bark, which is used to halt fermentation. The wood is pale yellow and resinous. The tree has low, thick, rounded buttresses and carries a dense, rounded crown.

Identification: The very straight trunk measures up to 120cm/47in in diameter and has deeply fissured, flaky, pale reddish-brown to dark brown bark. The young twigs have conspicuous, 1.5cm/½in-long stipules (paired leaf-like appendages) at the base of each axil. The leaves are 11cm/4½in long and have strongly marked veins. The sparsely flowered panicles (branched flowerheads) arise from the leaf axils and are 10cm/4in long. Each flower is 1cm/½in across, cream and has five twisted, pointed petals. The fruit measures 1 x 2cm/½ x ¾in and has five flat oblong wings, two 5cm/2in long and three 10cm/4in long.

Distribution: Sri Lanka.
Height: 45m/150ft
Shape: Rounded
Evergreen
Pollinated: Insect
Leaf shape: Ovate-elliptic

Above: Large stipules at the base of the leaf stems give rise to the species name.

Above left: This dipterocarp fruit has wings of different sizes.

THE ST JOHN'S WORT FAMILY

The trees in the Guttiferaceae family have oil glands and ducts on their leaves, which give a clear spot effect. Many also yield resins. Most are tropical trees or shrubs, and some are semi-epiphytic, using other plants to support them. They often produce latex, which may be white, yellow or even orange, and many have stilt roots. This family includes several useful timber trees and some species grown for their fruit.

Autograph Tree

Clusia rosea (Jacq.) L.

This tree earns its name from its leaves, which are so thick that one can carve words into them – historically, they have even been used as playing cards. The tree may start life on rocks or as an epiphyte, becoming a strangler with aerial roots forming many trunks. It grows quickly into a sprawling, irregular-shaped tree with horizontal branches and a dense crown. Being adapted to salt spray, high winds and sandy, saline soil, and with surface wandering roots, it is naturally found and planted in coastal locations.

Distribution: Caribbean, Florida Keys, and south-east Mexico.
Height: 15m/50ft
Shape: Spreading
Evergreen
Pollinated: Insect
Leaf shape: Obovate

Identification: The tree has yellow sap and thick, bright green leaves 8–20cm/3–8in long. The lightly fragranced flowers have thick, waxy petals. They appear intermittently throughout the year, but are particularly abundant in late summer. Solitary and white ageing to pink, they have many bright yellow stamens and are 5–8cm/2–3in across. The fruit is round, pale green, 5–8cm/2–3½in across, and bursts open to reveal red seeds embedded in black, poisonous resin.

Left: The lovely scented flowers are short lived, becoming brown after only a few days.

Right: The thick, tough, waxy leaves are designed to withstand harsh coastal conditions.

Ceylon Iron Wood

Mesua ferrea L.

This handsome, slow-growing tree, with a dense crown, grows in forests and is widely planted. In India the tree is sacred, and in Sri Lanka it is planted by Buddhist temples. In the wet seasons the new, young foliage creates an impressive sight as it hangs in limp red-pink tassels. In drier spells the scented flowers appear.

Identification: The trunk has flaky grey to reddish bark, and has small buttresses. Mature leaves are dark green above and pale below, resulting in an overall effect of grey-green. The 10–15cm/4–6in across, solitary flowers have a cluster of bright yellow stamens. The fruit is round or oval to cone shaped, hard, brown, 2.5–5cm/1–2in across and contains one to four dry, flattened, shiny seeds.

Above: The tree begins life with a conical habit, which broadens with maturity.

Right: The leaves have a pale waxy bloom below.

Far right: The beautifully scented flowers last only for a day.

Distribution: Sri Lanka, India, Himalayas to Malaysia.
Height: 25m/82ft
Shape: Oval to columnar
Evergreen
Pollinated: Insect
Leaf shape: Lanceolate

Alexandrian Laurel

Calophyllum inophyllum L.

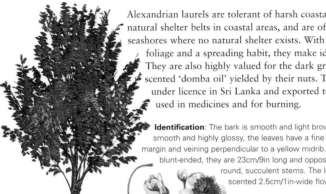

Alexandrian laurels are tolerant of harsh coastal climates, forming natural shelter belts in coastal areas, and are often planted along seashores where no natural shelter exists. With low branches, dense foliage and a spreading habit, they make ideal shade trees. They are also highly valued for the dark green, thick, strongly scented 'domba oil' yielded by their nuts. This oil is collected under licence in Sri Lanka and exported to India, where it is used in medicines and for burning.

Identification: The bark is smooth and light brown. Deep green, smooth and highly glossy, the leaves have a fine yellow line around the margin and veining perpendicular to a yellow midrib. Thick, leathery and blunt-ended, they are 23cm/9in long and oppositely arranged along round, succulent stems. The loose clusters of highly scented 2.5cm/1in-wide flowers appear in summer.

Far left: The fruit has a single seed and is 1.5–3.5cm/½–1½ in long with a smooth yellowish brown or reddish skin.

Distribution: Coastal, north Australia, South-east Asia, India and Africa.
Height: 15m/50ft
Shape: Spreading
Evergreen
Pollinated: Insect
Leaf shape: Oblong to obovate

Right: The genus name Calophyllum *means beautiful leaf.*

Santa Maria *Calophyllum brasiliense* Cambess.
This highly adaptable tree from northern South America, Mexico and the West Indies is tolerant of salty air and saline conditions around its roots. It grows to 15m/50ft in height and has a dense rounded crown of glossy, dark green foliage. The elliptical leaves have pale veining, a notch at the end and are 20cm/8in long. The small, loose clusters of white flowers are produced in spring and give off a sweet scent. The fruit is round and yellowish green.

Gamboge *Garcinia xanthochymus*
Hook. f. ex. Anderson
This tree is best known for its yellow pigment, also called gamboge, which was once used in painting. The pigment is extracted as juice from the dark yellow, round, pointed, 8cm/3in fruit. The gamboge tree, from northern India and the western Himalayas, grows to 12m/40ft tall and has a dense, rounded canopy. The leaves are glossy green, narrow and 45cm/18in long. The flowers are small and white.

St Domingo Apricot *Mammea americana* L.
From the West Indies and South America, this 18m/60ft, evergreen tree is grown for its sweet, scented fruit and timber. The tasty fruit is round and juicy, light brown to grey with a thick, warty outer skin. The golden to red pulp melts in the mouth. It measures 8–20cm/ 3–8in and weighs up to 2kg/4½lbs. The hard, durable timber polishes up well. In the West Indies the flowers are also used to make the liqueur "Crème de Créole". The dense, columnar crown has obovate, blunt-ended leathery green foliage and carries fragrant white flowers.

Mangosteen

Garcinia mangostana L.

The delicious, sweet, yet slightly acidic fruit of this tree is considered among the world's finest. Unfortunately, the mangosteen is difficult to grow and rarely seen outside of its native Malaysia. Additionally, the wonderful fruit does not travel well, and even in Malaysia the tree takes 15 years before it begins to fruit. The mangosteen tree is handsome in its own right, with a dense crown of symmetrical branches.

Identification: The oppositely arranged, 18–20cm/ 7–8in long leaves are thick, smooth and a deep plain green when mature, pinkish red when young. The simple flowers are greenish white and resemble a single rose. The fruit appears twice a year, in the summer and winter. It is 6–7cm/2¾–3in across, round, and has a thick purple rind. At the base of the fruit are five to eight small, triangular woody plates arranged like the petals of a flower. Inside, the fruit is divided into white fleshy segments.

Distribution: Malaysia.
Height: 13m/43ft
Shape: Columnar
Evergreen
Pollinated: Insect
Leaf shape: Elliptic-oblong

Above and above right: The thick, glossy foliage is pink when young and forms a dense crown on healthy trees.

Right: The mangosteen has segments resembling garlic cloves.

THE DILLENIA FAMILY

Dilleniaceae is a small family, encompassing only 20 or so genera and about 500 species from the tropics. It includes trees, shrubs, climbers and herbs. They often have pinkish or orange bark and have hard reddish wood. The leaves are usually serrated with a rough surface, and in some plants the leaf stems are winged. The five-petalled flowers have numerous stamens and are short lived.

Simpoh Air

Dillenia suffruticosa (Griffith) Martelli.

This fast-growing pioneer species grows as wide as it is tall and may become shrub-like. It grows in scrubby areas or disturbed forest. It is planted as a shade tree, being particularly attractive when in flower, and for the fleshy fruit which is used in jellies, preserves and curries.

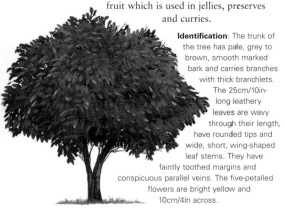

Identification: The trunk of the tree has pale, grey to brown, smooth marked bark and carries branches with thick branchlets. The 25cm/10in-long leathery leaves are wavy through their length, have rounded tips and wide, short, wing-shaped leaf stems. They have faintly toothed margins and conspicuous parallel veins. The five-petalled flowers are bright yellow and 10cm/4in across.

Distribution: Peninsular Malaysia.
Height: 9m/30ft
Shape: Spreading
Evergreen
Pollinated: Insect
Leaf shape: Oblong

Above: The large, scented flowers are found in racemes of 5–15 flowers.

Right: The leaves are clustered at the branch tips.

Below: The fruit is round, surrounded by enlarged sepals, and opens to become star shaped, revealing a red lining and seeds within a thin red aril.

Elephant Apple

Dillenia indica L.

This spectacular tree is common in cultivation. It is grown for the combination of stunning unusual foliage, beautiful scented flowers and large edible fruit. The fruit is, in fact, heavily swollen overlapping sepals, rolled into a ball containing a sticky green mass of seeds. It is musk scented, tasting like an unripe apple, and is apparently popular with elephants. The fruit it used to make cooling drinks and jellies. The tree has an open broad crown above a short dark trunk, with leaves concentrated towards the branch tips.

Identification: The trunk carries rich orange-brown bark and few branches. The leaves are heavily corrugated, up to 75cm/30in long, toothed, leathery, smooth on the upper surface but rough below. The flowers appear in late spring and early summer, and are fragrant, 20cm/8in across, creamy yellow to pure white with a mass of central golden stamens. The fruit reaches 15cm/6in across and is green.

Distribution: East India and South-east Asia.
Height: 18m/60ft
Shape: Domed
Semi-evergreen
Pollinated: Insect
Leaf shape: Elliptic-oblong

Left: The enormous solitary flowers face downwards; they are the largest of all Malaysian flowers and last only a day.

THE ELAEOCARPUS AND LIME FAMILIES

The Elaeocarpaceae and the lime family, Tiliaceae, are related to the sterculia, bombax, mallow and lecythis families. Most Elaeocarpaceae are trees and shrubs from India to New Zealand. They were once included with the lime family, to which they are similar. Members of the variable lime family are found worldwide. They have simple leaves and flowers with five or occasionally no petals, and berry- or nut-like fruit.

Blueberry Ash

Elaeocarpus cyaneus Sims.

Blueberry ash is naturally found in a wide range of habitats, including forested areas, wooded gullies, rocky ridges and in coastal scrub. This very tough tree withstands salt-laden air, wind, sun, shade, poor soil, and has even been known to survive temperatures below freezing. In Australian gardens it is often grown as a large shrub for its pretty aniseed-scented flowers and vivid blue fruit, which is popular with birds.

Identification: The trunk may have a slightly buttressed base and carries a dense, bushy crown. The 10–15cm/4–6in-long leaves are shiny, leathery, toothed, with prominent net veining. Over a long period, from spring to autumn, the 1cm/½in-long, creamy white to pink, fringed, bell-shaped flowers appear in lax, axillary racemes up to 15cm/6in long. The attractive fruit appears from autumn, lasting for many months. It is 1cm/⅖in long, round and deep to bright blue. The flowers and fruit are sometimes seen simultaneously.

Right: The edible fruit is not blue due to pigments; the skin is actually green, but it is designed to reflect blue light.

Distribution: East coast Australia to Tasmania and Frasier Island.
Height: 15m/50ft
Shape: Columnar-conical
Evergreen
Pollinated: Insect
Leaf shape: Oblong-lanceolate

Corkwood

Entelea arborescens R. Br.

The wood of this fast-growing tree is incredibly light, half the weight of cork. It is used by the Maoris to make fishing-net floats and frameworks for small boats. The tree is the only species of its genus and naturally grows as a pioneer species and in young woodland. It is highly tolerant of salt-laden wind and used in sand dune restoration. In addition, it is planted as windbreaks and hedging. When young it has an upright oval form and may be grown as a shrub. It can survive in areas with light frosts.

Right: The large, bright to light green leaves are soft and felt-like.

Identification: The alternate leaves are 10–23cm/4–9in long with similar length leaf stalks and a heart-shaped base. They may be inconspicuously lobed and have a double-toothed margin. All the leaves, shoots and flowers are covered in short soft hair. The white flowers with central yellow stamens form in spring and summer. They are 2.5cm/1in wide and in terminal cymes 7–13cm/2¾–5in long. The autumn fruit is in clusters, each is round, 2.5cm/1in diameter and covered in long rigid bristles.

Right: Sweetly scented flowers in erect panicles are followed by brown, bristly fruit composed of four to six sections.

Distribution: New Zealand North Island.
Height: 6m/20ft
Shape: Wide spreading
Evergreen
Leaf shape: Ovate

THE STERCULIA FAMILY

The Sterculiaceae family is found mainly in the tropics and includes trees, shrubs, climbers and herbs. The plants are not easy to recognize, they have simple leaves that alternate on each side of the stem and which may be divided. The flowers have three to five sepals and may have either five or no petals. The fruit may be fleshy, leathery or woody, and the seed may or may not have an outer covering.

Australian Flame Tree

Brachychiton acerifolius Cunn. ex. F. Muell.

This rather variable species is stunning when in flower. The profuse, foamy sprays of wide, bell-shaped flowers are vibrant red and may develop in large numbers in late spring to early summer. The distinctive swollen trunk stores water even though the tree occurs naturally in wet coastal rainforests. Aborigines use the fibres from the bark for weaving, and the seeds are a source of dye.

Identification: The trunk is greenish and bottle shaped. The leaves occur alternately on each side of the twigs and have three to seven lobes, which are particularly obvious when they are young. Mature leaves are mid-green, glossy, 9–25cm/3½–10in long and held on an 8–23cm/3–9in-long stem. The flowers appear in sprays 30cm/12in long and are all the more stunning as they occur when the tree is leafless. The fruit is 9–12cm/3½–4½in long.

Distribution: Queensland and New South Wales, Australia
Height: 30m/100ft
Shape: Conical or oblong
Deciduous
Pollinated: Bird
Leaf shape: Palmate

Left: The variable leaves often have far fewer incisions as the tree matures. The colourful flower 'petals' are the sepals. The woody fruit splits to release edible seeds.

Java Olive

Sterculia foetida L.

Distribution: Central Africa, Madagascar, India to Malaysia and northern Australia.
Height: 30m/100ft
Shape: Spreading
Semi-evergreen
Pollinated: Insect
Leaf shape: Compound palmate

Right: The leaf stems and twigs of young plants are coated in sticky hairs.

A fast-growing tree found in rocky and sandy coastal locations. The species name refers to foul-smelling flowers, which are enough to deter anyone from planting it. Even so, flowering is short lived and it is grown as a shade tree becoming as wide as it is tall. The fruit is botanically remarkable as it splits soon after pollination, and the seeds finish development completely exposed.

Identification: The smooth grey to orange-brown trunk carries horizontal branches. The elegant leaves are 10–30cm/4–12in long and have between five and eleven narrow, pointed, lanceolate lobes. Each lobe is deep olive green with a very prominent yellowish midrib. The flowers, which are held on branched structures, occur on deciduous trees in early spring before the leaves appear, but can be seen year round on evergreen trees. Each flower is 2.5–5cm/1–2in wide, has fleshy orange or red sepals with yellow markings and is woolly inside. The pear-shaped fruit develops quickly. Red, woody and 7–13cm/2¾–5in long, the fruit splits to reveal red cavities containing the 10–15 blue-black seeds.

Left: These seeds can be roasted and eaten.

Black Kurrajong *Brachychiton populneus* (Schott. & Endl.) R. Br.

This evergreen tree is found on rocky Australian hillsides. It is also grown by farmers as a shade tree and for animal fodder. The black kurrajong has a thick, heavy trunk topped by a bushy crown and grows to 18m/60ft tall with a 13.5m/45ft spread. The deep olive green leaves vary from ovate to narrow and lanceolate, and have three or five lobes, the central lobe being the longest. The bell-shaped flowers are 1.5cm/⅔in wide, pale yellow, greenish-yellow or cream and have yellow or purple spots inside to attract bees. They form in branched structures, which appear in the axils in summer.

Queensland Lacebark *Brachychiton discolor* F. Muell.

A rainforest tree from New South Wales and Queensland in Australia. In the wild it is evergreen, but if grown in cooler climes it may become deciduous. It grows quickly to 24m/80ft tall and has a thick trunk with green bark and a dense, spreading crown. The leaves are much like those of the black kurrajong (above), dark green above and silvery below. The clusters of flowers appear in spring or summer and while the tree is leafless where it is deciduous. They are bell shaped, velvety and vary from deep pink to lavender. The fruit is a 15cm/6in-long, rusty brown, elliptical, furry pod.

Panama Tree

Sterculia apetala (Jacq.) Karst.

This species is the national tree of Panama, which is found in tropical and subtropical forests and alongside rivers, where it thrives. It is grown in gardens and as a street tree, and has become naturalized in the West Indies. The Panama tree is fast growing and has many uses in addition to its fine stature as an ornamental, shade-bearing tree. It is a useful species for reforestation and erosion control.

Distribution: Central America, northern South America and the West Indies.
Height: 40m/130ft
Shape: Rounded
Deciduous
Pollinated: Insect
Leaf shape: Compound palmate

Identification: The trunk can be up to 2m/6ft in diameter and has grey, smooth bark. The five-lobed leaves cluster towards the branch ends; the lobes are 15–50cm/6–20in long. The flowers are 2.5–3.5cm/1–1½in wide, in branched structures. The woody fruit is yellow to grey and 30cm/12in long, and opens to reveal the 2.5 x 1.5cm/1 x ½in black seeds.

Far left: The edible seeds are rich in starch and fats.

Queensland Bottle Tree

Brachychiton rupestris (Mitch. ex. Lindl.) Schum.

This tree develops a massive, bulbous, branchless, bottle-shaped, water-storing trunk and is often planted as a novelty in parks and gardens. It is also planted on farms and streets. Unless well watered, this species is slow growing at first and does not form the characteristic swollen trunk until it is about ten years old. In the wild, the Queensland bottle tree is found inland in fertile valleys and along low ridges. The moist, fibrous, inner bark can be eaten.

Identification: The slightly fissured bark is greyish green. The leaves are deep green and form a dense crown but are liable to drop in prolonged dry spells. They vary in shape from narrow and elliptical to wide and divided. The small, yellowish clusters of bell-shaped flowers appear from late spring to early summer towards the tips of the branches, where they are hidden among the foliage. The short, boat-shaped fruit is woody and produced in late summer.

Right: This bottle tree grows on fertile soil and can be surprisingly fast growing when well watered.

Distribution: South-east Queensland
Height: 9–12m/30–40ft
Shape: Irregularly domed
Semi-evergreen
Leaf shape: Variable

Right: The mature foliage is long and slender, whereas the juvenile foliage may be wide and lobed.

Cola Nut

Cola acuminata (Pal.) Schott. & Endl.

'Cola' is a world-renowned drink, yet few people know that it is also a tree. The 'nuts' (really seeds) of this tree are two per cent caffeine and were originally used in the cola drink. The tree is cultivated in Sri Lanka, the West Indies, Malaysia and West Africa. In the tropics its seeds are chewed for medicinal purposes, for their stimulating effects and to enable people to undertake feats of endurance. They are no longer used in the drink to which they gave their name and are now little used in the West. The tree grows in humid lowlands.

Distribution: Tropical West Africa.
Height: 12m/40ft
Shape: Spreading
Evergreen
Pollinated: Insect
Leaf shape: Oblong-ovate

Above: The long-lived cola tree may yield fruit for 100 years.

Below: The ugly cola fruit contains the 'cola nuts'. White nuts are the most popular for chewing and demand the best price.

Identification: The leaves are leathery, dark green and 10–15cm/4–6in long. The flowers are found in the axils and at the ends of twigs in branched clusters of 15 throughout the year, or, on some trees, only in winter. The flowers are 1.5cm/½in across and have no petals. However, they do have five pale yellow sepals, each with central purple markings. The green, warty fruit is a 13–18cm/5–7in-long pod containing between six and ten pink, purple or white seeds. The seeds may be dried, before consumption, becoming dark brown.

African Mallow

Dombeya wallichii (Lindl.) Schumann

Distribution: Madagascar.
Height: 9m/30ft
Shape: Domed
Evergreen
Pollinated: Insect
Leaf shape: Broadly elliptic, variable

This tree is grown for its large, eye-catching flowers and its large, soft, felty leaves. It often takes the form of a large shrub with numerous trunks and has a very dense crown.

Identification: The bright green, heart- to diamond-shaped leaves have three lobes with jagged edges and are large, measuring 30cm/12in long and an even greater distance across. The flowers are 2.5cm/1in wide, fragrant, have overlapping petals and are cup shaped. Ranging from deep pink to red, they are crowded on to round, hanging heads 15cm/6in across and appear from midsummer into winter. The flower petals turn brown and remain on the tree after they have died, giving the African mallow a rather scruffy look as its small fruit develops.

Left: The dried flowers remain hanging on the tree while the fruit develops inside.

Cacao

Theobroma cacao L.

Cacao is cultivated in Central America, the West Indies, tropical Africa, Java and Sri Lanka for its beans, which are the source of cocoa. Today Ghana is the world's leading exporter of cocoa products, but the plant originated in Central America. It was there that the beans were first harvested. Before the arrival of Europeans, cocoa, chilli and other spices were incorporated into a hot drink that was consumed by royalty and had the name 'theo-broma', meaning 'godly-food'. Today cocoa is the key ingredient in one of the world's favourite foods – chocolate. Cocoa bean pods are harvested and opened to collect the beans, which are fermented for a couple of days and then dried in the sun to cure them. These cured beans are roasted, ground and heated to extract the cocoa butter and cocoa solids.

Distribution: Central America
Height: 9m/30ft
Shape: Domed
Evergreen
Pollinated: Insect
Leaf shape: Oblong-elliptic

Identification: The deep green, leathery leaves are smooth, often with dry, crispy edges or tips and 25cm/10in long. Flowers emerge directly from the trunk and older branches all year round and are particularly abundant in spring. Creamy yellowish or pinkish, they are 1cm/½in wide and have five petals. The fruit is an ovoid, longitudinally ribbed pod 20cm/8in long. It may be brown, maroon or orange.

Right: The fruit contains 50–100 beans. The 2cm/¾ in-long beans are set in a slimy white pulp, which has a lemony flavour. When cut, the fresh beans may be deep royal purple inside.

Left: Pods vary in colour, size, shape and texture. They may have smooth or warty skin.

Far left: Leaves are pale maroon and drooping when young; this is thought to deter pests.

Dombeya spectabilis Bojer
This deciduous tree grows to 12m/40ft in height and comes from Madagascar and north-eastern South Africa. Its 20cm/8in-wide leaves may be heart shaped, broadly oblong or even round. They are rough and covered with soft hairs above and white or rusty-coloured hair below. The large, round clusters of flowers appear during the spring dry season while the tree is leafless. Each flower is small, white or cream and sometimes has a hint of pink.

Triplochiton sceleroxylon Schum.
The pale coloured wood of this West African tree became popular during the Second World War because it is strong and easy to work. *Triplochiton sceleroxylon* is an evergreen tree to 55m/180ft of humid lowland forests and waterways. It is a fast-growing pioneer species, often found grouped in patches, and is a popular choice for reforestation programmes. Its only downside is that it is unreliable in its flowering and fruiting.

The smooth, pale brown trunk has buttresses up to 6m/20ft tall. It is topped with a small, sparse crown of smooth, narrow, mid-green leaves. Each leaf is 30cm/12in across and divided into seven lobes with pale veining. The conspicuous, pretty flowers appear throughout the winter and spring. They are red or purple with paler, sometimes white, margins, 2.5–3cm/1¼in across, and are found in dense clusters. The brown, leathery fruit is winged, carries one or two seeds and appears from early spring.

Cola nitida (Vent.) A.Chev.
This handsome, evergreen, African tree grows to 18m/60ft in height. It produces seeds that are high in caffeine and chewed or used in drinks. The seeds taste bitter at first but have a lingering, sweet flavour that remains in the mouth after eating. This tree produces more caffeine than any other cola species, and its nuts are both collected wild and grown in West Africa for the local and export markets. The tree has greyish-brown bark and tough, glossy, elliptic leaves 30cm/12in long.

Looking-glass Mangrove *Heritiera littoralis* Dryand
Found from East Africa to Australia on the landward side of mangroves and in riverine areas where there is less saline influence. When mature, this 25m/80ft tree forms impressive ribbon-like buttress roots. The pale reverse side of the looking-glass mangrove's leaves appears reflective. The starchy seeds are edible once the tannins have been removed. The hard, dark red wood, which sinks in water, is used in construction, and boat- and furniture-making.

The evergreen trees are densely branched. The bark is smooth, becoming furrowed and flaking when mature, and is white, pale grey or pinkish. The 12–25cm/4½–10in-long leaves are leathery, dark green above and silver below. Tiny, bell-shaped, summer flowers form in lax, branched, axillary panicles, and each is pinkish or green and downy. The 8cm/3in-long fruit is pale brown and ovoid with a small keel along one side, and is very hard and smooth.

THE BOMBAX FAMILY

The bombax family of tropical trees is especially well represented in South America, and includes some outstanding species. Many have thick or swollen trunks for water storage and spectacular flat-topped, spreading crowns. Their leaves are often lobed and clustered towards the tips of the thick branches. Bombacaceae flowers, with five petals and many stamens, are usually large and showy. The fruit capsule is sometimes winged and contains fine hairs.

Baobab

Adansonia digitata L.

This incredible tree can grow to a very great age. The trunk becomes grossly swollen and may be as much as 30m/100ft in circumference, making the baobab one of the widest trees in the world. In extremely old specimens the trunk becomes hollow and may hold up to 1,200 litres/2,100 pints of water. The inner bark also provides fibre for ropes.

Identification: The bark is pale, and the dark green, glossy leaves are divided into between five and nine leaflets, each 15cm/6in long with a pale midrib. The tree may be without leaves for a large part of the year. The flowers appear before or with the new foliage. They hang singly from branches on cords, are 15cm/6in wide, have fleshy, crinkled, off-white petals with numerous purple or yellow stamens, and open at night. The brown fruit hangs on long stalks. Each is 30cm/12in long by 10cm/4in wide and holds 30 seeds in sour pulp.

Distribution: Throughout tropical Africa.
Height: 24m/80ft
Shape: Sparsely domed
Deciduous
Pollinated: Bat
Leaf shape: Round (orbicular) and divided

Left: The flowers have a strong melon-like scent.

Left: One myth suggests the baobab was cursed, pulled from the ground and replanted upside down.

Right: The fruit contains an edible acidic dry pulp.

Kapok

Ceiba pentandra (L.) Gaertn.

Distribution: Throughout tropics (America, Africa and Asia).
Height: 60m/200ft
Shape: Conical
Semi-evergreen
Pollinated: Bat
Leaf shape: Round (orbicular) and divided

Right: Mature trees yield up to 900 fruits. These are harvested and laid out in the sun until they open.

This tree was sacred to the ancient Maya of Central America and today is often seen in market places. It probably originated in South America but has become so widespread that it is difficult to be certain of this. The kapok has a distinctive outline; its huge, thick trunk is heavily buttressed and often covered with thick spines. The thick, heavy branches are held at right angles to the trunk, and the tree eventually becomes as wide as it is tall. Kapok fruit yields fine silky filaments, which are used to stuff pillows and life vests.

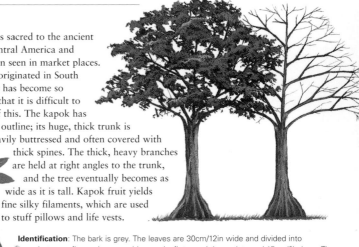

Identification: The bark is grey. The leaves are 30cm/12in wide and divided into between five and seven mid-green leaflets, each lanceolate and 15cm/6in long. The fragrant flowers appear in spring, when the tree is leafless (if deciduous). They are 15cm/6in across, woolly and white, creamy pink or yellow. The fruit pod is 15cm/6in long, narrowly elliptical, leathery and dark.

Water Chestnut

Pachira aquatica Aubl.

The seeds of this tree are eaten raw or roasted. Although they are called water chestnuts, they are completely unrelated to the water chestnuts used in Chinese cooking. This species occurs on damp ground and along watercourses. It has a very dense canopy and a heavy, buttressed trunk.

Identification: The bark is grey. The leaves are divided into between five and nine leaflets. They are smooth, 10–30cm/4–12in long and bright green with lighter midribs and veins. The flower buds are obvious, solitary, thick, brown, velvety spikes poking out from the leaf axils. The flowers have five narrow petals up to 35cm/14in long, pale buff on the top and brown underneath. These encircle hundreds of 15–20cm/6–8in-long stamens, which may be red, purple, pink or white. The fruit pod is up to 38cm/15in long x 13cm/5in across, velvety, reddish brown and contains the seeds in pulp.

Distribution: Tropical America and West Indies.
Height: 18m/60ft
Shape: Spreading
Evergreen
Pollinated: Bat
Leaf shape: Round (orbicular) and divided

Left: The flowers are fragrant and showy but open at night, each lasting for only 24 hours.

Dead Rat Tree *Adansonia gregorii* L.
This 18m/60ft-tall tree comes from a small region in north-western Australia. Outside its native home it is grown for its novelty value. The pale, rough-barked trunk grows to enormous proportions and is used by the tree to store water. The leaves are divided, and the hanging flowers are like those of the better-known baobab. The fruits, which look like dead rats hanging from the tree, contain sour, edible pulp.

Gold Coast Bombax *Bombax buonopozense* P. Beauv.
This deciduous tree occurs from Sierra Leone to Gabon in savannah and forests. It has large, conspicuous, deep red flowers, which appear in winter and spring when the tree is leafless. The Gold Coast bombax grows to 36m/120ft tall and has buttress roots. The thick, corky bark is fissured and has thick, conical spines. The leaves are divided into six or seven leaflets, each 15cm/6in long. The solitary flowers have five hairy, leathery petals, each of which is 10cm/4in long. The fruit contains up to 1,800 tiny seeds in silky floss.

Wild Chestnut *Pachira insignis* (Sw.) Savigny.
The edible seeds in the pod of this tree are the 'chestnut'. This buttressed tree from the West Indies and Mexico grows to 18m/60ft. It has large leaves divided into five to seven egg-shaped to oblong, glossy leaflets. The spidery-looking flowers are beautiful yet fleeting. They have five fleshy, pale pink, crimson or brownish petals, which are long and narrow, and elegantly curl back in on themselves. Held within the petals are many pale, delicate stamens. The fruit pods are 20–25cm/8–10in long.

Red Silk Cotton Tree

Bombax ceiba L.

Now found throughout the tropics, this tree is popular for its dramatic flowering display, and in India the thick flower petals are added to curries. The seed pod contains kapok but of an inferior quality to that of the real kapok tree. The tree is fast growing and has soft wood. The trunk is heavily buttressed and may have thick spines when young, as may the branches, which form in whorled tiers.

Identification: The bark is grey. The glossy leaves are divided into between three and ten leaflets, each 25cm/10in long, dark green above and paler below. The flowers appear along the branches in late winter while the tree is briefly leafless. They are 28cm/11in across and have five succulent, curved petals that are bright shining scarlet, pale red or vermilion and surround many bright red stamens. The fruit develops in late spring. It is a brown pod, 15cm/6in long and contains kapok fibres and small seeds.

Distribution: Tropical South America.
Height: 36m/120ft
Shape: Spreading
Deciduous
Pollinated: Bird
Leaf shape: Round (orbicular) and divided

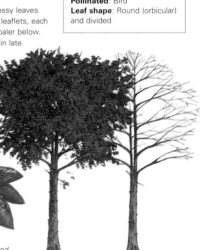

Above: As the flowers drop to the ground they form an ephemeral red carpet.

Balsa Wood

Ochroma lagopus Sw.

Distribution: Central and South America.
Height: 21m/70ft
Evergreen
Pollinated: Bat
Leaf shape: Cordate

Balsa is renowned for its incredibly light wood, which is used for floats, rafts, aircraft construction and insulation, among other things. Balsa wood is the lightest wood known, weighing just 9kg per cubic metre/7lb per cubic foot. The tree is incredibly fast growing and is common in its native haunts, colonizing secondary rainforest in dense patches.

Above: The fast-growing, short-lived balsa can prove a weed in some localities. In Spanish, the name translates as raft or dinghy.

Left: Each giant flower lasts only one night and may produce up to 20ml/4tsp of nectar to attract bats during that time.

Left: The huge leaves are unusual within the forest canopy. The largest leaves are seen on young trees.

Identification: The straight trunk has smooth, brown bark. The leaves are easily recognized, as they are immense – 60cm/24in long with leaf stems equally as long. Rough textured and weakly divided into angular lobes, the leaves occur in groups of five to seven. Each leaf is pale green with toothed margins, and downy below. The solitary flowers are funnel shaped, pale brown or yellow. The semi-woody fruit is produced in spring, and is rather curious: brown, velvety and 18cm/7in long, it is ridged longitudinally and stands erect on the branches. When the fruit splits open it reveals floss, making it look like a soft brown brush.

Durian

Durio zibethinus Murray

The durian is known as the 'king of the fruits'. These rainforest trees have been cultivated for hundreds of years in Malaysia, where the fruit is a delicacy. To the uninitiated, the pungent, putrid smell of the fruit is nauseating. However, the smooth flesh tastes delicious. Full of energy, it may be eaten as a vegetable if cooked before ripe. When ripe, it may be eaten raw or cooked to make cake, sweets or biscuits. The distinctive smelling fruit is also very popular with forest animals such as elephants.

Identification: The tree has a straight brown trunk, broad base and almost horizontal branches. The leaves are dark green above, silvery with brown scales below and 20cm/8in long. The flowers are greenish white or pinkish and emerge directly from the trunk and older branches in clusters of 3–30. The fruit is round, up to 38cm/15in across, yellowish green and has coarse hard spines covering the surface. It divides into four or five segments, each containing 5cm/2in long seeds.

Distribution: Malaysia and the East Indies.
Height: 36m/120ft
Shape: Rounded and irregular
Evergreen
Pollinated: Insect and bat
Leaf shape: Elliptic

Far left: During the day, insects pollinate the flowers, while at night fruit bats may pollinate or eat them.

Middle left: The sombre-looking foliage is distinctive in Malaysia.

Left: The fruit takes up to twelve weeks to form and is only ripe when it drops to the ground.

Floss Silk Tree

Chorisia speciosa A. St.-Hil.

The floss silk tree is grown for its beautiful and delicate cup-shaped flowers, which are quite different from those of other members of this family. It is thought that no two floss silk trees have identical flowers. This species grows quickly and has soft wood. The trunk is swollen at the base and has thick thorns; the number and density of thorns varies between trees. The branches are angular and sprawling.

Identification: The bark is green when young and turns grey as the tree ages. The leaves are divided into between five and seven leaflets, each long and narrow with a toothed margin and a long leaf stalk. The flowers appear in the leaf axils through the autumn and winter. They are 8cm/3in across and may be red, pink, white or yellowish with gold or white throats and purple or brown dots and striations. The large, capsular fruit is pear shaped and contains cotton-like silky white kapok.

Left: The trunk swells as it matures and may lose its lower spines with age.

Right: The mid-green leaves drop in autumn and winter.

Distribution: Brazil.
Height: 15m/50ft
Shape: Spreading
Deciduous
Leaf shape: Round (orbicular) and divided

Above: Speciosa means 'showy', describing the beautiful flowers.

White Floss Silk Tree *Chorisia insignis* Kunth. This fast-growing tree from Peru and north-eastern Argentina has an open, sprawling crown and grows to 12m/40ft tall. The smooth trunk has green to grey bark, with a few thick spines, and is swollen – it may measure up to 1.8m/6ft in diameter. The deep green, deciduous leaves comprise five to seven broad overlapping leaflets, each 15cm/6in long. In autumn the 15cm/6in-wide, trumpet-shaped flowers appear in clusters at the branch tips. The flowers have five waxy petals and are pale yellow when they open but change to orange or purple before finally becoming white. They may have brown markings but are highly variable. The old pale flowers hang on the tree after they have faded and died. The woody fruit contains seeds in kapok floss.

Wild Kapok *Bombax valetonii* Hochr. This tree is very similar in appearance to the kapok tree, *Ceiba pentandra*. The wild kapok, however, is native to Malaysia, Indonesia and Java where it is occasionally found in the forest. It grows to 30m/100ft and develops a dense flattened crown in maturity. The leaves are divided into five to nine blunt-ended, elliptical leaflets, each up to 38cm/15in long, which become smaller on mature trees. The flowers appear in the winter on leafless branches. They are 9cm/3½in long with pale-green petals and numerous white stamens. They are thought to be pollinated by bats. The dark brown fruit is a hard, round, narrow pod up to 23cm/9in long and contains silky floss.

Shaving Brush Tree

Psedobombax ellipticum (H. B. K.) Dugand.

This fast-growing tree is grown for its beautiful winter flowers, which open at night, and its colourful reddish-bronze young leaves, which contrast well with the pale green branches in spring. This species may have one or many short stout trunks.

Identification: The bark is pale grey with vertical green stripes. The leaves often droop when mature and are divided into five to seven leaflets. Each leaflet is dark green with a lighter midrib and veins, 15–30cm/6–12in long, elliptic to egg-shaped with the stalk at the narrow end and fine hairs on both sides. The leaves drop in the winter, and flower buds that resemble large acorns develop through the winter; in spring they enlarge rapidly into brown velvety spikes 10cm/4in long. The spikes open to reveal masses of thick 15–20cm/6–8in-long white or deep pink stamens. The fruit pods are woody, pear shaped to round containing kapok floss and seeds.

Below: The flowers and foliage are often mistaken for those of the water chestnut tree.

Distribution: Guatemala, southern Mexico and the West Indies.
Height: 9m/30ft
Shape: Spreading
Deciduous
Pollinated: Bat
Leaf shape: Round (orbicular) and divided

THE LECYTHIS FAMILY

Lecythidaceae includes trees and shrubs – many of the trees are large rainforest emergent species. The plants have a characteristic odour, tough fibres in their stems and leaves with toothed margins. The family is closely related to the myrtle family, and this is reflected in the flowers, which have numerous stamens and are often large and showy. The fruits are large berries or capsules and the seeds nut-like.

Cannonball Tree

Couroupita guianensis Aublet

A mature cannonball tree with fruit and flowers is an impressive sight. The large, waxy flowers hang the full length of the trunk and are interspersed with tough, sinuous cords holding large, cannonball-like, reddish brown fruit.

Identification: The brown bark is fissured, almost corky. The leaves, which may be oblong-elliptic, elliptic or broadly lanceolate, are bright green, leathery, 20–30cm/8–12in long and clustered at branch tips. Flowers grow in 60–90cm/2–3ft-long clusters held by long, thick cords emerging from the trunk and grow longer every year.

Above and right: The spherical fruit is 25cm/10in wide. When ripe, it falls to the ground, exploding and releasing its foul-smelling red pulp.

Distribution: Northern South America including the Amazon basin.
Height: 30m/100ft
Shape: Columnar
Deciduous
Pollinated: Bat
Leaf shape: Variable

Right: Flowers are 8–12cm/3–4½in wide, and strangely scented.

Brazil Nut Tree

Bertholletia excelsa Boupl.

This emergent rainforest tree has a small crown topping a trunk that is clear of branches for much of its height. The fruit holds 10–15 Brazil nuts and is a favourite food of cat-sized rodents called 'agoutis'. Agoutis, which live on the ground, open the fallen fruit to feed on the nuts. Like squirrels, they have the habit of burying some for later, and a few are never dug up again, helping the tree to spread. These trees do not fare well in plantations, and nuts are still collected from the wild.

Identification: The alternate leaves are dark green, leathery and large. Before dropping they turn brownish red. The flowers appear on thick branches above the foliage in long, branched clusters. Each individual flower is yellow and 2.5cm/1in wide. The fruit is attached to a long woody stem. It is round, brown, hard and 10cm/4in across. The fruit contains the hard-shelled, angular seeds that we know as Brazil nuts.

Below: The hard fruit takes about 15 months to develop. A large tree may yield 300 fruits in one season.

Distribution: Amazon basin.
Height: 30m/100ft
Shape: Oval
Evergreen
Pollinated: Bee
Leaf shape: Oblong

Far left: Brazil nut trees require cross-pollination (with another tree) to produce fruit.

Left and right: The leaves have wavy edges.

Fish Poison Tree

Barringtonia asiatica (L.) Kurz.

The pounded or grated leaf, bark or fruit of this tree when thrown into water will stupefy fish. This tree thrives in damp conditions and usually grows near water. In coastal locations it shows itself to be tolerant of saline soil, salt air and sea spray. The fish poison tree often grows with multiple buttressed trunks, which repeatedly divide to form a dense crown.

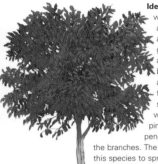

Identification: The bark is grey, while the 60cm/24in-long leaves are bright green, thick, leathery and glossy. Strongly veined, they grow in whorls at the branch tips and become reddish purple before dropping. The flowers are 20cm/8in across and have four white, fleshy, curved petals surrounding masses of central white stamens with red, purple or pink tips. The flowers are held in pendulous clusters at the ends of the branches. The fruit floats, which has enabled this species to spread through the coastal tropics. It is brown, 10cm/4in long, heart shaped and square in cross section.

Above: The scented flowers open at night.

Distribution: Coastal north Australia, South-east Asia, Pacific islands, Sri Lanka and India.
Height: 21m/70ft
Shape: Spreading
Evergreen
Pollinated: Moth and bat
Leaf shape: Obovate

Right: The single seed is surrounded by a fibrous husk.

Monkey Pod *Lecythis ollaria* L.
This very slow-growing tree from eastern tropical Africa reaches 13m/43ft tall and has a large spreading crown of elliptic leaves atop a short trunk. It gets its name from its fruit, which has a detachable lid and contains nuts. According to some accounts, monkeys sticking their hand into the fruit after removing the lid often appear to get stuck – the ball of a monkey's fist with the nut in it is sometimes too big to pull back out of the hole.

Stinkwood *Gustavia augusta* L.
This evergreen timber tree or shrub from Guyana and the Amazon grows up to 22m/73ft. The leaves vary from egg- to teardrop-shaped, with the stalk at the narrow end, and grow in tufts from the branch tips. They measure 48cm/19in long by 13cm/5in wide and are pink when young. The scented flowers have six to nine white petals tinted pink below and appear in clusters, each up to 20cm/8in across. The fruit is spherical and 8cm/3in in diameter.

Napoleon's Button *Napoleonae imperialis* P. Beauv.
This evergreen tree or shrub found from Nigeria to Guinea grows to 7m/23ft. The leaves are 22 x 9cm/9 x 3½in, elliptic to egg-shaped with basal glands. The plant sports interesting complicated flowers. Each flower includes a frilled, brick red, circular tutu-like surround edged in yellow, and two inner crowns. The tree gets its name from its berry, which is 3.5 x 4.5cm/1¼ x 1¾in and is rarely produced.

Cream nut

Lecythis pisonis Cambess.

This tree is grown ornamentally for the stunning effect created when the purple flowers and new young pink leaves unfurl, turning the entire crown pink and mauve. It is also highly regarded for its tasty nuts, which can be hard to find because monkeys and other animals are fond of them too.

Identification: The trunk carries ascending branches and a dense crown. It has grey bark with deep vertical fissures. The smooth, leathery leaves have specks on them, and have toothed margins and a prominent midrib. The flowers form in clusters at the ends of the twigs and branches. The hard fruit is cinnamon coloured, 20cm/8in long, and contains the delicious, red to brown, elliptical seeds, each of which is 5cm/2in long.

Distribution: Eastern tropical America.
Height: 30m/100ft
Shape: Domed
Deciduous
Pollinated: Insect
Leaf shape: Oblong-elliptic

Right: The rough-skinned fruit has a closely fitting lid and contains delicious seeds.

Below: The large, purple to white flowers have a dense central disc of stamens surrounded by six petals.

THE MALLOW FAMILY

*Most members of the Malvaceae family are herbaceous shrubs, many from temperate areas. The trees are
fast growing and have soft wood. They all have palmate, lobed leaves, which are serrated along
the margins. Mallow flowers have five petals, are usually asymmetrical and are often showy; many of the
family are grown as garden ornamentals. In all but one species the fruit is a collection of dry seeds.*

Mahoe

Hibiscus tiliaceus L.

Growing in lowlands, swampy and coastal areas
and forming impenetrable thickets and scrub,
this tree or large shrub varies enormously in
shape and size. The branches are thick and
drooping with dense foliage, and the trunk may
be contorted. The mahoe is adapted to salty
coastal air and sandy soil, and is sometimes
grown in gardens as a trimmed hedge.

Distribution: Coastal old
world tropics (Africa through
to Asia).
Height: 15m/50ft
Shape: Spreading
Evergreen
Pollinated: Insect
Leaf shape: Round (orbicular)
to heart shaped and lobed

Identification: The leaves are 13–20cm/5–8in wide, leathery and
covered in fine hair below. They are deep green in colour, have
prominent light green to red veining and are pale underneath. The
trumpet-shaped flowers appear throughout the year and last only a day.
Solitary with overlapping petals each 4–7cm/1½–2¾in
long, they occur in the leaf axils near branch tips and
are yellow or white with a red centre and deep red
stigma. After dropping from the tree, the flowers fade
to pink or maroon. The fruit capsule is ovoid, velvety,
greyish green and 1.5cm/⅝in long.

*Right: The mahoe
flower opens in the
morning, closes around
4pm and drops off the tree by
the next morning.*

Portia Tree

Thespesia populnae (L.) Sol. ex. Corr.

This tree is often confused with the mahoe, and there are
numerous similarities between them. The portia tree is very
salt tolerant, growing on seashores and in sandy places, and
has a dense, spreading crown. The trunk, although
sometimes contorted, has good, hard timber with chocolate-
brown-coloured heartwood, which is used for furniture.

*Above: A portia can be mistaken
for a mahoe but has rugged bark
and yellow flower stigmas.*

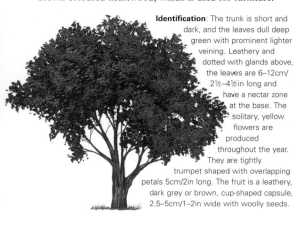

Identification: The trunk is short and
dark, and the leaves dull deep
green with prominent lighter
veining. Leathery and
dotted with glands above,
the leaves are 6–12cm/
2½–4½in long and
have a nectar zone
at the base. The
solitary, yellow
flowers are
produced
throughout the year.
They are tightly
trumpet shaped with overlapping
petals 5cm/2in long. The fruit is a leathery,
dark grey or brown, cup-shaped capsule,
2.5–5cm/1–2in wide with woolly seeds.

Distribution: Coastal
throughout all tropics.
Height: 20m/66ft
Shape: Rounded spreading
Evergreen
Pollinated: Insect
Leaf shape: Heart to ovate

*Above and left: The flowers open
in the evening attracting night-
flying moths. From daybreak they
fade to orange, pink or maroon to
attract day-flying insects, and stay
on the tree for a few days.*

THE BIXA FAMILY

This small family consists of a handful of shrubs and small trees. Bixaceae have large leaves that are often lobed. These have resin cells within them and small appendages (stipules) at the base of the long delicate leaf stem. The flowers have four or five petals, many yellow stamens and are held in branched clusters of racemes. The fruit are sectioned capsules containing many seeds.

Annatto

Bixa orellana L.

Tribal peoples use bright red dye from the annatto's greasy seeds cosmetically, and plantations have been set up to supply the export market to Europe and North America, where the pigment is used for lipstick and for colouring foods, such as red cheeses. This densely crowned tree or shrub with multiple branching has pretty flowers and is popular in tropical gardens, where it is grown as an ornamental or hedging plant.

Identification: The alternate leaves are light green with prominent veins, glossy, 20 x 15cm/8 x 6in and a reddish tone when young. The bark is light brown. The flowers occur in clusters at the ends of twigs or small branches. Each flower is pink or white with purple tones, 5cm/2in across and has masses of fluffy, central stamens. The fruit is a flattened ovate-shaped capsule, 5cm/2in long. Coated in dense soft spines, it may be white, red, pink or brown. The seeds inside are deep red in colour.

Distribution: Tropical America and West Indies.
Height: 7m/23ft
Shape: Domed
Evergreen
Pollinated: Insect
Leaf shape: Broadly ovate

Left: Attractive, dense foliage makes Bixa ideal for hedging in tropical gardens.

Right: The lovely flowers appear for most of the year. Although they are short lived, they appear in continual succession, soon followed by attractive seed pods.

Buttercup Tree

Cochlospermum vitifolium

This fast-growing tree with soft, brittle branches is grown for its intense yellow flowers, which are borne on bare branches. It is sometimes grown as a hedge, and there are varieties with double flowers. The buttercup tree is also commonly called the wild cotton tree due to the white floss that covers the seeds. This floss is used like kapok to stuff cushions and soft toys. The buttercup tree has a rather open, sparsely branched canopy. Some botanists consider it to be the sole genus in its own family, Cochlospermaceae.

Identification: The 30cm/12in-wide, vine-like leaves are deeply divided into between five and seven lobes, each toothed along the edges. Held in erect branched clusters, the flowers occur for three months in late winter and spring while the tree is leafless. The brown, elliptic fruits are 8cm/3in-long capsules with a velvety texture. Split into five sections, they contain kidney-shaped, dark brown seeds covered in floss.

Distribution: Tropical America.
Height: 12m/40ft
Shape: Spreading
Deciduous
Leaf shape: Round (orbicular) and lobed

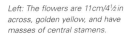

Left: The flowers are 11cm/4½in across, golden yellow, and have masses of central stamens.

THE SAPODILLA FAMILY

These tropical and subtropical trees and shrubs of the Sapotaceae family are an ecologically important part of the South American rainforest. They all have milky sap and leaves with smooth margins. The small flowers are whitish, greenish or tan and have four to eight petals fused into a tube at the base. The often edible fruit is fleshy, and the seeds are big, shiny and dark brown with a lighter coloured scar.

Chicle Tree

Manilkara zapota (L.) P. Royen

The sweet fruit of this tree is very popular in tropical America, where it is eaten raw and made into syrups and preserves. The trunk produces a gum, which may be tapped every two or three years. Called 'chicle', this was the original base for chewing gum, but it is now rarely used. Chicle trees are grown in plantations in tropical America and the Far East. The thick branches, closely set in tiers, have incredibly dense foliage.

Distribution: Mexico, Belize, Guatemala, northern Colombia.
Height: 35m/115ft
Shape: Domed
Evergreen
Pollinated: Insect
Leaf shape: Elliptic

Identification: The bark is grey to brown and made up of small interlocking plates. The 13–15cm/5–6in-long, leathery leaves are glossy dark green with a prominent midrib and clustered towards the branch tip. The flowers are small, greenish or creamy white, tubular and found in the leaf axils, while the 8cm/3in-wide fruit is spherical to egg shaped and has rough, matt brown skin. The flesh varies in colour from cream to yellowish or even reddish brown.

Left: The leaves are glossy and attractive.
Right: The fruits are produced all year and have a grainy (pear-like) texture.

Gutta Percha

Palaquium gutta (Hook.) Baillon

This tree is the main source of gutta-percha, a rubber-like latex, which is elastic and soft when heated and sets hard when cooled. Gutta-percha is used in moulds and for insulating underwater cables and wires. It was originally extracted by cutting the trees down and slashing the bark. Recently this species has become protected, so now the latex is tapped. Each tree may be tapped only once every year, or it stops yielding. Gutta-percha may also be extracted from the leaves, if required. As with many other plant products, gutta-percha has been largely replaced by synthetic alternatives, and the market for the natural product has reduced.

Identification: The dark green leaves are 10cm/4in long, leathery with shining golden to cinnamon-coloured velvety hairs below. Young branches are also coated in these hairs. The green, strongly-scented flowers form in clusters in the leaf axils. The fruit is an egg-shaped berry, 2–4cm/ ¾–1¼ in with one or two seeds.

Above: These trees were once common in lowland forest areas but are now a protected species.

Distribution: Malaysia, Sumatra, Borneo.
Height: 12m/40ft
Shape: Conical
Evergreen
Leaf shape: Obovate-oblong

Left: The fruit has six thin cavities within.

Left: The leaves' lower golden surface is exposed when they shimmer in a breeze.

Star Apple

Chrysophyllum cainito L.

This slow-growing tree occurs in wet lowlands and foothills. The fruit, which is found only on mature trees, is eaten when soft to the touch and has a cool, refreshing, sweet flavour. The name 'star' apple refers to the shape of the fruit – in cross-section the seed chambers radiate from the centre like a star. The tree has a short trunk and may be as broad as it is tall. Its thick, pendant branches have weeping tips and carry a dense mass of foliage.

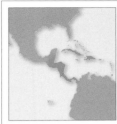

Identification: The bark is grey-brown and becomes deeply fissured as the tree ages. The 10–15cm/4–6in-long leaves are deep shiny green above and lustrous with copper-coloured velvet below. The young branches also have a copper-coloured down. Small white, purplish or yellow flowers appear in summer and are barely visible, due to the thick foliage. The smooth-skinned, round fruit ripens in spring and is up to 10cm/4in across. The fruit ripens to either a dark purplish red or to white, depending on the variety.

Distribution: Central America and West Indies.
Height: 30m/100ft
Shape: Domed to columnar
Evergreen
Pollinated: Insect
Leaf shape: Oblong-elliptic

Left: The delicious fruit has white or purple flesh and dark brown to black seeds.

Right: The fruit's skin must not be eaten, because it contains bitter latex.

Tanjong Tree *Mimusops elengi* L.
This slow-growing evergreen tree from the forests of India, Burma, Malaysia and the Pacific islands grows to 24m/80ft in height. The flowers are collected for their perfume, and the fruit, although acidic, may be eaten. The tanjong tree has a short trunk with reddish bark and a dense oblong crown with weeping branches. Its size and attractive shape make it well suited to small gardens or courtyards. The shiny, dark green leaves are elliptic, have distinctive wavy margins and are 8–15cm/3–6in long. The drooping, star-shaped flowers have eight petals and are 2cm/¾in across, white or cream and clustered in the leaf axils, where they are barely visible due to the leaves. The fruit is deep yellow or orange and very showy. Egg shaped and 2cm/¾in wide, it has a groove on one side and hangs from 5cm/2in-long stems in clusters. It has a floury texture and contains one large, dark seed.

Beef Wood *Manilkara bidentata* (A.D.C.) A. Chev.
This evergreen tree from the West Indies, Panama and South America produces gum balata, a latex similar to, and sometimes used as a substitute for, gutta-percha. It also has very hard, dense wood, which is highly durable. The beef wood tree has a short trunk and a massive oblong crown, and may reach 30m/100ft tall. The narrowly oblong leaves are 25cm/10in long, leathery, shiny and deep green above and greyish and velvety below. They have prominent yellow midribs. The small flowers are white and form in clusters in the leaf axils. The fruit is spherical, edible, is 2cm/¾in across and is yellow.

Damson Plum

Satin Leaf *Chrysophyllum oliviforme* L.

This slow-growing, long-lived tree has particularly attractive foliage. The leaves have shimmering velvety red or copper undersides, leading to its other name, 'satin leaf'. It is grown in towns to form an avenue or as a shade tree, and has edible fruit, which varies in flavour from plain and insipid to quite tasty.

Identification: The trunk is reddish brown, scaly, sometimes thorny and carries weeping branches. The glossy, 10–20cm/4–8in-long leaves are dark green above and a rich tone below, while the 5mm/¼in-long, five-petalled flowers are white, cream, grey or greyish green. The latter appear in clusters in the leaf axils throughout the year and are particularly abundant in late summer and early autumn. Like the flowers, the fleshy fruit is well hidden among the leaves. When ripe, the fruit is dark purple, shiny, up to 4cm/1½in long and contains one seed.

Distribution: West Indies and southern-most Florida.
Height: 12m/40ft
Shape: Oval
Evergreen
Pollinated: Insect
Leaf shape: Ovate-oblong

Above: Although naturalized in Hawaii, the damson plum has become endangered in its native Florida.

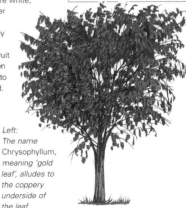

Left: The name Chrysophyllum, meaning 'gold leaf', alludes to the coppery underside of the leaf.

MISCELLANEOUS DILLENIIDAE

These families (caper family, Capparidaceae; moringa family, Moringaceae; flacourtia family, Flacourtiaceae; ebony family, Ebenaceae; and carica family, Caricaeae) are all related within the class Dilleniidae. They are generally small families or are poorly represented in the tropics. Indeed the moringa family has only the one genus, encompassing only three species.

Spider Tree

Crataeva religiosa Forster

As the Latin name suggests, this tree is sacred to people in its native South-east Asia. It has several medicinal uses, for example, the leaves and bark are used to treat stomach upsets. The spider tree grows naturally in shady places, often along streams, but may be seen in drier areas too. The yellowish-white wood is smooth and even grained.

Identification: The bark is smooth with horizontal wrinkles, and grey in colour, speckled with large white spots (lenticels). The young stems are pale green. The leaves are trifoliate (three leaves grow from one leaf stem) and clustered towards the ends of the branches. The 10cm/4in-wide flowers appear in winter and cover the crown: they open green or white, and have long, deep purple or reddish, spidery stamens. As they age, they fade to yellow or orange. The edible fruit is a smooth, hard, round or oval berry, 5–8cm/2–3in long and green with white specks. The seeds are contained within yellow pulp.

Distribution: South-east Asia, Pacific and northern Australia.
Height: 6m/20ft
Shape: Domed
Deciduous
Pollinated: Insect
Leaf shape: Trifoliate

Below: Each leaflet is deep green and measures 15cm/6in long.

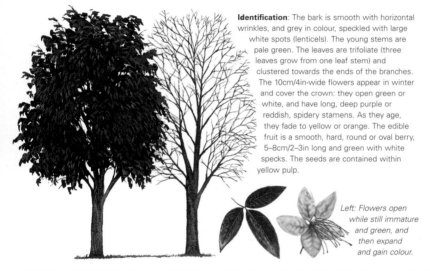

Left: Flowers open while still immature and green, and then expand and gain colour.

Horseradish Tree *Moringa oleifera* Lam.
Originating from northern India, this tree is used by people across Asia, India and northern Africa. Leaves, flowers, fruit and tuberous roots are edible. The thick main root is used as a substitute for horseradish, although the taste is inferior. Immature seed pods are cooked like beans, and the leaves are used in curries and pickled. Pods are rich in vitamin C. Seeds contain valuable oil, and flowers and bark have traditional medicinal uses. The seeds coagulate solids in solution, one crushed seed is said to clear 90 per cent of the coliform bacteria in 1 litre/1¾ pints of river water in 20 minutes.

This tree has an open, airy crown, a straight soft-wooded trunk and reaches 7m/23ft. The bark is thick and corky. The ferny, tripinnate, matt, pale green leaves are up to 75cm/30in long with a long leaf stem and composed of numerous 2cm/1in-long oblong leaflets. The white to pale yellow, honey-scented flowers are 2cm/¾in across, and appear in airy 10–25cm/4–10in-long drooping panicles chiefly in the spring. They are pollinated by insects. The 45cm/18in-long pods are mainly produced in late spring. They are green ripening to brown and three sided, faintly ribbed and tapering to a point. The fruit contains many 3–4cm/1¼–1½-in long grey to brown seeds with white wings.

Indian Prune *Flacourtia rukam* Zoll. & Moritzi
This small evergreen tree is widespread from India to Malaysia in rainforest, mountainous areas and particularly alongside streams. It is grown for its fruit, the white flesh of which is juicy but sour. When the fruit is rubbed in the hands before eating, it becomes sweet.

The tree, up to 17m/56ft, has smooth brown bark and crooked branches. The trunk and old wood often carry 10cm/4in-long spines. Spines are hard, strong and often in branched clusters. The elliptic leaves have a toothed margin and a short leaf stem. The small flowers are male or female, depending on the tree. They are green-yellow, form in small groups (where leaves arise from the twigs), do not have petals and are 5mm/¼in wide. The fruit takes about 12 weeks to develop. It is dark purplish red when mature and up to 2.5cm/1in wide.

Lovi-lovi *Flacourtia inermis* Roxb.
An ornamental tree, similar to the Indian prune, that grows up to 10m/33ft. Fruit is profuse, bright red, round and shiny, and although sour, is used to make jams and jellies. The 10cm/4in-long leaves are elliptic with long tapering tips and serrated and scalloped margins. Flowers are male and female, and produce the round, red fruit.

Ebony

Diospyros ebenum Koenig ex. Retz.

Many trees are commercially labelled as 'ebony' but this species, with its jet black heartwood, is considered the best. In the wild, it grows as a middle storey tree in dry, evergreen forests. The wood, which is heavy and may have yellow or brown streaking, is a luxury product used for carving, turnery and making furniture. The value of its wood means the species is now rare.

Identification: The bark is dark grey and peels off in rectangular pieces. The leaves, held on short leaf stems, are bright green with large, darkish glands on the underside. The foliage is very dense and somewhat gloomy in appearance. The young shoots are covered in soft down. Ebony has separate male and female flowers, which are small and off-white. The female flowers are produced singly, while the male flowers appear in clusters of three to fifteen. The fruit is round, 1–2cm/½–¾in across and green, ripening to black.

Distribution: India and Sri Lanka.
Height: 18m/60ft
Evergreen
Pollinated: Insect
Leaf shape: Oblong-elliptic

Left: The fruit is held in a woody green cup, which is the old flower sepal.

Left: The thick, glossy leaves alternate on the stem and are 5–18cm/2–7in long, smooth and have wavy edges.

Papaya

Carica papaya L.

The popular papaya fruit is tasty, juicy and has a distinctive flavour. It is grown throughout the tropics, and the fruit is exported to temperate regions. It is very fast growing, easy to cultivate and crops heavily, even from a young age. This herbaceous 'tree' has a single stem or may branch a little into a flat crown when older, and the leaves only ever remain on the growing tips. The stem always remains soft, becoming woody only at the base even when mature. The enzyme papain is contained within the leaves and fruit and is used for tenderizing meat.

Above: Deep indentations in the trunk remain where the leaf stems were once attached.

Distribution: South America.
Height: 6m/20ft
Shape: Columnar or spreading
Evergreen
Pollinated: Insect
Leaf shape: Round (orbicular) but heavily lobed

Identification: The stem remains light with old leaf scars evident. Leaves are 60cm/24in long, dark green and heavily incised into five to seven lobes, each further incised. Leaf stems are 60cm/24in long. The fleshy flowers appear year round, borne on the stem, and are creamy or greenish white, and 6cm/2in across. Trees may be either sex or both. The fruit is orange-yellow when ripe, pear shaped or round, smooth and up to 30cm/12in long but usually 20cm/8in long.

Left: Papaya leaves may help to aid digestion when taken medicinally.

Above: The papaya is a popular, yet short-lived, cropping tree.

Left: Papaya fruits are common in the tropics. They hang close to the stem among the leaf stems.

THE MIMOSA SUBFAMILY

Mimosas, cassias and beans are all sub-divisions of the very large pea family, sometimes called 'legumes'. Mimosoideae are well known for their finely divided, bipinnate leaves, although not all members of the subfamily have leaves with this structure. Mimosa flowers have small petals, extended stamens and appear in eye-catching clusters. Parts of these plants give off a distinctive, bean-like smell when crushed.

Knob Tree

Acacia nigrescens Oliver

This plant has fearsome curved spines on its trunk and branches to deter herbivores, yet goats and giraffes still manage to browse on it. The tree grows naturally on heavy, black soil in lowland deciduous bush and lightly wooded grassland. The leaves and pods of this species make valuable fodder for livestock, and the twigs and branches are collected for firewood.

Identification: The trunk has soft, thick, pale bark and is covered with large, knobbly spines. The spines grow in pairs below each leaf node and remain on the tree throughout its lifetime. The leaves are divided into between one and four pinnae, each carrying one or two pairs of leaflets. The leaflets are ovate to elliptical, 1–2.5cm/½–1in long and mid-green. The flowers form in spikes in late winter and are cream or white. The smooth, straight, dark brown pods are oblong, 7–15cm/2¾–6in long and 1.5–2.5cm/½–1in wide. They contain 1–1.5cm/½–⅝in-wide seeds.

Distribution: Tanzania, Botswana, northern South Africa and Lesotho.
Height: 25m/83ft
Shape: Domed
Deciduous
Pollinated: Insect
Leaf shape: Bipinnate

Far left: The scented flowers form in 10cm/4in-long spikes.

Ice Cream Bean

Inga edulis Mart.

This fast-growing tree is used in its native home to provide shade in coffee plantations. It is also grown for its seed pods, which contain sweet, white pulp that tastes like vanilla ice cream.

Above left: Seeds are encased in soft pulp.
Above right: Winged leaf stems are typical for the Inga genus.

Distribution: West Indies, Central America and northern South America.
Height: 12m/40ft
Shape: Spreading
Evergreen
Pollinated: Hummingbird and bee
Leaf shape: Pinnate

Identification: The trunk has smooth, grey bark and may be multi-stemmed. The spreading branches are heavily clothed with leaves, providing dense shade. The branches are somewhat brittle and occasionally break under their own weight. The leaves are 60cm/24in long and have three or four pairs of dark green leaflets with lighter veining. Each leaflet is 10cm/4in long, rough textured and elliptical. The stem between each pair of leaflets is winged. The flowers appear sporadically throughout the year but are most common in spring and summer. They have small, brown petals and long white stamens, and are clustered together like tight powder-puffs. The greenish-brown pods are 30–60cm/12–24in long, roughly oblong in cross section and velvety.

Powder-puff

Calliandra haematocephala Hassk.

This plant is grown for its amazing flowers – large, soft powder-puffs of intense scarlet or the darkest pink. It may be grown as a large shrub or pruned to give it a more tree-like shape. The branches droop and sprawl somewhat but are amply covered with thick foliage. The flowers first appear when the plant is quite small.

Identification: The leaves are composed of two pinnae, each 25cm/10in long and consisting of five to ten pairs of leaflets. Each leaflet is oblong to sickle shaped, deep green when mature and 4cm/1½in long. When young, the foliage weeps and is a soft coppery pink. The 10cm/4in-wide flower clusters contain hundreds of individual flowers with their petals obscured by the numerous, 6cm/2½in-long, red stamens. The flowers appear mostly in the autumn and winter months.

Distribution: Bolivia.
Height: 9m/30ft
Shape: Spreading
Evergreen
Pollinated: Hummingbird and insect
Leaf shape: Bipinnate

Left: The tight flower buds are reminiscent of small berried fruit, which burst open to reveal their long stamens.

Right: The flowers are short-lived, lasting only a day or two.

Mangium Wattle *Acacia mangium* Willd.
This fast-growing tree from the rainforests of northern Queensland, Australia, may reach 30m/100ft tall. It has a pyramidal crown atop a straight trunk and is grown in plantations for its hard, durable wood, which is used in building and for wood pulp. In South-east Asia the tree is a problem, as it is spreading rapidly outside plantations. The leaves are typically bipinnate in seedlings, but as the tree matures, the leaf stems and stems between the leaflets start to form into flattened, leaf-like, parallel-veined structures called 'phyllodes'. These are up to 30cm/12in long and pale green. Through the year pale yellow flowers appear, crammed into soft spikes 8–10cm/3–4in long and 1–2cm/½–¾in wide. The seed pods are dark brown and twist together to form spiral clusters.

Koa *Acacia koa* A. Gray
Native to Hawaii, this tree is found on slopes throughout the island in all except the driest locations. On Hawaii it is a popular choice for reforestation but is little used elsewhere. The wood is red and was once used for war canoes. The koa grows quickly and reaches 30m/100ft tall with an open, spreading crown of thick, contorted, horizontal branches. In ideal conditions, the trunk may reach 3m/10ft in diameter. The koa is tolerant of salty air and soil and on coasts forms a smaller, more contorted tree.

The leaf stems are expanded into evergreen phyllodes (*see A. mangium*), sickle shaped and 15cm/6in long. The spring flowers are pale yellow and form spherical clusters.

Ear Pod Tree

Enterolobium cyclocarpum (Jacq.) Griseb.

This upright tree is grown for the novelty value of its pods, which look uncannily like human ears. These pods may be eaten when young and are often collected for animal fodder. The bright red seeds are used for jewellery and the timber is of high quality. The ear pod tree can grow as wide as it is tall and has thick, ascending branches.

Distribution: Venezuela.
Height: 30m/100ft
Shape: Spreading
Deciduous
Pollinated: Insect
Leaf shape: Bipinnate

Identification: The bark is light grey and smooth, while the leaves are bright green and feathery, consisting of four to eight pairs of pinnae, each with 12–24 pairs of leaflets. The leaflets are 1.5cm/⅔in long and oblong to sickle shaped. The tree blossoms in spring, producing sprays of tiny white flowers clustered into balls. Each flower has greenish-white, 5mm/¼in-long petals and longer, white stamens. The seed pods often appear in the dry season, when the tree is leafless. They are deep russet brown, shiny and 8–16cm/3–6¼in long.

Left: The pods are produced in large numbers and contain a dry, sugary pulp, a valuable fodder at the end of the dry season.

Bead Tree

Adenanthera pavonina L.

Distribution: Sri Lanka.
Height: 18m/60ft
Shape: Domed
Deciduous
Pollinated: Insect
Leaf shape: Bipinnate

Seeds of this tree are bright scarlet and reportedly edible if roasted but are more often used as beads after softening in boiling water. In Asia they are used by chemists and jewellers as weights. The wood is strong, durable, red and often called 'red sandalwood' as it is frequently substituted for the real thing. The tree is upright with a light open canopy and fine, feathery foliage. It is grown throughout the tropics and has established itself in the wild in Florida.

Left: The pods ripen from green to brown.

Right: The flower petals fade to dull orange after opening.

Identification: The bark is smooth and grey. The leaves are mid-green, up to 40cm/16in long and divided into between one and six pairs of side stalks, each with 5–20 pairs of leaflets. The leaflets are 2.5–5cm/1–2in long, oblong and have blunt ends. The orange-blossom scented white, cream and yellow flowers appear in spring, tightly packed into narrow clusters up to 25cm/10in long and growing from the leaf axils. The pods are 10–23cm/4–9in long, 1.5cm/⅔in wide, flat and curved. As the pods open they twist to reveal the shiny seeds.

Above: The 'beads' are revealed as the pod twists open.

Yellow Rain Tree

Albizia saman (Jack) F. Muell.

The grass underneath this tree is often green when surrounding grass has dried out and died. This was once attributed to the tree making rain overnight, hence its name. In reality the leaves close at night and during showers, allowing rain to fall on to the grass below when that beneath other trees receives far less or none. The yellow rain tree is widely planted in the tropics for shade – its crown, which has a symmetrical form with ascending branches, attains a spread of 60m/200ft. The pods contain a sugary pulp, which is favoured by cattle and used for fodder.

Identification: The bark is grey and lightly fissured. The leaves are 30cm/12in long with three to six pairs of side stalks, each carrying six to eight pairs of leaflets. Each leaflet is 2.5–5cm/1–2in long, mid-green above, pale green below and oblong to diamond shaped. The delicate flowers occur throughout the year and are particularly common from spring to summer. They have small petals but long stamens, which together give the look of an airy, pink-tipped powder-puff. The pods are 15–25cm/6–10in long, flat, black and contain brown seeds.

Distribution: West Indies, Central America.
Height: 35m/115ft
Shape: Spreading, domed
Semi-deciduous
Pollinated: Insect
Leaf shape: Bipinnate

Left: The leaves close up an hour or more before sunset and open an hour or so after sunrise. It is thought that this allows moisture through the canopy and enables numerous epiphytes to live on the tree's trunk and branches.

African Locust Bean

Parkia javanica (Lam.) Merrill

This fast-growing tree is both visually attractive and useful. The straight, smooth trunk is heavily buttressed, and the foliage is fine and feathery. The tree is used locally as a source of dye, soap and foodstuffs, including the white, powdery contents of the fruit pod. It is found growing in moist lowland forests and is cultivated in parks and gardens in tropical and subtropical regions.

Identification: The trunk is clear of branches for much of its height. Each leaf has 20–30 pairs of side stalks, each of which in turn carries 40–80 pairs of leaflets. Each leaflet is 1cm/½in long, narrow and pointed. The numerous cream flowers form in winter in large globular heads on long hanging stems. The flower heads appear singly and in groups in the leaf axils and on the ends of the twigs and branches. The flowers produce a large quantity of thin nectar to attract fruit bats. The fruit is a smooth, tough, dark brown, twisted pod 38–51cm/15–20in long and 4cm/1½in wide. The fruits often form groups, which may be seen hanging from the branches in early spring.

Distribution: Malaysia through Burma to India.
Height: 46m/150ft
Shape: Spreading
Evergreen
Pollinated: Bat
Leaf shape: Bipinnate

Above left: The boiled beans may be eaten as a vegetable.

Left: The flowers attract fruit bats.

Petai *Parkia speciosa* L.
This slow-growing evergreen tree from Malaysia can reach 45m/150ft tall and has a domed or flattened crown. In good conditions it will branch low and makes a handsome, shapely tree. It is also grown for its edible seeds, which are collected while the pods are immature and still green. The dark green leaves are bipinnate with 10–20 pairs of side stalks carrying oblong leaflets. The flowers grow on long hanging stems with a globular body at the end. This body contains many cream flowers, which have a pungent, sickly scent that attracts pollinating bats. Six to ten dark brown or black pods develop from the globular body, each up to 50cm/20in long and 6cm/2½in wide.

African Locust *Parkia filicoidea*
Welv. ex. Oliver
The African locust is a useful tree to the savannah farmers of eastern central Africa. The husk and pulp of the seed pods are a staple food for people, and most parts of the tree have medicinal properties. The foliage is used as fodder for cattle, and the flowers are so nectar-rich that beehives are put into the tree branches. The African locust grows to 20m/66ft tall and forms a dense, spreading crown. The bark is grey-brown and fissured and the bipinnate leaves composed of up to 40 pairs of side stalks, each with up to 65 pairs of oblong leaflets. The entire leaf is up to 40cm/16in long. The red or orange flowers are clustered into hanging heads 6cm/2½in in diameter. The pods are brown and up to 30cm/12in long.

Manila Tamarind

Pithecellobium dulce (Roxb.) Benth.

This plant has thorns on all its branches and, when kept pruned as a shrub, makes a good spiny hedge. The Manila tamarind has several other uses: yellow dye is made from its bark, a drink is made from the fruit pulp, and its pods are collected for animal fodder. It is suited to dry conditions and has a light and airy canopy with ascending branches.

Identification: The pale grey bark has longitudinal ridges. The leaves have one pair of side stalks, each with only a single pair of leaflets. Each leaflet is 2.5–5cm/1–2in long, blunt ended and matt greyish green when mature. The young leaflets are dull maroon. The overall effect of the leaves makes the tree look congested. The tiny, greenish flowers are packed into round heads 2cm/¾in wide, which are held on branched clusters springing from the leaf axils. The pods are 12–15cm/4½–6in long, 1.5cm/½in wide, lobed and spirally twisted.

Below right: As the pods mature they twist up. They contain three to nine shiny black seeds in pink and white edible pulp.

Distribution: Mexico and Venezuela.
Height: 15m/50ft
Shape: Domed
Evergreen
Pollinated: Insect
Leaf shape: Bipinnate

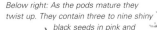

THE CASSIA SUBFAMILY

The legumes include well over 400 genera spread across the globe, and they are particularly common in the tropics. The family includes annuals, herbaceous plants, shrubs, trees and climbers. The trees play an important role in the forests of South America and Africa. The Caesalpinioideae subfamily is distinguished by flowers with five petals, and one odd-sized petal is enclosed by the others.

Hong Kong Bauhinia

Bauhinia x *blakeana* L.

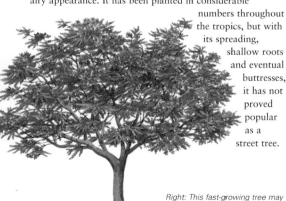

Leaves of orchid trees, such as the Hong Kong bauhinia, are quite unmistakable – they are shaped like a camel's hoof. This fast-growing tree was discovered as a naturally occurring hybrid in 1908 and is thought to be a cross between *B. variegata* and *B. purpurea*. As it is sterile, the Hong Kong bauhinia does not produce seed pods, making it popular for street plantings. In 1965 this tree was chosen as the emblem of Hong Kong. It is generally considered the most beautiful of the orchid trees.

Identification: The smooth trunk is often multi-stemmed and carries a dense crown with slightly hanging branches. The deep olive green leaves are thick, tough and 20cm/8in across. The 15cm/6in-wide flowers are profuse from late autumn until early spring and have a unique fragrance. Their petals are deep pink, purple or red with darker streaks on one odd petal.

Distribution: China and Hong Kong.
Height: 10m/33ft
Shape: Domed
Evergreen
Pollinated: Sterile
Leaf shape: Round (orbicular) and two lobed

Left: The thick leaves have raised yellowish veins.

Flame of the Forest

Flamboyant tree *Delonix regia* (Hook.) Raf.

Also called the flamboyant tree, the flame of the forest flowers in late spring and early summer, when it becomes one mass of intense vermilion blossoms, completely obliterating from sight any foliage across its incredibly wide, flat-topped crown. The tree is also eye-catching in fruit, when hundreds of long pods hang from its horizontal branches. Even when only in leaf the tree has a pleasant, airy appearance. It has been planted in considerable numbers throughout the tropics, but with its spreading, shallow roots and eventual buttresses, it has not proved popular as a street tree.

Identification: The smooth bark is light brown or grey, and the trunk carries thick branches, which are never straight. The leaves are delicate, 60cm/24in long, bright green above and lighter below. The flowers have four red petals and one larger white petal with yellow and red streaks. The dark brown, flattened seed pods are up to 60cm/24in long.

Distribution: Madagascar.
Height: 20m/66ft
Shape: Spreading
Deciduous
Pollinated: Bird
Leaf shape: Bipinnate

Above: Profuse, beautiful flowers give rise to masses of hard woody pods, which remain on the tree even when splitting open.

Right: This fast-growing tree may grow to 7.5m/25ft in four years.

Rose of Venezuela

Brownea grandiceps Jacq.

This slow-growing, handsome tree is notable for its display of impressive flowers and fine foliage. Despite being the largest flowering member of its genus, it is not heavily planted in the tropics. The leaves display an interesting piece of behaviour – they cover the flowers by day to protect them from the sun, then move aside to reveal them at night. The rose of Venezuela grows naturally in mountain forests.

Distribution: Northern Venezuela.
Height: 18m/60ft
Shape: Domed
Evergreen
Leaf shape: Pinnate

Identification: The dense crown has leaves up to 90cm/36in long divided into five to eleven pairs of long, narrow leaflets. Young leaves are translucent pink or bronze and hang, when mature they are bright green, leathery and flat. The delicate flowers are bright red and tubular with long, protruding anthers. They occur in clusters of about 50, in large hanging balls towards the branch tips. Each cluster is 25cm/10in wide. The wide, flattened seed pods are 25cm/10in long.

Left: Flowers appear year round and are particularly abundant in spring and early summer.

Peachwood *Haematoxylon brasiletto* Karsten
The peachwood is the source of haematoxylin dye, which is extracted from the red-brown heartwood. This evergreen, South American tree has spines and grows in arid areas. It has pinnate leaves with just a few blunt-ended, egg-shaped leaflets. The small flowers are yellow, and the little pods split open to release seed, which is dispersed by the wind.

Pride of Burma *Amherstia nobilis* Karsten
This incredibly beautiful flowering tree comes from Burma and India, where the flowers are offered by Buddhists at their temples. The flowers are 10cm/4in wide, deep pink or vermilion with one petal marked yellow and white. The pride of Burma is difficult to grow but when mature reaches 13m/43ft in height. Its bipinnate leaves are 1m/1yd long.

Yellow Flame Tree *Peltophorum pterocarpum* (D. C.) Barker ex. K. Heyne.
The yellow flame tree is grown for the deep shade cast by its wide crown, its profusion of strongly scented, glowing golden flowers and its velvety, copper-coloured pods. This species occurs from northern Australia to India. It grows to 66m/100ft tall and has pinnate leaves, 60cm/24in long, branched flower clusters and 10cm/4in-long pods.

Pink Shower Tree *Cassia grandis* L. f.
The thick canopy of coral pink flowers this tree produces falls quickly in early spring to form a pink carpet below. This species comes from Central America. It has a spreading crown and grows to 18m/60ft tall. The leaves are pinnate, 30cm/12in long and mid-green. The black, cylindrical pods may be up to 38cm/15in long and contain flat yellow seeds.

Tamarind

Tamarindus indica L.

The sweet yet tart pulp surrounding the seeds of this tree is cooked and used in Worcestershire sauce, chutneys and drinks. It is also regularly used as a raw ingredient in Asian cooking. The tree also has various local medicinal uses and, although slow growing, yields beautiful red timber. Well adapted to dry conditions and tolerant of wind, it makes a good street tree and is planted throughout the tropics. Originally from Africa, the tamarind has become naturalized throughout Asia and the Caribbean.

Distribution: Africa.
Height: 21m/69ft
Shape: Rounded spreading
Evergreen
Pollinated: Insect
Leaf shape: Pinnate

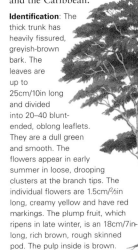

Identification: The thick trunk has heavily fissured, greyish-brown bark. The leaves are up to 25cm/10in long and divided into 20–40 blunt-ended, oblong leaflets. They are a dull green and smooth. The flowers appear in early summer in loose, drooping clusters at the branch tips. The individual flowers are 1.5cm/⅔in long, creamy yellow and have red markings. The plump fruit, which ripens in late winter, is an 18cm/7in-long, rich brown, rough skinned pod. The pulp inside is brown.

Above and below: The tamarind pods contain sticky, brown, sweet-sour pulp with little scent, but high acid content.

THE BEAN SUBFAMILY

Within the legumes many species have leaves that close up during stress or at night and which may be moved by the plant through the day. The bean subfamily, Faboideae, has flowers with five irregular petals: a large upper petal covers the others while the flower is in bud; two side petals form wings upon opening; and the two lower petals, often fused, form a keel.

Common Coral Tree

Erythrina crista-gali L.

This fast-growing plant has soft wood and is grown as a multi-stemmed tree in tropical regions and as a herbaceous plant in warm temperate areas, where it is cut to the ground by the cold each winter. The stems are covered in thick, 1cm/⅜in-long, curved thorns, and even the leaf stems carry spines. The large, long-lasting flower panicles are produced throughout the year and are the showiest in the genus.

Distribution: Brazil.
Height: 9m/30ft
Shape: Spreading, irregular crown
Evergreen
Pollinated: Bird
Leaf shape: Trifoliate

Left: As it matures, the tree gains rough fissured bark and gnarled contorted branches.

Above and below left: These stunning flowers are adapted to pollination by birds through their red colour, tubular shape, copious amount of nectar and sturdiness.

Identification: The trunk has ridged bark and grows into a gnarled form. The leaves are deep green, smooth and leathery with elliptic leaflets each measuring 8cm/3in long. The flowers are scarlet to deep pink and 5–8cm/2–3in long. They form an inflorescence containing up to 100 flowers, which often hangs. The flowers appear in cycles of six weeks. The smooth pods are up to 30cm/12in long and contain grey seeds.

Tahiti Chestnut

Inocarpus edulis Forst.

The large fleshy seeds of the Tahiti chestnut are eaten in its native island home; they are boiled and roasted while still unripe and said by some to taste as good as roasted almonds. The foliage is also very appetizing to livestock. The Tahiti chestnut grows in humid valleys and damp swampy locations. It grows quickly into a handsome tree with straight, heavily fluted, buttressed trunks. This species has clear sap that turns scarlet upon contact with the air. The sap is used as a dye and also medicinally.

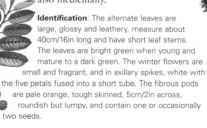

Distribution: Tahiti and neighbouring islands.
Height: 20m/66ft
Evergreen
Pollinated: Bird
Leaf shape: Oblong

Right: The leaves, flowers and fruit of this tree are not typically bean-like.

Identification: The alternate leaves are large, glossy and leathery, measure about 40cm/16in long and have short leaf stems. The leaves are bright green when young and mature to a dark green. The winter flowers are small and fragrant, and in axillary spikes, white with the five petals fused into a short tube. The fibrous pods are pale orange, tough skinned, 5cm/2in across, roundish but lumpy, and contain one or occasionally two seeds.

Burmese Rosewood

Pterocarpus indicus Willd.

This tree is famous for its fine, termite-resistant timber, which is hard, yellow to brick red in colour, has an interlocking wavy grain and is rose scented. Burmese rosewood commands a high price and polishes to a high shine: it is used in furniture-making, turnery and for panelling and flooring. A red dye may be extracted from the wood, and red gum exuded from it is used locally for medicinal purposes.

Identification: The trunk has finely fissured, light brown bark with well developed, large, flat, spreading buttresses in mature trees. The branches are wide spreading, elegantly arched and may trail to the ground. The leaves are pinnate, 50cm/20in long, deep green and have seven to eleven ovate, pointed leaflets. Found in racemes, which protrude from the axils, each is 1.5cm/⅔in across.

Distribution: East Indies.
Height: 40m/130ft
Shape: Spreading and domed
Semi-evergreen
Pollinated: Bee
Leaf shape: Pinnate

Right: 'Pterocarpus' means 'winged-fruit'. The seed pods are 3–5cm/1¼–2in across, flat and brown with a circular wing.

Far right: The golden-yellow flowers are produced in summer.

Swamp Immortelle *Erythrina fusca* Lour.
This tree is found across a very wide natural range that includes the tropics of America, Africa and Asia. It is a deciduous tree with a rounded crown that may grow to 24m/80ft tall and have a spread almost equally as large. The swamp immortelle is grown for its scarlet flowers, which are densely crowded into 25cm/10in-long sprays. The flowers appear in spring and summer, and have a brick red upper petal and brownish-maroon to cream wings and keel. The tree grows with a crooked, buttressed trunk, which loses its thick curved spines when mature. The leaves have three deep green, smooth and leathery elliptic leaflets, each measuring 8cm/3in long. The narrow pods are 30cm/12in long.

Mountain Immortelle *Erythrina poeppigiana* (Walp.) Cook.
Growing up to 24m/80ft in height, this tree comes from eastern Peru and Brazil and is sometimes used as a shade tree in cocoa plantations. In spring, and to a lesser extent in late summer, it can be seen from a long way off due to the abundant scarlet to deep pink flowers covering its dome-shaped crown. The flowers are pollinated by small birds. The mountain immortelle has thorny bark covering a soft-wooded trunk, which usually exceeds 1m/1yd in diameter. The leaves have three leaflets: the lower two are 10cm/4in across, and the terminal leaflet is 15cm/6in wide. The pods are 12cm/4½in long and contain two seeds.

Pride of Bolivia

Tipuana tipu (Benth.) Kunth.

The pride of Bolivia is a fast-growing tree that forms a thick, straight trunk with buttresses. This tree is common in Bolivia, and one valley there has so many of them that it is known simply as Tipuana. Once it has passed through a young, ungainly stage, the pride of Bolivia normally grows into a wide, spreading tree with horizontal, zigzagging branches. It has been planted around South America, in North America and in the south of France for its spring and summer flowers, attractive shape and abundant shade.

Identification: The dark brown trunk is usually short in cultivated trees. The leaves are 30cm/12in long and composed of 13–21 leaflets, each dark to yellowish green and oblong. The butterfly-like flowers vary from pale yellow to orangey yellow. They are in terminal clusters. The autumn fruit is a winged key, 5–10cm/2–4in long and brown.

Below: This drought tolerant species produces its flowers in spring and summer.

Distribution: South America.
Height: 30m/100ft
Shape: Spreading
Semi-evergreen
Pollinated: Insect
Leaf shape: Pinnate

THE ROSE FAMILY

Rosaceae is a well-known family of herbs, shrubs and trees and is poorly represented in the tropics. It includes many fruiting and ornamental plants of commercial importance. Roses and their relatives have alternate leaves and are often thorny. The flowers have five petals, which overlap in bud and are held equidistant in racemes, or open one after another on their own stalks in cymes. The fruits vary enormously.

Indian Cherry

Prunus cerasoides D. Don.

This is a fast-growing tree, found in mixed pine and broadleaf forests, and often in disturbed areas in mountainous regions. It is also planted in gardens as an ornamental tree. The fine wood is used for furniture, panelling and floors. The fruit is edible but acidic and is said to have medicinal properties.

Identification: The trunk is narrow, reaching only 38cm/15in in circumference. It has grey to reddish-brown bark, which peels horizontally when mature. The shiny leaves are a deep green above, pale green below, have finely toothed edges and a long tapering point. They measure 9–12cm/3½–4½in long and 3–5cm/1¼–2in across. Young leaves are maroon. The racemes usually appear while the tree is leafless. Each flower is 2cm/¾in long and turns from deep pink while in bud to mid-pink upon opening. The smooth, oval fruit is 1.5cm/½in long, bright red when ripe and contains one large seed.

Distribution: Northern Thailand, eastern Himalayas and western China.
Height: 16m/50ft
Shape: Rounded
Deciduous
Pollinated: Insect
Leaf shape: Ovate to oblong

Above left: The flowers appear in the spring.
Left: The leaves yield a green dye, and the fruit yields a grey-green dye.

Red Stinkwood

Prunus africana Hook. F.

Distribution: Africa.
Height: 36m/120ft
Shape: Rounded
Evergreen
Pollinated: Insect
Leaf shape: Elliptic

This slow-growing tree is found in humid and semi-humid highland rainforest. It is grown for timber and fuel by foresters and planted on farms for ornament, shade or protection from wind. The hard wood is used in construction and furniture-making but is not durable if used in the ground. This species is also currently being grown for its bark, which appears to have potential as a treatment for prostate cancer. Illegal over-collection of the medicinal bark is threatening this tree's survival. In 1994 it was registered as endangered.

Identification: The bark is brown and slightly fissured. The leaves are dark green, smooth, have toothed margins and reach up to 15cm/6in long and 4.5cm/1¾in across. The flowers appear throughout the year but peak in the winter months; they are small, off-white and found in groups of 7–15. The fruit appears mostly in the summer; it is dark brown when mature, 5mm/¼in long and 1cm/½in wide. The fruit contains reddish-brown pulp surrounding one or two delicate seeds and is very popular with birds and monkeys.

Right: When damaged the glossy leaves smell of almonds.

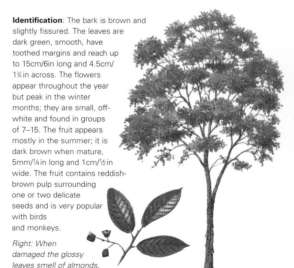

THE PROTEA FAMILY

The Proteaceae are found in warm regions of the southern hemisphere and are well represented in Australia and South Africa. Many species produce showy, long-lasting flowers used in the cut-flower industry. The flowers' petals and sepals are combined into a structure known as a 'perianth', which is often curled. The leaves are often thick and waxy or hairy – adaptations for water retention.

Rewa-Rewa

Knightia excelsa R. Br.

The beautiful red and brown wood of this tree is highly regarded by woodworkers and used for fine work such as inlay. The tree is easily recognizable in its native bush and woodland habitats as the only columnar tree one is likely to see. It has been planted in California and, until the severe frosts of 1947, was naturalized in the far south-west of England.

Identification: The leaves are 10–15cm/4–6in long, 3–4cm/1–1½in wide, have toothed margins and are very hard. When young, they are coated in fine, soft hairs. The tree does not produce many flowers, and those that it does are usually hidden by foliage. They have a spidery appearance with the stigma emerging on long styles and are held in 5–10cm/2–3in-long clusters, which emerge from the branches in pairs. Thick maroon velvet covers the outside of the perianth and the stigma and stamens are creamy yellow.

Above: The winter flowers produce an exceptional amount of nectar, which may be collected.

Distribution: New Zealand North Island.
Height: 30m/100ft
Shape: Columnar
Evergreen
Pollinated: Bee
Leaf shape: Narrowly oblong-obovate

Silky Oak *Grevillea robusta*
This fast-growing, showy, evergreen tree from the tropical rainforests of Australia's eastern coast reaches 30m/100ft tall. It is grown on farms for fodder, firewood, timber, shading, marking boundaries and protection from wind. It is also grown as an ornamental tree or bedding plant in tropical and warm temperate regions for its masses of long, spidery, golden yellow and orange flowers, which appear in spring. The 15–23cm/ 6–9in-long leaves are pinnate with lobed leaflets and greyish- or yellowish-green. The fruit is a yellowish-brown capsule and contains two lightweight, winged seeds.

Macadamia Nut

Macadamia integrifolia Maiden & Betche

The delicious nuts for which this species is famous are found inside the fruit. Macadamia nut trees are grown throughout the tropics, particularly in Australia and Hawaii, where they were introduced in 1890. The trees grow naturally in eastern Australia's rainforests but most grown commercially are selected grafted varieties. The wild tree is handsome with a dense, wide crown.

Identification: The leaves are leathery, glossy, dark green and up to 30cm/12in long. They appear in whorls, have wavy-toothed margins and yellowish midribs. The tiny flowers form dangling tassels, 10–30cm/4–12in long in winter and spring. Each flower is white, cream or pale pink. The fruit is usually ready in late summer, when it hangs in long clusters. Each fruit is spherical, 2.5cm/1in across and green with a broad scar revealing the inner husk. The shell and husk are hard to break and poisonous.

Distribution: Queensland and northern New South Wales, Australia.
Height: 21m/70ft
Shape: Domed
Evergreen
Pollinated: Insect
Leaf shape: Oblanceolate

Above: The fruit takes up to nine months to mature.

THE MYRTLE FAMILY

Many Myrtaceae are evergreen trees and shrubs having leaves with a distinctive spicy scent. They usually
have smooth margins and grow opposite one another on the stem. The bark is often papery, peeling or
splotched with pale and reddish patches. The flowers are arranged in various ways
but often have many stamens, giving them a 'powder-puff' look.

Clove

Syzygium aromaticum (L.) Merr. & Perry

Although most members of this genus are grown for their tasty fruit, this species is not. Instead, it yields cloves – immature flower buds, which are collected and dried in the sun for use in cooking, medicine and perfumery. Another product, clove oil, is extracted from the leaves and unripe fruit.

The fruit of this tree tastes quite repugnant, having an overwhelmingly bitter flavour. Cloves are widely cultivated throughout the tropics and are particularly important to the economy of Zanzibar. In the wild this handsome tree is a rainforest species. It has a dense canopy and pretty, pink young leaves.

Identification: The short trunk has smooth, pale brown bark. The highly glossy, scented leaves are dark green above, paler below, heavily dotted with glands, have undulating margins and are 8–12cm/3–4½in long. The scented flowers are produced in threes on a short panicle. Each is pale pink, yellow or green and 2cm/¾in across. The fruit is oblong, red or purple when ripe and 2.5cm/1in long.

Distribution: Moluccas islands.
Height: 15m/50ft
Shape: Conical
Evergreen
Pollinated: Insect
Leaf shape: Elliptical

Left: Clove leaves yield oil traditionally used in dentistry.

Right: Flower buds ready for harvest.

Malay Apple

Syzygium malaccense (L.) Merrill & Perry

Distribution: Malaysia
Height: 23m/75ft
Shape: Oblong
Evergreen
Pollinated: Insect
Leaf shape: Ovate

Right: The tree's showy flowers may be eaten in salads, and the youngest leaves and shoots may be eaten raw or cooked.

Once seen, this tree is unforgettable; throughout the year cerise pink, shaving brush-like flowers explode from the trunk and mature branches, wherever there are no leaves. As well as being grown for its fruit, the Malay apple is sometimes cultivated in tropical parks and gardens as an ornamental plant or grown as a windbreak. The fruit has an apple-like taste, sweet yet slightly tart. It is eaten raw and also made into preserves and wine.

Identification: The short, buttressed trunk has fissured flaky bark that is light to reddish-brown. The handsome, bright green leaves are smooth, glossy and thick – almost succulent. They measure 15–30cm/6–12in long and tend to hang under their own weight. Young leaves are pink. The flowers are held in clusters on short stems. Each is 5–7.5cm/2–3in wide and has a multitude of stamens. The fruit is pear-shaped, smooth, 5–7.5cm/2–3in long and changes from pale pink to purple as it ripens.

Golden Penda

Xanthostemon chrysanthus Bailey

This handsome, upright tree is regularly planted in tropical and subtropical gardens in Australia. It is grown for its fine foliage, which contrasts well with the sprays of golden yellow, showy flowers produced in winter or after heavy rain.

Identification: The bark is a light cinnamon-brown colour. The smooth, glossy leaves have long tapering points, are leathery, 20cm/8in long and 4cm/1½in wide. The upper surface of a mature leaf is dark green with a bright green midrib, and the lower surface is bright green. When young, leaves are reddish-bronze. The flowers are densely packed at the branch ends in cymes, each with five to ten individual blossoms. The flowers have masses of long stamens, making them look like shaving brushes. The round fruit is dark, almost black, and 1cm/½in across.

Left: Fine specimens of the golden penda are found all over Cairns in Australia, where it is the city's floral emblem.

Distribution: North-east Australia & New Caledonia to Malaysia.
Height: 16m/52ft
Shape: Rounded to columnar
Evergreen
Pollinated: Insect
Leaf shape: Narrowly elliptic-obovate

Mindanao Gum *Eucalyptus deglupta* Sm.
This tree has wonderful, colourful, flaky bark which peels off longitudinally to reveal smooth striations of green, cream, brown and pinkish brown below. Native to the Philippines, the Mindanao gum is widely planted in the tropics as a fast-growing timber tree, reaching at least 20m/66ft. The ovate leaves are 8–18cm/3–7in long, and the 1cm/½in-long flowers are white with many stamens. The fruit is woody, cup shaped and 5mm/¼in across.

Rose Apple *Syzygium jambos* (L.) Alston.
The rose-water-scented fruits of this tree are eaten raw and used in confectionery and preserves. The tree is from South-east Asia. A 12m/40ft-tall tree, the rose apple has a dense, evergreen, rounded crown of 20cm/8in, lanceolate, glossy green leaves. It produces clusters of 6–8cm/2½–3in-wide, white, pale yellow or green shaving brush-like flowers at the branch tips. The fruit is round, 4cm/1½in across, pale green, yellow or pink with white flesh.

Jambolan *Syzygium cumii* (L.) Skeels.
This fast-growing tree from India, Burma and Indonesia grows to 30m/100ft tall. It produces edible fruit, and its wood is used in construction. The short, thick, yellow-brown flaky trunk carries a dense oblong crown. The 15–20cm/6–8in leaves are elliptic, smooth, glossy and dark green with wavy margins. The fragrant flowers are in small pendant clusters in spring and summer. Each is funnel-shaped, white fading to pink and 2.5cm/1in long. The fruit is a 2.5–5cm/1–2in-long, dark purple, oval berry.

Crimson Bottlebrush

Callistemon citrinus

This aptly named tree is stunning in late spring and summer when covered in its glowing crimson flowers. It is often seen pruned into a dense shrub in tropical, subtropical and temperate gardens. If left to its own devices, it will branch close to the ground and form an arching crown of lax branches. From a seedling it grows quickly to about 3m/10ft tall then slows down. This species can tolerate light frost. In the wild in Australia it is seen in coastal localities.

Identification: The leaves are 4–9cm/1½–3½in long, dark green and very tough. The young shoots are silky soft and downy, and the cylindrical flower spikes 10cm/4in long and erect. The round fruit is a woody capsule 1cm/½in wide and contains many minute seeds.

Distribution: Eastern Australia.
Height: 4.5m/15ft
Shape: Spreading rounded
Evergreen
Pollinated: Birds
Leaf shape: Lanceolate

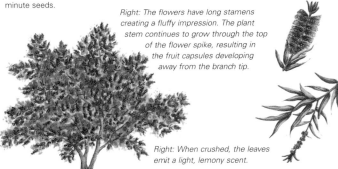

Right: The flowers have long stamens creating a fluffy impression. The plant stem continues to grow through the top of the flower spike, resulting in the fruit capsules developing away from the branch tip.

Right: When crushed, the leaves emit a light, lemony scent.

Allspice

Pimenta dioica (L.) Merr.

The fruit of this tree, sold as allspice, is often mistakenly thought to be a mixture of different spices. This error is understandable quite apart from the fruit's name, because allspice has a scent similar to a combination of clove, nutmeg and cinnamon. Allspice trees are widely grown in Jamaica, from where the spice is exported. The fruit is collected before it is completely ripe and dried in the sun for up to ten days. After drying, the fruit looks similar to pepper, so the genus is named *Pimenta*, from the Spanish for 'pepper'. In many languages the common name used for allspice is still their equivalent of 'pepper'. The berries are an essential part of Caribbean cuisine and have medicinal properties.

Distribution: Caribbean, southern Mexico and Central America.
Height: 12m/40ft
Shape: Oblong
Evergreen
Pollinated: Insect
Leaf shape: Oblong-elliptical

Identification: This dense crowned tree is aromatic in every part. The trunk is short and has pale grey peeling bark. The leaves are glossy, mid-green with prominent veining below and are 15–20cm/6–8in long. The flowers appear in spring and early summer in short panicles, which are in axils near the branch tips. Each flower is white or pale green, scented and tiny. The valuable fruit is produced in summer, and is black when ripe but picked when green, and 5mm/¼in across.

Left: The allspice tree's stems, bark, leaves and flowers are all scented, filling the air around the tree with a thick aroma. The tree also yields an oil used in perfumes and liqueurs.

Weeping Paperbark

Melaleuca quinquenervia (Cav.) Blake

Distribution: Eastern coastal Australia, New Guinea and New Caledonia.
Height: 18m/60ft
Shape: Columnar to spreading
Evergreen
Pollinated: Bird
Leaf shape: Elliptic-lanceolate

This tree occurs naturally in swampy ground but is very adaptable to even dry soils and has been planted throughout the tropics. In the Everglades, in Florida in the United States, the tree has become naturalized and is proving a threat to the local, indigenous species. On the other side of the world, in Hong Kong, the weeping paperbark has a very different reputation. There it is widely planted by the government to stabilize swampy farming ground, and considered an invaluable aid in land reclamation.

Identification: The thick, shaggy, peeling bark is pale cinnamon-brown to white. The tree emits volatile oils that deter insects. The smooth, shiny, hard leaves are a bluish grey green, flat, 4–10cm/1½–4in long and have parallel veins. The leaves are harvested and distilled to produce an essential oil that has numerous uses. The flowers occur throughout the year and are particularly abundant in spring. The fruits, which persist for many years, are 5mm/¼in-wide, woody capsules packed tightly along the stem.

Right: The white flowers form bottlebrush-like inflorescences 10cm/4in long. The flowers release large amounts of pollen, causing problems for hay fever sufferers.

Guava

Psidium guajava L.

This fruit tree is grown extensively throughout the tropics and into temperate areas, where it has proved itself capable of surviving slight frosts. It is popular because it is such an accommodating, undemanding plant and readily produces its tasty fruit. Although it has a slightly unpleasant grainy texture, the fruit is eaten raw and is highly nutritious, containing large amounts of vitamin C.

Above: Guava fruits are made into drinks, conserves and confectionery.

Distribution: West Indies to Peru.
Height: 10m/33ft
Shape: Domed
Evergreen
Pollinated: Insect
Leaf shape: Oblong-elliptic

Identification: The distinctive brown bark flakes off leaving mottled, green patches on the trunk and branches. The leathery leaves form a dense crown. They are up to 15cm/6in long, downy below, a yellowish grey-green and heavily veined. The white flowers have hundreds of stamens and appear mostly in spring and early summer. They are slightly scented, about 2.5cm/1in wide and occur in the axils. The fruit is a yellowish-green or pinkish tone when ripe.

Left: The round, lumpy fruit is heavily scented and measures 7cm/2¾in across.

Jamaica Pepper *Pimenta officinalis* Lindl.
The fruits of this Jamaican tree have a peppery flavour and a range of uses, including cooking, aromatherapy and pot pourri. The species is similar to allspice, although Jamaica pepper does not grow quite as tall and has flattened branches that are more oblong in cross-section. An essential oil called pimento is extracted from the leaves of Jamaica pepper and is used in the manufacture of perfume.

Bay Rum Tree *Pimenta racemosa* (Mill) Moore
This West Indian tree grows to 12m/40ft and is aromatic in every part. The leaves and twigs contain a pale yellow oil called myrcia or bay oil that is extracted from them by distillation in water. The oil is used in cosmetics, medicine and flavouring. The leaves are sometimes distilled in rum, when it is called 'bay rum'. The bay rum tree's bark is pale and peels, while the leaves are thick, bright green and oblong. The tree has white flowers tinged red. The pea-sized black fruit is popular with birds and can be used in cooking. The tree has proved itself an invasive weed in Hawaii.

Flax-leafed Paperbark *Melaleuca linariifolia* Sm.
This eastern Australian tree yields an essential oil from its leaves. It grows quickly to 15m/50ft tall and has a beautiful, dense, rounded crown of fine leaves. The flax-leafed paperbark is an extremely versatile tree and has even been grown in the very south-west of England. The very narrow leaves are 4cm/1½in long, and the 5cm/2in-long, bottlebrush-shaped flower is white, pale green or pale yellow.

Strawberry Guava

Psidium litorale Raddi.

A narrow, leggy, upright shrub or small tree, the strawberry guava has a dense crown and produces small fruit in large quantity. The fruit is juicy and has a similar taste and texture to strawberries, although it is a little more acidic and grainy. The strawberry guava is a slow-growing tree cultivated in tropical and warm temperate regions. In the latter it may be severely cut back by the winter cold, whereas in the former it may become naturalized and a serious plant pest.

Distribution: Eastern Brazil.
Height: 6m/20ft
Shape: Columnar
Evergreen
Pollinated: Insect
Leaf shape: Oblong-obovate

Identification: The tree has smooth, reddish or deep brown bark that flakes to reveal a mottling of greyish green below. The short-stalked leaves are smooth, glossy, thick and tough. Bright green, they have lighter midribs, are downy below and measure 7.5–10cm/3–4in long. The single white or yellow flowers are 2.5cm/1in across and scented. The round fruit are smooth skinned, 2.5–5cm/1–2in across, red or yellow when mature and have white flesh containing many seeds.

Right: The fruit may be eaten raw, but is usually used to make jams and jellies.

THE LOOSESTRIFE FAMILY

The Lythraceae family includes herbaceous plants, trees and shrubs but only a few are well known, and only a handful are used in horticulture. The trees have simple, smooth-edged leaves positioned opposite one another on the stem. The star-shaped flowers have petals that are crumpled up when in bud and appear in panicles, racemes or cymes. The fruit is a capsule or berry containing many seeds.

Queen's Crepe Myrtle

Pride of India *Lagerstromia speciosa* (L.) Pers.

This tree is grown as an ornamental plant for its large panicles of showy, pink flowers – the name 'speciosa' actually means 'showy'. It grows wild in humid forests and along forested waterways. The queen's crepe myrtle has a dense crown that loses its leaves in the cooler winter months. The tree flowers in summer.

Identification: The unusual bark is pale grey and often flakes off in large chunks, leaving concave indentations and resulting in the trunk having a yellowish mottling. The leaves have prominent veining and may have scalloped margins. They are 18cm/7in long and 7cm/2¾in wide, dark green and rough. The flowers form in erect panicles up to 60cm/24in tall on the top of the tree. Each individual flower is 8cm/3in across and has six crinkled, pink petals, which fade to purple as they mature. The small fruit sits in a star-shaped structure formed by the sepals, and the ovoid woody capsule has six sections. Each section of the fruit contains a winged seed.

Distribution: India, Sri Lanka, Burma, southern China and South-east Asia.
Height: 24m/80ft
Shape: Spreading and round
Deciduous
Pollinated: Insect
Leaf shape: Elliptic

Above left: Leaves turn bright red before dropping.

Left: Cultivated forms have flowers in different shades of pink or mauve.

Henna

Lawsonia inerma L.

Henna dye is used to temporarily colour hair, skin, nails and teeth a rich, burnt orange colour. In Indian marriage ceremonies, for example, the bride has intricate henna patterns painted on her hands, arms and feet. Henna dye is made from a paste of the crushed and powdered leaves of the henna tree. The tree is heavily cultivated (and is naturalized) in India for its dye and is widely grown as a shrub or hedging plant. In Western countries henna is used as an ingredient in cosmetics.

Identification: The heavily branching twigs are grey and may carry spines. The leaves are greyish green, 4–6cm/1½–2½in long and 4cm/1½in wide. The flowers may be white, cream, greenish-yellow, pink or red and appear throughout the year. They are sweetly scented, 1cm/½in wide and held in panicles 20–25cm/8–10in long. The 5mm/¼in, round fruit contains numerous seeds and is reddish.

Distribution: North-east Africa (Egypt, Sudan, Ethiopia) through the Middle East to northern India.
Height: 8m/26ft
Shape: Bushy
Evergreen
Leaf shape: Elliptic

Left: The flowers are heavily scented.

Far left: Henna trees are grown throughout the tropics. India and Pakistan export the dried leaves.

THE RED MANGROVE FAMILY

Many of the trees and shrubs in the Rhizophoraceae family are mangroves, living in brackish and salty water along tropical coasts. Several allow their seeds to germinate while still attached to the branches, giving them a better chance of getting established in-between tides. Leaf shape and size varies considerably, but flowers are star shaped, and either solitary or produced in groups in the axils.

Red Mangrove

Rhizophora mangle L.

Distribution: Coastal tropical America and West Africa.
Height: 30m/100ft
Shape: Domed or irregular
Evergreen
Pollinated: Wind or self
Leaf shape: Elliptic

Right: The thick waxy leaves are well adapted to harsh coastal conditions.

The red mangrove is an incredibly important species, ecologically speaking. Able to withstand truly saline conditions, it grows right down to the low tide mark, forming dense, often storm-proof thickets along coastlines and providing shelter for young fish and nest sites for birds. The red mangrove is able to survive where it does by excreting excess salt and by having pores on its roots that allow gaseous exchange when exposed to the air. This species is incredibly slow growing and forms distinctive branching stilt roots. As time passes, the main trunk dies until eventually the aerial roots alone support the plant.

Identification: The bark is pinkish-red when young and grey when mature. The leaves sit opposite one another on the branch and are deep green with a prominent paler midrib. Thick, succulent and glossy, they may be up to 20cm/8in long. The flowers appear throughout the year in groups in the axils. They are cream, 2cm/¾in wide and have four thick petals. The fruit is 2.5cm/1in long, brown and contains a single seed. The seedling may grow to 30cm/12in before dropping from the tree.

Asiatic Mangrove

Rhizophora mucronata Lam.

Mangrove swamps, if they can be penetrated, make good locations for rearing fish for food. The calm waters around these trees provide a protective habitat for a rich diversity of fish, crustaceans and molluscs. The Asiatic mangrove grows from a seedling already developed on the branch before dropping. If it is unable to secure a footing in the soft mud when it lands, it may float around for up to a year and still grow upon contact with soil. This particular species is harvested for its wood and bark, which provide an extract used for dyeing and tanning.

Identification: The leaves are bright green above and pale green dotted with red specks below. They have a sharp pointed tip and are 11–18cm/4½–7in long. The white to pale yellow flowers are produced in bunches of three to five in the axils near the growing tips. The pendulous fruit is 4–5cm/1½–2in long, ovoid to conical. The seedling may reach up to 75cm/30in long before it drops from the tree.

Distribution: Coastal tropics India to Australia.
Height: 25m/82ft
Shape: Spreading
Evergreen
Pollinated: Wind or self
Leaf shape: Elliptic

Left: The dark brown fruit has a rough, bumpy surface.

THE EUPHORBIA FAMILY

A large family of over 200 genera, the Euphorbiaceae includes herbs, climbers, shrubs and trees, many with white poisonous sap. The leaves are highly variable, and the small flowers are often without petals. The flowers are either male or female and occur on individual stalks in bunched clusters called cymes or on branched structures known as panicles. The fruit is usually split into three sections.

Rubber

Hevea brasilensis (A. Juss) Muell. Arg.

This erect, fast-growing tree is the source of natural rubber. When the tree reaches five or six years old it is 'tapped' by cutting a long slanting channel into the bark at about 1m/3ft from the ground. A white, milky latex flows from the channel and is collected in cups. The latex is then strained, standardized to a set density and coagulated by the addition of acetic acid. The resultant white spongy material, rubber, may be processed in a number of ways and is smoked for preservation.

Identification: The bark is patchy, pale brown or grey and smooth. The spirally arranged leaves have long stalks and smooth, elliptic, dark green leaflets, each 20cm/8in long. During a dry period, these turn orange and fall off, to be followed by the appearance of the flowers. Small, greenish white and scented, these are held on panicles, which grow from the axils. The fruit is a smooth, greenish-brown, 3cm/1¼in-long, three-sectioned capsule.

Distribution: Amazonian (Brazil) and Orinoco (Venezuela) river basins.
Height: 40m/130ft
Shape: Variable
Semi-evergreen
Pollinated: Insect
Leaf shape: Trifoliolate

Left: The trees are tapped with diagonal cuts in the bark.

Right: The three-sectioned fruit explodes when ripe.

Sandbox Tree

Hura crepitans L.

Distribution: West Indies, Mexico, Central America and northern South America.
Height: 60m/200ft
Shape: Spreading rounded
Evergreen
Pollinated: Insect
Leaf shape: Heart

Right: The flowers are small and dark red.

Every part of this tree is highly poisonous, and the sap may cause blindness if it contacts the eye. The fruit resembles a miniature brown pumpkin, and when ripe it bursts open explosively, discharging its seeds over quite some distance. In the past, these fruits were harvested then filled with sand and used as quill stands. Now they are occasionally filled with molten lead and sold as paperweights.

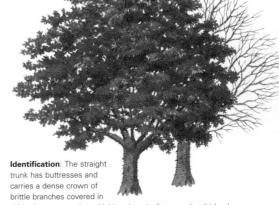

Identification: The straight trunk has buttresses and carries a dense crown of brittle branches covered in thick, dangerous spines. Held on long leaf stems, the thick, glossy leaves are dark green, up to 30cm/12in long, with light veining on the upper surface. The female flowers are carried on a thick, pendulous spike 15cm/6in long, and the male ones on a structure resembling an ear of corn. The 8cm/3in-wide fruit has a grooved surface and is made up of 15–20 sections, each containing a flat, pale brown seed.

Candleberry Tree

Aleurites moluccana (L.) Willd.

This fast-growing native of hillside forests has been cultivated for hundreds of years and is now naturalized throughout the tropics. Annually each tree produces up to 46kg/100lbs of poisonous nuts, which are 50 per cent oil and burnt for light, hence the tree's common name. The nutshells are used as beads and yield a dye, while the timber is a popular choice for canoe and house-building.

Identification: The thick, straight trunk has relatively smooth grey bark. Leaves are clustered towards the branch tips, have oil glands and are slightly scented if crushed. Each leaf is 10–20cm/4–8in long, divided into three or five lobes and has pale rusty down on the underside. Young leaves and shoots are coated in fine white down. Tiny, white, bell-shaped flowers are produced throughout the year in long, terminal panicles. The rough skinned, hard, pale green fruit is a 5cm/2in-wide ball.

Distribution: Moluccas and South Pacific Islands.
Height: 18m/60ft
Shape: Domed
Evergreen
Pollinated: Insect
Leaf shape: Broadly ovate

Left: The fruit contains one seed and is poisonous when raw but can be eaten cooked.

Left and right: The juvenile and mature leaves differ in shape.

Common Tree Euphorbia *Euphorbia ingens* E. Mey.
This is a spiny, succulent tree species. It reaches 12m/40ft in height and comes from the Natal area of eastern South Africa. The common tree euphorbia has a stout, fissured, brown trunk with many erect branches reaching up to form the crown. Each branch is formed from a stacked series of green segments shaped like upside-down hearts. The edges to the segments may have paired, dark brown spines along them. The flowers appear in threes next to the spines in summer and are yellowish green.

Mahang *Macaranga gigantae* Muell. Arg.
This 18m/60ft, short-lived, soft-wooded tree is common in Malaysia. It is grown for its unusually large leaves which reach 80cm/32in long and across. Leaves are divided into three or five large lobes and are hairy on the underside. The minute male and female flowers are found in separate panicles up to 30cm/12in long.

Coral Plant *Jatropha multifida* L.
This little tree from South America reaches 6m/20ft tall and has amazing leaves and colourful flowers. The leaves are round and up to 30cm/12in across but heavily divided into up to twelve leaflets, each of which has many incisions towards its tip. The leaves and seeds are poisonous but used locally for medicine. The small, red flowers appear throughout the year in flat-topped clusters above the tree. Each cluster stands on a long, upright stem.

Peregrina

Jatropha integerrima Jacq.

This tree is grown for its continuous display of vibrant, intense cerise pink or scarlet flowers. In the wild it often grows as a multi-stemmed tree, and it may be pruned or trained in gardens to retain its young, shrub-like habit or force it to grow as a single-stemmed specimen. In temperate countries it is sold as a houseplant.

Identification: The bark is dark brown and fissured. The glossy leaves alternate on each side of the stem, are deep green with paler veining and have a pair of glands near the base. They are 4–15cm/1½–6in long, vary from elliptic to egg shaped, have smooth margins and may be partially and irregularly lobed with a long slender point. The flowers are in long cymes protruding from the axils or the ends of branches. Each is either male or female, 2.5–5cm/1–2in wide and has five petals; the male flowers have yellow anthers. The fruit is nearly round in shape, 1–1.5cm/½–⅔in wide and split into three sections when ripe.

Distribution: Cuba, West Indies and Peru.
Height: 6m/20ft
Shape: Columnar
Evergreen
Pollinated: Insect
Leaf shape: Irregular

Right: The flower cymes bear many more male than female flowers.

THE SOAPBERRY FAMILY

The Sapindaceae family contains a large number of very diverse but mostly tropical trees, shrubs and climbers. The leaves may be simple, pinnate, bipinnate or even tripinnate. The small flowers, normally with three to five petals, form in branched clusters or in bunches with each flower on an individual stem. The fruit is also highly variable but is always composed of three sections.

Soap-nut

Sapindus emarginatus L.

The inedible fruit of this tree contains a substance called saponin, which lathers up in water. It is used in the manufacture of soap, or used whole, either fresh or dried, as a soap substitute. The fruit and roots also have medicinal value, and the flowers are a valuable source of nectar for honey production. Soap-nut trees grow naturally in dry, open areas of lowland monsoon forest and may be seen planted as ornamental trees in parks and gardens.

Identification: The trunk has rough, off-white bark and carries an open crown made up of numerous branches. The leaves are 10–20cm/4–8in long and have four to six opposite or almost opposite leaflets. Each leaflet is 5–18cm/2–7in long, elliptic to egg shaped and blunt ended or has a notched tip. The flowers are greenish white with rusty coloured down on the outside and occur in large, spreading clusters at the ends of twigs and branches. The spherical, 1.5–2.5cm/⅔–1in-wide fruit has thick flesh and is clustered in pairs or threes.

Distribution: Sri Lanka, India and Burma.
Height: 40m/130ft
Shape: Domed
Deciduous
Pollinated: Bee
Leaf shape: Pinnate

Left: The fruit may be used as a soap substitute.

Fern Tree

Filicium decipiens

This slow-growing and long-lived tree is highly valued for its fine foliage and dense crown. It is tolerant of a wide range of growing conditions and is particularly prevalent in India where it is often seen planted along roadsides. The fern tree has hard, heavy, reddish-coloured timber, which is used in construction and the making of cartwheels and cabinetry.

Identification: The short trunk has rough, dark, reddish-grey bark and highly visible large leaf scars. The 30–40cm/12–16in-long leaves are made up of anything from 12–25 closely spaced, stemless, glossy leaflets. Between each leaflet the stem is flattened and wing-like at the edges. Each leaflet is 10–15cm/4–6in long, narrowly oblong with a pronounced notch at the tip, has undulating margins and is deep dark green. The flowers appear mostly in the winter – each is tiny and inconspicuous and has cream petals. They form into 15cm/6in-long branched clusters, which sprout from the leaf axils. The oval, fleshy fruit is purple, shiny and 1.5cm/⅔in long.

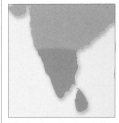

Distribution: Southern India and Sri Lanka.
Height: 25m/80ft
Shape: Domed
Evergreen
Leaf shape: Pinnate

Left and above: The tree is often multi-stemmed. It carries tiny resinous spots on the leaves, stems and flowers.

Right: The impressive spirally-arranged foliage of the fern tree. When very young the foliage gives the plant the look of a fern.

Ackee

Blighia sapida Koerig.

The tasty fruit of the ackee is a popular ingredient in West Indian cooking, but extreme care must be exercised when preparing it. The thick, creamy flesh can be fried or boiled as a vegetable but contains highly poisonous seeds, which must be removed before cooking.

Identification: The tree is fast growing and forms a handsome, dense crown. The trunk is short and thick with grey bark. The leaves consist of three to ten egg-shaped to oblong leaflets, each of which is glossy, mid-green above and paler below, 15–30cm/6–12in long with prominent veining. The scented flowers are hairy, white and hang from the tree. The smooth-skinned fruit is spherical to pear shaped and triangular with rounded corners in cross section. When ripe, it turns rosy pink, apricot, or red and measures 7.5–10cm/3–4in long. The fruit divides into three sections, each containing a shiny black seed surrounded by white flesh.

Distribution: West Africa.
Height: 15m/50ft
Shape: Rounded
Evergreen
Pollinated: Insect
Leaf shape: Pinnate

Left: The ackee fruit are deadly both before ripening and soon after bursting open.

Rambutan

Nephelium lappaceum L.

Rambutan fruits are particularly popular in Malaysia and parts of China. The translucent white flesh is firm, sweet and juicy, and where it is not available fresh, it is often sold in canned form. 'Rambut' means 'hair' in Malay, and this aptly describes the fruit, which is covered in thick, curled, soft, fleshy spines.

Identification: The tree has smooth brown bark and mid-green leaves, each 18cm/7in long and divided into between two and six pairs of opposite leaflets. Each leaflet is oblong-elliptic, smooth, shiny and has a prominent midrib. The flowers appear in spring in large, spreading branched clusters. The fruit, which is ovoid, 5–6cm/2–2½in long, yellowish, pinkish or orangey red, hangs in great bunches in late summer. Its hairy skin peels easily away to reveal white flesh enclosing a single large black seed.

Distribution: South-east Asia.
Height: 20m/66ft
Shape: Spreading
Evergreen
Pollinated: Insect
Leaf shape: Pinnate

Above: The profuse flowers are small and white.

Below: In wild plants the fruit may lack the sweet, juicy white flesh for which rambutan are renowned.

Litchi *Litchi chinensis* Sonn.
The litchi or lychee produces wonderfully tasty fruit, highly rated in China and exported worldwide. The litchi is related to the rambutan and similar in taste. It originates from southern China, where it is now under threat as the result of over-exploitation for its beautiful timber. It is grown across the warmer regions of Asia, but attempts to introduce it to other parts of the world have been mostly unsuccessful. The litchi grows slowly into a 15m/50ft-tall, rounded, evergreen tree with a dense crown and narrow trunk. The attractive pinnate leaves are 30cm/12in long and divided into two to eight pairs of elliptic, deep green leaflets. The plentiful spring flowers are small, greenish white and hang in 30cm/12in-long branched clusters. The fruit appears in summer, is 4cm/1½in long, ovoid and has brown, warty, hard skin. Inside the white fragrant flesh surrounds a single large seed.

Longan *Dimocarpus longan* Lour.
An evergreen fruit tree from the forests of south China, the longan is similar in appearance to the litchi apart from its bark, which is brown and fissured vertically. This species usually lives for over 100 years, with a few specimens reaching more than 1,000. Leaves are identical to the litchi, but the flowers are in erect branched clusters and provide a rich source of nectar for honey production in spring. The fruit is smooth, round and brown and tastes similar to watery litchis.

THE CASHEW FAMILY

The Anacardiaceae family includes a number of economically important tropical trees. It also contains shrubs and some temperate plants. Many members of the family have resinous bark and poisonous leaves with a white spirit-like odour. Leaves are pinnate or simple and arranged alternately or in whorls. Flowers are five-petalled stars, held in branched clusters, while the fruit has firm flesh surrounding a single seed.

Mango

Mangifera indica L.

Possibly the best known and most popular of all tropical fruit, the mango is thought to have been cultivated for more than 4,000 years. Mangoes are most widely grown in India, where legends surround the tree, and numerous varieties have been developed. The genus name comes from a mixture of Hindi and Latin; 'mango' is the original Hindi name for the tree and 'fera' is the Latin verb 'to bear'. The fruit of the mango tree is juicy.

Distribution: India to Malaysia.
Height: 30m/100ft
Shape: Domed
Evergreen
Pollinated: Insect
Leaf shape: Lanceolate

Right: The fruit appears in late summer and varies greatly in shape, size and colour.

Identification: The trunk is buttressed when mature and carries a dense crown. The drooping leaves are red when young and deep green and glossy when mature. The flowers appear at the ends of twigs and branches in late winter in loose, branched clusters. Each cluster contains thousands of tiny individual blossoms, which may be pink, yellow, green, brown or white.

Right: The leaves reach up to 30cm/12in long.

Cashew Nut

Anarcardium occidentale L.

The tasty, kidney-shaped cashew nut is produced individually inside a fleshy husk. The husk contains an extremely acrid, resinous sap, which can burn human skin. Once the husk is removed, the nuts are roasted, explaining their relatively high price.

The stem from which the nut hangs swells into a 10cm/4in-long, fleshy, pear-shaped organ, which is red when ripe. Called the 'cashew apple', this can also be eaten.

The cashew nut tree is fast growing and untidy-looking, and can bear fruit from a young age. The cashew tree favours areas with long, hot dry seasons.

Identification: The bark is light grey to brown. The smooth, leathery leaves are 15cm/6in long, mid-green and blunt ended or notched at the tip. The tiny yellow flowers occur early in the wet season in erect, branched clusters at the ends of twigs and branches. They are fragrant at night and fade to pink when mature. The fruit, which contains a single nut, is grey or brown and 4cm/1½in long.

Distribution: West Indies and tropical America.
Height: 10m/33ft
Shape: Spreading, irregular
Evergreen
Pollinated: Insect
Leaf shape: Oval-obovate

Right: The cashew apple resides above the nut. It is eaten raw and is used in a fermented drink.

Brazilian Peppercorn Tree

Christmas berry tree *Schinus terebinthifolius* Raddi.

All parts of this tree have a spicy scent and may cause irritation if they come into contact with skin. The small, pink to red fruits are the pink peppercorns of commerce, often mixed with green and black peppercorns for their decorative effect. The fruit appears at Christmas time, giving the species its other common name, the Christmas berry tree. The tree is fast growing and forms a dense crown of brittle branches, which may naturally ooze sap. It grows readily from seed and has become naturalized in many parts of the world, including Hawaii and Florida, where it is now an invasive weed.

Identification: The leaves are 10–18cm/4–7in long, dark green and divided into seven blunt-ended, elliptical leaflets (three pairs and one terminal). Each leaflet is 2.5–5cm/1–2in long and has pale veins. The tiny white or greenish-white flowers form in dense, erect, branched clusters 5–15cm/2–6in long. The fruit is spherical and 5mm/¼in across.

Distribution: Tropical Central and South America.
Height: 9m/30ft
Shape: Rounded
Evergreen
Pollinated: Insect
Leaf shape: Pinnate

Left: The pink 'peppercorn' fruits are produced in abundance. They do not have a peppery flavour, rather a sweet, subtle flavour, but look very similar to peppercorns.

Pepper Tree *Schinus molle* L. non hort. ex. Engl.
Native to the deserts of Peru's Andean region, this tree thrives in sandy dry places in tropical and temperate regions and may become a pest. It grows quickly to 15m/50ft tall and has a rounded crown, graceful weeping branches and fine blue-green, pinnate foliage. The small, pink fruit may be substituted for peppercorns.

Hog Plum *Spondias mombin* L.
This handsome tree occurs wild in rainforest areas of the West Indies, Central America and northern South America. The orange to yellow fruit forms in clusters and tastes acidic, often with an unpleasant flavour similar to the smell of white spirit. The tree has thick, fissured, pale cinnamon-coloured bark on its heavy trunk and a spreading crown of light green, pinnate foliage.

Red Mombin *Spondias purpurea* L.
This tree reaches just 9m/30ft tall and may grow as a large, sprawling shrub. It comes from tropical America and the West Indies and has 10–25cm/4–10in-long, light green, pinnate leaves. The branched clusters of tiny pink or purple flowers appear in spring and produce small yellow, orange, red or purple fruit with an acidic, plum-like flavour.

Mango cultivars
The fruit from mango tree seedlings is highly variable and often disappointing. Many promising mango cultivars are now propagated by cuttings or grown as dwarf-grafted trees. The small fruit 'Puhu-amba', for example, is seedless, while the large oval fruit 'Alphonso' is considered the best tasting and is widely grown.

Golden Apple

Spondias dulcis Parkinson

This fast-growing tree is seen in rural areas, gardens and occasionally in city parks throughout South-east Asia. It is grown for its large green to yellow fruit, produced all year round but particularly abundant in winter. When ripe, the fruit is said by some to taste of pineapple, but many people find it sour and unpleasant. This handsome tree has an open structure with few branches, large leaves and a beautiful trunk.

Distribution: Indonesia and Polynesia.
Height: 20m/66ft
Shape: Spreading
Semi-evergreen
Pollinated: Insect
Leaf shape: Pinnate

Identification: The trunk has smooth, almost white bark. The leaves are generally clustered towards the branch tips; they are up to 75cm/30in long and have between 9–27 lanceolate leaflets, each of which is 10cm/4in long, deep green, glossy and may have toothed margins. The tiny flowers are yellowish or greenish-white, fragrant and appear in large branched clusters, particularly in the spring. The fruit is oval, 7.5cm/3in long, suffused with maroon and is soft and juicy when ripe.

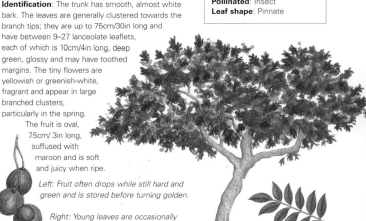

Left: Fruit often drops while still hard and green and is stored before turning golden.

Right: Young leaves are occasionally eaten raw or steamed.

THE MAHOGANY FAMILY

This family includes many important timber trees, some with sweetly scented timber. It also contains trees and shrubs with edible fruit or valuable seeds. The Meliaceae are tropical or subtropical trees and shrubs with pinnate or bipinnate leaves. The flowers have four or five petals and appear in branched clusters. The leathery-skinned fruit often contains seeds with wings.

Mahogany

Swietenia mahogani (L.) Jacq.

Distribution: Central America and West Indies.
Height: 20m/66ft
Shape: Rounded
Evergreen
Pollinated: Insect
Leaf shape: Pinnate

This very slow-growing, long-lived tree is famous for its hard, red, glowing timber, which polishes to a high shine. It has been a favourite choice of cabinet-makers ever since it was first discovered in the seventeenth century and is now threatened in the wild due to over-collection. In some places it is grown as a shade or avenue tree and it becomes spreading when fully mature. It is cultivated throughout the tropics and flourishes in drier climates, such as that of India.

Identification: The buttressed trunk has dark, reddish-brown, scaly bark and carries a crown that becomes open when the tree reaches maturity. The leaves have five to seven pairs of 7cm/2¾-in long, ovate to sickle-shaped, dark green leaflets. The insignificant flowers are greenish yellow or white, scented and form in branched clusters from the leaf axils in spring and summer.

Right: The fruit is an oval, woody capsule, 10cm/4in across, and contains 45–55 winged seeds.

Chinaberry

Bead tree *Melia azedarach* L.

In India this tree is venerated and grown for its pretty, honey-scented flowers, which are used as temple offerings. It is often called the 'bead tree', as its poisonous seeds have a hole through them, making them ideal for threading. It was once grown in Italy specifically for the making of rosaries. The chinaberry is a short-lived tree that grows quickly and easily in dry tropical and subtropical areas. In some places it is considered a weed.

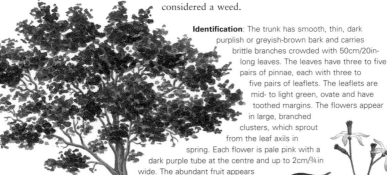

Identification: The trunk has smooth, thin, dark purplish or greyish-brown bark and carries brittle branches crowded with 50cm/20in-long leaves. The leaves have three to five pairs of pinnae, each with three to five pairs of leaflets. The leaflets are mid- to light green, ovate and have toothed margins. The flowers appear in large, branched clusters, which sprout from the leaf axils in spring. Each flower is pale pink with a dark purple tube at the centre and up to 2cm/¾in wide. The abundant fruit appears in autumn; it is oval, pale yellow or orange and 2.5cm/1in long.

Distribution: From Iraq to Japan down to Australia.
Height: 12m/40ft
Shape: Spreading
Deciduous
Pollinated: Bee
Leaf shape: Bipinnate or tripinnate

Right: The chinaberry may produce its fragrant flowers all year round, and from a very young age, even when the tree is still a seedling.

Neem

Azadirachta indica Adr. Juss

This fast-growing tree has a multitude of uses. Every part of it is used – its timber is termite resistant, its fruit produces medicinal oil, while its leaves and bark are collected and ground up for their insecticidal properties. Neem is planted throughout the arid and semi-arid tropics and is popular in India as an ornamental, shade, street or reforestation tree.

Identification: The erect, straight trunk supports an open crown. The glossy, mid-green leaves are up to 60cm/24in long and have pairs of toothed, sickle-shaped, 7cm/2¾in long leaflets. The star-shaped flowers are small, pale green, yellow or white and form airy, branched clusters from the leaf axils in spring. Flower clusters are usually partially hidden by foliage. The fruit is small, smooth-skinned, oblong and develops in the autumn. When ripe, it is orange, yellow or green-yellow.

Right: The fruit is up to 2cm/¾in long, and contains one stone in a thin, sweet pulp.

Far right: Leaves are placed in books to deter insects.

Distribution: Sri Lanka, India and Burma.
Height: 20m/66ft
Shape: Spreading
Evergreen
Pollinated: Insect
Leaf shape: Pinnate

Australian Teak *Flindersia australis* P. Br.
This evergreen tree grows wild in rainforests on Australia's subtropical east coast. It is cultivated in plantations for its valuable timber. The Australian teak has a thick trunk and grows to 36m/120ft tall. Its leaves are pinnate and its starry, white flowers are in clusters at the ends of twigs and branches. The fruit is hard, woody and covered in short spines.

Honduran Mahogany *Swietenia macrophylla* King.
Once an extremely important timber tree in Central and South America, the Honduran mahogany is incredibly valuable. It grows in lowland rainforests but huge areas have now been depleted due to over-collection. Unfortunately, this species is difficult to establish in plantations, due to pests. It grows with a straight, buttressed trunk to 45m/150ft tall and has rough, brown bark. The pinnate leaves are 38cm/15in long and have up to six pairs of leaflets. The flowers are insignificant, but the woody, brown fruit is 15cm/6in across and hangs on 30cm/12in stems.

Langsat *Lansium domesticum* Corr.
The langsat has long been cultivated in South-east Asia but is little known outside of its native area. The pale yellow, round fruit is popular for its refreshing aromatic, watery pulp but varies in flavour. It forms in tight, drooping clusters directly from the older wood. This slow-growing tree reaches 15m/50ft tall and does not fruit until it is 15 years old. It has glossy, elliptic to oblong leaves.

Cigar Box Cedar

Jamaican cedar *Cedrela mexicana* Roem.

This tree produces a mahogany-like timber, which is used for cabinetry and making cigar boxes. The wood is light reddish brown, aromatic and termite resistant. The cigar box cedar is sometimes called the Jamaican or Honduran cedar and has been over-exploited in its native forests. The genus name *Cedrela* was given because of the similarity of the wood's scent to that of true cedars, *Cedrus*. The cigar box tree is fast growing, has brittle branches and forms an untidy, thin, open crown.

Identification: The trunk has pale brown bark and reaches 90cm/36in wide. The leaves are up to 60cm/24in long and divided into between six and eight pairs of leaflets. Each leaflet is oblong to elliptic, smooth, pale green and up to 12cm/4½in long. The small white flowers appear at the ends of twigs and branches in pyramidal branched clusters 30cm/12in long. The fruit is a hard, brown, oblong, 4.5cm/1¾in-long pod, which splits open to release winged seeds.

Distribution: West Indies and Central and South America.
Height: 35m/115ft
Shape: Narrow
Evergreen
Pollinated: Insect
Leaf shape: Pinnate

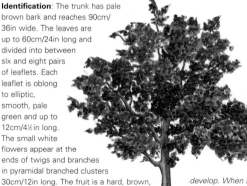

Above: The woody fruit takes nine to ten months to develop. When ripe it splits into five sections revealing a woody central core and numerous winged seeds.

THE RUE FAMILY

Many of these plants are strongly scented, often with a citrus-like aroma, and yield valuable oils. The oils are found in translucent glands, often visible in the flowers, fruit, leaves and bark. The Rutaceae family is comprised mostly of trees and shrubs and is well represented in Australia and South Africa. A number of the trees and shrubs have thorns, but throughout the family botanical features are highly variable.

Cape Chestnut

Calodendrum capense (L. f.) Thunb.

This beautiful slow-growing tree is abundant in forests in its native range, where it is also an important timber source. Although preferring the company of other trees and plenty of moisture, it is planted throughout Africa and sub-tropical regions. The Latin name is translated as 'beautiful tree of the cape' and each year huge clusters of pale pink scented flowers clothe the canopy.

Right: In some localities the foliage drops briefly in the autumn.

Identification: The smooth, grey trunk reaches 1m/3ft in diameter. The leaves are deep green, 15cm/6in long, 7.5cm/3in wide and have many parallel veins. Terminal flowers appear in spring or summer; each is 9cm/3½in across, has five pink petals, five pink stamens and five stamens impersonating petals. The autumn seed pods are brown, hard, round, 4cm/1½in long and covered in blunt spines. When ripe they split into a five-petalled star and release black, triangular seeds.

Distribution: South Africa through to Kenya, not coastal.
Height: 18m/60ft
Shape: Domed
Semi-evergreen
Pollinated: Insect
Leaf shape: Ovate

Right: The flowers appear in clusters of 8–12.

Curry Leaf

Murraya koenigii Koenig ex. L.

The warm, strong, spicy, and slightly bitter flavour and aroma of the leaves of this plant have been exploited as a flavouring for curries in Indian cuisine. The distinctive scent cannot be substituted with any other spice. Although often found in mulligatawny soup and Madras curry mixes it does not play a major role in most curries. Additionally the bark, leaves and roots are used as a tonic, and the berries are edible, having a peppery flavour. The plant grows as a dense shrub or small tree in drier areas of its range.

Identification: The trunk remains narrow and carries a dense crown of foliage. Each leaf is composed of 10–20 leaflets up to 5cm/2in long. Leaflets may be hairy, are bright green and paler below. The small, fragrant yellowish white flowers are found in loose panicles in summer. The small berries are black.

Distribution: Sri Lanka, India and Pakistan.
Height: 6m/20ft
Shape: Round-headed
Evergreen
Pollinated: Insect
Leaf shape: Pinnate

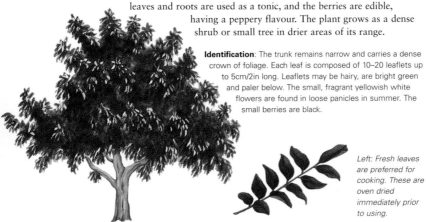

Left: Fresh leaves are preferred for cooking. These are oven dried immediately prior to using.

Right: The 1cm/½in flowers form panicles of up to 90 flowers.

Orange Jessamine

Murraya paniculata (L.) Jack.

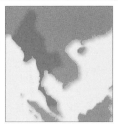

This beautifully scented plant has its leaves and bark powdered to make the sweetly scented Thanaka powder. This is a famous scent in Asia and widely used by Burmese and Thai women. The small, scented, white flowers, reminiscent of orange blossom, are also used for perfumery in Java and make popular offerings in temples. This lovely dense plant is grown throughout the tropics. It may be grown as a bush and is often seen as a houseplant in temperate zones.

Distribution: Burma, Thailand and northern Malay Peninsula.
Height: 6m/20ft
Shape: Round-headed
Evergreen
Pollinated: Insect
Leaf shape: Pinnate

Identification: This tree is often multi-stemmed and carries a dense crown of dark green glossy foliage. Each 20cm/8in-long leaf is composed of six to nine elliptic 4cm/1½in-long leaflets. The flowers form in spring, summer and autumn. They are in dense clusters over the crown of the tree. Each flower is 2cm/¾in across with four or five thick creamy white petals. The fruit is a red berry 1cm/½in across. This plant is grown as hedging, a shrub, a tree, topiary, and may even be treated as a bonsai.

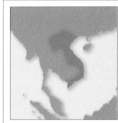

Left: The scent from these waxy flowers fills the air in tropical gardens.

Mountain Pride *Spathelia sorbifolia* (L.) Fawcett & Pendle
An unusual tree from the West Indies with an elegant stem to 15m/50ft and no branches. The crown consists of a tuft of large feathery evergreen pinnate leaves, each with 20–40 pairs of oblong to lanceolate-shaped leaflets. The huge terminal flower panicle may reach several metres in length and carries large red to purple flowers. The fruit has two wings.

African Cherry Orange *Citropsis schweinfurthii* (Engl.) Swingle & Kellerm
This small tree from central Africa from Sudan to Congo is related to *Citrus*. It has spines, leathery pinnate leaves with winged midribs, white flowers and clusters of small, orange, sweetly flavoured fruit. The leaflets are narrowly lanceolate, the flowers are large and the 4cm/1½in fruit has three or four segments to it.

Caffre Lime *Citrus hystrix* D. C.
This citrus grows only to 5m/16ft. It is grown in tropical Asia through to Sri Lanka for the very warty, 10cm/4in-long, pear-shaped fruit. The yellow fruit has little juice and is used in medicine, as food flavouring and in shampoos but is not eaten. The bright green leaves are also used as a curry spice.

Tetradium ruticarpum (A. Juss.) Hartley
From the valleys of the Himalayas through India to Taiwan comes this small evergreen tree with dense foliage. The branches are clothed with pinnate leaves and flowers with a soft velvety down. The small flowers are carried in panicles 7–10cm/2¾–4in across.

Calamondin

x *Citrofortunella microcarpa*
(Bunge) D.O. Wijnands

This plant is a result of a rare natural cross between two closely related genera, in this case *Citrus* and *Fortunella*. It carries characteristics of both parents. The *Fortunella* parent, kumquat, lends a dense shrubby habit, small leaves and a hardy constitution, whereas the *Citrus reticulata*, mandarin orange, lends thorns, tasty fruit and ease of peeling. So the calamondin has smallish, easy to peel fruit with an acidic flavour. It grows well in truly tropical areas through to those with very occasional mild frosts. With its upright habit, dark glossy foliage and multitude of small brightly coloured fruits the calamondin makes a fine ornamental and is well suited to growing in containers.

Distribution: Laos and Vietnam.
Height: 7.5m/25ft
Shape: Columnar
Evergreen
Pollinated: Insect
Leaf shape: Elliptic

Identification: The glossy leaves are about 7cm/2¾in long and paler green below. Flowers are in clusters, each 2.5cm/1in wide, and white with an intoxicating scent. The orange fruit is up to 6cm/2½in across and round.

Right: The attractive calamondin is grown as a houseplant in temperate zones.

MISCELLANEOUS ROSIDAE

These small families are all related within the class Rosidae. The mistletoe family, Loranthaceae, are semi-parasitic plants. The torchwood family, Bursuraceae, is a small tropical family often producing resins. The caltrop family, Zygophyllaceae, includes few trees, while the wood sorrel family, Oxalidaceae, is composed almost entirely of herbaceous plants.

Brush Box

West Australian Christmas tree *Nuytsia floribunda* (Labill.) R. Br. ex. Don.

Distribution: Western Australia.
Height: 9m/30ft
Shape: Domed, spreading
Evergreen
Pollinated: Bird
Leaf shape: Linear

Right: The sheer weight of the flowers often breaks the branches.

This tree is a sinister parasite that saps resources from other plants. Unlike many parasites, it is terrestrial, attacking plants underground. Underground stems travel more than 100m/328ft from the trunk, and on contact with another plant's root their own roots encircle the host and pierce it to absorb foods. Seeds and seedlings are rare, instead the plant sends up suckers from underground stems, resulting in clusters of the trees in the sandy damp areas it likes. The trees are awkward and heavy-set with brittle, lightweight branches. At Christmas time though, they become smothered in vibrant, golden-orange, honey-scented flowers.

Identification: The mid-brown to grey trunk can reach 1.2m/4ft in diameter. The rigid leaves are up to 7.5cm/3in long and 5mm/¼in wide. The six-petalled flowers are packed into dense racemes 10–15cm/4–6in long, crowded at the end of the branches. The fruit is a nut 1cm/½in long.

Java Almond

Canarium luzonicum (Blume) A. Gray

In its native home this fast-growing tree has many local uses. A gum with a fresh lemony scent, known as brea gum or elemi, is extracted from the trunk. The gum is used in healing ointments, for soothing muscles and as a dietary supplement. The gum provides a valuable volatile oil thought to have anti-ageing properties. The flowers are popular with bees and useful in bee keeping. The fruit has an edible kernel, somewhat similar in taste to an almond, from which oil is also extracted. The oil is used for cooking and burning in lamps. The tree also makes a fine ornamental specimen and works well as an avenue. It is particularly popular in Java as a shade tree.

Distribution: Philippines.
Height: Large
Shape: Domed
Evergreen
Pollinated: Insect
Leaf shape: Pinnate

Below: The fruit contains one hard, pointed stone, which has an edible kernel inside it.

Identification: The trunk has enormous buttresses, which are nearly uniform in thickness throughout. Leaves measure up to 45cm/18in long and have seven to nine small ovate to oblong leaflets. Leaflets vary from 7cm/2¾in to 20cm/8in in length. The small, scented white flowers have three petals and are clustered into terminal panicles. The fruit forms in large hanging clusters in summer. Each fruit is oval, 4cm/1½in long and dark purple when ripe.

Lignum Vitae

Guaiacum officinale L.

The wood of this pretty, extremely slow-growing tree has outstanding characteristics. It is possibly the heaviest wood in the world, weighing 1,307kg per cubic metre/67lb per cubic foot. It even sinks in water. It is the hardest wood used commercially and has a high content of oily resin. This resin gives a good level of lubrication, lending the wood resistance to rot, termites, fungus, borers and harsh chemicals. It is particularly favoured for use on boats, where bearings of this wood will outlive metal. The name 'lignum vitae' translates as 'wood of life'; in sixteenth-century Europe the tree was thought to have great healing properties. Due to over-harvesting these plants are now facing a very high risk of extinction in the wild.

Identification: The short trunk has dark grey bark and may ooze greenish resin. The crown is dense. The 10cm/4in-long leaves are composed of four to six obovate, blunt ended, 2.5cm/1in-long leathery leaflets. The beautiful, fragrant, felty flowers appear twice a year, and are 2.5cm/1in across with four or five petals. The fruit is often seen with the flowers, and is yellow or orange, heart shaped with a moist leathery skin and 2cm/1in across.

Distribution: West Indies, Panama, Colombia and Venezuela.
Height: 9m/30ft
Shape: Spreading
Evergreen
Pollinated: Insect
Leaf shape: Pinnate

Far left: The deep blue flowers fade to silvery blue.

Left: The colourful fruit holds up to five hard oblong seeds.

Star Fruit

Averrhoea carambola L.

In the West, the insipid fruit of this tree is a popular garnish, due to its distinctive star-shaped cross section. In the tropics, however, the vitamin C rich fruit is often delicious, sweet and very juicy, but it is very delicate and bruises easily. Many different forms of the fruit exist, some of which may be cooked in stews or curries. The Chinese value the fruit as an antidote to high blood pressure, and the juice can also be used to remove stains from linen and for polishing brass. It is cultivated in California, northern Australia, India, southern China and areas of Africa. The leaves have the interesting characteristic of closing up at night or when touched, in a similar way to a sensitive plant.

Identification: The moderately short trunk carries a very dense crown of long twigs. Usually the alternate leaves each have nine or eleven leaflets. Leaflets are ovate, mid-green above, paler below, thin and 2.5–7cm/1–2¾in long. Flowers appear throughout the year but generally in two main flushes. They form in panicles on the twigs, branches and the trunk. Each tiny flower is pink, red or mauve with five overlapping petals. The fruit forms in great profusion; when ripe it is deep yellow, 10–15cm/4–6in long, five-angled and appears as if carved from wax.

Distribution: Malaysia.
Height: 9m/30ft
Shape: Oblong to rounded (variable)
Evergreen
Pollinated: Insect
Leaf shape: Pinnate

Left: The dense network of long twigs droop down towards the branch tips, particularly when laden with fruit.

Left: The terminal leaflet is always the largest.

THE IVY FAMILY

The ivy family, Araliaceae, spans temperate and tropical regions and encompasses trees, shrubs, climbers and herbs. Some are prickly and in tropical countries may be epiphytic or semi-epiphytic. They are grown for their foliage yet often have an unpleasant scent. Their alternate leaves vary immensely, whereas flowers are more distinctive, small and usually arranged in umbels. The fruit is often a small black berry.

Snowflake Tree

Trevesia palmata 'Micholitzii' (Roxb. ex. Lindl.) Vis.

'Micholitzii' is the most commonly grown form of this jungle tree. The extraordinary leaves are large and complex. They are shaped like a snowflake, though with many more points. The leaf is also coated with a snowy woolly pubescence and white speckles, giving an additional snowy feel. The plant makes few branches, many specimens have no branches at all, and is sometimes grown as a large shrub.

Identification: The trunk and stems are covered in short sharp spines. The hanging branches are white with pubescence. The leaf stems reach over 60cm/24in in length. The leathery leaves are virtually round and 60cm/24in across. They are mid-green with white markings and have central webbing and 7–11 lobed sections with toothed edges. The spring flowers are pale green to cream, 2cm/1in across, have 8–12 petals and are clustered into umbels arranged on 45cm/18in-long terminal panicles. The fruits are fleshy, oval and 1cm/½in across.

Distribution: Northern India eastward to Vietnam and southern China and southward into peninsular Malaysia.
Height: 6m/20ft
Shape: Oblong
Evergreen
Leaf shape: Palmate

Left: The youngest leaves and growing tips are eaten in Thailand.

Left: The flower and fruit-bearing stems arch heavily away from the plant.

Umbrella Tree *Schefflera actinopylla* Endl.
In its native forests of Queensland and New South Wales, Australia, the 18m/60ft evergreen umbrella tree may start life as an epiphyte, eventually strangling the host plant. It is popular for its fast-growing nature, unusual, colourful flowers and fruit, and thick glossy foliage. It is columnar while young, developing a multi-stemmed oblong crown with age. It has been very widely planted throughout the tropics as an ornamental, but in many countries has become a weed. In cooler climates it is successful as a houseplant. It often has many slender, soft-wooded, brown trunks carrying few branches but a dense canopy. Individual trunks will become quite sturdy with age. In humid climates plants may send down aerial roots from mature branches. The leaves are thick, glossy, dark green, 60cm/24in across and divided into 9–15 oblong leaflets. The curved leaflets hang, looking like an umbrella. The red flowers are 5mm/¼in across and clustered into umbels along numerous 1m/1yd-long, terminal spikes in summer. The tiny flower petals fall off as they open. The flowers are pollinated by insects, resulting in long attractive spikes carrying the fruit. Fruit is deep red to black, round and 1.5cm/½in wide.

Puka *Mertya denhamii* Seem.
From New Caledonia comes this impressive 6m/20ft, slender, round-headed tree. On mature trees the immense leaves reach 1.2m/4ft in length and are clustered at the tips of the branches. Each leaf is leathery, oblanceolate and has toothed margins. The tiny, pale green flowers cluster in panicles in spring and summer. The black fruit is 1.5cm/½in long.

Rice Paper Tree *Tetrapanax papyrifer* (Hook.) K. Koch
Originating from Taiwan, this moderately hardy, fast-growing, suckering tree or shrub reaches 6m/20ft. The lightweight trunks contain white pith used in Asia to make a type of Chinese rice paper. These narrow trunks rarely branch but carry enormous palmate leaves, each up to 75cm/30in across. The tiny, cream, autumnal flowers are packed into round umbels, arranged in panicles. The small fruit is round and black.

False Aralia *Schefflera elegantissima* (Veith ex. Mast.) Lowry & Frodin
This evergreen plant is common in cool temperate areas as a beautiful, low-maintenance, foliage houseplant. In this form it is unrecognizable as the same plant found growing in the under-storey of tropical rainforests. The habit and leaves of a mature plant are very different to those of a young one. The juvenile leaves are fine, elegant and delicate with dark colouring, light midribs and toothed and wavy edges. A juvenile plant has many narrow, straight un-branched stems, whereas mature plants have branches, and the foliage is much larger. The trunks are pale with no branches close to the ground. The leaves are divided into 6–10 leaflets.

Mallet Flower

Schefflera pueckleri (K. Koch) Frodin

Incredibly, this beautiful, densely-crowned tree was only brought into cultivation in the 1960s. This tree naturally occurs in damp forested areas and prefers shady conditions. In the wild it normally grows with multiple trunks, but as it ages it may take on climbing characteristics and become a huge forest liana. In cultivation, it may be grown as a large shrub, wide spreading tree or narrow specimen. In temperate zones, it is becoming widely available as a fast-growing houseplant and is also successfully included in interior planting schemes.

Distribution: Northern India through to Vietnam.
Height: 12m/40ft
Shape: Oblong
Evergreen
Leaf shape: Palmate

Identification: The deep green, smooth, leathery, glossy leaves are composed of seven to ten pendulous leaflets, each 10–18cm/4–7in long, narrowly oblong with a pronounced midrib. The leaf and leaflet stems are often red. The odd, greenish, mallet-shaped flowers are up to 3cm/1¼in across. They have thick, fleshy, leathery petals, which drop off as a cap, and numerous crowded white stamens. In the wild, three to seven flowers form into short, stout, spreading, terminal panicles directly from the main stem or older wood, but these are rare in cultivation. The rounded, fleshy fruit can have a diameter of up to 4cm/1½in.

Left: The leaves are thick, tough, smooth and shiny. Each leaflet hangs down creating an umbrella-like shape to the entire leaf.

Ming Aralia

Polyscias fruticosa (L.) Harms.

This popular and fast-growing tropical garden plant is often seen as a large shrub or hedge, for which it is well suited. If grown as a tree, the columnar habit makes it a useful 'architectural' feature. It makes a fine, graceful specimen, often with multiple trunks. The elegantly cut foliage tends to form in rounded tiers up the trunks. It is also grown as an attractive houseplant in temperate zones. Many different varieties have been developed, which are popularized through the houseplant industry.

Distribution: India through to Polynesia (Burma, Vietnam, Indonesia).
Height: 8m/26ft
Shape: Columnar
Evergreen
Leaf shape: Pinnate, bipinnate and tripinnate

Identification: The leaves are variable but most often tripinnate. Each is up to 75cm/30in long with dark green speckled stems. The leaflets are up to 10cm/4in long, ovate, smooth, leathery, dark green and heavily toothed on the margins. The insignificant flowers form throughout the year in umbels, arranged in terminal panicles 15–20cm/6–8in long. Up to 40 tiny, off-white flowers form each umbel. The fruit is ovoid and may reach up to 2.5cm/1in in length.

Left: There are different forms of the ming aralia. Some forms have finely divided foliage, others have congested, twisted leaflets similar to parsley.

THE COMBRETUM FAMILY

The Combretaceae family includes trees, climbers and shrubs. Its members vary significantly and have few consistent features. Many of the trees have large yet narrow buttresses and yellow inner bark, and the flowers usually have greatly reduced petals and protruding anthers. The fruit, which is dry, is dispersed by water or wind, and has wing-like structures protruding from it.

Leadwood

Combretum imberbe

This tree, a protected species in its native South Africa, may live more than 2,000 years, and may remain standing for an equally long time after death. Its leaves are popular with browsing animals, such as giraffes, elephants and impala. It also produces an edible gum. The leadwood tree is named after its exceptionally hard and heavy wood. Ash produced from burning the wood is sometimes used as toothpaste.

Identification: The trunk has silvery grey bark fissured into rectangular pieces and carries a dense network of branches. The leaves have undulate margins. They are 5cm/2in long, 1.5cm/⅔in wide, dull green and heavily spotted with tiny white glands on both surfaces. Young leaves are bright green and develop from pinkish-brown shoots. The creamy yellow, orange or red flowers appear in winter on long spikes. The fruit is leathery and contains a single seed.

Distribution: Tanzania to northern South Africa.
Height: 20m/66ft
Semi-evergreen
Leaf shape: Elliptic-oblong

Left: The fruit forms in spring and summer, and is dispersed by the wind on four papery wings.

Left: A flower spike.

Tropical Almond

Terminalia catappa L.

The nuts of this tree are incredibly hard and popular with humans and animals. The tree is highly tolerant of salt and is often grown along beaches to provide shade and help stabilize the soil. Its reddish timber is used for boat construction. The tropical almond is a good-looking tree with horizontal tiers of foliage that spread out to make it wider than it is tall.

Identification: The trunk is short and dark, and the smooth, glossy leaves cluster towards the branch tips. The leaves are deep green turning bright orange, red or purple before dropping at any time of year. The flowers occur mostly in summer on 23cm/9in-long spikes, produced near the branch tips. The fruit is greenish-yellow or red, almond shaped and 5cm/2in long.

Distribution: Tropical coastal Asia.
Height: 24m/80ft
Shape: Spreading
Deciduous
Pollinated: Insect
Leaf shape: Obovate

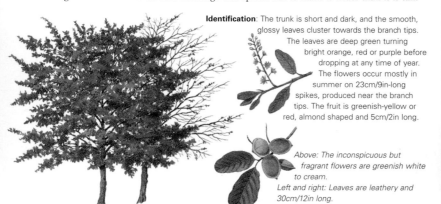

Above: The inconspicuous but fragrant flowers are greenish white to cream.
Left and right: Leaves are leathery and 30cm/12in long.

THE VERBENA FAMILY

This large family contains well known and useful plants. It is found mostly in the southern hemisphere and includes herbs, climbers, shrubs and trees, some of which are aromatic. Verbenaceae often have square-shaped twigs, and flowers with a long tube divided into five petals. The fruit is a hard capsule or fleshy with a hard stone, divided into four sections, each with one seed.

Teak

Tectona grandis L.

The wonderful hard timber of the teak tree was first brought to Europe in the early 1800s. It has remained a constantly popular choice for quality furniture production ever since. As a result, the monsoon forests of which it is native have been stripped of their specimens, and now few wild trees remain. Originally elephants would have been used to extract the timber before it was floated downriver out of the forest. Now, the fast-growing teak is planted in large plantations across its indigenous area.

Identification: The straight trunk carries many tiered branches and has pale grey, soft, fissured, peeling bark. The leaves are of colossal size, up to 80cm/32in long and 40cm/16in wide with undulating margins and prominent veining. They are rough and leathery, mid-green above and covered in soft white hairs below. The tiny cream flowers are found in large panicles 45cm/18in long in early summer. The fleshy fruit is round, 2cm/¾in across and purplish red or brown.

Right: The old bark peels off in small, thin, oblong pieces, revealing the yellow inner bark.

Left: The flowers appear after the tree has put on its new leaves in the wet season.

Distribution: Tropical India to Vietnam.
Height: 35m/115ft
Shape: Oblong
Deciduous
Pollinated: Insect
Leaf shape: Widely elliptical

Meru Oak

Vitex keniensis

This tree is native to the moist evergreen mountain forests and rocky hillsides of Kenya and Tanzania but has a wide distribution including deciduous woodland, savannah, coastal and upland regions. It has valuable, hard teak-like timber used for furniture, boat-making and building poles, but has only been cultivated in plantations since the 1950s. It is valuable to farmers because it has the ability to fix nitrogen in the soil.

Identification: The trunk has thin, lightly fissured bark and is clear of branches at the base. The leaves are divided into five obovate leaflets, each 5 x 8cm/2 x 3in, leathery, deep green above and paler below. The flowers form in the spring in a 15cm/6in cyme. Each is less than 1cm/½in long and white and mauve. The elliptic, fleshy fruit takes five months to develop. When ripe it is soft, black, 1.5cm/⅔in long and has a tough leathery skin.

Right: The ripe fruit is popular with birds and monkeys. Although edible by humans it is rarely eaten. The leaves are coated on both surfaces with soft hairs and glands.

Distribution: Central and southern Africa.
Height: 40m/130ft
Shape: Rounded
Deciduous
Pollinated: Insect
Leaf shape: Palmate

THE DOGBANE FAMILY

This family is renowned for its toxic properties. Plants contain a large quantity of poisonous, milky latex, which in some species is of value to humans. The family is also valuable for its contribution to ornamental horticulture. Most of the Apocynaceae are tropical, and many are shrubs. The simple leaves are usually opposite, the five-petalled flowers are funnel shaped and the fruit is usually dry and in pairs.

Frangipani

Plumeria rubra L.

The legendary frangipani is regarded as one of the world's most beautifully scented flowers. It is thought a botanist named Frangipani first distilled the perfume in the sixteenth century and so the common name arose. The trees are regularly seen growing in temple grounds of Buddhists, Hindus and even Muslims and the flowers used as offerings. In Hawaii garlands made of these flowers are used on special occasions and to greet visitors. Although the flowers may be white, red, yellow or pink the form *P. rubra* f. *acutifolia* with white flowers with golden centres is most widely planted.

Distribution: Southern Mexico to Panama.
Height: 8m/26ft
Shape: Domed
Semi-evergreen
Pollinated: Insect and self
Leaf shape: Elliptic-obovate

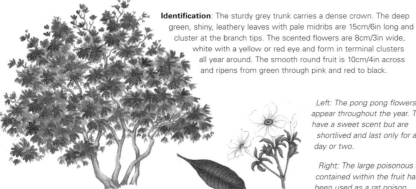

Identification: The fleshy round stems are rubbery and green when young, woody and pale grey when mature. Branching is sparse and candelabra-like. The thick, 30cm/12in-long leaves with paler midribs cluster at the branch tips. The 8cm/3in-wide twisted flowers form in terminal clusters. The fruits are pairs of 15cm/6in-long leathery pods.

Left: Each funnel-shaped flower has five waxy petals and an intoxicating perfume.

Pong Pong

Sea mango *Cerbera odollam* L.

Naturally found in coastal forests and mangrove areas, this plant has been cultivated successfully in gardens in swampy areas, with saline soil or salty air. In addition to the attractive tropical foliage it has large, colourful fruit. The fruit is reminiscent of mango in appearance, which has resulted in its other common name of 'sea mango'. However, the fruit is poisonous. The tree is closely related to the frangipanis with which it shares a number of characteristics.

Distribution: Coastal, India through to northern Australia.
Height: 15m/50ft
Shape: Rounded to oblong
Evergreen
Pollinated: Insect
Leaf shape: Narrowly obovate

Identification: The sturdy grey trunk carries a dense crown. The deep green, shiny, leathery leaves with pale midribs are 15cm/6in long and cluster at the branch tips. The scented flowers are 8cm/3in wide, white with a yellow or red eye and form in terminal clusters all year around. The smooth round fruit is 10cm/4in across and ripens from green through pink and red to black.

Left: The pong pong flowers appear throughout the year. They have a sweet scent but are shortlived and last only for a day or two.

Right: The large poisonous seed contained within the fruit has been used as a rat poison.

Dita Bark

Alstonia scholaris (l.) R. Br.

Distribution: Throughout the tropical regions of Asia, Africa and northern Australia.
Height: 30m/100ft
Shape: Oblong
Evergreen
Leaf shape: Narrowly oblong

A drug is sourced from the bark of this tree to treat malaria, the white sap can be extracted as rubber and the soft, pale lightweight timber has many uses, including for coffins and as plyboard, but it must not be used in contact with food. The timber was used historically in southern India for writing-tablets in schools, and this application explains the species name 'scholaris'. It is a fast-growing tree from monsoon regions and rainforests.

Identification: The straight trunk has pale, smooth bark and branches radiating out in horizontal tiers from its upper two thirds. The whorls of glossy, leathery leaves are clustered towards the branch tips, and each is deep green, paler and heavily veined below and 15–23cm/6–9in long. In summer the terminal clusters of beautifully scented tiny greenish-white to cream flowers appear. The fruit is a 60cm/24in-long, deep blue pod that splits open to release many seeds.

Far right: The tiny scented flowers form in clusters 8–13cm/3–5in wide all over the tree's crown.

Penang Sloe *Kopsia flavida* Blume
This small evergreen tree originates from Malaysia. It may reach 8m/26ft and carries a rounded crown of dark green foliage. Each leathery leaf is elliptic and 9cm/3½in long. The ornamental summer flowers are white to yellow, 3.5cm/1⅜in long, with a long narrow tube divided into five oblong petals. They occur in terminal clusters. The smooth oval fruit is 2.5cm/1in long.

White Frangipani
Plumeria obtusa L.
One of the most popular frangipanis is this 8m/26ft-tall evergreen tree from Mexico and the Caribbean islands. It is endowed with intensely fragrant pure white blossoms. As with other frangipanis, the terminal clusters of flowers develop all year round in constantly wet areas, or in the wet season only in monsoon areas. The attractive leaves are dark green, glossy, obovate and 15–30cm/6–12in long. Dwarfing varieties have been developed to be more shrub-like.

West Indian Jasmine *Plumeria alba* L.
Less well known is this large spreading *Plumeria* of 16m/52ft native to the West Indies. It has 30cm/12in-long, 8cm/3in-wide, deep green lanceolate leaves. The leaves have soft, pale coloured down underneath and margins that curl under. The scented flowers appear in summer in dense clusters. They are white with a yellow eye.

Yellow Oleander

Thevetia peruviana (Pers.) Schum.

The sap and fruit of this tree are extremely poisonous, and yet the deadly poisonous seeds contain chemicals that are extracted for use in heart medicines. Curiously the seeds are also thought to be lucky, and are carried as charms or worn as pendants. In addition to the typical yellow flowers, forms exist with white, orange or apricot flowers. In some plants they are pleasantly scented, while others have no scent. Often used as a fast-growing hedge or screen, the foliage gives an unusual soft appearance.

Identification: The brown trunk is often multi-stemmed and rarely upright. The bright green, glossy leaves cluster at the tips of the branches forming a dense crown. Each leaf is 10–15cm/4–6in long. The terminal clusters of a few flowers appear throughout the year. Each flower is tubular shaped and 8cm/3in long. The fruit is a rounded, four sided, 4cm/1½in-wide, hard, fleshy pod. When ripe it is black.

Below: The yellow oleander with its fine, spirally arranged leaves thrives in dry sites.

Distribution: South-east Mexico, Belize and the West Indies.
Height: 9m/30ft
Shape: Domed
Evergreen
Pollinated: Insect
Leaf shape: Lanceolate

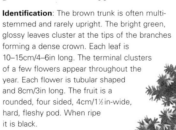

THE BUDDLEIA AND POTATO FAMILIES

The buddleia family, Loganiaceae, and potato family, Solanaceae, are both in the class Asteridae. Loganiaceae have simple leaves and funnel-shaped flowers with four or five petals. Solanaceae is a larger family, also including trees, shrubs, climbers and herbaceous plants, found throughout warmer temperate and tropical zones. Their leaves may be simple or lobed, many carry spines, and some are poisonous.

Tembusu

Fagraea fragrans L.

Although not widely planted in the tropics, this tree is common in Singapore. It is seen in public gardens and makes a good choice for avenues. Apart from being rather slow growing, it has a number of endearing characteristics. It has a narrow form, particularly when young, with distinctly ascending branches, retains its foliage to the ground for many years and has an airy crown. All the trees in an area flower simultaneously, usually twice a year, when the entire crown is clothed in heavily scented flowers for many weeks. The ensuing fruit is a feast for fruit bats and birds.

Right: The tembusa is naturally found in wet and swampy localities.

Below: The deeply fissured bark has ridges which interconnect.

Distribution: Malaysia and Indonesia.
Height: 40m/130ft
Shape: Oblong–variable
Evergreen
Pollinated: Moth
Leaf shape: Elliptic

Identification: The narrow trunk or trunks have dark brown heavily fissured bark. Leaves cluster at the branch tips. They are mid-green with a paler midrib and up to 13cm/5in long. The flowers form in large terminal clusters of up to 100. Each is funnel shaped, white upon opening, fading to cream, with protruding stamens and 2.5cm/1in across. The fruit forms in clusters too. Each is 5mm/¼in wide, round, shiny and orange to crimson when ripe.

Tree Potato

Solanum wrightii Benth.

This incredibly fast-growing tree has been recorded at 9m/30ft high with an equal spread in only two years. Inevitably this cannot last, and trees are said to lose their condition after only four years. The flowers open as deep purple and fade to white over a couple of days. As they are in clusters and appear throughout the year, the tree almost always has a colourful collection of purple, mauve and white flowers. In some gardens it is kept pruned as a shrub; this treatment inhibits flowering but extends the life and encourages the hairy ornamental leaves to become huge.

Identification: The soft-wooded, pale grey trunk is often multi-stemmed. The bright green leaves vary enormously in size depending on the way the plant is grown, in shrubs they can reach 45cm/18in in length, whereas in trees they are more normally 25cm/10in long. Each is deeply incised into angular lobes and covered in coarse hairs. The midrib and main veins carry thorns. The round fruit is 5cm/2in across, round and orange-yellow to brown when ripe. It contains four cavities filled with pulp and flat seeds.

Distribution: Bolivia and adjoining area of tropical Brazil.
Height: 12m/40ft
Shape: Domed
Evergreen
Pollinated: Insect
Leaf shape: Ovate

Left: The flowers are crumpled up in bud. When open they are 8cm/3in across and have a cluster of central golden stamens. They have five petals and form in small clusters.

THE BORAGE FAMILY

The majority of the Boraginaceae family are herbs with just a few trees, shrubs and climbers included. Many of the woody species are tropical. They have simple hairy leaves, usually alternately arranged and smooth edged. Stems are often covered in stiff hairs, too. The five-petalled flowers are occasionally alone but most often in axillary cymes. The fruit has one to four seeds and is usually dry and hard.

Salmwood

Cordia alliadora L. (Ruiz & Pavon) Oken

This attractive, fast-growing yet long-lived pioneer species is often found on disturbed land within humid and dry regions. It is grown throughout its native range for its quality timber, used in numerous products including veneers, furniture, and boat and housing construction. The flowers are a major source of nectar for beekeeping, producing a thick pale honey. The crushed leaves have a distinctive onion-like odour. Some trees have hollow swollen nodes which are inhabited by ants.

Identification: The thin trunk may have small buttresses, has smooth, pale grey or brown bark, and carries a thin, open crown. The dark green leaves reach 18cm/7in and are covered in hairs below. Flowers appear mostly in summer, and a large tree may produce as many as ten million in one season. They are 1cm/½in long and in 10–30cm/4–12in-long inforesences. The dry, brown fruit is up to 1cm/½in long with a parachute formed from the expanded petals.

Distribution: Northern Mexico through to northern Argentina and Paraguay and the islands of Cuba to Trinidad.
Height: 40m/130ft
Shape: Oblong
Evergreen
Pollinated: Insect
Leaf shape: Elliptic

Left: Trees can flower from as young as two years, although viable seed is only produced from five-year-old trees. In mature specimens, up to one million seeds can be produced annually.

Geiger Tree

Cordia sebestena L.

The attraction of this tree is in its virtually continual succession of bright vermilion flowers and its tolerance of dry conditions and salt-laden air. It is a popular ornamental tree in gardens and along streets throughout its native range. It is sometimes also grown as a shrub. In addition, the tree has a number of medicinal uses, particularly in relation to breathing difficulties. The sweet edible fruit is used in some areas as a remedy for coughs, while the bark, flowers or fruit may be used to make a sugary syrup.

Identification: The trunk is rarely straight and may be multi-stemmed. Interestingly, the stiff leaves are hairy and rough on the upper surface and smooth below. They are dark green above and paler below, 15cm/6in long and may have a slightly toothed margin. The veins are paler than the leaf and depressed on the upper surface. Each flower is funnel shaped, 4cm/1½in long and a similar width. The petals are crinkled like crepe, and there are central yellow stamens. The flowers are in terminal clusters and are particularly abundant in the summer. The white fruit is oval and 1cm/½in long.

Distribution: West Indies and Venezuela.
Height: 8m/26ft
Shape: Oblong to spreading (variable)
Evergreen
Pollinated: Insect
Leaf shape: Ovate

Left: The clusters of flowers include bisexual and male ones; the male flowers are smaller but occur in a greater number.

THE BIGNONIA FAMILY

Bignoniaceae is one of the more readily recognized families. They are native to the tropics and subtropics and include trees, shrubs, a few herbs and many climbing plants. Their funnel-shaped flowers are usually found in panicles or racemes and are some of the most flamboyant. Their compound leaves are opposite. The fruit is normally long, splitting into two to release numerous flat winged seeds.

Sausage Tree

Kigelia africana (Lam.) Benth.

The huge brown, sausage-shaped fruit hanging on long cords has given this tree its name. Originally a forest tree, it is now grown for curiosity and shade throughout the tropics. Although the hanging flower panicles reach 2m/6ft in length, the tree is not noted for its floral display. Only one or two flowers open at any one time on a panicle, and they open overnight and have an unpleasant scent. In central Africa the tree is considered sacred, and the fruit is used medicinally and to flavour beer but is not eaten.

Identification: The smooth, grey barked trunk carries a dense head of spreading branches. The 30cm/12in-long leaves cluster near branch tips; they comprise 7–13 leaflets, deep green, oblong, glossy, and 4–18cm/1½–7in long. The early summer, trumpet-like flowers are dark red or purple and 9–13cm/3½–5in long. Smooth, woody fruit, up to 60cm/24in long, hangs for many months and contains large seeds in pulp.

Left: The fruit weighs up to 4kg/9lb. Atypically for this family it does not split open and the seeds do not have wings.
Right: The sausage tree is tolerant of arid conditions and is planted in India. When young, the foliage has a reddish hue.

Distribution: Tropical Africa (Sudan to Senegal to Swaziland).
Height: 18m/60ft
Shape: Rounded spreading
Evergreen
Pollinated: Bat
Leaf shape: Pinnate

Calabash Tree

Crescentia cujete L.

Distribution: Throughout Central America, northern South America, West Indies and southern Mexico.
Height: 13m/43ft
Shape: Spreading
Evergreen
Pollinated: Bat
Leaf shape: Obovate

Calabashes are gourds, and were originally used as water carriers, but are now more likely to be seen as musical instruments, cups, ornaments or bags. Calabash maracas still feature in Afro-Caribbean music. The fruit is hollowed out, highly polished and often carved on the outside. To make an hourglass or other shapes, the fruit is tied with string while immature.

Identification: The short trunk has fissured light grey bark and carries a dense to open crown of heavily foliaged, rarely branched, long, spreading, semi-pendulous branches. The leaves are in clusters of three to five, and they jut out along the length of the branches in an inelegant fashion. Each leaf is dark green, glossy and 10–15cm/4–6in long. The unpleasantly scented flowers form directly from the trunk and larger branches; they are off-white with purple markings and 5cm/2in long. The fruit is ovoid or round, brown when ripe and up to 30cm/12in long.

Right: Calabashes are green while immature ripening through yellow to brown.

Jacaranda

Jacaranda mimosifolia (Aubl.) D. Don.

While leafless the clear mauve flowers of the jacaranda cover the crown, creating a unique and unforgettable sight. The flowers fall to form a blue carpet below. In addition, this fast-growing tree has delicate ferny foliage justifying its use as a pot plant and in gardens of humid tropical areas, where it flowers less reliably. This is one of the rare trees commonly called by its botanical name.

Distribution: Paraguay, southern Brazil and northern Argentina.
Height: 15m/50ft
Shape: Domed
Deciduous
Pollinated: Insect
Leaf shape: Bipinnate

Identification: The trunk has grey bark. The airy, well-shaped crown is as wide as the tree is tall. The leaves measure 20–45cm/8–18in in length and consist of 8–20 pairs of pinnae, each carrying 10–28 pairs of leaflets. Each downy leaflet is bright green, ovate to elliptic and 1cm/½in long. The dense terminal panicles of 5cm/2in-long trumpet-like flowers appear in spring and summer. The fruit is a 5cm/2½in-wide, flattened, round to oblong, rich brown, leathery pod containing winged seeds.

Above and right: The jacaranda is a beautiful tree. The fine, fern-like foliage casts delicate shade below.

Jicara *Crescentia alata* H. B. K.
From southern Mexico through to Costa Rica grows this 9m/30ft evergreen tree. It has long, thin, stem-like branches and a short trunk. The trees were thought to have Christian significance, as the leaves form the shape of a cross. Each trifoliate leaf is composed of a winged leaf stem, which looks like a leaf and three leaflets arranged at right angles to one another. The entire leaf is 12cm/4½in long and dark green. The flowers form in pairs on the trunk and larger branches; they are 6cm/2½in long, greenish-yellow to brown with purple markings. The round gourd-like fruit reaches 13cm/5in across.

Asian Bell Flower *Radermachera sinica* (Hance) Hemsl.
A fast-growing evergreen tree with a very symmetrical form from south-east China. It forms an ornamental round-headed tree of 9m/30ft and may also be grown as a shrub or as a houseplant in temperate areas. The large bipinnate leaves are up to 1m/3ft long with a triangular outline and have a soft, ferny look. Each leaflet is deep green, smooth, glossy and 5cm/2in long. In spring and early summer large panicles of fragrant white or pale greenish yellow flowers appear. They are flared wide open, have crinkled petals and are 8cm/3in long. The fruit is a thin bean-like pod up to 40cm/16in long.

Yellow Trumpet Flower

Tecoma stans (L.) Juss. ex. H. B. K.

This fast-growing plant forms a large shrub or small tree. It can be grown as a hedge or screen and is popular in gardens, as it is reliable and flowers over a long period, particularly in the spring and autumn. If pruned after flowering, the tree is encouraged to produce more flowers. It grows well in arid and semi-arid zones but may cause problems for some people, as the flowers produce a large quantity of pollen.

Identification: This tree is often multi-stemmed, and the trunks have smooth light grey to brown bark. The opposite leaves are 20–25cm/8–10in long and consist of five to eleven leaflets. Each leaflet is 6–8cm/2½–3in long, lanceolate, light green, smooth, thin and heavily toothed. The 4cm/1½in-long flowers are clustered in rounded terminal panicles. The fruit is a 20cm/8in-long, leathery, rich brown, thin bean-like pod. It contains the two winged seeds.

Distribution: West Indies, Mexico, Central America and northern South America including Peru.
Height: 9m/30ft
Shape: Spreading
Evergreen
Pollinated: Insect
Leaf shape: Pinnate

Above and left: The flowers are an attractive trumpet shape and a beautiful golden yellow.

Right: Leaves are somewhat variable.

Tabebuia chrysantha

(Jacq.) Nichols

Distribution: Mexico to Venezuela.
Height: 30m/100ft
Shape: Rounded spreading
Deciduous
Pollinated: Insect
Leaf shape: Compound palmate

Right: Breathtaking in flower, this tree produces a profusion of golden trumpets. In the wild, it grows in forested, riverine and coastal localities and is a feature of secondary forest.

This genus has earned a reputation as being one of the most worthwhile trees for planting in the Americas. There are numerous species to choose from, providing a vast choice of colour, and the majority have outstanding displays of flowers over a long period, particularly in the winter months. Many are tolerant of coastal conditions, flooding or dry conditions and are rarely attacked by pests and diseases. This species has deep yellow flowers in large clusters while it is leafless. Its timber yields a mulberry-coloured dye, and it is also valued for making furniture, flooring and bowls.

Identification: The tree often has an irregular trunk, and the narrow branches have a zig-zagging habit, creating an open haphazard crown. The leaves fall in late winter or spring; they are up to 25cm/10in across and divided into five hairy, ovate leaflets up to 18cm/7in long. The trumpet-shaped flowers have pink streaks inside, are lightly scented, 8cm/3in long and appear towards the branch tips from late winter through to summer. The fruit pods are slightly hairy.

Candle Tree

Parmentiera cerifera Seem.

This tree is grown for the oddity of its fruit which hangs in great abundance on the trunk and branches of mature trees. The fruit has a distinctive apple-like scent and bears a strong resemblance to old-fashioned hand-dipped candles, which is how the common name came about. In its native habitat the fruit is eaten and in many areas is used as cattle fodder.

Identification: The tree often has many trunks and may grow as a large shrub. The leaves drop only briefly and consist of three ovate leaflets, each less than 2cm/¾in long, and have a winged leaf stem. The waxy flowers appear individually or in groups directly from the trunk and larger branches throughout the year. They are bell shaped, pale greenish to creamy yellow, up to 7cm/2¾in long and open in the evening. The smooth, fleshy, cylindrical fruit is pale yellow, measures up to 60cm/24in long and appears mostly in the drier months.

Distribution: Panama.
Height: 8m/26ft
Shape: Rounded
Deciduous
Pollinated: Bat
Leaf shape: Trifoliate

Left: The candle-shaped fruit has very waxy skin. Unusually for this family it does not split open.

Right: The leaves turn yellow when they fall from the trees.

Far left: These unusual-looking trees are said to have medicinal properties. They have spread out of cultivated areas and become naturalized in Australia.

Cow Okra *Parmentiera aculeata* (HBK) Seem.
A small tree of 10m/33ft from secondary forest in Central America and Mexico. It is grown for the edible fruit, medicinal properties of the roots, shade and ornament. In Australia this plant has become a weed, posing a threat to the native flora. It may grow with a shrubby multi-stemmed habit, and has ascending branches and grey fissured bark. The trifoliate leaves have thorns at the base and are dark green with paler veins. Leaflets vary in size up to 15cm/6in in length. The flowers emerge directly from the trunk(s) and older branches throughout the year. They are funnel-shaped, greenish cream with purple markings and 5cm/2in long. The greenish-yellow fruit resembles okra, it is 15cm/6in long, 6cm/2½in wide and has deep furrows along its length.

Pink Cedar *Tabebuia heterophylla* Britt.
This 10m/33ft *Tabebuia* is native to the West Indies. It is grown as a tree or a large shrub. It has rough bark and evergreen foliage. The compoundly palmate leaves comprise five obovate leaflets, each up to 15cm/6in long. The flowers appear throughout the year, particularly in late spring and summer. They may be white to pink, and varieties with pure white flowers and with deep-pink flowers have been selected. Flowers are funnel-shaped, 5cm/2in long and in loose axillary and terminal panicles. The pods are up to 20cm/8in long.

Pink Trumpet Tree

Tabebuia rosea (Seem.) Hemsl.

This tree is grown for its stunning floral display and handsome foliage, and as a shade tree for coffee and cocoa throughout the tropics. In areas without a pronounced dry season, flowering is reduced, and the tree may be virtually evergreen. It is also grown for timber in forestry plantations, and the heavy durable wood is used in construction and furniture-making.

Identification: The massive straight trunk has rough, furrowed grey bark, is often buttressed and carries well-spaced branches. Dark green leaves are up to 30cm/12in across and form from three to five elliptic leaflets of varying size, the largest measuring 15cm/6in in length. Numerous terminal and axillary inflorescences carry clusters of trumpet-shaped, pale to dark pink to mauve flowers with crinkled petals in spring and sporadically through the year. The fruit is a dark brown, straight, round pod which splits to reveal winged seeds attached to a central core.

Distribution: Mexico to Venezuela to Ecuador.
Height: 27m/90ft
Shape: Oval to cylindrical
Deciduous
Pollinated: Insect
Leaf shape: Compound palmate

African Tulip Tree

Spathodea campanulata Pal.

This outstanding tree is easy to spot and to recognize. It is grown throughout the tropics for its spectacular display of intense orange-red flowers radiating against the dark foliage. A pure yellow form is occasionally seen, too. In some places these fast-growing trees are used to mark land ownership boundaries. Their soft wood is brittle, often resulting in damage in windy conditions.

Identification: The pale trunk carries only a few thick branches but a dense crown. The 60cm/24in, dark green leaves are composed of 9–21 ovate leaflets, each about 10cm/4in long. The terminal flowers appear throughout the year but are more pronounced in the wet season. Domes of tightly packed buds open in succession over many weeks. Each tulip-shaped flower is 10–15cm/4–6in long, yellow inside, and red outside with a frilly golden edge to the petals and an unusual scent. The smooth, woody pods are 20cm/8in long, 5cm/2in wide and split open to release hundreds of winged seeds.

Distribution: Uganda.
Height: 25m/82ft
Shape: Oblong
Evergreen
Pollinated: Bat
Leaf shape: Pinnate

Left and right: The finger-like flower buds are full of water and when squeezed will squirt water.

THE MADDER FAMILY

This is an important and virtually wholly tropical family of trees, shrubs, climbers and herbaceous plants. A number of the family Rubiaceae have economic and/or ornamental value. The family is easy to recognize. Leaves always have smooth margins, are most often oppositely arranged and simple. Flowers are usually tubular with four or five flared petals, and the fruit is usually divided into two sections.

Quinine Tree

Cinchona officinalis L.

Distribution: Ecuador and Peru.
Height: 10m/33ft
Shape: Oblong to rounded
Evergreen
Pollinated: Insect and hummingbird
Leaf shape: Ovate-lanceolate

One of the most important medicinal discoveries of all time was the quinine tree. The bark of *Cinchona* plants has provided the anti-malarial drug quinine since at least 1638, when it cured the Countess of Cinchon in Peru. Commercial plantations were not developed though until the 1800s in Asia. After World War II synthetic anti-malarial drugs were developed, but due to a build-up of resistance, quinine continues, to some extent, to be used. The trees naturally grow in humid lowland forests.

Identification: There is great variation within each *Cinchona* species, and hybrids are readily produced. The leaves of *C. officinalis* are generally smooth, shiny, mid-green and 7.5–15cm/3–6in long. The tubular flowers vary from red to pale pink. They are covered in fine silky hair, are often heavily fragrant, and found in terminal and axillary panicles. The ovoid fruit is 1.5cm/⅔in long, and splits into two to release numerous winged seeds.

Right: The cinchona bark is usually harvested by either coppicing the trees every six years or by carefully shaving the bark off two sides of the trunk at any one time, without damaging the cambium.

Leichhardt Tree

Nauclea orientalis (L.) L.

This tree is naturally found growing in coastal locations, alongside rivers, in swamps and in boggy areas of rainforest. It is useful for stabilizing river banks.
Traditionally, the tree has been used by Aborigines: the trunk was carved into canoes, the leaves and bark were used as fish poison, pain relief and medicine, while the fruit is edible and the bark also yields a yellow dye. The tree is grown for shade.

Identification: The light brown or grey trunk is deeply furrowed and carries an attractive, stately, well balanced crown with spreading branches. The foliage is thick, smooth and glossy. Leaves are 13cm/5in long and bright green with paler veins. The tiny, delicate yellow fragrant flowers are arranged in attractive, softly spiky balls, 5cm/2in in diameter. The flowers arise from the leaf axils in late spring and summer. The fruit is a round, soft, red berry containing black seeds.

Distribution: Coastal areas of Queensland, Australia; New Guinea and Indonesia.
Height: 20m/66ft
Shape: Conical
Evergreen
Pollinated: Insect
Leaf shape: Ovate to obovate

Left: The fruit is composed of numerous tiny capsules, each splitting into four and containing minute black seeds.

Indian Mulberry

Morinda citrifolia L. non Bedd.

This small, fast-growing tree is grown commercially in India and Burma for the red dye in its root. Historically, the tree provided dyes of many colours from its different parts, to the Polynesians. Every part has medicinal properties. The putrid-smelling, yet edible, fruit was only eaten by indigenous people when food was scarce. The name *Morinda* is derived from *Morus* and *indica*, meaning 'Indian mulberry'.

Right: Indian mulberry leaves have traditionally been used in poultices and to treat wounds. The species name 'citrifolia' suggests the leaves were thought to resemble citrus.

Identification: The pale yellowish trunk and stout four-angled branches carry a deep green, glossy crown of foliage. Each smooth leaf is 15–25cm/6–10in long with prominent paler veins and midrib. Small white tubular flowers form clusters in the leaf axils throughout the year. They develop from a globular head, which progresses to form the lumpy compound fruit. The fruit is ovoid, soft and 8cm/3in long.

Distribution: Pacific islands, north Australia, New Guinea, Indonesia, Malaysia.
Height: 9m/30ft
Shape: Domed
Evergreen
Pollinated: Insect
Leaf shape: Elliptic

Left and above right: The fleshy and juicy fruit is green when immature, grey to creamy yellow when ripe.

Genipap *Genipa americana* L.
This semi-evergreen 14m/46ft tree from Guyana and the West Indies has edible aromatic fruit. The fruit must be kept after picking until it softens. It has an acid taste similar to dried apple and is used to make marmalade and refreshing drinks. The tree has grey bark, ascending branches and sparse foliage. The leathery glossy leaves are 12–25cm/4½–10in long, oblong to lanceolate and dark green. The flowers form in axillary clusters, which are 2.5cm/1in across, open white and fade to yellow. The round fruit is 9cm/3½in across, cinnamon brown and contains purple juice, mucus and many flat brown seeds.

Cinchona pubescens Vahl.
This 24m/80ft tree from Ecuador and Peru is one of the principal species used in commercial quinine production. It grows in hotter, more humid lowland areas than the other species and has proved a tough, competitive species with disease resistance. In recent years modern technology has allowed *C. officinalis* plants, with the highest quinine content, to be grown on the strong roots of *C. pubescens*. It has soft, hairy, elliptic leaves up to 30cm/12in long and often red below. The pale pink, 2cm/¾in-wide flowers are in dense, pyramidal inflorescences. The oblong fruit capsule is 3cm/1¼in long.

Robusta Coffee

Coffea canephora Pierre ex. Frohner.

Beans from this species account for about a quarter of traded coffee. It is used primarily in espresso and cheaper instant coffee, as it has a poorer flavour yet higher caffeine content. The plants grow more vigorously and yield more abundantly than *C. arabica*. They are tolerant of poor growing conditions and are disease resistant. Breeding programmes are under way to introduce this resistance into other coffee species. Two different strains are apparent: an upright form and the more widely planted spreading form. Commercial plants are pruned to 3m/10ft to facilitate harvesting of the beans.

Identification: The handsome, deep green, slightly hanging leaves are 20cm/8in long. The pungently sweet-scented, white star-like flowers appear in clusters along the branches. The smooth, ovoid fruit forms in dense clusters, takes about ten months to ripen, and is 2cm/¾in long and red when ripe.

Top: The leaves have wavy margins and deeply set veins.

Left and above: The fruit contains two pale brown, flattened seeds, which are the coffee beans.

Distribution: Congo, Gabon, Zaire, Angola, Uganda.
Height: 10m/33ft
Shape: Variable
Evergreen
Pollinated: Insect
Leaf shape: Ovate

THE PALM FAMILY

The palms, Arecaceae, are monocotyledons. There are about 150 genera, the majority of which come from tropical and subtropical regions where they are a common feature in wild and cultivated areas. Most palms have a hard, woody upright stem or stems, and recognizable arching leaf fronts. Many provide invaluable products including foodstuffs, cordage, timbers, waxes and oils.

Burmese Fish-tail Palm

Caryota mitis Lour.

The aptly named fish-tail palms have unusual and distinctive foliage, each leaflet representing a fish tail. This species is an under-storey plant from humid rainforests, and a popular garden plant throughout the tropics. It is multi-stemmed. When each stem reaches its full height it commences flowering, and subsequently fruits.
Flowers appear from the top, successively opening down the length of the stem to the ground.

Identification: Each stem may reach 10cm/4in in diameter. The suckering habit ensures that fronds are found along the entire height of the plant. The erect fronds are overall triangular in shape, reaching 2.4m/8ft in length, with deep green, shiny leaflets. Leaflets are triangular, have a ragged distal edge and measure up to 18cm/7in long. The tightly packed inflorescences produce masses of hanging stems clothed with white flowers followed by fruit.

Distribution: Burma to Philippines.
Height: 9m/30ft
Shape: Multi-stemmed, palm
Evergreen
Pollinated: Insect and/or wind
Leaf shape: Bipinnate

Above: This palm puts a huge amount of energy into an enormous number of fruits. When the fruit is ripe, the fruiting stem dies.

Right: Fruits ripen to dark red or black, and they each measure 1.5cm/⅔ in.

Sealing Wax Palm

Lipstick palm *Cyrtostachys lakka* Becc.

Distribution: Thailand, Malaysia and Borneo.
Height: 9m/30ft
Shape: Multi-stemmed, palm
Evergreen
Pollinated: Insect and/or wind
Leaf shape: Pinnate

Right: The elegant arching, deep green fronds and fine red stems are a striking sight.

One of the most memorable plants from a first trip to the tropics will surely be this palm. The deep glossy red frond bases clasping the stems are a unique feature, satisfying its descriptive common names of 'sealing wax' and 'lipstick' palm. It is native to damp humid forests and coastal swamps but can prove problematic in cultivation. Nonetheless it is such a garden-worthy plant that it is persistently cultivated throughout the tropics.

Identification: The palm is multi-stemmed with narrow, grey to brown stems, reaching 15cm/6in wide, marked with white leaf scar rings. The sparse upright arching fronds are found throughout the plant's height, due to its suckering nature. Each frond is 1.2m/4ft long, has a red midrib and smooth, dark green, 45cm/18in-long leaflets. The flower inflorescence also has a red stem and numerous small flowers. The fruit is round, red or black when ripe and contains one seed.

Loyak

Licuala grandis H. A. Wendl.

This diminutive palm is a popular choice for gardens throughout the tropics and is an unusual houseplant in temperate zones. The broad distinctive leaves, pleated like corrugated cardboard, are most unusual and striking. They form on long spiny stems creating an elegant yet compact head above the fine stem. This understorey palm is found in isolated patches in forests.

Identification: The 8cm/3in-thick stem retains the previous fronds' bases and is covered in a dense mat of tightly woven brown fibres. The crown is composed of approximately 20 leaves, which arch away from the plant on their 90cm/3ft-long upright stems. The leaves are smooth, bright green, heavily toothed around the margin, and undulating. Each leaf is up to 75cm/30in long. The attractive round fruit is 1cm/½in across and red when ripe.

Left: The yellowish flowers are 1cm/½in long and in 1m/1yd-long narrow panicles.

Distribution: Solomon and Vanuatu (New Britain) islands (south and east of Papua New Guinea).
Height: 3m/10ft
Shape: Single-stemmed, palm
Evergreen
Pollinated: Insect and/or wind
Leaf shape: Orbicular to diamond (fan)

Nibung *Oncosperma tigillarium* (Jack) Ridley
This is a multi-stemmed palm from the coastal areas of South-east Asia. It may have up to 40 very slender, pale grey stems, which grow to 20m/66ft high. These are covered in long, ferocious, black spines. The small crowns of feathery palm fronds hang elegantly on top of the stems. The fruit of this palm is purple to black.

Senegal Date Palm *Phoenix reclinata* Jacq.
Native to a wide area of tropical Africa and Madagascar, this multi-stemmed palm is found in open woodland, scrub thickets and beside rivers. Plants consist of up to 25 thick, yet gracefully curving stems reaching 9m/30ft. Stems are topped with a dense crown of arching fronds up to 4m/13ft long, with vicious spines at the base. Female plants produce eye-catching fruit which is bright orange and found in large clusters. This fruit is eaten raw or cooked and used to make wine. In addition, the seeds may be roasted and ground to make a coffee substitute.

Coco de Mer *Lodoicea maldivica* (Gmel.) Pers.
This impressive giant palm from the isolated Seychelles islands is highly endangered. It produces the largest single seeded fruit of any known plant, weighing in at up to 20kg/44lbs. The seed is like two large coconuts fused together. These characteristics led to the seeds being over-collected and sold to tourists in the 1970s. The plants are now heavily protected, but due to their incredibly slow growth, and the fact that each seed takes many years to ripen, recovery will be indeterminately slow. The palm grows to 30m/100ft and carries a crown of colossal deep green fan shaped leaves.

Bismarck Palm

Bismarckia nobilis

This magnificent palm is the only species in its genus and has become rare in the wild. It is incredibly beautiful, and is grown for its huge leaves held in a dense crown above a straight trunk. The leaves vary in colour between plants from blue-green to grey-green; the most highly prized are those with steely blue-grey foliage. It is highly adaptable, growing well in tropical and subtropical conditions, and is drought-tolerant. Although slow growing, it is popular and widely planted.

Identification: The rough stem reaches up to 30cm/12in in diameter and is mid-brown. The thick leaves measure up to 2.5m/8ft across and are very heavy. They are folded and divided into long tapering points. When young, they may have a reddish margin. The flowers form on a 1.2m/4ft inflorescence and produce hanging clusters of large, ovoid, shiny dark brown fruit that contains large seeds.

Distribution: Madagascar.
Height: 25m/82ft
Shape: Single-stemmed, palm
Evergreen
Pollinated: Insect and/or wind
Leaf shape: Palmate (fan)

Left: The huge silver leaves are adapted to dry conditions and held rigidly away from the trunk.

Foxtail Palm

Wodyetia bifurcata A. K. Irvine

Only discovered in the early 1980s, this species is named after the Aborigine, Wodyeti, who died in the 1970s. It made a rapid entry into the horticultural world and is now popular throughout tropical and subtropical regions. Initially fears were raised over the future of wild populations. However, the plants proved to be fast growing, highly adaptable, tolerant of garden conditions, and produced a large quantity of seed; so there was no incentive to poachers to collect from the wild. They are grown for their fluffy, plume-like, heavily arching fronds.

Identification: The grey or tan stem is slightly bottle-shaped. The long clasping leaf bases are pale green. The crown consists of only about a dozen fronds, each up to 3m/10ft long. The leaflets are dark green and extend from the midrib in every direction to form the foxtail. The large, branched inflorescences give rise to a mass of attractive, 6cm/2½in-long, oval, orange or red fruit.

Distribution: Northern Queensland, Australia.
Height: 12m/40ft
Shape: Single-stemmed, palm
Evergreen
Pollinated: Insect and/or wind
Leaf shape: Pinnate

Left: At one time there was a black market in the sale of this fruit.

Left: Considering its origin, this palm is tolerant of both drought and frost. It is becoming a very popular landscaping subject in tropical and subtropical zones.

Royal Palm

Roystonea regia (H. B. K.) Cook.

When one sees a dramatic awe-inspiring avenue of palms in the tropics, it is likely to be *Roystonea*. Their fast, strong growing nature, straight upright trunk and dense crown of feathery fronds makes them ideal for formal planting. In the landscape gardening industry they are highly regarded and widely planted, in both tropical and subtropical regions. The growing tip, called the palm heart or cabbage, is often eaten as a vegetable, but this involves killing the palm in its harvest.

Identification: The thick, smooth, pale grey or white trunk has distinctive rings and becomes swollen in the centre with age. The huge arching fronds reaching up to 6m/20ft in length are composed of numerous, deep green, narrow pendulous leaflets, each up to 1m/1yd long. The small white flowers are found densely packed on 1m/1yd branched plumes. The fruit is oval and 1.5cm/⅔ in long.

Below: In the wild, the royal palm can be found growing in swampy locations.

Distribution: Cuba
Height: 30m/100ft
Shape: Single-stemmed palm
Evergreen
Pollinated: Insect and/or wind
Leaf shape: Pinnate

Right: Ripe fruit is reddish purple.

Below: The elegant leaves arise from a deep green shaft.

Bottle Palm

Hyophorbe lagenicaulis (L. H. Bail.) H. E. Moore

This incredibly slow-growing palm found in the fertile volcanic soils of Round Island in the Mascarenes is facing extinction in the wild. The specimens which were once collected from the wild, depleting the numbers, are now found growing in gardens throughout the tropics. Ironically, these will ensure its survival. It is grown for the novelty value of its distinctive and architectural form. The sparse crown is also architectural, each arching frond held rigidly in place.

Identification: The bulging stem is grey and smooth with closely-spaced rings. The crown consists of about six fronds. The deep green fronds have heavy-duty midribs, and the two rows of rigidly held leaflets form a V-shape in cross section above it. Tiny flowers form in densely branched inflorescences around the top of the trunk.

Distribution: Mascarene Islands.
Height: 4.5m/15ft
Shape: Single-stemmed, palm
Evergreen
Pollinated: Insect and/or wind
Leaf shape: Pinnate

Left: When mature, the trunk is swollen into a short fat bottle shape.

Right: Fruits blacken when ripe.

Left: Each frond is about 2m/7ft long.

Piccabeen Palm *Archontophoenix cunninghamiana* H. A. Wendl. & Drude.
An elegant palm from Australia's subtropical east-coast rainforests. It grows to 15m/50ft with a straight, smooth stem and fine, upright, arching deep green leaves. The small, pale lilac flowers and bright red fruit grow in pendulous panicles. It is a popular landscaping plant.

Manila Palm *Veitchia merrillii* (Becc.) H. E. Moore
Native to the humid rainforests of the Philippines, this single-stemmed palm grows to 6m/20ft. It has a compact crown of stiff, bright green, arched fronds carrying upright leaflets. Often a number of seeds may be sown together, giving rise to an apparent multi-stemmed specimen.

Solitaire Palm *Ptychosperma elegans* (R. Bc.) Bl.
This graceful palm originates from the humid rainforests of north-east Queensland. It grows to 12m/40ft with a slender stem reaching only 15cm/6in in diameter. The few stiffly arching fronds carry broad olive-green leaflets. The flowers and subsequent orange-red fruit appear on large, dense, many-branched inflorescences.

Ruffle Palm *Aiphanes caryotifolia* (H. B. K.) H. A. Wendl.
From northern South America, this palm's widespread habitat includes deciduous and rainforests. It is common in disturbed areas and is cultivated locally for the edible red fruit and seeds. It grows to 9m/30ft, with a single stem clothed in long black spines. The softly arching fronds have roughly triangular leaflets with jagged edges.

Triangle Palm

Dypsis decaryi Jumelle

This striking palm, native to the drier forested area of Madagascar, has been successfully grown in tropical and Mediterranean regions of the world. The short, sturdy stem is topped by clasping leaf bases arranged in threes, one above the other, and thus is triangular in cross section, a feature unique within the palm family. The large, upright fronds elegantly arch at the tips and arise in a triangular shape. They are bluish-green and have long elegant threads hanging from them to the ground.

Identification: The trunk is grey with rings. The clasping frond bases may be covered in blue-grey felt. The fronds are up to 3.5m/12ft long and carry very narrow, bluish leaflets held upright, forming a V-shape in cross section. The leaflets nearest the stem extend into long threads. The small cream flowers are found on short panicles in and around the leaf bases. The small oval fruit is green or yellow when ripe.

Distribution: Southern Madagascar.
Height: 6m/20ft
Shape: Single-stemmed, palm
Evergreen
Pollinated: Insect and/or wind
Leaf shape: Pinnate

Left: The leaves are used for thatching in Madagascar.

Right: In the wild, this palm is an endangered species because the fruit is collected and eaten.

Coconut

Cocos nucifera L.

Tropical beaches would be incomplete without coconut palms arching towards the ocean. They can grow in sand and are incredibly tolerant of windy, salty conditions. Every part of this palm can be used: the leaves for thatch, the growing tip for palm cabbage, the flower for a local drink called toddy, the fruit for food, drink and oil, the fruit husk for matting and fuel, and the trunk for construction. The origins of the coconut are uncertain; it was cultivated long before records began. It is grown inland and in coastal areas throughout the tropics.

Distribution: Unknown.
Height: 30m/100ft
Shape: Single-stemmed, palm
Evergreen
Pollinated: Insect
Leaf shape: Pinnate

Below and left: The tough leaves can withstand strong coastal winds. Older leaves turn yellow before dropping off.

Identification: Slender, often curved trunks are swollen at the base, where new roots emerge. The lightly arching fronds grow to 6m/20ft with long, hanging, deep green leaflets. The 1m/1yd-long branched inflorescence carries small, cream flowers. The fruit is a hard, triangular sphere, 30cm/12in long and green or yellow.

Left: A coconut fruit may float at sea for many months and still be viable to germinate.

Betel Nut

Areca catechu L.

Distribution: Malaysia, Philippines, Indonesia.
Height: 20m/66ft
Shape: Single-stemmed, palm
Evergreen
Pollinated: Insect
Leaf shape: Pinnate

This fast-growing forest palm is cultivated throughout humid areas of Asia. Commonly, the seeds are sliced and a tobacco leaf and a little lime added, then this is wrapped inside betel pepper leaves and chewed as a mild narcotic. The red juice stains the mouth and rots the teeth. The fruit is also said to reduce hunger, stimulate digestion, prevent indigestion and have medicinal properties. Each mature tree yields 200–250 nuts a year and they bear from 6–8 years, until they are about 35 years old.

Identification: The straight, smooth, green stem carries 2.5m/8ft-long deep green, glossy, erect fronds. The closely-spaced leaflets are 50cm/20in long and 5cm/2in wide, forming a dense crown. The small pale yellow flowers are found on a 1m/3ft-long weeping inflorescence. The fruit is egg-like in size and shape, with white flesh and a yellow, orange or red husk.

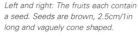

Left and right: The fruits each contain a seed. Seeds are brown, 2.5cm/1in long and vaguely cone shaped.

Right: The leaves form a compact crown.

Assai

Euterpe edulis C.

Large stands of this fast-growing graceful palm dominate damp areas of rainforest in the Amazon basin. The fruit is edible and can be used to make a nutritious drink, assai, by soaking in water. The palm hearts are also popular, although their harvest kills the palm. The heart is harvested from the young growing tip when the palm is three-and-a-half years old. The hearts are canned and exported from South America. Other species of *Euterpe* are multi-stemmed and so need not be killed during the harvest of the heart.

Left: This is a fast-growing, tolerant palm.

Identification: The smooth trunk is slender, usually reaching about 15cm/6in in diameter. It is grey with long green clasping leaf bases at the top. The deep green fronds are up to 3m/10ft long and elegantly arching. Fronds consist of narrow weeping leaflets up to 90cm/36in long. The small white flowers on erect panicles produce large quantities of purple or black fruit, 5mm/¼in across.

Distribution: Amazon basin, Brazil.
Height: 30m/100ft
Shape: Single-stemmed, palm
Evergreen
Pollinated: Insect
Leaf shape: Pinnate

Right: The fruit is popular with forest birds and mammals.

Left: Assai foliage is particularly elegant.

Jelly Palm *Butia capitata* (Mart.) Becc.
This tough palm from the open drier areas of southern Brazil, Paraguay, Uruguay and northern Argentina grows in tropical to cool temperate environments. It grows to only 6m/20ft with a thick trunk of up to 1m/3ft diameter. The 2.5cm/1in-across yellow fruit is found in huge clusters and is harvested to make jellies and wine.

Carnauba Wax Palm *Copernicia prunifera* (Mill.) H. E. Moore
A slow-growing, 12m/40ft, slender palm from low-lying areas of north-eastern Brazil. The distinctive stem is clothed on the lower half only with old leaf bases. The tough carnauba wax found on the lower leaf surfaces is collected and used commercially in polish and foodstuffs.

Toddy Palm *Borassus flabellifer* L.
An impressive palm reaching 21m/70ft with a massive trunk over 1m/3ft in diameter and a crown of fan-shaped, blue-green leaves, each to 3m/10ft in diameter. In its native India through to Indonesia and southern China this palm is valuable in every part. The immature seeds are canned and exported as toddy palms.

Jaggery Palm *Caryota urens* L.
This popular but short-lived, single-stemmed palm, native from India to Malaysia, grows to 20m/66ft. The 6m/20ft-long bipinnate fronds have fish-tail-like leaflets. When flower stems are cut off, a sweet sap, or toddy, is collected from the wound. One tree can yield about 800lt/176 gallons a year, which when boiled becomes like brown sugar and is called 'jaggery'. The palm also yields tasty sago from its pith.

African Oil Palm

Elaeis guineensis Jacq.

An immensely important commercial palm product is palm oil, derived from the fruit of this palm. Vast areas of Malaysian tropical rainforest have been cleared to grow monocultures of the lucrative oil palm, but it has not been exploited in Africa, where it originated. Palm oil is used in cooking oil, lubricants, waxes, soaps and detergents. In Africa this palm is tapped for toddy (a drink made from sap). It is native to swampy and riverside locations where it tolerates flooding.

Identification: The trunk is thick and lumpy. The crown is dense with hanging fronds, each 4.5m/15ft long. The fronds consist of 50–60 dark green, hanging leaflets, each 60cm/24in long. The leaf stems carry thick, sharp spines. Male and female flowers occur on separate inflorescences. Male flowers resemble tight clusters of long, fat cream catkins. Female flowers are cream and in dense, short-stemmed clusters. The dense bunches of fruit may weigh up to 70kg/150lb; each is 5cm/2in long and black to red-brown when ripe.

Distribution: Wet tropical West Africa (Senegal to Congo).
Height: 20m/66ft
Shape: Single-stemmed, palm
Evergreen
Pollinated: Wind and weevil
Leaf shape: Pinnate

Above: The fruit occurs in large spiny clusters. It yields yellow to red palm oil from the fibrous flesh, and white palm kernel oil from the seed.

MISCELLANEOUS MONOCOTS

Monocotyledons are often recognized by having parallel veins, although this is not always the case, and when young, by their single seed leaf. Very few monocotyledons, except for the palms, grow into trees. The stems (trunks) of these plants tend to be pithy and fibrous with a woody surface and do not branch as readily as dicotyledons. Leaves grow from the compact growing points at the tips of the stems.

Common Screw Pine

Pandanus utilis Bory

Planted throughout the tropics, this fine looking plant, with a strong upright form, is tolerant of coastal conditions. The common name derives from the distinctive spiral arrangement of the leaves, and the fruit that resembles a large pine cone. The fibrous leaves are used for thatching, making Manila hats and to make bags to line sacks of sugar for export.

Identification: The cylindrical stem becomes thinner towards the base of thick stilt roots. These roots grow straight down into the soil. The stem is marked with lines where leaves were previously attached. It branches in tiers and carries dense heads of 1m/3ft-long, 8cm/3in-wide, thick, leathery, green leaves at the tips. The leaves have fine red teeth along the edge. Plants are either male or female. Male flowers are found in long branched spikes and female flowers in compact heads. The hanging compound fruit is yellow to red when ripe, 15cm/6in long and composed of about 100 separate fruits.

Distribution: Madagascar.
Height: 18m/60ft
Shape: Conical, spreading
Evergreen
Pollinated: Wind and insect
Leaf shape: Sword

Left: The hard edible fruit has a small amount of pulp in it and is attractive to mammals. Leaves and fruit are used in tropical floral arrangements.

Traveller's Palm

Ravenala madagascariensis Adans.

The magnificent traveller's palm graces the entrance of many prestigious buildings in the tropics. Its striking, formal, two-dimensional silhouette is a result of the leaf stems growing in an east to west orientation. It is believed that lost and thirsty travellers may find their way from this plant and also find water in the base of each cup-shaped leaf stem. The plant is not a palm, but more closely related to bananas and the bird-of-paradise flowers of florists; it is the only species in its genus.

Identification: The straight, pale brown trunk is topped by immense 3m/10ft-long leaves. The long leaf stems arise very closely from the crown. The bright green leaves are often shredded by the wind. From between the leaf stems emerge dense, often congested, large green bracts holding the inconspicuous white flowers. Flowers appear year round and particularly in the winter. The bracts become hard and woody and enclose the large black seeds, coated in an extremely unnatural looking blue aril.

Above: Green bracts contain the pale flowers.

Distribution: Madagascar.
Height: 25m/82ft
Shape: Fan-like
Evergreen
Pollinated: Lemur
Leaf shape: Oblong

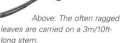

Above: The often ragged leaves are carried on a 3m/10ft-long stem.

Left: The leaf stems form a distinctive pattern as they emerge from the trunk.

Rhodesian Tree Aloe

Aloe excelsa A. Berger.

A number of aloes grow very slowly into 'trees' of a few metres. They are stunning plants, with their bold form, distinctive succulent foliage and prominent winter flowers, and are a valuable addition to cactus gardens. They originate from drier regions and dislike wet winters but are very tolerant of drought conditions.

Above: The dense spires of flowers open in succession from bottom to top.

Identification: The brown stem rarely branches, and it is rough with the remains of old leaf bases. The 75cm/30in-long leaves form a rosette at the top of the stem, emerging close to one another. They are very thick and succulent, green and arched. Each leaf is concave on the upper surface and keeled below with short spines along the edges. Older leaves become brown and withered but hang on the stem for some time. Each small tubular flower is yellow, orange or red. They are closely packed into tight spikes on the top of an upright, many-branched, 1m/3ft-tall stem.

Right: The fruit is densely packed along the panicles.

Distribution: Zimbabwe.
Height: 8m/26ft
Shape: Like single-stemmed palm
Evergreen
Leaf shape: Sword

Quiver Tree *Aloe dichotoma* Masson
Native to incredibly dry areas of Namibia and southern South Africa, this slow-growing tree may eventually reach 9m/30ft, with a massive smooth-barked trunk. The trunk divides into many thick branches, producing a dense flat-topped crown. The thick leaves are grey-green with minute yellow spines along their margins. The tiny yellow flowers appear in winter, packed on to branched spikes 30cm/12in high.

Pandanus odoratissimus L.
This particularly useful plant is widely grown in the Pacific islands. Large fruiting varieties have edible seeds and flesh, and the leaf fibres are utilized in clothing, bags and mats. In India it is grown for a perfume, obtained from the tiny male flowers. From southern Asia, the Pacific islands and northern Australia, it grows to 6m/20ft with a heavily divided trunk, many stilt roots and clusters of spiny sword-shaped green leaves. Compact female flower heads produce 30cm/12in-long, hard, ovoid, compound fruit.

Banana *Musa* spp.
Bananas are not really trees at all. They are gigantic herbaceous plants, the 'trunk' being composed of many layers of leaves. They provide fruit, vegetable, fibre and ornamental flowers to tropical countries. Each water-filled green stem is topped with huge oblong bright green leaves. The whitish flowers are enclosed within a massive red, yellow or green flower bud, appearing among the leaves. Many fruits develop simultaneously on an arching stem. When the fruit has ripened the banana stem dies while a new one grows.

Dragon Tree

Dracaena draco (L.) L.

The genus name *Dracaena* means 'female dragon' and *draco* means 'dragon'. The infamous dragon tree is so named due to its deep red sap, once thought in European legend to be dragon's blood. The sap is used as a dye. This impressive, stout tree is very slow growing and lives for hundreds of years. An enormous old specimen in northern Tenerife is now quite a tourist attraction. In Mediterranean regions it thrives in coastal locations and is tolerant of drought. It is also grown as a houseplant in temperate regions.

Identification: The short wide trunk is pale brown with a rough surface and divides repeatedly into short sturdy branches. Each branch is topped by a small compact rosette of stiff, blue-green leaves. Each leaf is up to 60cm/24in long and 5cm/2in wide. The small, insignificant greenish white flowers are in large panicles and are followed by small orange berries.

Far right: The seed from the fleshy fruit does not germinate easily, and as a result, there are only a few dragon tree specimens growing in the dry mountainous regions of their homeland.

Distribution: Canary Islands
Height: 15m/50ft
Shape: Spreading
Evergreen
Leaf shape: Sword

GLOSSARY

Axil Upper angle between stalk and leaf.

Bipinnate (of leaves). Having leaflets which are also divided in pinnate manner.
Bract A small leaf or scale placed below calyx.

Calyx Collective name for sepals, at base of flower below petals.
Cambium A layer of cells from which annual growth of bark and wood occurs.
Catkin A cylindrical cluster of male or female flowers.
Chlorophyll Green colouring matter of plants.
Chloroplast Part of tree cell containing chlorophyll.
Compound (of leaves). With leaf divided into leaflets.
Cordate (of leaves). Heart-shaped.
Cotyledon The first leaf or leaf-pair within seed.
Cuticle Protective film on leaves.

Deciduous Shedding leaves annually or seasonally.
Dicotyledon Plant with double leaf or leaf-pair within seed.
Dioecious Having male and female cones or flowers on separate trees.
Drupe Fleshy fruit containing stony seed-cover, for example, plum.

Elliptic (of leaves). Oval in shape, with widest point at midsection.
Epidermis Protective layer of cells on leaves and stalks.
Evergreen Bearing leaves all year.

Fastigiate (of trees). Having conical or tapering outline.

Gymnosperm A plant bearing seed unprotected by seed vessels, for example, conifer.

Heartwood Dense wood within inner core of tree trunk.

Inflorescence Arrangement of flowers on a single stem.

Lanceolate (of leaves). Narrow oval shape, tapering to point.
Lenticel An aeration pore in bark.
Linear (of leaves). Narrow, elongated.
Lobed (of leaves). Having rounded indentations.

Meristem Growing tissue in trees.
Monocotyledon A plant with single leaf or leaf-pair within seed.
Monoecious Having male and female flowers on same tree.

Needle A slender, elongated leaf.

Oblong (of leaves). Being longer than broad, with parallel sides.
Obovate (of leaves). Egg-shaped, with broadest end furthest from stem.
Orbicular (of leaves). Round.
Osmosis Transfer of solutions between porous partitions; process whereby liquid moves from one cell to another.
Ovate (of leaves). Egg-shaped, with broadest end nearest stem.

Ovoid (of flowers). Egg-shaped.
Ovule Female reproductive structure which develops into a seed after fertilization.

Palmate (of leaves). With three or more leaflets arising from the same point.
Panicle A head of stalked flowers.
Petiole Leaf stalk.
Phloem Soft tissue within tree trunk.
Photosynthesis Use of sunlight to create nutrients within leaves.
Phreatophyte Tree or other plant with long taproots.
Pinna(e) Primary division of pinnate leaf.
Pinnate (of leaves). Having leaflets in pairs on either side of petiole.
Pubescence; pubescent A layer of short, fine hairs; downy.

Samara A winged fruit, e.g. ash key.
Sapwood Soft wood between heartwood and bark.
Scale Small, modified leaf.
Sessile (of leaves). Without stalks.
Simple (of leaves). Not divided into leaflets.
Stamen Male part of a flower; releases pollen.
Stigma Tip of female reproductive organ in a flower; receives pollen.
Stomata Pores in the epidermis of leaves.

Transpiration Loss of moisture through evaporation.
Trifoliate (of leaves). Having three leaflets.
Tripinnate (of leaves). Having three or more pinnae.

Xerophyte Tree or other plant capable of conserving and storing water.
Xylem Woody tissue within tree trunk.

INDEX OF COMMON NAMES

NOTES

Notes

NOTES

NOTES

NOTES

NOTES